June 20, 1966

To a fine person who i met just
for a short time and have grown so fond of.
I am taking the opportunity to send a small
gift about a people.
I think you would appreciate,

With fondest regards.

Mrs. Gertrude Gideon

A PICTORIAL HISTORY
OF THE JEWS
IN THE UNITED STATES

Works by Morris U. Schappes

A Documentary History of the Jews in the United States: 1654-1875
Emma Lazarus: Selections from her Prose and Poetry
The Letters of Emma Lazarus, 1868-1885

A PICTORIAL HISTORY OF THE JEWS IN THE UNITED STATES

MORRIS U. SCHAPPES

FOREWORD BY
THE REV. DR. DAVID de SOLA POOL

NEW REVISED EDITION
MARZANI & MUNSELL NEW YORK

Table of Contents

List of Illustrations

Foreword

In "A Pictorial History of the Jews in America" Morris U. Schappes presents a vivid story of what Jews have contributed to the country over three centuries. What makes a Jew is history expressed through the law of Moses, the moral vision of the Biblical prophets, the spiritual aspirations of the Psalmist, the wisdom of the rabbis, and the spirit of martyrs. These traditions the Jew brought with him to America. They gave him the will to persist and preserve his unique historic consciousness and help build up the character of the United States.

The pictures and illustrations in this volume illumine the words in the text and make the more vivid the story told of the three hundred years of Jewish life in the United States. We come face to face with rabbis and judges, congressmen and artists, writers and merchants, diplomats and musicians, scientists and bankers, actresses, artists, farmers, pioneers, kosher butchers and revolutionaries. The past and the present depicted in this volume enable us to catch a glimpse of the future of the Jews in the United States.

D. de Sola Pool

New York, June 8, 1965

The Reverend Doctor David de Sola Pool is Rabbi Emeritus, Congregation Shearith Israel, founded in 1654 and the oldest in the United States, and is the Vice President of the American Jewish Historical Society. He is the author of Portraits Etched in Stone, Early Jewish Settlers, 1682-1831 *and of* An Old Faith in the New World, Portrait of Shearith Israel, 1654-1954.

Introduction

This book was initiated in June, 1955 under the impact of the celebration in 1954-1955 of the three hundredth anniversary of Jewish settlement in North America.

The entire manuscript has been read by Dr. Herbert Aptheker, Dr. Joshua Bloch, Simon Federman, Jacob Mestel, Dr. Herbert M. Morais and Paul Novick, and parts of it have been examined by individuals of special competence who have made helpful suggestions. All of these added to the merits of this work; its deficiencies are the responsibility of the writer. I am indebted beyond my powers of expression to Dr. Joshua Bloch, whose meticulous, exhaustive scrutiny of the manuscript saved me from many an error and whose enthusiasm for the book sustained me in a difficult undertaking.

Many photographs in this volume have been drawn from the exhibition of reproductions of historic documents, prints and photographs assembled by the historian Dr. Herbert M. Morais, and on view from February 12 to April 1, 1955 at 189 Second Avenue, New York.

Dispensing with a bibliography, I have tried to list in the Reference Notes all the works actually used as source materials and to give credit there to special assistance rendered. The names of authors used, but not the titles of their works, are included in the special Index to Notes.

The General Index, prepared by the librarian Henry Black, is elaborate, including not only the names of all persons mentioned but also place names and subjects.

Finally, I am peculiarly and continually indebted to my wife, Sonya, whose encouragement, criticism, endless patience and helpfulness with editorial chores have expedited the completion of this book.

M.U.S.

New York, April 21, 1958

Introduction to Second Edition

To bring this history of American Jewish life up to date, I have added Chapter 14 as a Postlude. My design in this chapter has been to follow substantially the pattern and, in so far as possible, the sequence of themes I had used in the Mid-Century Profile with which the first edition closed. My purpose has been briefly to bring up-to-date the facts contained therein and to dwell upon such new problems as emerged or became central in the years 1950-1965.

In addition to correcting typographical errors, I have also availed myself of the opportunity offered by the reprinting of the bulk of the volume to correct errors on pages 32, 54, 70, 191 and 226, and to make slight changes, usually for the purpose of updating material, on pages 98, 118, 122, 148, 169, 170, 171, 172, 182, 188, 196, 197, 205, 207, 213, 214, 215, 217, 218, 221, 222, 234, 246, 255, 263, 274, 275, 276, 279 and 282.

I am deeply appreciative of the honor done to me by the Rev. Dr. David de Sola Pool in writing the Foreword to this edition.

M.U.S.

New York, August 17, 1965

To
the memory of
Dr. Joshua Bloch
(1890-1957)
advocate of social justice,
rabbi, scholar, mentor
and friend

The Landing of Columbus, October 12, 1492. The Columbus expedition was composed of people of many nationalities. Among the crew were several Marranos or secret Jews.

PROLOGUE

Again and again, for centuries on end, Jews were going to rediscover America, each for himself, each the forerunner of another. But the Discoverer, the one who boldly beat the uncharted ocean path that others followed to seize, to conquer and to settle the New World, was Columbus.

1492 was, in the phrase of Emma Lazarus, "a two-faced year." One face looked upon the tragic expulsion of the Jews of Spain from their thousand-year old home. The other face witnessed the unlocking of a Hemisphere on which, centuries later, Jews in clusters or in millions could seek a refuge. In historical perspective, the poet saw the two faces clearly in 1883, when anti-

Semitic pressures in Eastern Europe were driving Jews in vast numbers to our shores. But as a contemporary, Columbus himself made only one fleeting reference to the grim expulsion.

In the *Journal* of his voyage of discovery, he began by invoking "the name of our Lord Jesus Christ." Then he bowed before Ferdinand and Isabella, the Monarchs: "Your Highnesses, as Catholic Christians, and princes who love and promote the holy Christian faith . . . determined to send me . . . to the . . . countries of India . . . to learn . . . the proper method of converting them to our holy faith . . ." He was to seek out India by going, for the first time, westward. So,

3

Residuaz table festoz mobiliuz										
Aureus numer?	litera dominica	Intervallu Concurrentes	febraz feptuage	matii qdzagesi	aplis pafcha	maii rogationes	Jonii pentecofte	Jonii corpe ati	beb a pet ad Jo dies fuperflui	beb a pad aduent
3	e	8 4	9	2	13	18	1	12	3 2	26
	f	8 5	10	3	14	19	2	13	3 1	26
11	g	8 6	11	4	15	20	3	14	3 0	26
	A	9 0	12	5	16	21	4	15	2 6	26
19	b	9 1	13	6	17	22	5	16	2 5	25
8	c	9 2	14	7	18	23	6	17	2 4	25
	d	9 3	15	8	19	24	7	18	2 3	25
	e	9 4	16	9	20	25	8	19	2 2	25
	f	9 5	17	10	21	26	9	20	2 1	25
	g	9 6	18	11	22	27	10	21	2 0	25
	A	10 0	19	12	23	28	11	22	1 6	25
	b	10 1	20	13	24	29	12	23	1 5	24
	c	10 2	21	14	25	30	13	24	1 4	24

Expliciüt table tablaz aftronomice Raby abraham zacuti
aftronomi ferenifimi Regis emanuel Rex poztugalie et cet
cü canonib⁹ traductis alinga ebrayca in latinü p magiftrü
Jofeph vizinü difcipulü ei⁹ actoris opera et azte viri folez
tis magiftri ortas curaqz fua nö mediocri inprefione cöple
te exiftüt felicib⁹ aftris año apma rez ethereaz circuitione
1496 fole exiftéte in 15 g̃ 53 m̃ 35 ⅔ pifciuz fub celo leyree

Abraham Zacuto's astronomical tables, published in
1496, were used by Columbus.

he remarked, "after having driven out all the
Jews from your realms and lordships . . . your
highnesses commanded me that, with a sufficient
fleet, I should go to the said parts of India. . . ."

Thus expulsion and discovery were contemporaneously interwoven. On March 31, 1492, the
inhuman order was issued: the Jews had four
months, until July 31, to convert to Christianity
or to get out of the country. Soon the roads to
the borders of Portugal and the seaports began
to swell with tens of thousands of Jewish families
who were choosing exile. With the Moors driven
from Spain and the Jews on the way out, the
Monarchs turned to discoveries for added riches.

Columbus would have sailed from a big port
like Cadiz, but Cadiz had been designated as a
port from which the Jews would be departing.
So on May 12, when Columbus left Granada to
organize his expedition, he went to the tiny port
of Palos instead. Perhaps on the highway he saw
the scene as Emma Lazarus drew it: "The Spanish
noon is a blaze of azure fire, and the dusty pilgrims crawl like an endless serpent along treeless
plains and bleached highroads . . . all brothers
now, all merged in one routed army of misfortune. . . ." Jewish artisans made up the bulk
of this routed army of misfortune.

By July 31—the seventh of the Hebrew calendar
month of Ab, two days before the fast-day anniversary of the destruction of the Second Temple
in the year 68—the Jews, some 200,000 of them,
had left, 8,000 families sailing from Cadiz alone.
A few who had tarried followed the next day—
and thus Spain became "Juden-rein," cleansed
of Jews, at least of those who openly professed
to be Jews.

On August 3, a day or two after the purge,
Columbus sailed westward from Palos, in order,
as Emma Lazarus saw it, "to unlock the golden
gates of sunset and bequeath a Continent to Freedom!" Thus the poet, and there is vision in the
poetry, just as there is truth in the judgment of
the historians, Charles and Mary Beard, that "in
the main the men who organized and commanded
expedition after expedition into Asia, the Americas, and Africa had their hearts set on the profits
of trade and the spoils of empire." What Columbus was to discover was a new vast arena for
the striving of man for profits and freedom.

Columbus himself may have been of Marrano
descent, that is, of a family of Jews who had been
converted to Christianity but who secretly maintained their contact with and practice of Judaism.
But whether he was or not, professing and also
Marrano Jews were certainly a factor in his voyage, both in the background and the foreground.
Like all mariners of the time, he was aided by
the developments in astronomical science, to
which Jews like Abraham Zacuto and Jose Vecinho made important contributions, and Jews
who were map-makers and nautical instrument
makers were useful to all the adventurous captains, to Columbus, too.

When Isabella turned a deaf and queenly ear
to Columbus' appeal that she sponsor his journey,
it was Luis de Santangel who decisively persuaded
the Queen to back the venture and even rounded
up a large part of the funds needed to outfit the
expedition. Santangel was a Marrano whose great-
grandfather had been a Jew, and who was now

the comptroller of the royal household. It was to Santangel that Columbus wrote his first letter announcing his discovery.

There was a crew of over 90 on the three tiny vessels, the *Santa Maria,* 100 tons, the *Pinta,* 50 tons, and the *Niña,* 40 tons (compare the modern Hudson River ferryboat, 700 tons). There were Marranos among them too. With Columbus on the *Santa Maria* was Rodrigo Sanchez de Segovia, selected by Isabella herself to be the comptroller on the voyage—and a first generation Marrano, for his own parents had been born Jews before conversion. With him was Luis de Torres, who, confronted with the royal expulsion order, chose baptism just before he sailed. Hired as an interpreter knowing Arabic and Aramaic, he is reported to have been the first European to have set foot on the land Columbus discovered, and

one of the first two to see tobacco smoked and, more important, corn grown. And on the *Pinta* as ordinary seaman and servant to Captain Martín Alonso Pinzón, there was Bernal, a Marrano who only a couple of years earlier had been fingered by the Inquisition as a "Judaizer," but had escaped conviction and therefore the funeral pyre. There may have been other Marranos, too, among those who sailed westward.

The land that was discovered was not a haven for professing Jews. The Monarchs of Spain and Portugal applied the expulsion decree to all their territories. Professing Jews had to wait more than a century before they could make their way to the new lands. And when they did go, it was not from Spain and Portugal, but from one of the great advancing rivals in pursuit of profits and empire, Holland.

"Torture of the Pulley Inflicted." The Holy Court of the Inquisition used torture of the severest kind to force confessions. The above shows the use of torture by pulley.

Model of New Amsterdam in 1660. In September 1654, 23 Jewish refugees from the Inquisition arrived in New Amsterdam. Above is replica of small town in 1660.

CHAPTER I: The First Settlements: New Amsterdam and Newport

If Jews had a future in the Western Hemisphere, and then specifically in territory now the United States, it was because of developments in Holland and England in the sixteenth and seventeenth centuries. Western Europe began to be an arena for vast conflicts and changes, economic, political, social, legal, religious and cultural, and the settlement of the New World was one of the results.

The feudal system, in which the big landowners ruled the land and all who lived and worked on it, had become an obstacle to social progress. The growing class of merchants, eager to expand production and trade, were intolerably hemmed in by feudal restrictions. It was in Holland and England that the biggest changes took place as the new capitalism rose to challenge the old feudalism.

Spain and Portugal, still largely feudal powers but already claiming the entire Western Hemisphere between them, became the international obstacle to the emerging capitalist enterprisers, with their overseas appetites, of Holland and England. In 1579 Holland wrested itself from Spanish rule; it declared its independence in 1581, abolished feudal and Catholic domination, and set out to build a social order giving full expression to the desires for profit of the merchant capitalists. Protestant Calvinism embodied in the Dutch Reformed Church became the official religion. Yet Holland welcomed the immigration of dissenters from other countries because they were economically useful and was soon known for its toleration of religious differences. By the end of the century an expanding community of openly

7

Recife or Pernambuco, center of Jewish life in Brazil to 1654. Recife, capital of Dutch Brazil, fell to the Portuguese in January, 1654. Its 500 Jews had the alternative of fleeing or facing the threat of the Inquisition.

professing Jews was functioning in Amsterdam. Sometimes Spanish and Portuguese Marranos would migrate to Amsterdam and publicly profess Judaism.

In the first half of the seventeenth century, Dutch and English naval power thrust rapidly into the Atlantic basin, loosening the hold of Spain and Portugal on territorial possessions, on trade routes, and on the gruesomely profitable African slave trade. On the North American seaboard, England, Holland and Sweden established settlements. England colonized Virginia in 1607, New England beginning in 1620 and Maryland in 1634. Holland in 1624 settled the New Netherlands, of which New Amsterdam was the commercial and political center. Sweden in 1638 obtained a temporary toe-hold in the Western Hemisphere by founding a colony at what is now Wilmington, Delaware.

For Holland one instrument of this economic penetration was the Dutch West India Company,

formed in 1621, with Jewish capitalists participating actively from the very beginning. Jews were particularly useful to Holland in another way. Because of their contacts with Marranos, they were able to obtain economic and even military information helpful to Holland in its conquest of Portuguese islands and other possessions.

After such a victory, under newly established Dutch rule, Marranos would often come out openly as Jews. But when, in the seesaw of economic and military fortunes, the Portuguese reconquered a colony held by the Dutch, they were merciless with such Jews. Thus to be caught in the middle was especially dangerous.

When in 1630 the Dutch wrested from the Portuguese the settlement of Recife (now Pernambuco) on the Brazilian bulge, it became the site of the first Jewish community in the Western Hemisphere. Hundreds of Jewish settlers from Holland, supplemented by Marranos already on the scene, formed a well-organized community.

At its peak in the mid-1640's, it included about 1,000 persons, complete with synagogue, a rabbi and other religious functionaries, and even a due process for settling disputes between Jew and Jew inside the Jewish community. Beginning with 1645, however, when the Portuguese began seriously to try to re-establish their control of Recife, the Jewish population declined. It dropped to about five or six hundred by the time the Portuguese actually reconquered Recife in January, 1654.

The new Portuguese governor gave the Jews three months, until April 26, to get out. By that date, Brazil too was "Juden-rein." In 16 ships, the 150 Jewish families, as well as Marranos fleeing the re-established Inquisition, sailed for Holland or for other Dutch possessions. One group,

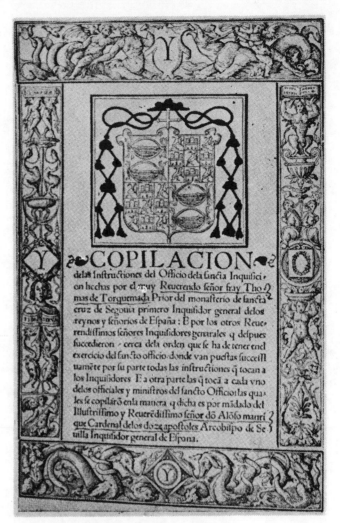

Spain brought the Inquisition to the new world. These instructions were carried by the Inquisitor, Cerezuela, to Lima, Peru, 1570.

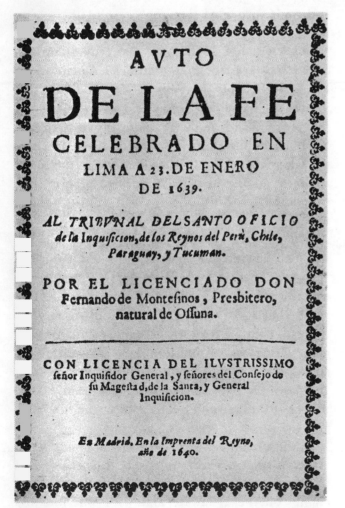

Title-Page of the account of the Auto da Fé in which DeSilva figured. In the 1639 Auto da Fé in Lima, Peru, 11 Jews, including Francisco Maldonado DeSilva, were burned to death. In 1649, a similar event took place in Mexico.

after many mishaps, finally got passage on the French frigate, the *St. Catherine*, for New Amsterdam. Thus it was that 23 Jews landed in that Dutch West India Company colony in the first week of September, 1654.

The colony was small, its less than 200 dwellings housing perhaps 1,000 persons. Yet New Amsterdam lacked the homogeneity of the New England settlements. As a trading center, New Amsterdam had something of a cosmopolitan character. A sharp ear had recently heard 18 different languages in its streets and shops. There were farmers, householders and shopkeepers, traders, sailors and artisans. There were Negroes, free as well as slave.

In 1653 the local population had, after four years of struggle against Governor Peter Stuyvesant, won from the Dutch West India Company the right to a very limited municipal self-government. That same year, the Lutherans had begun to trouble Stuyvesant by petitioning him and the council for the right to public worship and to send for a minister. Stuyvesant was relieved when the Company backed him up in saying no to that petition, but he was annoyed by the persistence of the Lutherans in holding religious services within their houses.

It was to this bubbling town that the 23 Jews came. Having landed, their first problem was to pay for their passage. On board the *St. Catherine* the adults among the 23 had agreed with the Captain that they would be bound jointly to pay the passage-money. But even when all their goods had been sold at auction and the proceeds given to the Captain, they were still in debt. To guarantee payment, David Israel and Mose Lumbroso were placed under civil arrest until the Captain agreed to wait for money to arrive from Amsterdam.

Refugees from the Portuguese, the newcomers had certainly expected to be welcome in a Dutch colony. But Governor Peter Stuyvesant met them with open hostility. He had not objected to the Jews who had come that very summer from Holland to New Amsterdam to trade, for they had returned to Holland, and there were only two Jews in the town, Jacob Barsimson and Salomon Pietersen, when the 23 arrived. When the newcomers said they wanted to stay, however, Stuyvesant asked them to go away. The Jews refused.

Stuyvesant hesitated to issue a deportation order. He had failed two years before when he had tried to prevent Jews from settling in the Dutch West India Company colony in Curaçao, and he remembered that, as recently as March 1654, the Company had written to him in favor of unrestricted immigration. Therefore on September 22, 1654 he wrote to the Company for permission to drive the Jews out. To make out his case, Stuyvesant used anti-Semitic arguments that were common then and are still used in modern times. He charged Jews with "customary usury" and "deceitful trading with the Christians." Moreover, these Jews were poor—which was true—and would have to be supported by the Deacons that winter—which also proved to be the case. These

three economic reasons Stuyvesant wrapped up in a fourth and explosive charge: that Jews are "hateful enemies and blasphemers of the name of Christ."

The Directors of the Company in Amsterdam, however, rejected Stuyvesant's request, although, they assured him, they shared his fears. In general the Company was hard put to find settlers, and for that very reason it had encouraged Jews, Catholics and others to go to its overseas possessions. Specifically in this case, the Directors were subjected to the pressure of the Amsterdam Jewish community, some of whose members were principal shareholders in the Company and could point to the outstanding loyalty of Jewish settlers to Holland and the Company. So on April 26, 1655 the Company ordered Stuyvesant to allow the Jews to stay in New Amsterdam and to travel and trade, provided they took care of their own poor.

But it was not for nothing that Stuyvesant was called *Hardkoppige Piet* (hardheaded-pigheaded-Pete). Stubbornly he resisted carrying out the intent of his instructions. "To give liberty to the Jews," he wrote to the Company on October 25, 1655, "will be very detrimental there, because the Christians there will not be able at the same time to do business. Giving them liberty, we cannot refuse the Lutherans and Papists." This was the same anti-Semitic compound he had shown the year before, with religious bigotry wrapped around the hard core of economic advantage. Therefore the Jews had to fight continually for two years to enforce in practice the rights they had been granted. Petition after petition was filed, in New Amsterdam and in Amsterdam. Time and again the Jews of Amsterdam added their weighty protests. One by one the Jews won the economic rights to travel and trade, to own real estate and to buy a house, and to bake and sell bread at retail.

In the summer of 1655, an issue of a civic right arose. Although there was need to increase the town militia because of trouble with the Swedish colony on the Delaware and with the Indians, Jews were first excluded from the right to stand guard—and then a special tax was levied on them for the exemption. Some of the Jews paid the tax, but two workers among them, Jacob Barsimson and Asser Levy, petitioned on November 5 for the right to stand guard or at least to be excused from the tax, which they maintained they could not afford to pay "as they must earn their living by manual labor." Although this petition was denied, Levy later did win the right to stand guard.

Levy, a vigorous character, also figured in the fight for the "small burgher right." This conferred certain citizenship rights, as well as the right to apply for a retailer's license, but not the right to hold office, restricted to Great Burghers. Levy's application was turned down, despite the fact that Jews in Holland had won the right. More influential Jews in New Amsterdam, including Joseph d'Acosta, a principal shareholder in the Dutch West India Company, intervened with another petition. They also submitted as evidence a Jewish burgher's certificate from Holland. Stuyvesant and the Burgomasters on April 20, 1657 therefore ordered the right to be extended to Jews.

In addition to the economic and political issues, there was the matter of religious rights. At that time the fight for religious equality was a basic struggle for human liberty, which directly affected everybody, because religious institutions and ideas were dominant in every field of human activity. Wherever there was an official established Church, those who were outside that church had to endure handicaps not only in respect to freedom of worship, but also in taxation, voting, and other economic and political respects. Therefore when the Jews, Lutherans, Quakers and other groups strove for the right to organize their religious bodies, to hold public worship and to conduct their religious life without penalty, they were fighting for a fundamental democratic principle. This principle of separation of Church and State was not established in law in our country until it was written into the United States Constitution and Bill of Rights a century and a half later, and even then there remained the problem of the effective enforcement of the law.

While the Jews of New Amsterdam, as we have seen, organized themselves first for mutual defense against exclusion and economic restrictions,

A seventeenth century baker at the oven.

it may be assumed that they also organized themselves for religious purposes. Among the 23 there were four adult males, Abram Israel, David Israel, Asser Levy and Mose Lumbroso, and two widows, Judith de Mercado and Ricke Nunes, and their families; probably the wives of the adult males and possibly 13 young people and children. Rosh Hashanah in 1654 fell on September 12. Was there a *minyan* (quorum of 10) for a religious service? Only if, in addition to the four adult male newcomers plus Barsimson and Pietersen, there were also four boys 13 years of age or over, and therefore eligible for a *minyan*.

In March, 1655 a number of Jews arrived in New Amsterdam from Holland, one of them, Abraham de Lucena, bringing with him a Sefer Torah for the new Jewish community. For the first Passover in New Amsterdam there was certainly a *minyan* for the service. Yet the Jewish population fluctuated so much, owing to Stuyvesant's stubbornly grudging attitude, that by 1663 when de Lucena was back in Amsterdam he had taken the Sefer Torah with him for lack of a *minyan* in the colony.

The oldest Jewish cemetery in the United States, dating from 1682, is in Chatham Square, New York.

The first religious issue the Jews pressed before the town authorities was that of a separate cemetery. On February 22, 1656, the need having arisen—it is not known who died—the petition of the Jews was granted and "a little hook of land" outside the city limits on the tip of Manhattan Island was set aside as a Jewish burial place. The location of this first Jewish institution on our territory is today unknown. The oldest existing Jewish cemetery, which is in the lower Bowery in New York, dates back to 1682; the oldest tombstone there, with its inscription entirely in Spanish, is that of Benjamin Bueno de Mesquita, who died in 1683, the only known Jewish grave of the seventeenth century.

The right to public worship in a synagogue was not won by the Jews of New Amsterdam under Dutch rule, although they had the right in Holland itself. Stuyvesant and the New Amsterdam leaders of the official Dutch Reformed Church interfered, and on February 1, 1656 passed a law forbidding public worship by any other religious denomination, thus affecting Lutherans, Mennonites, Puritans and Catholics as well as Jews.

Separate petitions by Jews and by Lutherans were in vain, although both groups won the right

to private worships in their houses, even that, however, being denied to the newly arrived Quakers. On June 14, 1656, the Directors of the Company, pressed again by the Jews of Amsterdam, instructed Stuyvesant to let Jews "exercise in all quietness their religion within their houses," for which purpose, incidentally, they were to be allowed to "build their houses close together." It was only under English rule, some 30 years after New Amsterdam had become New York, that the Jews there, by 1695, had their own synagogue.

Occasionally individuals asserted rights connected with Judaism. Thus the stalwart Barsimson on June 3, 1658 refused to answer a summons to appear in court on the Jewish Sabbath, and the court sustained his action. On October 15, 1660, as he was being licensed as a butcher, Asser Levy asked to be exempted from having to slaughter hogs on grounds of his religion. The request was granted, as was that of Moses Lucena when he was licensed and sworn in as a public butcher two weeks later. Either or both of them may have served the Jewish population as *shohet* (animal slaughterer according to Jewish rite).

Relations with Christians were varied. Business relations were common. In 1671, Levy having

A seventeenth century butcher at work.

worked himself up from a "manual laborer" to a man of considerable property, the Lutherans borrowed money from him to help build their first church in New York—the right to public worship had been won under the English, who ruled the city from 1664 to 1672 and then continually from 1674. It was in 1671, also, that Levy served on a jury that tried Peter Stuyvesant himself on a charge of having failed to pay a former employe of the Dutch West India Company. Incidentally, the jury acquitted Stuyvesant. In 1678 Asser Levy entered into a business partnership in building a slaughter-house with Garrett Jansen Rose.

Hostility to Jews was expressed not only by Stuyvesant or some of the church authorities. Some instances of anti-Semitic activities against individual Jews have found their way even into court records. On August 12, 1658, Jacob Cohen charged that a customer had said to him, "You are a Jew; you are all cheats together," because of a dispute about the weight of nails. The official Weigher testified that Cohen's weight was accurate. On October 2, 1668 it was demonstrated in court that a miller had mixed rye and pease into wheat flour ordered by Rabba Cooty because he had been instructed to make the flour "as coarse as he pleased, it being only for a devilish Jew."

In the economic life of the time, the Jews played a varied part. In New York in 1687, there were not only Jewish shopkeepers, merchants and West Indian traders, but also artisans and craftsmen. There was an auctioneer, a baker, a brazier and a butcher, three chandlers, a cordwainer (shoemaker), two distillers, a goldsmith, a peruke-maker, a saddler, a tailor, a tobacconist, a watchmaker, and, in 1691, a soldier. Jews bought slaves with the same conscience and for the same reasons as non-Jews: to solve the urgent problem of the shortage of labor primarily for their business enterprises and also for domestic work. In 1670, Rabba Cooty had an agent buy a slave Negro boy for him, but could not pay the price. When Asser Levy died in 1681, a rich man, his inventory included a Sabbath lamp, "a parcel of old books," and a Negro boy "valued at 20 pounds."

Only because of active struggle for their rights, supported by the Jews of Amsterdam and the over-riding desire for a prosperous colony by the Directors of the Company, had the Jews won a foothold in North America in the seventeenth century. They won it first in New Amsterdam under the Dutch and maintained it in New York under the English after 1674.

There was another attempt made by Jews to settle on the coast, in the New England town of Newport. It is reported, but not substantiated in the records, that in 1658, only a few years after the landing in New Amsterdam, 15 Dutch Jewish families came to Newport. The reason Dutch Jews would go to this particular one of all the English colonies is not far to seek: it was the only one in which, Roger Williams had proclaimed, Jews might have the right to practice Judaism without molestation by the governing body. As far back as 1644, in a pamphlet published in London, Williams had supported his argument for separation of Church and State by declaring that Jews, despite their religious differences, could be law-abiding citizens. In 1652, in two London pamphlets, he had declared himself in favor of the readmission of the Jews to England, after Amsterdam Jews had raised the issue by an appeal to Cromwell.

But once they came, if they did, the reasons to stay were weak. Newport in 1658 was a commercially unimportant village of some 200 white families, its trade possibilities inhibited by the English Navigation Act of 1651. The act was aimed specifically at the Dutch, whose competition it wanted to keep away from Newport and other English colonies. In 1660 another Navigation Act prohibited foreigners in English colonies from trading there—and that would include Jews. The Navigation Act of 1663 restricted imports only to goods arriving from England—a direct blow to colonial trade with the West Indies, New Amsterdam, and so forth. In a colony in which their economic opportunities were so restricted, the right of Jews to religious toleration or even equality was not enough to create a foundation for a stable residence. So if they came, they did not stay long.

Reliable records did not begin until 1674, when commercial relations between Jews in Newport and New York appeared, and not long thereafter

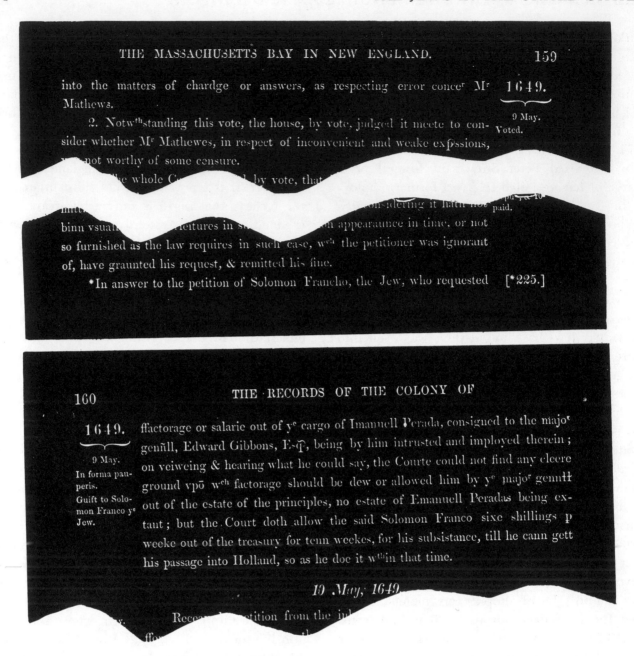

THE MASSACHUSETTS BAY IN NEW ENGLAND.   159

1649.

into the matters of chardge or answers, as respecting error conce^r M^r
Mathews.

9 May.
Voted.

2. Notw^{th}standing this vote, the house, by vote, judged it meete to consider whether Mr Mathewes, in respect of inconvenient and weake ex∫ssions,
... not worthy of some censure.

... the whole C...... by vote, that ......

paid.

..... considering it hath not ....
binn vsuall ..... feitures in s..... on appearance in time, or not
so furnished as the law requires in such case, wch the petitioner was ignorant
of, have graunted his request, & remitted his fine.

*In answer to the petition of Solomon Francho, the Jew, who requested   [*225.]

160   THE RECORDS OF THE COLONY OF

1649.

9 May.
In forma pau-
peris.
Guift to Solo-
mon Franco y^e
Jew.

ffactorage or salarie out of ye cargo of Imanuell Perada, consigned to the majo^r
genñll, Edward Gibbons, E-⊕, being by him intrusted and imployed therein;
on veiweing & hearing what he could say, the Courte could not find any cleere
ground vpō wch factorage should be dew or allowed him by ye majo^r genntł
out of the estate of the principles, no estate of Emanuell Peradas being extant; but the Court doth allow the said Solomon Franco sixe shillings p
weeke out of the treasury for tenn weekes, for his subsistance, till he cann gett
his passage into Holland, so as he doe it w^{th}in that time.

19 May, 1649.

Receaue.. petition from the in......
ffo......

May 9, 1649—Unable to collect a claim, the impoverished Jew, Solomon Franco,
was awarded six shillings a week for ten weeks by the government of the Massachusetts
Bay Colony, pending his getting passage to Holland.

a Jewish community was visible. On February 28, 1677 Moses Pacheco and Mordecai Campanall bought a plot of land for the use of the "Jews and their Nation, Society or Friends" as a burial place. A Jewish community was thus in evidence. In 1684 there were still signs of life, but they were faint, even though the number of Jews was increased by a small influx from Barbadoes in the British West Indies. In reply to a petition from the Jews on June 24 asking for a definition of their position with regard to such matters as the annoying Navigation Acts, the Rhode Island General Assembly declared "that they may expect as good protection here, as any stranger, being not of our nation residing amongst us . . . ought to have, being obedient to his Majesty's laws." Equality with other *strangers,* with no immediate possibility of changing the status of strangers, was no firm attraction. By 1690, apparently, the first congregation that may have been organized there seems to have died away. It is not until Newport became, toward the middle of the eighteenth century, the busiest seaport on the coast, that there emerged a vigorous Jewish population and community.

In the other colonies there were only individual Jews here and there, but no other Jewish group anywhere. Outside Newport, New England was inhospitable. These colonies were homogeneous, and the governing groups were intolerant of dissent and cold to strangers. In reference to Jews, there was simultaneously among the Puritans a veneration for their Biblical past and at least a suspicion as to their present ways. In 1635 the Massachusetts Bay Colony, in its code of laws, explicitly based itself on "Moses, his judicials," that is, on the laws recorded in the Five Books of Moses, chapter and verse being cited for definiteness. But on March 22, 1638 when Rev. Hugh Peter of Salem was denouncing the heresy of Anne Hutchinson, one of the evil things he could say of her was, "I believe that she has vile thoughts of us, and thinks us to be nothing but a company of Jews."

There was more cordiality to the Hebrew language than to Jews. Hebrew was regarded by the Puritans as a sacred tongue, and three books published between 1640 and 1694 used a few words in Hebrew type. Harvard College in 1655 began to require the study of Hebrew by its Christian students. About the same time, tracts began to appear aimed at the conversion of the Jews. Yet the ten or 12 Jews who dot the seventeenth century records of Massachusetts and Connecticut from 1649 to 1699 did not feel welcome enough to stay there or to attract others there.

In Pennsylvania the record is utterly bare of Jews, except for the decision of a group of Mennonites in 1662, in planning to establish a colony in Delaware County, to exclude "all intractible persons" such as Catholics, Quakers, Puritans, and "Usurious Jews."

Moving southward along the coast, we find the one Jew in Maryland in 1658, Dr. Jacob Lumbrozo, being held on a charge of blasphemy which carried a death penalty with it. After a while in prison, he seems to have benefited by a general amnesty declared in England. He remained in Maryland, but in order to own land he became a convert to Christianity. It was to be a full century before a Jewish community appeared in Maryland.

In Virginia there may have been two or three Jews in the 1620's but the first definite record is of a Jew in 1658, followed by a total blank for a century. In South Carolina, a Jew is recorded as a Spanish interpreter in 1695, and three or four Jewish merchants are naturalized in 1697, by virtue of a law pressed from the colonial Assembly by the large minority of French Huguenots in the colony. But no Jewish community appeared for several decades.

Thus by the end of the seventeenth century there was only one tiny but rooted Jewish community on the seaboard, in New York, with possibly a weaker one in Newport. These shores were far indeed from being an eagerly sought haven by Jews. In Eastern Europe in 1648 there had been tragic events. Tens of thousands of Jews were slaughtered, horribly caught in the middle between their Polish patrons and the Ukrainians rising in a mighty movement for independence from Poland. Jewish refugees from these horrors, however, if they fled into Europe, got to Central and at most Western Europe. The transatlantic crossing of East European masses of Jews was to come two centuries later, although in the eighteenth century a trickle of Jews from Central and Eastern Europe made its way to our seacoast to form new Jewish communities.

A view of the interior of the Touro Synagogue of Congregation Jeshuat Israel, Newport, R. I., dedicated in 1763, designed by the foremost colonial architect, Peter Harrison. Note the women's gallery and the reading desk in the center. The oldest synagogue building in the United States, it was declared a "national historic site" in 1946.

CHAPTER 2: Laying More Colonial Foundations

New roots were sunk and old roots strengthened as more Jews came to the seaboard colonies that were soon to become the United States. Yet this immigration was so slow that by 1775 there were only about 1,000 Jews here.

For the thirteen colonies these 75 years were a period of great expansion. More than one half million white immigrants crossed the Atlantic. The slave trade herded hundreds of thousands of African Negroes into our ports to meet the shortage of labor, especially for the plantation economy of the South. From about 300,000 in 1700, the total population multiplied to about 2,600,000 in 1774.

The white settlers who came were mainly those bolder spirits who had decided that economic distress, intensified by religious persecution, required the drastic relief of emigration.

16

French Huguenots and German Protestants first found their way to England, and then, with dissenting Puritans, Scottish Presbyterians and Irish Catholics, took ship to go west. One third of them, too poor to pay their passage, came as indentured servants, to work off their debt under contract for several years.

With agriculture the main base of the economy, more than 95% of the people lived on the farms and in villages. There were only five cities in 1774 with a population of 10,000 or more: Philadelphia, almost 40,000; New York, 25,000 to 30,000; Boston, 20,000; Newport, 12,000; and Charleston, 10,000. It was in four of these cities (Boston excepted), that most of the Jews lived. Centuries of feudal exclusion from agriculture in Europe had prepared the Jews primarily for urban life in the colonies.

The cities, however, were the centers of colonial commerce and budding industry. Because of British mercantilist legislation, trade was chiefly with England and the British West Indies, but intercolonial trade on the seaboard, which included extensive smuggling, was developing those economic ties that became the foundation for unity in the fight for independence. Exports were chiefly of farm and forest products, and of furs and skins. The industries were ship-building, iron-working and flour milling. The ship-builders helped develop not only commerce but also fishing and whaling.

Finally, this century witnessed the removal of France as a power in colonial North America. Winning the French and Indian War, England by 1763 came into possession of virtually all the territory from the Atlantic to the Mississippi and up into Canada.

It was into this background that the few hundred Jewish immigrants fitted themselves with energy, persistence and skill, despite anti-Semitic restrictions and hostility, which conditioned the activities and attitudes of the Jews.

New Jewish communities developed in Philadelphia and Charleston in the 1740's as Jews drifted into these bustling cities, but the only organized group Jewish immigration occurred in Georgia, the last colony to be established. Georgia was founded in 1733 largely for the strategic purpose of acting as a buffer to protect prosperous South Carolina from invasion by the Spanish power based in Florida. To recruit for such a venture, it was necessary to appeal to hardship cases, including persons imprisoned for debt.

The wealthy and haughty leaders of the Sephardic (Spanish and Portuguese) Jewish community in London saw their opportunity. Scores of Ashkenazic German and Polish Jews had been coming into London. Their poverty was a drain on the charity of the Jews, while their different language and manners, secular and religious, were a strain on the upper class sensibilities of the proud Sephardim and seemed to threaten their status. Therefore the rich Jews quickly raised funds to finance emigration of Jews to Georgia, despite the objections of the Trustees of the Colony. The emigration began in January, 1733. On July 10 there arrived in Savannah 67 Jewish men, women and children, Sephardim as well as Ashkenazim, including a couple of Jewish indentured servants. The number was swelled at once when Abigail Minis gave birth to twins: a daughter on July 10 and a son on July 12. Altogether there were 90 Jews in Georgia in the Colony's first years, about one-fifth the population of Savannah.

Efforts by the Trustees in London to have the Jews expelled were unsuccessful. Needing colonists, and grateful to one Jew, Dr. Samuel Nunes Ribiero, for having stopped an epidemic, Governor General James E. Oglethorpe informed the Trustees that the local population wanted the Jews to stay. The Jews remained, and on December 21, 1733 obtained allotments of land for cultivation like the other settlers.

Savannah, however, did not prosper. Many colonists set forth the reasons in a petition in 1738: they had no outright ownership of the land they tilled and therefore little incentive to improve land which after seven years would rotate to somebody else; they had no right to import slaves. The Trustees denied the petition to change these Charter regulations. Threats from the Spaniards in Florida caused some settlers, including eight Jews, to flee in the late summer of 1740. In 1741, when the land rotation became due, there was a general exodus from Georgia.

Barnard Gratz (1738-1801), by Charles Peale Polk.

almost all the Jews leaving with the others. Some Jews went to New York and Charleston, others to the West Indies and London. In 1749, when the Trustees finally agreed to private ownership of land and to the importation of slaves, many Georgians returned to the Colony, including some Jews. Yet a stable Jewish community did not emerge in Savannah until after the adoption of the Federal Constitution.

Economically, the Jews were generally part of the city middle classes. There were a couple of plantation owners in Georgia and South Carolina, but few working farmers. In the cities, there were some indentured servants, male and female, and an occasional wage-worker like Lazarus Isaac (an artistic glass-cutter), who tried to set up as an independent craftsman in Philadelphia in 1773. Failing to attract customers, he hired out as a cutter and flowerer for the now famous Stiegel glass works in Lancaster County, signing his contract in Hebrew, Lezar bar Yitzhak Segal.

Most Jewish craftsmen and artisans were self-employed as bakers, braziers, candle-makers, distillers, engravers, house painters, saddlers, shoemakers, silversmiths, snuffmakers, tailors, tobac-

conists and wigmakers. Shopkeepers were numerous and in the 1760's included even a woman in Philadelphia, Mrs. Hannah Moses, who sold cheap jewelry, children's rings, knives, snuffboxes, brass and enamel fountain pens, and other trinkets purchased from the merchant firm of Barnard Gratz and Benjamin Moses Clava.

Traces of peddlers at the time are few, but solid merchants left an easy trail, advertising their imports at first of drygoods and hardware and later of all kinds of luxury goods. Some served as suppliers for the armed forces. There is a small but interesting development of inter-colonial trade among Jews whose religious, social and sometimes family ties paved the way for and reinforced business relations. The biggest Jewish merchants sometimes also owned their ships in Charleston, New York, Philadelphia and especially in Newport, trading with England, the West Indies, and the African coast. Most important of these, after the death of Jacob Franks of New York in 1769, was Aaron Lopez of Newport.

Of Lopez a New England historian has written that "he almost epitomizes the commercial

Michael Gratz (c. 1733-1811) in 1808, by Thomas Sully.

A Yiddish letter of 1768 about a marital problem, from Barnard Jacobs in Chestnut Hill, Pa. to Barnard Gratz in Philadelphia.

history of Newport in its golden age just before the American Revolution." At his wealthiest he owned outright or in part at least 30 ships in intercolonial and international trade. Once a year from 1757, like equally pious Christians, he sent a ship to Africa for the superprofits of the horrible slave trade, of which Newport was the center for the entire country. In 1775, Lopez was the highest taxpayer in the city, paying almost twice as much as the highest non-Jewish taxpayer and more than all the other 17 Jewish taxpayers combined. Yet reverses during the Revolutionary War left him insolvent when he died in 1782.

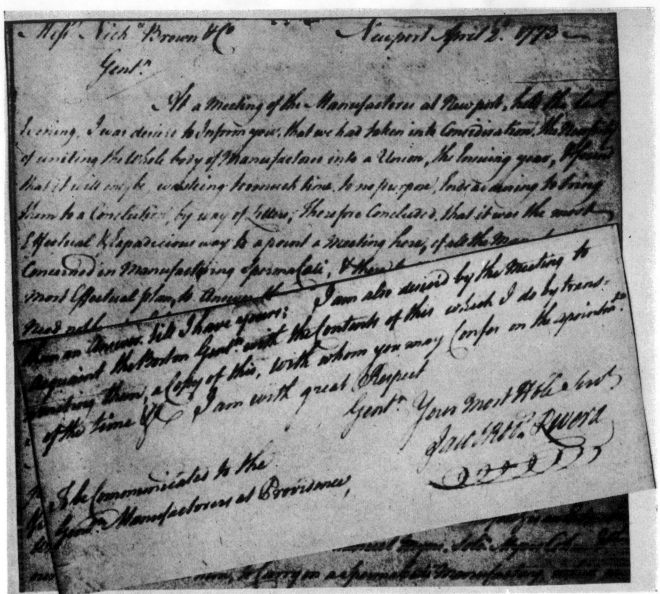

Jacob Rodriguez Rivera of Newport wrote to Nicholas Brown & Co. of Providence, R. I. on April 2, 1773 about "the necessity of uniting the whole body" of manufacturers of spermaceti candles, perhaps by including the Nantucket and New York producers. Rivera mentioned other Jewish spermaceti manufacturers: Sampson and Solomon Simson, Moses Isaacks, Manuel Myers and Solomon Myers Cohen. The United Company of Spermaceti Candlers, in which Jews were a significant minority, had sought since 1761 to control prices.

Lasting to the turn of the century was the firm of the brothers Barnard and Michael Gratz in Philadelphia, exporters, importers and distributors of an incredible variety of merchandise. In addition, after 1765 they became a basic part of a big enterprise, with Jewish and non-Jewish partners, to open up the West for the fur and Indian trade as well as for settlement. The land speculation of this combine embraced literally many millions of acres way out into the Illinois territory.

In the development of the infant colonial industry, Jews too played their small, but in one or two instances, effective part. Jews of Newport were a large factor in the development of the spermaceti industry, the making of candles from whale oil. Some were engaged in the manufacture of potash, Castile soap, snuff, and barrel staves; one, in South Carolina, had a great deal to do with the production of indigo as a dye.

A half dozen Jewish medical men round out the picture of how Jews made a living at this time. In addition to the Georgia doctor already mentioned, a surgeon and dentist from Bohemia, Elias Wollin, worked in New York in 1740, and Dr. Isaac Cohen of Hamburg practiced in the frontier town of Lancaster, Pa. in 1747. There was a Dr. Jacob Isaac in New York in 1753 and a Dr. Nathan Levy in South Carolina in 1772. It should be remembered that there were only two medical schools, and that up to 1783 they had graduated only 50 persons. The first Jew to become a doctor by learning medicine in this country was Isaac Abrahams, graduated from Columbia College in 1774 (when it was still Kings College).

The economic life of the Jews was of course connected with their political status. In comparison with the situation in Europe, this status was superior, in fact unique. Nowhere in Europe did Jews have the rights and opportunities they developed here. But in comparison with fellow white colonials, Jews did not achieve even formal equality with white Protestants, any more than did the Catholics. Even in Rhode Island, no Jews voted before the Revolution, nor is there evidence of Jews voting for the colonial legislatures anywhere except in New York.

Nevertheless, as early as 1718 in New York Jews were being elected to such a local office as constable. Nowhere in Europe could a Jew be even so humble a part of the apparatus of law enforcement.

Helpful was the enactment by the British Parliament in 1740 of a Naturalization Act enabling Protestants, Quakers and Jews (but not Catholics) to be naturalized in the British colonies after seven years' residence. To encourage colonization, Parliament thus extended rights it denied in England itself. During the next 30 years, about 50 Jews in the seaboard colonies were naturalized, 34 of them in New York. Yet in Rhode Island in 1762 Aaron Lopez was denied naturalization, and had to go to Massachusetts to obtain it. By this law, moreover, no naturalized citizen could hold office or any military or civil place of trust. A Parliamentary law of 1773 extending such rights to naturalized citizens did not clearly apply to Jews.

The Jews in this period had the right to

Jacob Rodriguez Rivera (c. 1717-1789), by Gilbert Stuart, about 1775.

public worship, but that was not yet even formal religious equality. Where there was an official established church, as in New York and South Carolina, everybody, including dissenters and Jews, had to pay taxes for the support of the official church.

Jews were potential targets of discrimination, restriction, abuse or attack. Anti-Semitism was revealed in various ways. In New York in 1737 the colonial Assembly refused to permit Jews to testify before it in a case of a disputed election. One disputant argued heatedly that Jews had no right to vote for the Assembly since they were disfranchised in England and had, he maintained, crucified Jesus. Members of the Assembly were moved to tears by his rhetoric, and a pogrom atmosphere was created. Not until 1761 is it certain that Jews voted again in New York.

In Georgia, in 1738, when the Christians petitioned the Trustees for the introduction of private property and slavery, the Jews wanted to sign the petition, but were denied the right to do so on the ground that such signatures would prejudice their case.

Aaron Lopez (1731-1782) and Isaac Elizer of Newport having petitioned for naturalization, the General Assembly of Rhode Island on October 30, 1761 decided that they
might be sworn in as lawful subjects of the King with the right to buy land and
transmit inheritance, but, since they were Jews, they would not have the rights to
vote or hold office. In 1762 their petition was finally denied.

In New York in May, 1743, a man dressed like a Gentleman, according to a newspaper account, led a crowd to interfere violently with a Jewish burial, so that "it was with much Difficulty the Corpse was interr'd." Interment did not mean undisturbed rest, either, for in 1746 and 1751 the New York Congregation publicly advertised a reward for seizure of the vandals who had desecrated the tombs and damaged the cemetery walls.

In Williamsburg, Va., in 1752 the anti-Semitic stereotype of Shylock was presented to a genteel audience "with great applause," and by 1774 this play had been performed in Annapolis, Philadelphia, New York and Charleston. In Pennsylvania in 1764, during the elections to the Assembly, an anti-Semitic attack on "Jew landlords" appeared in a German newspaper. In 1770 in Georgia, a bill to assign common land for a Jewish cemetery was killed by outspoken and nasty opposition.

Of course this was not anti-Semitism on the same level as it was operating then in Europe. But such random public expressions of it could not but make Jews uneasy, and aware in their depths that equality and security were not yet theirs.

Religious Jews organized themselves where-

By PERMISSION of the Honble ROBERT DINWIDDIE,
Esq; His Majesty's Lieutenant-Governor, and Commander in
Chief of the Colony and Dominion of Virginia.

By a Company of COMEDIANS, from LONDON,
At the THEATRE in WILLIAMSBURG,
On Friday next, being the 15th of September, will be presented,
A PLAY, Call'd,
THE
MERCHANT of VENICE.
(Written by Shakespear.)
The Part of ANTONIO (the MERCHANT) to be perform'd by
Mr. CLARKSON.
GRATIANO, by Mr. SINGLETON,
Lorenzo, (with Songs in Character) by Mr. ADCOCK.
The Part of BASSANIO to be perform'd by
Mr. RIGBY.
Duke, by Mr. Wynell.
Salanio, by Mr. Herbert.
The Part of LAUNCELOT, by Mr. HALLAM.
And the Part of SHYLOCK, (the Jew) to be perform'd by
Mr. MALONE.
The Part of NERISSA, by Mrs. ADCOCK,
Jessica, by Mrs. Rigby.
And the Part of PORTIA, to be perform'd by
Mrs. HALLAM.
With a new occasional PROLOGUE.
To which will be added, a FARCE, call'd,
The ANATOMIST:
OR,
SHAM DOCTOR.
The Part of Monsieur le Medecin, by
Mr. RIGBY.
And the Part of BEATRICE, by Mrs. ADCOCK.
No Person, whatsoever, to be admitted behind the Scenes.
BOXES, 7s. 6d. PIT and BALCONIES, 5s. 9d. GALLERY, 3s. 9d.
To begin at Six o'clock.
Vivat Rex.

The first performance of "The Merchant of Venice" is
advertised in "The Virginia Gazette," Williamsburg, on
August 28, 1752. This was among the very first plays
produced in the American colonies.

ever possible, although sometimes a decade or two passed, even when there were enough Jews in the vicinity, before a stable congregation was established. By 1750 the majority of Jews were definitely of Ashkenazic origin, yet the form of Jewish ritual that prevailed was that of the Sephardim. In New York by 1730 the congregation already had a majority of Ashkenazim, but the governing board used its power to maintain the Sephardic ritual. In Georgia, the two groups held separate services. One Jew there lamented vehemently that "the Spanish and Portuguese Jews persecuted the German Jews so much that no Christian could persecute another like that." The founding of a congregation in Georgia was delayed for many years; yet when it emerged it adopted the Sephardic rite, and the same thing occurred in Philadelphia. It was not until the end of the eighteenth century that Ashkenazim began to found their own congregations.

In the colonial period other religious functionaries began to appear besides the *Hazan* (the Sephardic cantor and reader who in our country evolved into the spiritual leader of the congregation), although they were decidedly in short supply. The *shohet* and the *mohel* (ritual circumcizer) became part of the scene, the latter often having to travel far and wide to do his

This Hebrew "Hechsher" (document certifying products as "Kosher"), signed by Abraham I. Abrahams of Congregation Shearith Israel in New York on February 27, 1767, declared that the Jews of Barbados could safely eat the meats exported to them by Michael Gratz.

work. Michael Gratz, wishing to export preserved kosher meat to Barbados in 1767, had to obtain a *hechsher* (certificate of ritual fitness) from New York. The beginnings of Jewish education of the young, under congregational control, emerged first in New York in 1731 and in Newport in 1760.

At this time, too, charity was still a congregational function exclusively, and aid was given from special funds to the sick and aged, the orphans and widows and otherwise needy. Congregations sometimes appealed for help in building a synagogue. Thus New York received aid in 1730 from the West Indies, Surinam, Curaçao and London, and Newport in 1760, with only 58 Jews in town, also asked for and received help to build the synagogue that is today a national shrine as the oldest extant synagogue in our country. From 1759, occasional aid was sent to the Jews of Palestine.

There was only one secular Jewish organization, a Wednesday evening supper and low-stake card-playing club in Newport in 1761, with membership limited to nine Jews. Anyone who dared talk there about "Synagogue affairs" was to be fined "four bottles good wine." Another form of social life was found in the Masonic organizations, to which Jews were admitted in Georgia, South Carolina, Pennsylvania, New York and Rhode Island, finding a base for frater-

A Hanukah lamp in use since colonial days at Congregation Shearith Israel, New York.

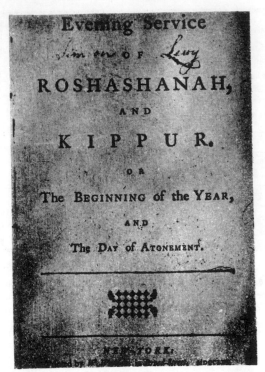

The first prayer-book for Jewish holidays published in the American colonies, New York, 1761.

nalism with non-Jews in the general religious and political liberalism that characterized the Masons of the time. Similarly, in Georgia the St. George's Society, a benevolent organization established in 1750 (later the Union Society), counted the Jew, Benjamin Sheftall, among its five founders.

The meager beginnings of Jewish cultural life made their appearance. The first Hebrew grammar printed in our country was published in Boston in 1735, composed by Judah Monis, who in order to become a teacher of Hebrew at Harvard in 1722 had had to embrace Christianity. The first work by a colonial Jew to be printed was an English translation of the Hebrew Prayer offered by Joseph Ysurun Pinto in the New York Synagogue on October 23, 1760, thanking God for the British conquest of Canada. In 1761 in New York there appeared an English translation of the Rosh Hashana and Yom Kippur service, followed in 1766 by the first translation into English of the Sephardic rite prayers "for Shabbath, Rosh-Hashanah, and Kippur," with Isaac Pinto as the translator. The first local Jewish sermon to be published appeared in English in Newport in 1773; it was preached in Spanish in the Newport Synagogue at Shevuoth (Pente-

cost) by Rabbi Haim Isaac Karigal of Hebron in Palestine.

In secular culture, faint traces were barely noticeable. If Isaac the Scribe was a Jew (the identity of Isaac Pinto has been suggested), then *The Chapters of Isaac the Scribe* in the *New York Journal* in 1772, and later in a still unlocated pamphlet, was the first Jewish literary work. Written in Biblical prose style, it described a voyage to England, devoting a chapter to Richie, the daughter of the recently deceased Jacob Franks, well-known New York merchant. Perhaps mention should be made that in 1744 a traveler in Philadelphia reported that "One Levy there played a very good violine" at a music club. Of more enduring value was the art and craftsmanship of the famous New York silversmith, Myer Myers.

On the eve of the Revolutionary Era, the thousand Jews in the colonies were sufficiently at home, despite restrictions, to be ready to join the fight for independence and democracy.

Silver Torah Scroll Bells, made about 1772 for Congregation Mikveh Israel of Philadelphia by Myer Myers (1723-1795), an outstanding silversmith whose work is now in many museums.

CHAPTER 3: Jews as Rebels of '76

Abraham Solomon fought the British at the Battle of Bunker Hill in 1775.

Francis Salvador, the first Jew to give his life in 1776, was glad with his dying breath that the enemy had been beaten, although in distant South Carolina he had not yet heard of the Declaration of Independence.

Philip Moses Russell as a surgeon's mate froze in the draughty huts of Valley Forge, tending the tattered and suffering wounded in 1778.

Benjamin Nones, an immigrant from Bordeaux, France, enlisted in 1777 in the American army and fought right through the war; his captain cited him for exceptional gallantry in action at the Siege of Savannah in 1779.

Esther Hays of Bedford in Westchester County, New York, wife of an American soldier, refused to turn informer, as the family tradition has it, when loyalists raided her house in 1779 while she was nursing a new-born infant in bed, and carried out their threat to set fire to her house.

Why did these Jews take their place in the Revolutionary War? Whatever the personal motivation of each individual named, or of the hundreds of others who took part in or supported it, these Jews were all in the war for the same basic reason as other new Americans. Although still suffering inequality as Jews, they shared the grievances and the aims of the new American nationality that had been developing out of the colonial soil, in combat against the economic and political tyranny of the British merchants, King and Parliament.

Most of the Jews in the 13 seething colonies were part of the merchant, shipping and shopkeeping middle class that suffered from British trade restrictions, British limitations on colonial manufacture, British taxation policies, British obstacles to speculation in Western lands, British interference, in sum, with the desire of the American middle classes to expand production, land settlement and their markets at home and abroad.

Similarly, the Jewish artisans and craftsmen—the shoemakers, glaziers, tailors, soap-makers, silversmiths, and so forth—shared the problems of their fellows in the same class. British trade laws caused loss of business and unemployment. The craftsmen had to pay more for the raw materials they bought. If they owed money, they were hard hit by British currency laws.

If the Southern plantation and slave owners, heavily in debt to British merchants and cramped by British land restrictions, turned to revolution —as did Washington and Jefferson and Madison —Jewish plantation and slave owners, a Salvador, a Sheftall and a Minis, were similarly moved by the same forces.

Thus among the vast majority in the colonies an anti-British coalition was shaped in the decade before '76. Led by planters, merchants, shopkeepers and professionals, the coalition had its popular base among the independent farmers and the city artisans and wage-workers. The farmers and city working people, however, had a special need for more democracy and representation in government to protect their own interests against merchants, employers and creditors. "Taxation without representation" was suffered by all colonials at the hands of Britain; it was also the affliction of the mass of the colonials at the hands of their own upper classes. But the cry for more democracy ran up against opposition not only by merchant and planter

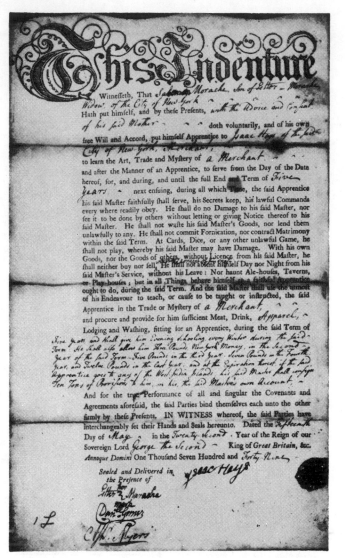

Indenture of Apprenticeship for five years of Salomon Marache by his widowed mother, Estter, to Isaac Hays, New York Jewish merchant, May 15, 1749. Although apprentices usually received no payment, Hays contracted to pay £27. Marache became a patriotic merchant, leaving New York when the British occupied it.

but particularly by the British power. Independence from Britain, therefore, became the popular demand of farmers, artisans and wage-workers, which pushed the other groups in the coalition forward when they hesitated. The war that British repression forced upon the colonies in April, 1775 began as a war for redress of grievance. Under pressure of the people, it became a war for national independence by July, 1776.

Now although there were very few Jewish farmers and a comparatively small number of craftsmen, the Jews were a tiny but staunch element in the coalition for a specific reason. As Jews they still had to win formal religious and political equality. This could best be achieved in a democracy that would enforce separation of church and state. Such separation could be attained more easily in the colonies with their great diversity of religions than in England. Independence from England therefore would have a special meaning for all sections of colonial Jews. The overwhelming majority of Jews supported the revolutionary cause because of their position in the colonial economy as Americans and their specific democratic needs as Jews.

Resistance to British policy first took the form of an economic boycott or, as it was called then, a non-importation program. The odious Stamp Act, imposing a tax on various legal and economic activities, was met by colonial merchants with an effective rolling wave of non-importation agreements. In Philadelphia, among the 375 merchants who in 1765 pledged themselves not to import British goods there were eight or nine Jews, the majority of Jewish merchants of the town. Such boycotts turned many a colonial merchant to new enterprises. The business careers of Barnard and Michael Gratz, backers of this agreement, were decisively changed by this action. From importing they had to turn largely to intercolonial trade and to Western land speculation. When in 1774 the British Quebec Act assigned the Western lands to Quebec, the Gratzes and their associates in such ventures had another reason to turn against Britain.

As resistance grew, defenders of British rule wheeled out the theory of the Divine Right of Kings. To fight Britain was to fight His Sacred Majesty, argued the conservative clergy. Upon simple and literal believers, this was intimidating argument. The eternal damnation that would be visited on those who fought God's King loomed as infinitely worse than that of fighting a King alone. How was King George to be stripped of his alleged Divine Right to rule as he willed? Only an authority generally accepted as Divine could do this. It was found in the Biblical account of ancient Hebrew history.

In Christian pulpit and pamphlet revolutionary clergymen and writers like Tom Paine cited the Old Testament. In chapter 8 of the first book of Samuel was it not clearly written that the Lord

The Non-Importation Agreement of Philadelphia, October 25, 1765, signed by 375 merchants, of whom nine were Jews.

(8)

When firſt the Iſraelites came out from the bondage of Egypt, they were a multitude without any other order than what had been kept up, very feebly, under the ancient patriarchal authority. They were ſuddenly collected into a body under the conduct of Moſes, without any proper national or military regulation. Yet in the ſhort ſpace of about three months after they had paſſed the red ſea, they were reduced into ſuch civil and military order, blended together by the advice of Jethro, as was well adapted to their circumſtances in the wilderneſs while deſtitute of property. Able men were choſen out of all their tribes, and made captains and rulers of thouſands, hundreds, fifties and tens : and theſe commanded them as military officers, and acted as judges in matters of common controverſy.

But the great thing wanting was a permanent conſtitution, which might keep the-people peaceable and obedient while in the deſert, and after they had gained poſſeſſion of the promiſed land. Therefore, upon the complaint of Moſes that the burden of government was too heavy for him, God commanded him to bring ſeventy men, choſen from among the elders and officers, and preſent them at the tabernacle; and there he endued

them

The use of ancient Jewish history in contemporary politics continued in the debate on ratification of the United States Constitution. Above is a page from a sermon, "The Republic of the Israelites an Example to the American States," preached June 5, 1788 before both houses of the New Hampshire State Legislature by Rev. Samuel Langdon, "Pastor of the Church in Hampton-Falls."

had warned the Israelites of all the afflictions that would befall them if they got themselves a king? And had not the heedless Hebrews gotten themselves a king, and suffered for it? Therefore the Lord was obviously against kings! As late as April, 1776 Paine was explaining this to his readers, quoting Hosea, chapter 13, verse 2, "I gave them a king in mine anger." In fact, it was argued, the Lord was on the side of the colonial rebels. It is not known whether any Jewish sermon preached during those days expounded this doctrine. More important is the fact that it was effective in mobilizing the consciences of pious

Christians for the revolution, as it had done and was still to do under similar circumstances in Europe.

As British repression stiffened the resistance and turned it more and more to the inevitable revolution, the majority of Jews took their stand with the majority of other Americans. Among the three million colonials, however, there were only about 1,000 Jews, clustered in Newport, New York, Philadelphia, Charleston and Savannah, with a small group in Lancaster, Pa. and individuals scattered here and there. So small a number could hardly be decisive or even influential in so huge a conflict. In fact, the American Revolution did more for the Jews here and, by its example, abroad, than the Jews here could possibly have done for the Revolution. But they played their honorable part, political, military and economic.

In the face of political restrictions in some colonies, the Jews did not find it easy to take part in the early stages of the political conflict, when legal institutions like the Colonial Assemblies were the channels of struggle. But as extra-legal organizations of resistance and revolution emerged, an occasional Jew appeared in them. After the Continental Congress in the fall of 1774, Provincial Congresses were organized in the colonies, rivaling the authority of the established colonial Assemblies. In the Provincial Congress in South Carolina, Francis Salvador took his place in December, 1774. An active advocate of independence, he also served in the second Congress. When on March 26, 1776 that Congress declared itself to be the first South Carolina State General Assembly, Salvador became thus the first Jew to hold state legislative office.

In Georgia, the local revolutionary organizations were called Parochial Committees. "One Sheftall, a Jew," the Colonial Governor complained in December, 1775, was the head of the Savannah Parochial Committee, which, according to the irate Governor, consisted of "a Parcel of the Lowest People, Chiefly Carpenters, Shoemakers, Blacksmiths, &c." And this Jew, Sheftall, was ordering British vessels out of the harbor without allowing them to unload, much to the horror of His Majesty's Governor! He was "a

Jonas Phillips (1736-1803), painting attributed to Charles Willson Peale.

Isaac Franks (1759-1822), by Gilbert Stuart — revolutionary soldier from June, 1776 to June, 1782.

very great rebel" indeed, and so was Philip Minis and his wife and daughter Judith. When the British captured Savannah in 1778, these two women were placed under house arrest and then expelled from town as "Great Whigs," that is, rebels.

Finally the work of all such extra-legal organizations culminated in the Declaration of Independence, that giant step forward proclaiming a new state on the Fourth of July, 1776. When on July 8 the Declaration was issued in Philadelphia and printed as a handbill, Jews shared the great wonder and excitement, and Jonas Phillips (who had been Jonah son of Feibush in Germany before he Anglicized his name in London) bought the handbill and sent it a few weeks later to a friend in Amsterdam with a Yiddish letter. News indeed!

In New York on July 9 Washington read the Declaration to his massed troops, and among those who cheered were Jewish soldiers like Isaac Franks and Hart Jacobs. (In January the revolutionary Committee of Safety had considerately excused Jacobs from standing guard on Friday nights because it was his Sabbath, but he had done "his full tour of duty on other nights.") With all patriots, the Jews were inspired by the words not only of independence but particularly of equality. "All men are created equal," it said, but that did not include Negroes, and even the statement condemning the slave trade had been stricken from the Declaration to please the South Carolina and Georgia delegations and the New England slave traders. But did equality include Jews?

In Newport, Moses Michael Hays asked for an answer on July 11, 1776. Called up before a Committee of the state Assembly, Hays declared he was a patriotic native-born American, but protested, "I am an Israelite and am not allowed the liberty of a vote, or voice in common with the rest of the voters . . ." He actively supported the Revolution as a merchant and supplier without waiting for Rhode Island to extend the right to vote to Jews. Independence came first, and would in fact open the way to fight for democracy.

It was for independence that, in their own way, the majority of the congregation in New

Moses Michael Hays (1739-1805).

Rev. Gershom Mendes Seixas (1745-1816) of Congregation Shearith Israel, New York, from a painting by J. F. Brown in 1929 from a contemporary miniature. The portrait now hangs in Columbia University, of which Seixas had been a Trustee, 1787-1815.

York voted in a unique debate in the summer of 1776. The British and their hired Hessian troops were about to capture New York, driving Washington north to Harlem Heights. What should the Jews do? Some in the congregation Shearith Israel argued for staying in the city under British occupation. After all, there was an old rabbinic law that "dina de malhuta dina," the law of the land is the law, and obedience is due to whatever powers rule. But an opposite idea was expressed by Gershom Mendes Seixas, *Hazan* and leader of the congregation, and by Solomon Simson, a young merchant who was president of the congregation. The issue in that square little synagogue on Mill Street was "Life, Liberty and the Pursuit of Happiness," in the words of the Declaration of Independence, against "dina de malhuta dina." The majority decided they would rather leave the city than stay and collaborate with the British and Hessian forces of occupation. On August 22, 1776 Seixas gathered the ritual objects and synagogue records and, with whatever household goods were easily movable, he and the other patriotic Jews left New York. For the first time in a thousand years

a Jewish community went into *voluntary* exile. Some went to Stratford, Conn., but most headed for the capital of the Revolution, Philadelphia, where in various ways they supported the revolutionary cause.

It was not because they were homeless that these Jews decided to leave New York. They left only in order to fight for the independence that would add rich meaning to these homes. And they did not return to New York until the British troops left it in 1783. A triumphal return! For in 1777 New York had adopted a Constitution which was the first in our country and in the world to "ordain, determine and declare, that the free exercise and enjoyment of religious profession and worship, without discrimination or preference, shall forever hereafter be allowed within this state to all mankind." Here was the beginning of legal Jewish emancipation.

For this, Jews had not only given political support to the revolution but had fought in it. Most of them enlisted and served as privates in the revolutionary forces. Enlistments were for short terms, and men like Asher Pollock of Newport and Benjamin Nones enlisted a half dozen times, year after year. Some became non-commissioned officers and two rose to the high rank of lieutenant-colonel: David Salisbury Franks and Solomon Bush. Wounded in the fighting at Philadelphia in September, 1777, Bush wrote to a Jew in Virginia that he was slowly recovering from a broken thigh though the surgeons had given him up for lost, and "my wishes are to be able to get Satisfaction and revenge the Rongs [sic] of my injured country."

There were Jews also enrolled in militia companies in Philadelphia and Charleston, and some of them were called into active service. In Charleston, in the part of the city where the Jews lived, one such militia company was organized by Captain Richard Lushington. All males in the area from 16 to 60 were required to be in this militia. Of the 60 persons enrolled about 25 were Jews, although not all of course were ablebodied and ready for service. Because of the high percentage of Jews, the company got to be called uncomplimentarily the "Jew Company." When part of it was called into action at Beaufort in 1779, Joseph Solomon was among those killed and Ephraim Abrams was wounded.

There were also, it may be noted, Jews among the Loyalists who made up almost one fifth of the colonial population, siding with the King and opposing independence. Among the Jews the Loyalists were to be found mainly in New York and Newport under British occupation. There were about 15 or 16 Jews in Oliver De Lancey's three Loyalist Battalions in New York. They were loyal to King George's "sacred person, Crown and Dignity," to use the words of the loyalist address of October 16, 1776. Did they waver when the New York State revolutionary Constitution extended the "free exercise" of religion to all, consciously including Jews? Whatever the personal intentions of the Jewish loyalists, they were in fact fighting against the only forces that could open roads of equality for Jews and for the country as a whole. It was only the Jewish revolutionaries who advanced the cause of freedom.

Lieutenant Colonel David Salisbury Franks, (d. 1793), by Charles Willson Peale.

As useful in the war as other efforts were the energies of Jewish merchants, shippers and brokers in selling supplies and raising funds for the government and the troops. Michael Gratz sold them blankets and clothing; Joseph Simon offered Pennsylvania rifles, superior to anything the British had; and Manuel Josephson supplied "guns, cutlasses and bayonets." Jacob Isaacs of Newport sold four cannon, and Aaron Lopez provided gunpower and a whale boat. Scores of others helped round up the materials of war for the ragged Continentals.

Part of the naval contest between Britain and the revolutionary cause was fought by venturesome privateers, armed merchantmen that roamed the ocean raiding enemy merchant vessels, sinking or better still capturing their cargoes. Among the Jews who outfitted vessels for

Manuel Josephson (1729-1796), from a painting attributed to Lawrence Kilburn.

this daring work were Moses Michael Hays of Boston, the Gratzes, and Isaac Moses, Benjamin Seixas, Abraham Sasportas and Moses Levy, operating from Philadelphia, to which they had come from New York and Charleston.

Jews were also among those that aided in the financing of the war, although there were so few really wealthy Jews that their direct contribution was small. An Isaac Moses in Philadelphia had the means in 1780 to advance £3,000 and a Jacob Hart, Sr. in Baltimore in 1781 lent the government £2000 for one year to help pay the soldiers. Even a more signal service was rendered by Haym Salomon. Not a rich man and therefore unable to lend money himself to the government, Salomon was energetic and resourceful enough to raise about $200,000 for the government. As the most effective of all the Philadelphia brokers, including five or six other Jews, in the sale of government securities, Salomon was at his own request permitted to advertise himself as "Broker to the Office of Finance." Moreover, the broker's fee that Salomon charged was smaller than that which the Office of Finance had to pay to other brokers.

Thus did the small Jewish population of the time make its small but varied and devoted contribution to establish *its* country's independence. But while they were working, fighting, dying for the cause, they still had to face the slings and arrows of outrageous anti-Semitism. The image of Shylock as the Jew continued to be stamped upon the public mind. In 1775, a Philadelphia publisher reprinted James Burgh's British manual, *The Art of Speaking*. In two scenes, Shylock is presented as a model of obstinacy, hypocrisy, cruelty, malice, blood-thirstiness, sneakiness and spite. Until 1804 this work was reissued in edition after edition in New York, Boston, Danbury and Baltimore.

Time and again and in many places the patriotic Jews faced the anti-Semitic taunt or attack, but their patriotism withstood these tests. Very shortly after the Jews who had gone into voluntary exile from New York reached Philadelphia and swelled the Jewish population, there was a political attack. The Pennsylvania Constitutional Convention had on September 10, 1776 issued its proposed draft. In Section 10 the

Jacob Hart (1746-1822) by Philip Parisen.

oath of allegiance required of voters was given as: "I do believe in one God, the Creator and Governor of the Universe." Immediately protesting letters from bigots appeared in the *Evening Post*. Were Jews and Turks to be allowed not only to become big landholders but also officeholders and thus make Pennsylvania "unsafe for Christians"? There were no Turks in Pennsylvania. The attack was successful. When the Constitution was adopted on September 28, 1776, the prescribed oath read: "I do acknowledge the Scriptures of the Old and New Testament to be given by divine inspiration." Jews had been excluded. The Jews waited. In 1783, the Jewish New Yorkers went back to New York, where the Constitution accorded them religious equality before the law. The Jews of Philadelphia that year petitioned for constitutional revision, but the petition was ignored. The change was not effected until 1790.

The Jews of Charleston had to react to a jibe in *The South Carolina and American General Gazette* in 1778. An article signed "An American" sneered at "the Tribe of Israel" as cowards who, with Savannah under siege, "fled here for an asylum, with their ill-got wealth—dastardly

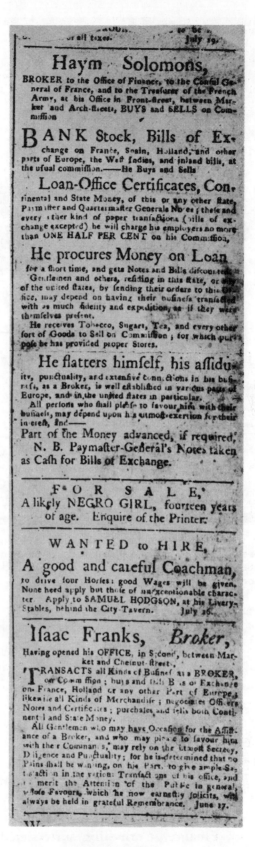

valuable acquisitions of men who, for their religious sentiments, were distressed in their own countries.— And if Jews in Europe or elsewhere, should incline to transport themselves to America, and would, for reason of some certain advantage of the soil, climate, or the trade of Pennsylvania, rather become inhabitants thereof, than of any other state; yet the disability of Jews to take seat among the representatives of the people, as worded by the said religious test, might determine their free choice to go to New-York, or to any other of the United States of America, where there is no such like restraint laid upon the nation and religion of the Jews, as in Pennsylvania.—Your memorialists cannot say that the Jews are particularly fond of being representatives of the people in assembly or civil officers and magistrates in the state; but with great submission they apprehend that a clause in the constitution, which disables them to be elected by their fellow citizens to represent them in assembly, as a stigma upon their nation and their religion, and it is inconsonant with the second paragraph of the said bill of rights; otherwise Jews are as fond of liberty as other religious societies can be, and it must create in them a displeasure, when they perceive that for their profession dissent to a doctrine, which is inconsistent with their religious sentiments, they should be excluded from the most important and honourable part of the rights of a free citizen.

Your memorialists beg farther leave to represent the religion of the Jews, or

Philadelphia Jewish leaders on December 23, 1783 petitioned for revision of the State Constitution to remove a clause barring Jews from holding office. The text appeared in "The Freeman's Journal," Philadelphia, January 21, 1784.

Haym Salomon (c. 1740-1785) placed a large advertisement in "The Pennsylvania Packet," July 20, 1782, after he had been granted permission to call himself "Broker to the Office of Finance," perhaps to meet the competition of Isaac Franks, revolutionary soldier who had come to Philadelphia and opened a brokerage office.

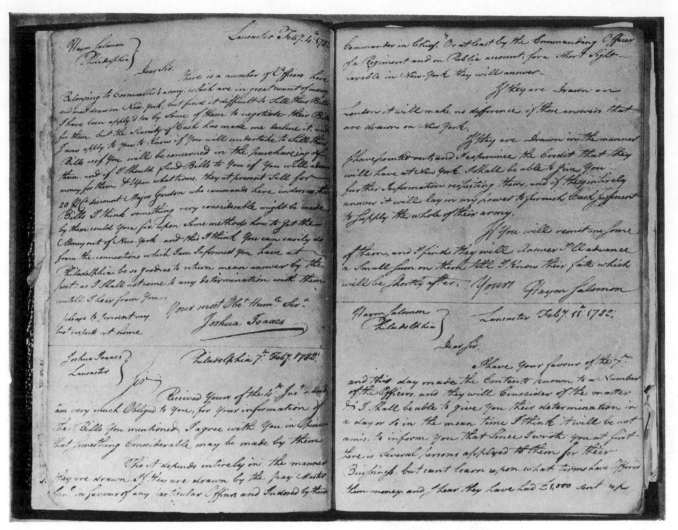

Pages from Haym Salomon's Letter-Book, showing correspondence in February, 1782 between Joshua Isaacs of Lancaster, Pa. and Salomon, about the possibility of making considerable profit by buying up the Bills of Exchange of imprisoned British officers of Cornwallis' army at a large discount.

turning their backs upon the country when in danger, which gave them bread and protection . . ." The newspaper soon carried a rejoinder by "A real American, and True hearted Israelite" disproving the charge, as such charges were to be disproved and renewed again and again. The frequency of the refutation only underlined the buoyancy and usefulness of the slander.

In another instance, Haym Salomon had to swallow a public insult. A few months after Salomon had begun to work as a broker for the Office of Finance, Cornwallis surrendered at Yorktown on October 19, 1781, ending the fighting in the war. Just after the news arrived in Philadelphia, Salomon was at the Coffee House. Seeing a hard-crusted Loyalist, Salomon teased

him: "I presume you know that your friend Lord Cornwallis is taken with all his army."

"Do you believe it?" said the Loyalist.

"To be sure I do," replied Salomon.

"Well my good friend, I can only tell you that you had better believe in Jesus Christ, that will save your poor soul from a worse fate than that of Lord Cornwallis, if, as you say, he has been captured."

The contemporary chronicler of this incident added: "The laughers were not on the side of the Israelite," and then he summed it up: "The Jews were yet a hated and a despised race."

A few months later, in the spring of 1782, the Jewish congregation in Philadelphia as a whole suffered a rude and costly affront. By this time, most of the Jews of Georgia and South Carolina had come to Philadelphia as refugees when their home cities had been occupied by the British. Together with the Jews from New York and Newport who were then in Philadelphia, the Jewish population there included almost all the Jews in the states. Congregational life had blossomed to the point where the leaders undertook to build a synagogue, the first in the city. Having with difficulty raised £540 to pay for a lot on which to build, the Jews suddenly found they could not use the lot, because it adjoined a Reformed German Church, and the Church objected that a synagogue next to them would "disturb" them. Finally the synagogue was built, on another lot around the corner. Yet consider the psychology of the congregation, which warned all those participating in the dedication exercise "to be particularly carefull [sic] not to raise their Voices higher than the Hazan's who will endeavor to modulate his Voice to a proper Pitch so as only to fill the Building"—and not be heard outside, where it might "disturb" those around the corner. All men *were* created equal, but even Jews active in support of the revolution felt they had to be careful.

A year and a half later there was another public smear of the Jews. In March, 1784 a former Loyalist Quaker lawyer, Miers Fisher, in support of a new state bank that would compete with the National Bank, appeared before the Pennsylvania Assembly with a diatribe against "Jew Brokers." "The Jews," he insisted, "were the authors of high and unusual interest," as he evoked the image of Shylock. This time he was answered in the *Independent Gazetteer* by an anonymous Jew and broker, one of the six in Philadelphia and perhaps even Haym Salomon himself. Indignantly he rejected "the indecent, unjust, inhumane aspersions, you cast so indiscriminately on the Jews of this City at large . . ." Vigorously he protested (a little too much?) that "I exult and glory in reflecting that we have the honour to reside in a free country where, as a people, we have met with the most generous countenance and protection . . ." Stoutly he pointed with pride to the fact that "we have in general been early, uniform, decisive whigs, and were second to none in our patriotism and attachment to our country!"

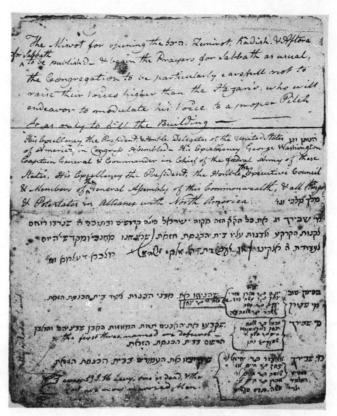

Manuscript instructions by Rev. Gershom Mendes Seixas that Congregation Mikveh Israel should not make too much noise at the dedication exercises of the Synagogue in 1782, and the text of his prayer for the Continental Congress, George Washington, the government of Pennsylvania, and "all Kings & Potentates in Alliance with North America."

It was a good resounding "answer." But the fact that there had to be so many good answers to public charges (private sneers and barbs you could, if you wished, "haughtily" overlook) was itself disturbing. Of course the Jews found democratically inclined non-Jews who defended them against misrepresentation. They were happy to read in *The South-Carolina Gazette and General Advertiser* of August 30, 1783 that "He who hates another man for not being a Christian is himself not a Christian. . . . The Jews have had a considerable share in our late Revolution. . . . Let our government invite the Jews to our state and promise them a settlement in it." And they were delighted when a Christian correspondent in *The Freeman's Journal* of Philadelphia on January 21, 1784 supported their petition for constitutional equality because it "would benefit the state, by inviting hither a great number of Jews, who for their wealth, their

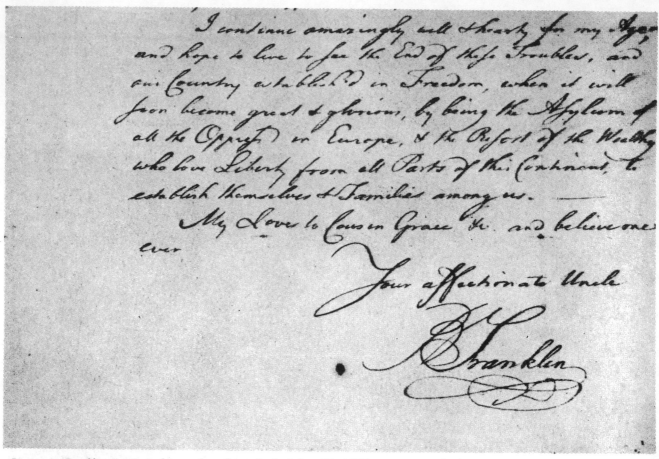

Benjamin Franklin wrote to his nephew from Paris, May 27, 1777, expressing the hope that "our Country . . . will soon become great & glorious, by being the Asylum of all the Oppress'd in Europe . . ."

information, and their attachment to the cause of liberty, might be of extensive and permanent service," although some Jews probably wished the correspondent had not added that equality would also help convert Jews to Christianity. Philadelphia Jews also took comfort in the response of Christians to the appeal of Congregation Mickveh Israel in 1788 for funds to save their synagogue from being sold to meet still unpaid debts of construction. Heading the list of these contributors was the octogenarian Benjamin Franklin with £5, followed by Pennsylvania Attorney-General William Bradford and Thomas McKean, signer of the Declaration of

Independence, with £3 each, and so on down, with names famous in Philadelphia history like Rittenhouse, Biddle and Rush.

Pleased with such defenses, Jews were worried by the continuing need for defense. But the war was over and won. Independence was established. The Declaration had said that all men were created equal. The most democratic among the Jews began to reflect that *all* did not include Negroes and that something would have to be done about that. As a whole, the Jews were determined that *all* did include Jews and they were prepared to continue to fight that it should.

The Address of the Hebrew Congregaton of Newport, R. I. to Washington, when he visited the city on August 17, 1790, and his reply. These, together with others by the Christian clergy and Masonic organizations, were printed in the Providence newspaper.

CHAPTER 4: Promise and Suspense: Under the Constitution

The years from the end of the Revolutionary War to the end of the century were years of promise and suspense—and of the striving to make the promise become reality. There was the economic reconstruction, the search for new overseas markets and for domestic financial stability.

There was the keen social conflict among groups of opposing economic and political interests. A national Constitution was drafted and published, an event new in world political history. Pleased and proud but wary, the American people firmly attached a Bill of Rights to the Constitution.

Isaac Moses (1742-1818), by John Wesley Jarvis.

chants and brokers listed in the directories of the period, as well as some 15 shopkeepers and three boardinghouse operators, including one run by a Mrs. Cohen. In Philadelphia, ten Jewish brokers and commission agents were active, and there were 40 merchants and shopkeepers. Charleston had an even more extensive Jewish merchant group. At the height of its prosperity as a shipping center for West Indian trade, Charleston was attracting Jews from other coastal cities and the West Indies, and by 1800 had the largest Jewish population in the country, about 500.

The Jews were never at this time among the top wealthiest merchants, but some of them were substantial business-men. Three in New York, Isaac Moses, Benjamin S. Judah and Moses L. Moses, were members of the Chamber of Commerce, a politically conservative group of the bigger merchants. When the New York Stock Exchange was established in 1792, five of the 23 founders were Jewish: Bernard Hart, Alexander Zuntz, Ephraim Hart, Isaac M. Gomez and Benjamin Mendes Seixas. As banks were created to help promote the expansion of pro-

And of all this Making of History, the Jews were a part—a small part, as befitted their numbers, which reached only about 2,500 in a total population of over five million by 1800, but a zestful part, fired with enthusiasm and hope at the very promise of equality, for which they had fought in the ranks.

Economic independence created problems that took several decades to solve. England tried to choke the economy of the new States by keeping their merchants out of English and West Indian markets. But soon American merchants were opening new markets in France, Holland, the Scandinavian countries, Russia, and even in China. Merchants of all kinds multiplied: wholesalers, brokers, commission agents and factors. All of them engaged in the historically useful function of developing the distribution of goods, thus stimulating the productive capacity of infant United States capitalism. Jews were especially active in this distribution phase of economic life.

In New York there were about 45 Jewish mer-

Harmon Hendricks (1771-1838), by Jacob H. Lazarus (1822-1891).

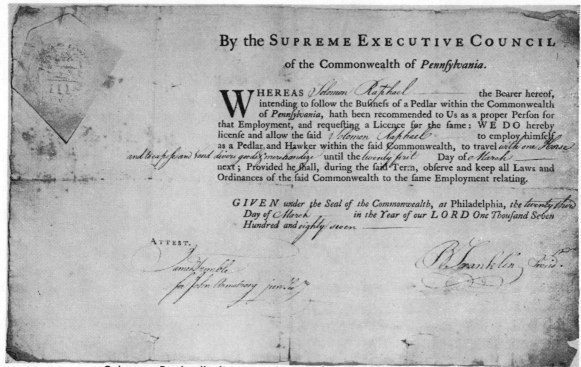

Solomon Raphael's license as a one-horse "Pedlar within the Commonwealth of Pennsylvania," issued on March 23, 1787 by Benjamin Franklin.

duction and commerce, Jews in a minor way became shareholders, seven of them owning 11 shares in 1784-1785 in the Bank of New York (out of a total of 500 shares at $500 each) but only three of them owning six and one half shares in 1791. When in 1798 the Bank of Manhattan was formed by Jeffersonians as a people's bank, four Jews, Naphtali Judah, Ephraim Hart, Solomon Simson and Harmon Hendricks, were among the 376 stockholders, and bought more than 300 shares altogether (out of a total of 40,000) at a par value of $50, while the wealthiest merchants were purchasing 1,000 shares each. This was the Jewish middle class.

But there were many also of the little people, the self-employed artisan and craftsman, and even a couple of laborers and indentured servants. Philadelphia listed the Jewish hatter and trunk-maker, the embroiderer and cooper, the carter and glass-engraver, the shoemaker and stevedore, the leathergoods worker and printer, the saddler and inn-keeper and two licensed peddlers. In New York there were the Jewish tobacconist, tailor and shoemaker, the chocolate-

maker, coppersmith and silversmith, the distiller, boatman and bookbinder, the butcher, spermaceti candle-maker and brazier, the furrier, copper-engraver and watchmaker. Charleston too had its smaller number of Jewish artisans. Since feudal guilds in the European countries of origin had excluded Jewish craftsmen and thus prevented the development of a Jewish artisan class and a Jewish tradition of craftsmanship, the wonder is that there were so many Jewish craftsmen in the new environment.

But the promise of the Revolution had been more than economic. There were the horizons opened by the unforgettable declaration of self-evident truths: that all men were created equal and had "unalienable Rights," among which were life, liberty and the pursuit of happiness. How would the Convention of 1787 that would draft the United States Constitution reflect these horizons? Particularly were the Jews concerned whether religious freedom and equality or religious discrimination would be written into it. The New York State Constitution was sound on that score, and Virginia had in 1786 passed its

Congregation Beth Shalome, Richmond, Va. This building was dedicated September 15, 1822.

Act for Establishing Freedom of Religion, which Jefferson regarded as one of his greatest achievements. (After that it was only three years before enough Jews had been attracted to Richmond, Virginia, to organize a community and establish a congregation, Beth Shalome.) But discrimination was still written into the constitutions or laws of other states that had Jewish groups, such as Pennsylvania and South Carolina. What lead would the national constitution give?

The Convention in Philadelphia worked in secret, with no publicity and no formal minutes. Three months passed. Finally the patriotic, pious and stalwart Jonas Phillips decided he would personally petition the convention to be sure not to repeat the discriminatory provision of the Pennsylvania constitution. Dating his letter the 24th Ellul 5547 or September 7, 1787, Phillips respectfully but firmly reminded the delegates that "it is well known . . . that the Jews . . . have been foremost in aiding and assisting the states with their lifes & fortunes, they have supported the cause, have bravely fought and bled for liberty which they can not Enjoy."

Phillips need not have worried, although it is well he expressed his concern for the historic record. The Jews were by no means the only ones that wanted religious equality. In every state there were numerous Christian Dissenters who had a vast stake in religious equality and the issue was decided mainly by them. More than two weeks before Phillips wrote his petition, the Convention had agreed on Article 6, providing

that all state and federal officials "shall be bound by Oath or Affirmation, to support this Constitution; but no religious Test shall ever be required as a Qualification to any Office or public Trust under the United States." No constitution anywhere in the world had such a clause, and it was far in advance of most of the state constitutions. Like all the other groups vitally concerned with freedom of religion, the Jews rejoiced when, at the end of September, the draft of the Constitution was submitted to the State Legislatures for ratification.

By the end of June, 1788 enough states had ratified it to bring the Constitution into force, although widespread popular pressure was still insistent on adding a Bill of Rights. In Philadelphia on Independence Day, 1788 the people demonstrated *en masse* to celebrate the ratification. Among the noteworthy details pointed to in the *Pennsylvania Packet* of July 9, 1788 was the fact that in the parade were "the Clergy of the different Christian denominations, with the rabbi of the Jews, walking arm in arm." Rev. Jacob Raphael Cohen was the happy man's name. The following month, a similar celebration was staged in New York, with contingents of craftsmen marching craft by craft. Poor but proud, Asher Myers strutted at the head of the coppersmith's division, while Jonas Lyon kept his stride among the furriers.

The new government began to organize itself. On March 4, 1789, the first Congress of the United States met in New York. When on April 30 George Washington was inaugurated there as the first President, Rev. Gershom Mendes Seixas was among the religious leaders present at the ceremony. Within a week, the Hebrew Congregation of distant Savannah sent Washington an address of congratulation, noting that he had "dispelled that cloud of bigotry and superstition which has long, as a veil, shaded religion—unrivetted the fetters of enthusiasm—enfranchised us with all the privileges and immunities of free citizens, and initiated us into the grand mass of legislative mechanism." Responding, Washington sagely rejoiced "that a spirit of liberality and philanthropy is much more prevalent than it formerly was . . . and that your brethren will

On May 6, 1789, a week after Washington's inauguration as President, the Hebrew Congregation of Savannah, Ga. sent him this Address of Congratulation, the only congregation in Savannah to do so.

benefit thereby in proportion as it shall become still more extensive."

There was another occasion for jubilation on September 25, 1789, when Congress submitted the Bill of Rights to the States for ratification as amendments to the Constitution. The first amendment read: "Congress shall make no law respecting an establishment of religion or prohibiting the free exercise thereof; or abridging the freedom of speech, or of the press; or the right of the people peaceably to assemble, and to petition the Government for a redress of grievances." There in the very first clause of the first amendment was written clearly what Jefferson called the "wall of separation" between church and state. What economic, political, so-

cial and religious frustrations and persecutions Jews had endured in countries where the feudal fusion of church and state existed! Never before had Jews lived under a government in which the principle of separation was so loudly and unmistakably affirmed. Article 6 was not enough. The people had affixed the first amendment, the Freedom Amendment, and if they put freedom of religion first it was because so many political and economic crimes had been committed in the name of one official religion or another. Unfortunately, the Senate had defeated another Amendment proposed by Madison—to forbid the States to interfere with freedom of conscience and religion. Had this passed, all the struggles later waged in the States might have been avoided, or would have taken place under more favorable circumstances.

The Newport Congregation summed up the situation memorably in August, 1790. For a long time they had hesitated to send their congratulation to Washington "to avoid giving umbrage" to the people of the one State which had at first rejected the Constitution in a popular referendum and then finally seen the State legislature ratify it by 34 to 32, the last of the original States to join the United States, on May 29, 1790. In August, Washington, however, came on an official visit to Newport to consolidate the position of the federal government, and the Newport Congregation joined with other bodies in sending addresses of greeting. Feelingly they spoke of how, "deprived as we have hitherto been of the invaluable rights of free citizens, we now . . . behold a Government, erected by the Majesty of the People . . . which to bigotry gives no sanction, to persecution no assistance . . ." Washington echoed the last majestic phrases, and added that he rejected the concept of "toleration" for the superior one of "equality."

Thus the Jews of Savannah and Newport, later joined by those of Philadelphia, New York, Charleston and Richmond, looked upon the new constitution and saw that it was good— better than any in the world. Did any of them note the limitations on the democracy defined in the Constitution—which made slavery constitutional for 750,000 slaves, one fifth of the total population, did nothing for 200,000 indentured servants, or for the Indian population, and ignored the rights of women? Or were there any who saw that basically this constitution, written in the image of the ruling circles of the country, made property rights supreme over the human rights of the propertyless and the exploited? There were those who saw one or another of these historic limitations, among the Jews as among the general population. They were to become the radicals of the next decade and the next centuries, exercising their rights under the Bill of Rights to work together with others for change and progress, while they defended the Constitution from those reactionaries who would undermine it.

The new doctrines also echoed and resounded across the ocean and to the south of us, quickening the aspirations of all the oppressed whose ears they touched. Behind barriers of legal restrictions or actually behind ghetto walls, Jews heard and hearkened. Within a half year after the Bastille fell in France, the Jews of France petitioned the National Assembly on January 29, 1790, demanding equality and pointing to the American example: "The word *toleration* . . . is no longer suitable to a nation that wishes to firmly place its rights upon the eternal foundations of justice. America . . . has rejected the word from its code . . ." Equality was rung like a bell. As far east as Moravia, in 1797 the readers of a volume in Hebrew (*Sefer Haberith* by Phinehas Elijah Hurwitz) were informed that in Charleston the Jews had equal rights.

At home, one effect of the new atmosphere and the new promise was that Jews began to move out more into the general stream of public life. When the New York State Legislature transformed King's College first into the University of the State of New York in 1784 and then into Columbia College in 1787, it named the Rev. Seixas as a Regent and then as a Trustee, and he served in the latter position until he resigned in 1815. In Richmond, the silversmith and merchant Isaiah Isaacs was elected to the municipal council in 1788 and 1790. Solomon Simpson of New York was elected Assessor in his Ward in 1794 and 1795.

An even larger number of Jews began to join the many civic, philanthropic and political organizations that were developing. A few Jews were attracted into the early abolition societies in Philadelphia and New York. Thus Benjamin Nones first freed his own slave by 1793 and then became active in persuading others to do so, succeeding in some ten cases in a few years. Others joined liberal groups like the General Society of Mechanics and Tradesmen in New York, the Humane Societies of New York and Boston, the Masons and the Militia. In Philadelphia and New York, some Jews joined the Society of the Sons of St. Tammany, designed to counteract the conservative and pro-British Sons of St. George. When in 1793 and 1794 the Jeffersonian political

The Beth Elohim Synagogue in Charleston, S. C. in 1794, which burned down in the great fire of 1838, as drawn by Solomon N. Carvalho.

clubs called Republican and Democratic Societies were formed, Jews were active in them in New York, Philadelphia, Baltimore and Charleston. Since the programs of these groups often overlapped, some Jews participated in two or even more of them.

Certainly the boundaries of freedom had been extended, and the Jews moved about in economic, civic and political affairs with less difficulty than ever before, anywhere. Jewish religious groups were sometimes accorded unexampled marks of respect. Thus in 1794, when the Beth Elohim synagogue was consecrated in Charleston, state and city officials headed by Governor William Moultrie were among those present. But there were still boundaries. In 1790 the Constitutions of Pennsylvania and South Carolina had been rewritten, and religious discriminations removed from them, but other states still had them. In Maryland, for instance, Solomon Etting, a leader of the Jeffersonians in Baltimore, headed a petition submitted by Jews in 1797 asking for constitutional change to accord them legal equality. The petition was pigeon-holed, and it was to take thirty

Solomon Etting (1764-1847), by John Wesley Jarvis.

years before its aim was attained.

Separation of church and state in the national government had not automatically brought about the same separation on the state and local levels. Sunday laws were a case in point, for by their provision the religiously observant Jew had to cease from work or business on Sunday as well as on Saturday. There was also the problem of whether Jews had a legal right to observe their Sabbath, as Jonas Phillips found out in 1793 in Philadelphia. For refusing to be sworn in as a witness in court on his Sabbath, Phillips was fined £10.

In 1794, Philadelphia enacted a Sunday law. Such laws and their strict enforcement were being pushed especially by the conservative clergy. Denouncing the popular Jeffersonian movement as atheistic, the clergy sought to promote religion by law. In New York their efforts to pass a State Sunday law came to a climax in 1798, but failed. Even though the Jeffersonians were not united, the strongest pressure for separation of church and state and against the proposed Sunday law came from them. Thus a writer in the Jeffersonian *Albany Register* for March 9, 1798 showed that the bill "discriminates and gives a preference contrary to the spirit and letter of the constitution . . . Under our liberal and free constitution, the Jew, the Mohomedan or the disciple of Confucius are entitled to the same protection as the Christian . . ." The Jews could not but be uneasy in the face of the strong pressure for more Sunday Laws and for the literal enforcement of those on the books. Sanction was still being given to bigotry.

Then there was the larger matter of anti-Semitism in attitude and propaganda. The European feudal fusion of church and state had given anti-Semitism a certain legal and institutional form, with restrictions written into the law. Now, with separation of church and state, that form was, on the national level, removed. But old anti-Semitic images persisted and were continually refreshed. This false image of the Jews lay ready to hand for the confused, and soon proved particularly useful to Federalist reaction.

There was of course the new democratic, liber-

tarian trend in part of the press to report news that placed Jews in a sympathetic light. In 1788 the *Pennsylvania Packet* gave a glowing account of the boxing match near London in which Daniel Mendoza, the Jewish champion of Great Britain, went down to defeat, but made it clear Mendoza lost only because he sprained an ankle. Shortly thereafter the same newspaper urged Christians to join with Jews in contributing money to two Palestinian messengers who had arrived from Hebron to collect funds to ransom Jews enslaved by the Turks. When in 1790 the French National Assembly was debating the rights of the Jews, newspapers in Philadelphia and in upstate New York reported the liberal sentiments with enthusiasm. The Philadelphia *American Daily Advertiser* on July 27, 1791 took the news that the Paris Jews would shortly open a synagogue, just as the Methodists were about to open a church, as evidence that "religious liberty reigns in France, and will sooner or later extend itself over the whole universe." Similarly there were favorable reports of the activities of Jews in the West Indies, Stuttgart, Danzig, Galicia and even St. Petersburg.

But amid the new and encouraging, there was also the old stereotype that had made the Jew synonymous with malicious money manipulation. The same newspaper that had in 1788 pointed to the fact that rabbi and Christian minister walked arm in arm in support of the Constitution could in 1790 print an anti-Semitic jingle. Commenting on a report by Alexander Hamilton, Federalist Secretary of the Treasury, the anonymous versifier snarled:

Each day a fresh report he broaches,
That Spies and Jews may ride in coaches.

In upstate New York newspapers, anti-Semitic anecdotes and doggerel spread the picture of the Jew as greedy and madly evil.

On the stage, anti-Semitic elements were presented. In New York, Jews appeared as scoundrels and hateful in English importations like the *Little Hunchback* in 1791, *The Young Quaker* in 1794 and 1797, and in 1798 in *The London Hermit* and *The Wandering Jew*.

The most harmful and popular of the plays was the American product, *Slaves in Algiers*, per-

The Philadelphia Aurora.

AURORA

ISSUED BY PROSM.

PHILADELPIA:

WEDNESDAY, AUGUST 13, 1800.

TO THE EDITOR.

Mr. Duane.

I enclose you an article which I deemed it but justice to my character to present for insertion in the Gazette of the United States, in reply to some illiberalities which were thrown out against me in common with many respectable citizens in that paper of the 5th inst. When I presented it to Mr. Wayne, he promised me, in the presence of a third person, that he would publish it. I waited until this day, when finding it had not appeared, I called on him, when he informed me that he would not publish it. I tendered him payment if he should require it. His business appears to be to asperse and shut the door against justification. I need not say more:

I am &c. B. NONES.
Philadelphia Aug. 11, 1800.

To the Printer of the Gazette of the U. S.

SIR,

I hope, if you take the liberty of inserting calumnies against individuals, for the amusement of your readers, you will at least have so much regard to justice, as to permit the injured through the same channel that conveyed the slander, to appeal to the public in self defence.——Lex

I am accused of being a Jew; of being a Republican; and of being Poor.

I am a Jew. I glory in belonging to that persuasion, which even its opponents, whether Christian, or Mahomedan, allow to be of divine origin—of that persuasion on which christianity itself was originally founded, and must ultimately rest—which has preserved its faith secure and unaltered, for near three thousand years—whose votaries have never murdered each other in religious wars, or cherished the theological hatred in general, so unextinguishable among those who revile them. A persuasion, whose patient followers have endured for ages the pious cruelties of Pagans, and of christians, and persevered in the unoffending practice of their rites and ceremonies, amidst poverties and privations—amidst pains, penalties, confiscations, punishments, tortures, and deaths, beyond the example of any other sect, which the page of history has hitherto recorded.

To be of such a persuasion, is to me no disgrace; though I well understand the inhuman language, of bigotted contempt, in which your reporter by attempting to make me ridiculous, as a Jew, has made himself detestable, whatever religious persuasion may be dishonored by his adherence.

But I am a Jew. I am so—and so were Abraham, and Isaac, and Moses and the prophets, and so too were Christ and his apostles. I feel no disgrace in ranking with such society, however, it may be subject to the illiberal buffoonery of such men as your correspondents.

I am a Republican! Think—

I am a ——— and for no other reason, for that reason am I a republican. Among the pious priesthood of church establishments, we are compassionately ranked with Turks, Infidels, and Heretics. In the monarchies of Europe, we are hunted from society—stigmatized as unworthy of common civility, thrust out as it were from the converse of men; objects of mockery and insult to froward children, the butts of vulgar wit, and low buffonery, such as your correspondent Mr. Wayne is not ashamed to set us an example of. Among the nations of Europe, we are inhabitants indeed every where—but Citizens no where unless in Republics. Here, in France, and in the Batavian Republic alone, are we treated as men, and as brethren. In republics we have rights, in monarchies we live but to experience wrongs. And why? because we and our forefathers have not sacrificed our principles to our interest, or earned an exemption from pain and poverty, by the dereliction of our religious duties, no wonder we are objects of derision to those, who have no principles, moral or religious, to guide their conduct.

How then can a Jew but be a Republican? in America particularly. Unfeeling & ungrateful would he be, if he were callous to the glorious and benevolent cause of the difference between his situation in this land of freedom, and among the proud and privileged law givers of Europe.

Benjamin Nones (1757-1826), Revolutionary War veteran and Jeffersonian Democrat, answers an anti-Semitic attack on him by a Federalist editor in the Presidential election campaign of 1800.

formed in 1794 in Philadelphia and Baltimore, published as a book in Philadelphia the same year, and staged frequently thereafter in several cities. With the United States involved in conflict with the Barbary pirates, including those of Algiers, the author of the best-selling novel of the period, Susanna Haswell Rowson, composed *Slaves in Algiers, or, A Struggle for Freedom* to snare current interest. The villain and ally of the Algerian enemy is a vicious character, Ben Hassan, a "little Israelite." For womanly virtue, Americanism, abolitionist sentiments and justice to triumph in the play, Ben Hassan has to be bested. The measure of the anti-Semitism can be taken from Ben Hassan's answer as to why he had become a convert to Mohamedanism. In a song he explains that having been a petty thief, usurer, and forger, he found the going heavy:

> So, having cheated the Gentiles, as Moses
>   commanded,
>
> Oh! I began to tremble at every gibbet I saw;
>
> But I got on board a ship, and here was safely
>   landed,
>
> In spite of the judges, counsellors, attorneys,
>   and law.

There were four Jews who were subscribers to the Philadelphia theater in which this play opened, but their reaction is not on record.

Ben Hassan, the first Jewish character in an American play, did not survive as an evil classic, but he reinforced the classic image of the hated Shylock in *The Merchant of Venice,* which was performed several times during this period. A conscious dramatic effort to offset the Shylock figure was made by the importation of Richard Cumberland's play, *The Jew; or, Benevolent Hebrew,* performed in London in 1794. Presented in Boston, New York and Philadelphia in 1795 and issued in book form in each of these cities the same year, the play was a success. Yet Sheva, the "Benevolent Hebrew," never became the byword for benevolence or the popular image of the Jew that Shylock is for malevolence and the Jew.

In the middle of the 1790's, anti-Semitism became a political issue. The conflict was sharpening between the Federalist controlling party, representing big merchants and land- and money-speculators, and the Jeffersonian democratic-republican movement, a coalition of small business people, working farmers, artisans and laborers, and Southern planters. Against our country's former ally, France, the Federalists were waging a cold war in the hope of turning it into a real war. With the people rising in opposition, the Federalists in 1798 passed the Alien and Sedition Acts, designed to deport all non-citizens critical of the government and to suppress all criticism. The Federalists, who feared the extension of democracy, were, in sum, anti-French, anti-alien, anti-Irish, anti-democratic, anti-Negro, anti-labor—and, it turned out, some were ready to use anti-Semitism as a political instrument, to the undoubted embarrassment of the occasional Jewish Federalist of this period, like Isaac Moses of New York.

To their standard cries that the Jeffersonians were foreign agents financed by "Paris gold" and nasty atheists undermining Christianity, Federalist editors added the charge that wicked and money-mad Jews were tied up with this movement. In New York, the patriotic and radical Jewish merchant, past president and a leader of Congregation Shearith Israel, Solomon Simpson, was one of the founders and Vice-President of the Jeffersonian Democratic Society. James Rivington, former Royalist and now a Federalist editor, in 1795 denounced the Society as an "itinerant gang" that "all seemed to be, like their *Vice-President,* of the tribe of Shylock," with a "leering underlook, and malicious grin." The Jeffersonian press rebutted this anti-Semitism. Shakespeare had distorted his sources, wrote one, and "if, by the word Shylock, you mean a Jew, from my knowledge of the Vice-President, I dare say he would think himself honoured by the appellation, Judaism being his religious profession, as Democracy is his political creed." Later Simpson was elected President of the Jeffersonian club.

Of course the "Shylock" epithet did not down. Alexander Hamilton himself, leader of the Federalists, referred to "Shylock the Jew" in the courtroom one day in 1797 to describe two merchants, and was rebuked in the Jeffersonian press. In New York State, a discussion of a proposed

For the NEW-YORK JOURNAL, &c.

To *the* WRITER *of the* PREFACE *to* DEMOCRAT.

IT is a good maxim not to ridicule religion, or the natural defects of the human body. The first shews the depravity of the head, the latter the malignity of the heart. If this observation is just, we may conclude from the extraordinary preface, lately published by J---n R---gh---n to a novel entitled the Democrat, that the writer's head is destitute of every liberal sentiment, as his heart is devoid of charity and compassion for the defects of his fellow-creatures, had such defects really existed.

I shall endeavour, in the course of a few observations, to place the preface in its proper point of view; but being unaccustomed to writing, the public are not to expect well-turned periods or elegance of diction, but in lieu thereof, I will endeavour to give them facts in plain and unadorned language; in doing this, I am in some measure under the disagreeable necessity of using a mode similar to that of the author of the preface, not indeed with a view of wounding the feelings of any person whatever, but merely to expose the absurdity of the practice itself. I shall only take notice of such part of the preface as respects the Democrats, of whose Society I am a member, and leave those whom it concerns to notice the rest.

Speaking of the Democratic Society, it has the following words—" This itinerant gang will be easily known by their physiognomy," &c. The public will doubtless admire your sagacity in discovering the Democrats to be a wandering gang. An abusive stile, Sir, is ever a very bad one; the word gang is made use of to denote ruffians and highway-men—Let us try how these elegant expressions will sound, when applied to other Societies—For instance, to the St. George's, St. Andrew's, St. Patrick, Tammany, Black Friars, or any other in this city. I believe, Sir, they will not be in a hurry to erect a statue to your memory, for the politeness of the expression, or the honour you meant to confer on them—" They all seem like their Vice President, of the tribe of Shylock."

Really, Sir, this is extremely sarcastic: the wits of the age ought to have your name wrote in letters of gold, for this brilliant proof of your talent. Perhaps some of the readers of your preface may be ignorant of the source from whence this pretty story took its rise; you ought to have the goodness to inform them, that by turning to Farneworth Page Sixtus the Vth, page 401, they would find it recorded at large; but this story, as erroneously represented by Shakespeare, could not be applied to the Vice-President, as it would not by any means suit his liberality of sentiment and general character (but it might, with truth, be applied to a certain gentleman who commenced a suit against D---v---d C---m---b---li for not allowing sufficient usury for his money;) this will be evident to every person who is acquainted with the character of the Vice-President, and that of the late printer of the Royal Gazette. If, by the word Shylock, you mean a Jew, from my knowledge of the Vice-

President, I dare say he would think himself honoured by the appellation, Judaism being his religious profession, as Democracy is his political creed.

It is an old remark, that the great Author of the Universe has so beautifully variegated his works, that scarce any two things appear alike. To your inventive genius it was left to discover, that all the members of the largest Society in the state, look exactly like their Vice President—Go on, Sir, and convince the Philosophers of the age, that you have no equal.

With your permission I will make use of an old adage—It must be a bad rule that won't work both ways—let us try it. Your most gracious sovereign, for instance, was unfortunately inflicted with insanity; by a parity of reasoning, all his liege subjects must be mad men. Again, let it be said that the President of the C---mb---r of C---mm---r---e has a peculiar leer or cast of the eye, the Society an underlook, ergo, the whole Chamber must have both a leer and an underlook. Once more, it is said that the great C---m---ll---s has something in his countenance resembling a Creole or African, ergo, all his adherents must be black. Do you not already see, Sir, the very great and essential service you have rendered your friends, by producing these elegant families, which never would have been thought of, or brought forward, but to expose your own absurdities; indeed, they ought to reward your zeal, though, like an unskilful counsellor, you have injured the cause you intended to promote.

Your enemies, as well as your friends, do you justice, and say you are no changeling; that you have acted, and still do act, consistently from your appointment of printer to his most gracious majesty to the present time. Courtier like, you have feared and flattered your superiors, and represented all those in the most ludicrous and false colouring, from whom you supposed you had nothing to fear.— While the British fleets and armies were wantonly burning our towns, and committing scenes that will scarcely at this day be believed, did not your zeal then, and does it not still continue to represent them as the bravest and most gallant people on the globe terrestrial? Did you not, on every occasion, represent the worthy and brave General Washington, and his army of heroes, as banditti, that could never stand before British troops? Did you not turn their well fought battles into so many defeats, and represent them as retreating with dismay over the Alleghany Mountains? Have you not, by your false and insidious publications, caused many brave Americans to be confined in the Provo, and Jersey prison-ship? Have you forgot your advertizing the rebel N---s C---g---r being brought in prisoner within the British lines, and how handsomely that gentleman has since rewarded you for your trouble*?— I am bold to say, Sir, that the whole of the Democratic Society, from the President to the Door Keeper individually, would be pleased with an opportunity to serve you precisely in the same way: but rest assured, merit like yours will never fail to meet its due reward

If I had a thousand mouths of brass they would be inadequate to trumpet

forth the many exploits you have made the bravest and most magnanimous people on the globe terrestrial perform, and it would require as many more to represent the dastardly and dreadful situation in which you have uniformly placed the Americans, and do still some of their best friends.

To conclude, Sir, I deny the allegations as set forth in your preface, respecting the Democratic Society and their Vice-President, as untrue, but say the facts contained herein are true, and leave the decision to the impartial public.

SLOW AND EASY.

* *Rewarded him with a good horse-whipping.*

For the NEW-YORK JOURNAL, &c.

To THE CI DEVANT PRINTER OF THE ROYAL GAZETTE.

Good Sir,

QUI caput ille facet, is a found old adage. If you have imprudently taken a share in affairs which ought not to concern you, you alone are to be answerable for all the evil consequences that may possibly attend your temerity. After the most lenient and indulgent treatment from a people, whom you had long been in the daily habit of calumniating, it was to have been expected, that the return on your part would at least have been the observance of a respectful silence, if it had not inspired you with the more lively emotions of gratitude and esteem. Instead of this, sir, what have you done? let facts speak, let them, if possible, inspire a blush on a countenance, torpid to manly sensibility, and dead to shame. Unfortunately, old whigs of this country have become divided in their sentiments, upon a variety of important political subjects. Candor must induce us to believe, that the majority of them really wish to promote the prosperity of their native land—it cannot be otherwise—it is impossible that the great body of the people should will an injury to themselves;—but why sir, do you take an active part in their differences? What have you—what have the old tories done to entitle themselves to the confidence of the public? The preface that you have lately published to an American edition of a work entitled " the Democrat," is doubtless one of the most impudent performances that has ever appeared in any age, or country: the invidious and personal remarks that it contains, not only upon a worthy individual, but also upon a numerous class of citizens, who are certainly, at least, more sincere in their attachment to the interests of America than yourself, merits censure; and if repeated, may perhaps involve you in consequences, that may prove disagreeable, if not dangerous to yourself. The preface itself is not, nor are you, Mr. R------, entitled to any observation; it will not however, be amiss to conclude by advising you, in the most friendly manner, to abstain from a course of conduct that may prove injurious to yourself, and perhaps subject you to consequences, for which the writer of these remarks will not undertake to be answerable.

HORTENSIUS.

Two letters in the "New York Journal" of December 17 and 19, 1795 rebut the anti-Semitic attack of a Federalist editor on Solomon Simpson (1738-1801), New York Jeffersonian leader.

bill on usury and the rate of interest provoked repeated use of the term, so that all too often even democrats fell into the pattern and reached for the epithet "Shylock," to the discomfort of Jewish democrats.

As the political struggle grew acute, anti-Semitism began to be used by Federalist editors, and even by a college president in Pennsylvania, against non-Jews. At first it was against Christians with "Jewish" names like the democrats Israel Israel in Philadelphia or John D. Israel in Pittsburgh. But then even an old Irish name like William Duane was not immune. One Federalist, attacking Duane, editor of the leading Jeffersonian newspaper in the country, the Philadelphia *Aurora*, assured his readers that "Duane was once a Jew Cloathsman in London," where he was known not as Duane but as "Jew Aine."

The climax of this political use of anti-Semitism came in the campaign of 1800, in which Jefferson was elected to the Presidency. The primary issue was the Alien and Sedition Acts, under which Federalist officials and judges had attacked the democratic-republican press, prosecuting 25 and convicting ten Jeffersonian editors and printers. In Pittsburgh John D. Israel's democratic editorial office was called "a Synagogue." In Charleston, Jews were accused of allowing Jeffersonians to electioneer in the synagogue; one Jew publicly denied the charge but maintained the right of the Jews to work for the defeat of the Alien and Sedition Acts by the election of the Jeffersonians to office.

But it was in Philadelphia, the capital of the nation, that the issue was most acute. The leading Federalist journal published a scurrilous account of a Jeffersonian convention, full of anti-Negro, anti-labor, anti-intellectual and anti-democratic venom, ending with an anti-Semitic sneer at Benjamin Nones. When the Federalist editor refused to publish Nones' reply even as a paid advertisement, the *Aurora* gladly printed it. Nones also had it issued as a handbill to be distributed in the streets. Revolutionary War veteran, pa-

triot, conscientious Jew and radical, Nones wrote an answer that deserves a place among the classic utterances of American democratic thought.

To the Federalist charge "of being a *Jew;* of being a *Republican;* and of being *Poor,*" he proudly pleaded guilty. His pride in being a Jew is not new, nor is his assertion that he is poor but honest—although there is political fire in his explanation that he will be able to pay his creditors as soon as the Federalist cold war against France permitted him to collect some debts due in France.

What is new is his response to the "charge" that he is a "Republican," a term of the worst abuse at the time, meaning that he was an extreme radical. Nones did not merely defend his *right,* but proclaimed his *duty as a Jew* thus to be in the forefront of the fight for progress. "I am a Jew, and if for no other reason, for that reason am I a republican." He had enlisted in 1777 to fight in the American Revolution, "and for three and twenty years I felt no disposition to change my political, any more than my religious principles."

There was very little indeed at the time that was written by Jews and published, but the words of Nones are the most enduring. There were two sermons by Rev. Seixas in New York that achieved publication, one on Thanksgiving Day, 1789, the first Thanksgiving under the new Constitution, and the other in 1798, a plea for an end to the cold war with France. They are worthy utterances, fine in sentiment but heavy and outmoded in their religious form and style. But the vigor of Nones in August, 1800 resounds to this day. He had given pith and point, and the ring of a manifesto, to the thought that Jews had to be wedded to the ideal of progress and the fight for it. Under the Constitution and its Bill of Rights, this was the banner that would lead Jews, together with the American people as a whole, forward. The new century was opening well. The people elected Jefferson. The Alien and Sedition Acts were dead letters.

CHAPTER 5: On the Tide of Expansion

Expansion is the key-word for the first 30 years of the nineteenth century, but it was complicated by a war to maintain United States independence and by the first crisis of our capitalist economy.

There was expansion of territory out to the Mississippi, achieved by ruthless conquest and expulsion of the Indians, so that there were 24 States in the Union in 1821, and Jewish congregations emerged in Cincinnati in 1824 and in New Orleans in 1828.

There was expansion of the population, from 5,308,000 in 1800 to 12,866,000 in 1830. Immigration totaled over 300,000, and took a spurt after the final defeat of Napoleon at Waterloo in 1815 put reaction in the saddle in all of Europe and brought about an economic crisis. The Jewish population almost kept pace with the general increase, rising to about 6,000 in 1826.

There was expansion of manufacture and of commerce, both foreign and internal, with the Ohio and Mississippi rivers as highways. Jews in the river ports of Cincinnati, Louisville and New Orleans were tied in with this commerce, while some in Philadelphia and New York turned to manufacturing.

There was an expansion of democracy, with the pressure coming from the farmers and the city laboring people. Property and taxpaying qualifications for voting were abolished in some states and some appointive offices were made elective. The people, rather than the State legislatures, began to choose the Presidential electors. Within this framework, the fight to abolish legal religious discrimination was waged. There was also, however, an enormous expansion of slavery, with its profound effect upon the economic and political life of the country. From a moral issue, slavery began to be transformed into the basic social issue that developed into the "irrepressible conflict."

It was a sign of the Jeffersonian times that from the beginning of the century more and more Jews were appointed or elected to public office. Shortly after his inauguration on March 4, 1801, Jefferson appointed Reuben Etting, a Jeffersonian leader in Baltimore, as United States Marshal for the district of Maryland. Thus a Jew was chief law enforcement officer of the federal government in a state in which no Jew could constitutionally hold any state or local public office or trust! Jefferson also appointed Solomon B. Nones, son of the revolutionary war veteran and Jeffersonian Benjamin Nones, as a consul-general in Portugal—a country in which the Inquisition had not yet been abolished. The governor of Pennsylvania in 1803 appointed Benjamin Nones to one of the five coveted posts as Notary Public in Philadelphia.

The list of Jews in the public service is too long to detail, but examples are significant. In 1810, the democrat Joel Hart was elected to the New York State Senate, and Myer Moses to the South Carolina House. In 1812, Chapman Levy of Camden was in the South Carolina House and in 1818 in the State Senate. In 1814-1815, Solomon Jacobs was Recorder of Richmond. In Charleston from 1806 to 1827 there were five Jews who were Justices of the Peace, and three Jews served as City Commissioners of Schools, Markets, Poorhouse,

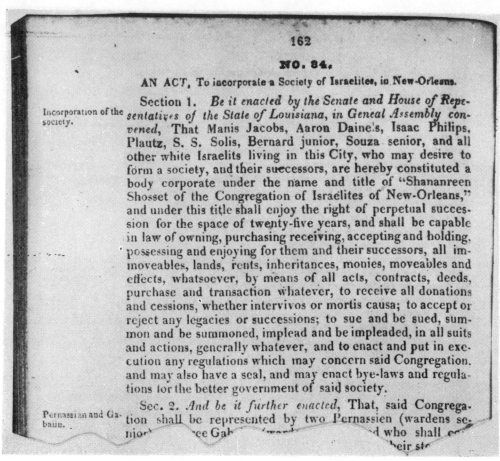

162

NO. 84.

AN ACT, To incorporate a Society of Israelites, in New-Orleans.

Incorporation of the society.   Section 1. *Be it enacted by the Senate and House of Representatives of the State of Louisiana, in Geneal Assembly convened,* That Manis Jacobs, Aaron Daine!s, Isaac Philips, Plautz, S. S. Solis, Bernard junior, Souza senior, and all other white Israelits living in this City, who may desire to form a society, and their successors, are hereby constituted a body corporate under the name and title of "Shananreen Shosset of the Congregation of Israelites of New-Orleans," and under this title shall enjoy the right of perpetual succession for the space of twenty-five years, and shall be capable in law of owning, purchasing receiving, accepting and holding, possessing and enjoying for them and their successors, all immoveables, lands, rents, inheritances, monies, moveables and effects, whatsoever, by means of all acts, contracts, deeds, purchase and transaction whatever, to receive all donations and cessions, whether intervivos or mortis causa; to accept or reject any legacies or successions; to sue and be sued, summon and be summoned, implead and be impleaded, in all suits and actions, generally whatever, and to enact and put in execution any regulations which may concern said Congregation. and may also have a seal, and may enact bye-laws and regulations for the better government of said society.

Pernassian and Gabaiin.   Sec. 2. *And be it further enacted,* That, said Congregation shall be represented by two Pernassien (wardens se- nio⸱⸱⸱ ⸱ee Gab⸱⸱⸱ ⸱⸱⸱⸱⸱ ⸱d who shall ⸱⸱⸱ ⸱eir st⸱⸱

The Act of Incorporation of the first Jewish congregation in New Orleans, March 25, 1828.

Streets and Lamps, and the Marine Hospital. In 1817 Leon Levy was elected State Treasurer of South Carolina, and the Federalist Henry Solomon was elected to the Philadelphia Common Council. In Charleston and Philadelphia Jews served as city health officers. By 1820 Mordecai Manuel Noah was a real power in the Tammany Society of New York, and in 1824 he was elected its Grand Sachem, than which at the time there was nothing politically grander. So well integrated were Jews in Tammany life and ways that they were even involved in its swindles and corruption. When Tammany Sachem Naphtali Judah was publicly exposed in 1818 as having swindled tens of thousands of dollars in a lottery, Tammany was loyal to him and re-elected him a Sachem in 1819.

In North Carolina there arose a public controversy about equal political rights for Jews that attracted nation-wide attention. Jacob Henry had already served a year in the State House in 1808 and had been re-elected in 1809 when his right to his seat was challenged. The North Carolina constitution discriminated against Catholics and Jews, and Henry, it was charged, had refused to take the proper oath of office on the New Testament. Aided by the Catholic element, Henry won a partial victory. In a magnificent speech that was widely reprinted and became an elocutionary classic for decades, Henry eloquently argued that "Conduct alone is the subject of human laws," and that man ought to suffer civil disqualification for what he does and not for what he thinks." The House allowed Jacob Henry to retain his seat by a tortured interpretation of the constitution to the effect that Jews and Catholics could hold legislative but *not* executive or other office. It was not until 1868 that the Constitutional Convention in the Reconstruction period, with a large num-

Part of the manuscript of the Address by Jacob Henry in the House of Commons of North Carolina, December 6, 1809, opposing a move to unseat him because he was a Jew.

Isaac Harby (1788-1828), a silhouette by an unidentified artist.

ber of Negro delegates, abolished this religious test for office.

A number of native-born Jews emerged in journalism and the arts. In Charleston there was Isaac Harby, editor, journalist, dramatist and literary critic, and Jacob Nuñez (later Newton) Cardozo, editor, journalist and leading economist. (Charleston for 34 years also had the first American Jewish artists, the portrait and miniature painter and teacher, Joshua Canter, who had studied art in Copenhagen before coming to Charleston in 1788, and John Canter, artist and drawing teacher at the College of Charleston, 1806-1807). In New York there was M. M. Noah, editor, journalist and popular playwright, Samuel B. H. Judah, playwright and verse satirist and Isaac Gomez, Jr., anthologist. Noah and Cardozo are still creditably remembered in histories of their fields.

The first on the scene and, owing to his untimely death "in abject poverty" in 1828 at the age of 40, the first off it, was Isaac Harby. Two long-forgotten plays staged and printed in Charleston in which a recent drama historian

still found "the touch of inspiration," a number of critical essays much praised by his contemporaries, and his output as a Jeffersonian Democratic-Republican political journalist sum up a literary career that was complemented, as we shall see, by pioneering as a Jewish religious reformer.

Vastly more influential was J. N. Cardozo, whose journalistic work began in Charleston in 1817 and lasted until 1872, the year before he died. He has recently been judged to have been "the ablest pre-Civil War economist of the country" by Joseph Dorfman in *The Economic Mind in American Civilization*. An early Federalist and always a Southern pro-slavery leader, Cardozo opposed the repeal of the property qualification for white male voters, objected to all legislation to aid the poor, and favored teaching the workers through mechanics' institutes, libraries and lectures to "submit to temporary deprivations of employment, as the law of our social condition." His *Notes on Political Economy*, published in Charleston in 1826, and innumerable editorials were widely quoted in the Southern press and in pro-Southern journals in the North.

In the New York that was in the 1820's replacing Boston as the literary capital of the country, Noah was the only one that achieved prominence. Yet it is interesting that with only about 1,000 Jews in a city approaching 200,000 population, there were three Jews in the literary field, even though fleetingly. Thus in 1820, Isaac Gomez, Jr. issued a volume of over 400 pages, *Selections of a Father for the Use of His Children*, consisting of excerpts from classic and modern authors on morality and the natural sciences, including some anti-slavery passages. More pungent was the literary career of Samuel B. H. Judah. Son of a wealthy merchant economically ruined in the War of 1812, Judah tried his youthful fling on the stage in the 1820's before turning to the profession of law. Three hastily and badly written plays were produced and printed. They were popular and critical failures, although one on the revolutionary battle of Lexington was part of the movement for a drama on national themes. A vengeful, satirical poem landed him in prison for libel, from which he was freed by gubernatorial pardon—to begin the study of law. Judging the plays "wholly worthless" and the author "a vain and shallow man," the *Dictionary of American Biography* nevertheless found it necessary to include Judah's biography.

By contrast, M. M. Noah achieved eminence as a member of New York's literary circle when it included luminaries like Washington Irving, James Fenimore Cooper and Wiliam Cullen Bryant. As a political editor he was in the field continually, and often in the thick of battle, from 1816, when he took charge of the *National Advocate,* the Tammany democratic organ, until he died in 1851, editor of *The Times and Noah's Weekly Messenger.* In between he had edited a Jacksonian democratic paper, then veered to a conservative Whig journal, and finally returned to the democrats. Reflecting the interests of New York merchants tied to Southern markets, Noah was pro-slavery, and opposed to independent working-class political action. On other issues, he, like Tammany, yielded to the pressure of the laboring element.

But it was as a playwright that he made his literary mark, with several spectacles dramatizing American history, and one dealing with the Greek revolution. The only one that has survived the sands of oblivion is *She Would Be a Soldier, or The Battle of Chippewa,* dealing with the War of 1812. A hit in New York in 1819, it was printed and produced repeatedly in subsequent seasons, holding the stage as late as 1848. In 1918 it merited a place in a collection of representative plays by American dramatists. Noah had made his minor contribution to our country's efforts to develop a national culture independent of British domination.

It is noteworthy that in all this literary work, apart from the journalism, of Harby, Gomez, Judah and Noah there was no direct reflection, except in one respect, of Jewish life or of the fact that the authors were Jews, although two of them, Harby and Noah, were conspicuously active Jewish communal leaders. The exception had to do with the Shylock stereotype. Gomez in his *Selections* and Harby in an essay vigorously expressed themselves on the harm done by the

Mordecai Manuel Noah (1785-1851), by John Wesley Jarvis.

portrayal of Shylock as a Jewish type. If they felt it necessary to react on this issue, it was because their concern with literature and with the Jewish people here merged. Writing before the attempt to "correct" or "improve" Shakespeare by "interpreting" Shylock as a "sympathetic" character, Harby was forthright in his perception and condemnation. All of Shakespeare's evil characters have some redeeming feature, "but in Shylock," Harby observed, "there is no trait of nobleness, 'no redeeming spirit,' which can possibly elicit our forgiveness of his bloody and desperate design —or give to his actions the plausibility of human motives. 'Tis all demoniacal and black atrocity." In Shylock and in a few other cases, Shakespeare, he concluded, "bowed his great genius to the prejudices of an ignorant age." The effectiveness of these condemnations can be inferred from the fact that they did not hinder the first American performance, in 1821, of Christopher Marlowe's anti-Semitic play, *The Jew of Malta,* with the great Edmund Kean himself in the role of the greedy, malevolent Jew, Barabas.

Mordecai Myers (1776-1871).

The great national test and trial shaping the history of this period was of course the War of 1812, a war for the reaffirmation of United States economic, political and territorial independence from Great Britain. British control of the world market was setting the price for cotton, tobacco, rice and other agricultural exports from the United States, and British investments exerted a heavy influence on our economic policy. Britain refused to recognize the legitimacy of our purchase of the Louisiana territory in 1803 and from her base in Canada actively hindered the settlement of our Western area by American farmers. British interference with American freedom of trade and the impressment of American seamen into the British navy made the issue acute. This was therefore a just war on our side, despite the fact that, with the aggressive greed characteristic of the developing capitalists, United States fur traders, whalers, slaveowners, farmers and land speculators trumpeted their desire to annex Canada and Florida. Canada, unfortunately, suffered the consequences of being a *place d'armes* for British military operations.

The participation of the Jews in the war effort was varied and widespread. From the Canadian frontier to New Orleans, on land and sea, as privates and officers, in the militia and the regular army, Jews were active. Mordecai Myers in New York and Abraham A. Massias in Georgia were captains in the regular army. Myer Moses in South Carolina, Joshua Moses in Pennsylvania and Aaron Levy in New York were captains in the state militias. In the Navy, Uriah Phillips Levy was Sailing Master of the *Argus*, which successfully raided British merchant vessels right off

This painting of Commodore Uriah Phillips Levy (1792-1862) by Thomas Buchanan Read is now in the Museum of the United States Naval Academy at Annapolis, Md. Levy holds a scroll reading: "Author of the Abolition of Flogging in the Navy of the United States."

the English coast for months before it was captured and Levy and the others were imprisoned. Thus began a distinguished naval career that, despite anti-Semitic pressures, brought Levy ultimately to the rank of Commodore, then the highest in the Navy.

In battles on the Canadian frontier, Captain Myers and Private Isaac De Young were both seriously wounded, the latter a veteran of ten engagements at the age of 18 years. In New Orleans, the 40-year-old Jewish merchant and militiaman Judah Touro suffered a grievous cannonball wound in a thigh.

While New England Federalist merchants treacherously traded with the enemy in Canada, the British fleet captured and burnt Washington, D. C., in August, 1814 in retaliation for the burning of York (now Toronto) by United States troops. In Baltimore, Philadelphia and New York the population rallied to build fortifications to defend their homes, and Jews like others dug in. Even Jewish Federalists were among the almost 40 Jews there enrolling in the militia in Philadelphia. Benjamin Nones, already in his fifties, formed a Company of veterans over 45,

A daguerreotype of Judah Touro (1775-1854), merchant and philanthropist.

and was elected its Second Lieutenant. In Fort McHenry near Baltimore there were eight Jews among the thousand defenders that withstood British "bombs bursting in air," saved Baltimore from attack, and inspired Francis Scott Key that night of September 13-14, 1814 to write "The Star Spangled Banner."

In the darkest days, the spirit that led to victory was notably expressed in a letter written by a sister of the still militant patriot of the Revolutionary period, Rev. Gershom Mendes Seixas, the elderly New York matron, Grace Nathan: "I cannot for the life of me feel terrified. I am so true an American—so warm a Patriot that I hold these mighty Armies—and their proud—arrogant— presumptious [sic] and over-powering Nation as Beings that *we* have conquered and *shall* conquer again. This I persuade myself will be so. And may the Lord of Battles grant that it may be so." And so it was.

The United States was aided in its victory by the fact that Britain was involved in war with Napoleon. Within a half year after the final battle of New Orleans in the War of 1812, Napoleon was finally beaten at Waterloo. A tide

Mrs. Grace Nathan (1752-1831), a miniature by Henry Inman.

PLAN

FOR ESTABLISHING A

Jewish Settlement in the United States.

---

1. An association of wealthy and respectable Jews are to subscribe a fund, to as large an amount as may be practicable, for the purpose of purchasing a tract of land in the United States, adequate to the object in view.

2. This tract of land I recommend to be purchased in the Upper Mississippi and Missouri territory, in a climate particularly well adapted for European constitutions, and where the fertility of soil is equal, if not superior, to any in North America. There are now for private sale, several large tracts contained in these two sections, and embracing several millions of acres, adjacent to the Mississippi and Missouri rivers, two of the most important navigable streams in the northern divisions of America, and destined, at no very remote period, to become the most populous and flourishing regions in the new world.

Page from a pamphlet published in London in 1819, W. D. Robinson's "Memoir Addressed To Persons of the Jewish Religion in Europe, On The Subject of Emigration To, and Settlement In, One Of The Most Eligible Parts Of The United States Of North America."

of reaction washed over Europe as feudal and monarchic forces clamped oppressive regimes down upon the people and wiped out the democratic reforms that had been won on the impetus of the French Revolution. A deep agricultural and economic crisis also struck the people. A new push was thus given to emigration from Europe, which had virtually stopped for 25 years first because of the great promise of the French Revolution and then because of the Napoleonic Wars.

For the Jews of central Europe, who had just begun to enjoy the fruits of political emancipation, the reaction meant not only the loss of their new rights and the instituting of new ghettoes

but also an outburst of pogroms in which Jews were murdered and their property burned and pillaged in a number of German cities. The hoodlums, encouraged or organized by the authorities, chanted the exterminating cry of "Hep, Hep," the word formed from the initials of the Latin slogan, "Hierosolyma est perdita," or "Jerusalem must be destroyed." In this way the peoples suffering from an economic crisis were incited against the Jews.

Our country was ready to welcome immigration because labor was always in short supply. The first immigration law enacted by Congress in March, 1819 did not restrict immigration. It sought to aid the immigrants, who were being cruelly over-crowded and underfed by profiteering shipowners, through regulating the amount of food and living space each passenger must be given.

In the same year, two Americans issued public appeals to the Jews of Europe to migrate to the United States. One was by a Presbyterian, W. D. Robinson, who published a pamphlet in London on October 20, 1819 proposing that "an association of wealthy and respectable Jews" buy a huge tract of land "in the Upper Mississippi and Missouri territory," and then finance and equip a large number of Jews to establish a settlement on it. There was no response to Robinson's plan, although three months later it was being quoted in a Maryland legislative debate in support of political equality for Jews, and a few years later a handful of English Jews did settle in Ohio.

The other call was issued by Mordecai Manuel Noah and was published in the Rhineland in the *Koblenzer Anzeiger* on July 2, 1819 (ten days after Noah's *She Would Be a Soldier* made a hit on the New York stage). Pointing to the "persecution and oppression" of the Jews of Europe "despite the sympathy of many good men," Noah remarked that the doors of Palestine are closed, "but another glorious country is beckoning to them from afar. Free America, with its immeasurably vast stretches of land . . . welcomes the suppressed peoples of the old world . . ." There, he declared, "a new Jewish state" could be founded and "equal Palestine in size." This was the beginning of the fantastic Grand Island project that culminated in September, 1825 in a blaze of empty pomp "compounded," as Noah's biographer, Isaac Goldberg, states, "of religiosity, theology, politics, patriotism, ethnology, delusions of grandeur and . . . real estate." It was then that Noah, in an Episcopalian church in Buffalo, N. Y., unveiled the "foundation stone" of "Ararat, A City of Refuge for the Jews," to be built on Grand Island, size 17,000 acres (about the area of Manhattan), lying in the Niagara River near Buffalo. Before the pathetic-comic finale, there had been an echo to Noah's call. Reports in the general press and in Jewish German newspapers kept interest awake. In 1822, Noah had received a suggestion from Berlin that he organize in the United States a cooperating branch of the Verein für Kultur und Wissenschaft der Juden (Society for the Advancement of the Culture and Science of the Jews) to discuss with them "the means of promoting the emigration of European Jews to the United States." And in New York in 1822 the *Commercial Advertiser* had supported the idea of Jewish immigration because "the wealth and enterprize of the Jews would be a great auxiliary to the commercial and manufacturing, if not agricultural interests of the United States." But after Ararat Noah met from the Jews of Europe the ridicule, and from the Jews in the United States the indifference, he deserved. German Jews were beginning to join the increasing general German immigration, but they were not coming to Ararat.

From the end of the War of 1812 to 1830 there were several other significant organizational, communal and ideological developments in Jewish life. The first was caused by the economic crisis

This "cornerstone" of Noah's projected Jewish city on Grand Island, N. Y. is now in the Buffalo Historical Society.

A legal document by which Jacob Levy, Jr. freed one of his slaves, March 5, 1817; from the records of the Manumission Society of New York City.

of the American economy that began in 1819 and lasted to 1822. Jewish charitable institutions until then had always been part of the congregations, and dispensed their aid to the sick, the widowed, the orphaned and the aged and to those otherwise afflicted with sudden disaster. The crisis brought forward the need to aid those whose ailment was social and consisted of able-bodied poverty born of crisis. So in Philadelphia late in 1819 there was established the Female Hebrew Benevolent Society to help "their indigent sisters of the House of Israel," and in 1820 a society of the same name appeared in New York. In 1822, the Hebrew Benevolent Society was organized in New York from among Ashkenazic members of the Spanish and Portuguese congregation, and the United Hebrew Beneficent Society was born in Philadelphia. In Charleston, the Hebrew Benevolent Society founded in 1784 was revitalized and expanded in 1824. In the northern cities these institutions later assumed some of the responsibility of assisting newly arrived needy German Jewish immigrants.

Another development was the victorious completion of the struggle begun in Maryland in 1797 to abolish the discrimination against the Jews embedded in the State Constitution. An unsuccessful flurry of activity in 1801, 1802 and 1803 was followed by a long period of inactivity, while the Jews smarted under the restrictions that kept them from holding office, practicing law, or filling any public position. The situation changed in 1817 when an immigrant Scottish

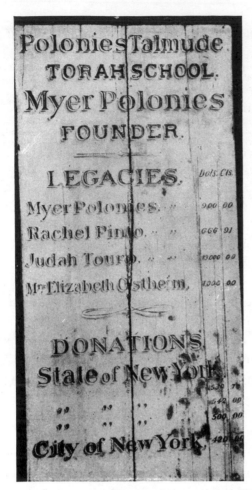

The Polonies Talmud Torah of Congregation Shearith Israel, New York, which opened May 2, 1803, is now the oldest extant Jewish religious school in the country.

Presbyterian, a democrat of Jeffersonian principles, was elected to the Maryland House of Delegates from rural Washington County. Thomas Kennedy had known no Jews, but he knew the United States Constitution. Under his persistent and enthusiastic leadership a struggle began in 1818 to get the two consecutive state legislatures to pass the law needed to amend the constitution. When his first bill was defeated, he introduced another after re-election. He did this year after year until in 1822 his bill passed for the first time.

Then the enemies of equality really became aroused. In the election campaign in 1823, one of the main issues not only in Kennedy's district but throughout the state was, as it was called, the "Jew Bill." The anti-Semitic propaganda was successful. Kennedy and 15 supporters in the House who were branded as the "Jew ticket" were defeated at the polls by the self-styled "Christian ticket." Another round began. In 1824 Kennedy, still on the issue of the "Jew Bill," was re-elected, and started the legislative battle all over again.

Newspapers in and outside Maryland discussed the issue extensively. Pamphlets were published with the speeches in favor of equality for the Jews. Charge and counter-charge were fully aired. The anti-Semites agitated noisily that the Jews were "Shylocks," that they had killed Jesus, that they would immigrate into Maryland and ruin the state. Firmly Kennedy and his principled associates in the legislature retorted: Jesus "was a Jew, was one of these persecuted and proscribed people." Shakespeare had drawn a false picture, and among the Jews in Maryland there was "the same proportion of estimable individuals as in any other class." Moreover, the Jews had fought bravely in the Revolutionary War and the War of 1812 for the equality they had the right to expect. And change in the state constitution was due not in the spirit of mercy or as a favor to the Jews, but as "justice, sheer justice." The United States Constitution should be followed as the model for Maryland.

Finally democracy won, decisively if not completely. The last vote taken, on January 5, 1826, showed 45 in favor and 32 against the Amendment that would permit persons "professing the Jewish religion" to hold office, practice law, and fill positions of public trust, *provided* such persons took a special oath declaring "a belief in a future state of rewards and punishments." Such is the law today. That same year the electorate of Baltimore elected Solomon Etting and Jacob I. Cohen, Jr. to the City Council, which immediately chose Etting as President of the City Council. The 150 Jews in Maryland had attained legal equality.

While this political struggle was being fought in Maryland, a movement for religious reform began among the native-born Jews of Charleston, which then had the wealthiest if not the largest Jewish population in our country. While rooted here in the needs of the middle class Jews in Charleston, the urge to reform was influenced by earlier developments along this line in Holland and Germany.

There the beginnings of the political equality won temporarily by the Jews in the wake of the French Revolution were accompanied by a movement for cultural emancipation from feudal traditionalism. Under the intellectual sway of Moses Mendelssohn (1729-1786), the German Jewish middle class was drawn into the German Enlightenment, and began to strive for mastery of the German language and culture as a way of achieving more economic, cultural and social equality with the German middle class. Differences that were an obstacle to such equality were to be eliminated or reduced. Thus arose the tendency to Reform Judaism, to revise the content and form of Jewish Orthodoxy. Although it left the masses of Jews untouched, the Reform movement spread to five or six cities in Germany by the 1820's. Its rationalistic attack on superstition also expressed the needs of a middle class that was then progressive in its attempt to apply reason to the solution of social problems.

In Charleston, middle class Jews faced similar situations, with the notable difference that they had more formal and practical equality than the Jews of Germany and did not have to face the repressions and pogroms that came after 1815 in central Europe. By December, 1824, discontent with the orthodoxy of Congregation Beth Elohim led to the presentation of a Memorial proposing reforms signed by 47 Jews, or about 40 per cent of the membership.

The Memorial observed that "apathy and neglect" among the Jews of Charleston were leading to decline in the congregation, and ascribed the apathy to "certain defects which are apparent in the present system of worship." It was proposed that a "more rational means of worshipping the true God" be instituted, as had been done in Holland and Germany, by shortening the services, using English translations of the prayers, having a weekly sermon in English, and abolishing such unseemly practices as the auctioning of religious honors at the services. Rejection of the Memorial led to the founding early in 1825 of the Reformed Society of Israelites, led by Isaac Harby, which soon had a membership of 50, representing with their families, as Harby pointed out, "upwards of two hundred dissenters." About

Rebecca Gratz (1781-1869), founder of the first Jewish Sunday School in the United States, and reported to be the prototype of Rebecca in Walter Scott's "Ivanhoe." The portrait is by Thomas Sully.

70 members remained in Beth Elohim, totaling some 300 persons.

Shorter services enabled the business man to hurry away to his place of business. More decorum at services and the use of instrumental music met the challenging standards of the Christian churches. But the Reform also affected religious principles. In the prayer book used by this Charleston Society there were omitted the portions of the Orthodox prayers that declare a belief in a personal Messiah, in the resurrection of the body when the Messiah comes, in the sacrificial cult, and in the return to Palestine. The United States was home and not exile for these Reformers.

Only "a tender regard for the opinions and feelings of their parents," Harby said, kept most of the native-born Jews from leaving Beth Elohim and joining the Reformed Society. This parental pressure, together with Harby's leaving for New York in 1828, led to the disbandment of the Society in 1833. Yet when Beth Elohim

I have not seen the criticism of Harrington you mention. but confess myself very well satisfied with the Tale. I do not think she could have managed her fable better. there was a necessity for some sacrifice of religious principal. and we are better pleased it should be kept out of view & have been made by the parents of Berenice. than by either her or Harrington. there is a strong instance too of religious tolerance in Montenero's educating his daughter a Christian. and in the harmony of their affections towards each other. which contains the moral she would inculcate in her tale. I think however a more interesting & natural story might have been produced. in making the characters of Jew & Christian associate. & assimilate in all the respective charities of social life. without bringing the passions into contact I believe it is impossible to reconcile a matrimonial engagement between persons of so different a creed. without requiring one or the other to yield. in all instances we have heard of in real life. this has been the case. and where a family of children are to be brought up. it appears necessary that parents should agree on so important a subject. I have known many Jews many christian women. whose wives have become strict conformists to the rites of one religion. and, families married to Christians who have entered the church. as in the instance of my Aunt Schuyler. one instance similar to Montenero I have heard of here. but the parties lived very unhappily. little jealousies were continually occurring. and at length when the husband died the widow & her daughters returned to her family & the synagogue. while the son was put in the navy and quite estranged from the family the poor fellow is also dead. but had he survived the division of interests and sentiments would have broken up the harmony of feelings that should subsist between such near relations.

I saw our old friend James Paulding in his way home. he appears to

Part of the manuscript of a personal letter discussing intermarriage, sent by Rebecca Gratz of Philadelphia to her friend, Mrs. Ogden Hoffman of New York, October 20, 1817.

itself was reorganized in 1836, it selected a rabbi who followed the practice of the Reform Temple in Hamburg, Germany. After this beginning in Charleston, there was a lull in Reform Judaism until, in the 1840's, German Jews who had been under its influence there came to our country, revived the movement and made it rapidly one of the main features of middle class Jewish life of the nineteenth century.

Two other religious developments took place in these first three decades of the century. The first was the breaking of the European Jewish tradition of organization which provided for only a single Jewish community in a given city, with complete authority over Jewish affairs. In the eighteenth century in our country there was also only one congregation in a city. But the German Jews in Philadelphia began to break the pattern in 1795, and by 1802 emerged from the preliminary stages of having an Ashkenazic *minyan* (quorum of ten adult males) gathering informally for religious services into a formally constituted congregation, Rodeph Shalom. That social class distinction was an underlying factor in this division along ritualistic lines of Ashkenazic and Sephardic may be inferred from the fact that by 1825 many of the members of Rodeph Shalom who had grown wealthier in the interim changed their membership back to the Sephardic Congregation Mikveh Israel, because of the greater prestige attached to that older and richer group.

In New York the first Ashkenazic congregation was organized in 1825. Although the Sephardic Shearith Israel had for a century had a membership which consisted mostly of Ashkenazic Jews, the secession did not come until 1825. By then a group of more recently arrived and poorer Jews from Germany and Poland were not only ill at ease with the Sephardic ritual but had also become critical of what they regarded as the religious laxity of the congregation. When a petition for the right to hold separate Ashkenazic services as part of Shearith Israel was rejected, these German, Polish and some Dutch and English Jews left Shearith Israel and established the Ashkenazic congregation Bnai Jeshurun.

Hebrew Marriage Certificate of 1822, in Charleston, S. C.

At about the same time, there began a trend toward the publication of apologetics, or works of defensive justification of one or another aspect of Jewish life. Three themes received particular attention: Christian missionary attempts to convert Jews, the occupational characteristics of Jews in Europe and here, and whether Jews were or could be patriotic. The first was comparatively the easiest to handle. The orthodox Jew was much less worried by the occasional Jewish convert to Christianity in the United States than by the much higher rate of intermarriage with non-Jews. Yet an increase of conversionist propaganda and organization was annoying enough to provoke response.

In 1820 a new society entered the field, The American Society for Meliorating the Condition of the Jews, under which benevolent name they sought converts. To persons of this Christian persuasion conversion of the Jews was vital because upon it depended the Second Advent of Jesus as Messiah. The picture of the Jews given

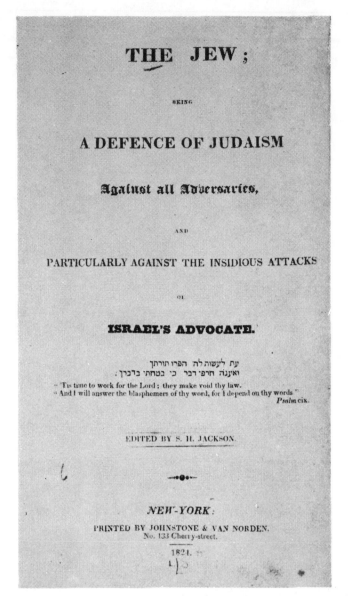

Title-page of the first Jewish periodical in the United States, 1824.

in this conversionist propaganda was, however, anti-Semitic. The first published reaction came from Abraham Collins, a member of the New York Hebrew Benevolent Society, who in December, 1820 issued a small volume entitled *Israel Vindicated* and signed "An Israelite," although there is evidence that a non-Jew, George Houston, wrote the text. Among the "calumnies propagated" by the aforementioned conversionist Society that are refuted are the cry that the Jews crucified Jesus, that they are an inferior and accursed people, and that their way of making a living is wicked. On the last, the author comments: "It will readily be conceded, that, in most countries of Europe, the Jews have carried com-

mercial speculation too far, and neglected the mechanic arts." But the reason for this situation was not Judaism, he explained, but the economic restrictions imposed upon Jews. Only when all religious, political, economic and social restrictions upon Jewish equality have been obliterated, can the Jew "be restored to his proper place in society."

Following Collins and "An Israelite," Solomon Henry Jackson, also a New Yorker, entered the lists, against the conversionists. First he appeared in 1823 with a pamphlet he composed and published, answering a sermon delivered by an English clergyman before the London Society for Evangelizing the Jews. In the same year and for the same purpose, Jackson began to publish the first Jewish periodical in the United States, *The Jew,* which was less a magazine than a running polemic, for two years, against *Israel's Advocate,* organ of the American conversionists.

The matter of Jewish occupational characteristics, already noted, had become the concern both of Jews and friendly non-Jews. Thus M. M. Noah, in a *Discourse* in 1818 at the consecration of the new synagogue of Shearith Israel, had suggested that the Jews should be turned from what he called the "crooked paths of traffic miscalled commerce" to industry and agriculture. The following year, when W. D. Robinson published his Memoir urging a Jewish settlement in the West, he discussed why there were so few Jewish artisans and farmers in Europe. He ascribed this condition correctly not to "any inherent aversion to cultivate the soil" or to labor, but to "the uncertainty of their social and political existence" in countries in which they were surrounded by hostility and restrictions. In the United States, he was confident, they would be able, if colonized in a body, to overcome the economic "habits in which they are unfortunately reared." Neither he nor Noah nor others understood that no significant change in Jewish occupational characteristics could occur in an expanding capitalist economy such as that of the United States, in which the greatest economic rewards, political power and social prestige go not to the workers and farmers but to the moneyed elements, the landlords, manufacturers, bankers, merchants and commercial middle-men of all sorts.

Simultaneously there began the practice, still in operation, by which Jews tried to convince anti-Semites that Jews were patriotic by pointing to the service so freely rendered by Jews in our country's wars. The defense is as repeated as the charge. With two wars now behind them, Jews could "point with pride" to 1776 and 1812. Noah felt impelled to do so in an appendix to a pamphlet he issued in 1816 containing documents about his service as United States consul in Tunis. "An American Jew" did it anonymously in a pamphlet in the election campaign in New York in 1823. Noah, appointed Sheriff in 1822, was now a candidate for this post, which had become elective while he was in office. His candidacy was greeted with unashamed anti-Semitism. Charles King, editor of the *New-York American,* had announced that Jews were not fit for office because they lacked "that single national attachment, which binds a man to the soil of his nativity, and makes him the exclusive patriot of his own country." Vigorously the anonymous American Jew retorted at length, citing 1776 and 1812. "We love our country," he protested, "not only because it is our country, but we love it because it gives us a privilege which our persecuted sect enjoys in no other country of the world." But Noah was defeated at the polls. His election in 1824 as Grand Sachem of Tammany was a consolation which could not, however, erase the fact, and the effect, of the anti-Semitic campaign of the previous year.

The pathetic dilemma of "An American Jew" was to persist and even grow deeper. Thomas Jefferson had understood the problem. In a letter to Noah in 1818, Jefferson had explained that, with regard to persecution and discrimination, our laws provided for equality, "but more remains to be done. For altho' we are free by the law, we are not so in practice. Public opinion erects itself into an Inquisition, and exercises its office with as much fanaticism as fans the flames of an Auto da fé. . . ." This public opinion, of course, was not spontaneous, but generated by a social order based on anti-social competition and exploitation. That was why in 1815 Nathan Nathans of Philadelphia wrote to his non-Jewish friend, William Meredith, that he had decided to go to the University of Pennsylvania rather than Harvard because "I think there will be some difficulty about my religion at Cambridge . . ." How often would Jews choose the second best because they could not, or had reason to fear they would not, get the best? Although the second best here might for a long time be better than anything obtainable elsewhere in the world, still the psychology of the Jews in the United States was being shaped in the pattern that there was always a dubious "but" after the proud assertion of equality.

Western Scene, a painting by S. N. Carvalho.

CHAPTER 6: New Immigration, New Organization

THE MAP of the United States kept bulging outward, to the South and especially the West, as the population rocketed, at a rate never again equalled, from 12,866,000 in 1830 to 23,191.000 in 1850. Seven new states, making a total of 31 in the Union, were added: Arkansas (1836), Michigan (1837), Texas and Florida (1845), Iowa (1846), Wisconsin (1848) and California (1850). Texas and California were carved out of United States conquests over Mexico; the other states grew by the toil and persistence of pioneers, combined with the Federal government's expulsion of the Indian population across the Mississippi River.

Immigrants rolled in on the Atlantic tide in unheard of numbers. In the 1830's there were four times as many, and in the 1840's eleven times as many as in the 1820's, and the tide was still rising. Almost half of the 1,965,000 immigrants were Irish, almost a third were German, among them thousands of Jews. It was national policy to welcome this immigration. President John Tyler, in a message to a special session of Congress on June 1, 1841, declared that "we hold out to the people of other countries an invitation to come and settle among us as members of our rapidly growing family, and for the blessings which we offer them we require of them to look upon our country as their country and to unite with us in the great task of preserving our institutions and thereby perpetuating our liberties." But because immigrant laborers and craftsmen were used to slash wages, an anti-alien, anti-Catholic movement, aimed especially at the Irish, grew up and became violent and murderous in the 1840's.

Economically there was rapid expansion of manufacturing and agriculture, with special attention to transportation to make possible the commerce needed to distribute these products. Roads and canals multiplied: in 1830 there were 1,270 miles of canals; in 1850, it was 3,700 miles—and railroads were being built and planned. But the cycle of boom-to-bust could not be avoided. The longest depression in American history began with the Panic of 1837 and lasted for a full six years into 1843.

Movements for social reform arose from the unrest of the people. The masses, especially in the North and West, demanded public schools. As cotton became king in this democracy, with cotton production leaping from 731,000 bales in 1830 to 2,133,000 in 1850, slavery became more widespread and oppressive—and the abolitionist movement reorganized itself and spread out. Women began to campaign for their rights as human beings. The depression temporarily wiped out labor's efforts to organize national trade federations, but it stimulated Utopian attempts to build small islands of collective enterprise in the sea of capitalism. Followers of Charles Fourier of France and Robert Owen of England founded some 60 such colonies, but their doom was as certain as the noble intentions of their originators to grope for a better way of life.

Within this framework, Jewish life developed in many ways. The size of the Jewish population multiplied from about 6,000 in 1826 to about 50,000 in 1850, with immigration the chief cause.

Solomon Nunes Carvalho crossed the Rocky Mountains in 1854 with the explorer John Charles Fremont, serving as daguerreotypist and artist to the expedition. This engraving is from Carvalho's book, "Incidents of Travel and Adventure in the Far East," New York, 1857. Carvalho's own drawings of the expedition are lost.

The main stream came from Germany, but there were perhaps a thousand from Austria, Hungary and Bohemia, and some from Russia and Poland.

The Jews who came from the German states were a small part (about five per cent) of a large migration that brought 587,000 Germans here from 1831 to 1850. What was it that moved such masses to make their long way to the seaports of Bremen or Le Havre, there to be crowded into the steerage of a small vessel of about 300 tons for the uncomfortable and dangerous voyage of some 45 days across the Atlantic? Those who ventured on these hardships were peasants fleeing crop failure and land hunger, and handicraftsmen displaced by the beginning of manufacturing. Political tyranny and the defeat of the 1848 Revolutions also combined with the disruptive effect of the rise of capitalism on the old agricul-

Advertising a clothing establishment in Providence, Rhode Island, 1852.

tural economy to add a spurt to German emigration.

For the Jews the basic factors were the same—but with a difference. As one such immigrant wrote home from Baltimore in 1850, there was "the pressure within the pressure," that is, "in the general German pressure there is a special Jewish pressure." This took the oppressive form of many special taxes for Jews, occupational restrictions, and, in Bavaria, limitation on the number of Jewish marriages permitted. Therefore the percentage of Jews in the German immigration, although small, was twice the proportion of Jews in the German population, especially when the crushing of the 1848 Revolutions frustrated the hopes of Jews for emancipation from discriminatory laws. Occupationally, also, the Jewish immigrants differed from other German immigrants. Exact knowledge is meager, but the following facts on Jewish immigration from Wuerttemberg from 1848 to 1855 are suggestive: of 171 whose occupations are given, eight were farmers, 64 were merchants and traders and their clerks, and 94 were craftsmen (more than half of them butchers, shoemakers and bakers).

From Russia and Russian-Poland in the 1830's and 1840's only several hundred Jews came to the United States, although many more emigrated into Central and Western Europe. Three events stimulated this emigration: 1) the decree of 1827 ordering conscription of Jews, including children of 12, for 25 years or more of military service (a decree extended to Poland in 1843); 2) the defeat of the Polish Insurrection against Tsarism in 1830; and 3) the 1843 order expelling all Jews living within 33 miles of the Prussian and Austrian frontiers. There was at this time practically no non-Jewish immigration from Russia and Poland.

Landing in our ports, usually New York but sometimes New Orleans, the Jewish immigrants, weary but eager, had to find at once a place to live and to make a living. Where they could make a living, there they settled. Large numbers stayed in the ports of entry, especially New York, the Jewish population of which swelled from 2,000 in 1836 to 10,000 in 1842 to 16,000 in 1850, when the total population of the city was more than a half million. Until 1825, the largest Jewish population had been in Charleston, but when that city began to lose its importance as a seaport owing to the decline of trade with the West Indies and the movement of cotton planting westward, the Jewish population stopped growing and New York emerged as the city with the largest number of Jews, a position it has held to this day.

Next to New York, the five metropolitan centers with over 100,000 population were, in that order, Boston, Philadelphia, Cincinnati, Baltimore and New Orleans. In 1850, the largest Jewish populations were also in these cities, but in a slightly different order: Philadelphia, New Orleans, Cincinnati, Baltimore and Boston. Furthermore, as the American economy and population spread westward both in the North and South, the Jews were right among them. Especially did the German Jews move westward with the mass of German immigrants, whose language they shared and with whom they could therefore have easier relations than with the English speaking population. The Census of 1850 noted 77 Jewish congregations in 40 cities in 21 of the 31 states of the Union. The 31 "Jewish Churches" had a total seating capacity of 16,575 and a property valuation of $371,600.

With others, the Jews moved westward in the North, settling in Syracuse, Rochester and Buffalo, in Cleveland, Detroit, Chicago and Milwaukee. They moved west in the central area, into Pittsburgh, Louisville, Wheeling, Fort Wayne, and St. Louis. They moved west in the deep South, into Mobile, Natchez and Vicksburg. Lured by the Gold Rush of 1849, they scurried with 100,000 other Americans into California, which had three congregations, two in San Francisco, when the Census takers came around in 1850.

It was the drive to make a living that took Jews, like others, westward. First the immigrant generally tried to establish himself in the port of entry. How he did it is suggested by the list of

Joseph Jonas (1792-1869), watchmaker and silversmith, pioneer Jewish settler in Cincinnati, 1817.

In business in Detroit in 1853.

occupations of 101 German Jews who in 1849 and 1850 applied for admission to a New York Jewish fraternal society. Fully 50 were engaged in merchandising, 46 were craftsmen (14 shoemakers, 13 tailors, five butchers, four cigarmakers, two capmakers, and a lithographer, glazier, cabinetmaker, tinsmith, barkeeper, goldsmith, machinist and barber). Then there were two physicians, a civil servant, an artist and a landlord. Of the 50 in merchandising, 30 were peddlers. In a small city like Easton, Pa., the peddler bulked even larger in the economic life of the Jews. In 1840 Easton had six German Jewish peddlers, in 1845, seven, and in 1850 all of 24, outnumbering the Jews in all other ocupations combined.

Peddling at that time, however, was not what it is now. Before the railroad made possible modern techniques of distributing consumer goods, the peddler was a necessary link between expanding manufacture and the otherwise inaccessible consumer in the rural areas in which the vast majority of the people lived. Today our image of

HOTELS AND RESTAURANTS.

**SUTTER HALL!—PIONEERS, AT-
TENTION!**

The undersigned would most respectfully announce to the Ladies and Gentlemen of Sacramento and vicinity, and the public at large, that they have purchased the building and its appurtenances, located at the corner of J and 29th streets, known as

SUTTER HALL!

And have fitted up and furnished it in the most elegant style, where they are prepared to receive and entertain Ladies and Gentlemen who may favor them with a visit.

They are also prepared to give COTILLION PARTIES on the shortest notice.

Our Bar is supplied with the best of Wines, Liquors, Cordials, &c., that can be obtained in California, and you will find OLD JOE HARRIS at all times ready and willing to wait on his friends.

☞ STRAWBERRIES AND CREAM from Kublan & Co.'s Gardens, opposite, served up at all hours.

☞ The OMNIBUS during week days will convey passengers to and from our house at 3 and 5 o'clock P. M., and on Sundays will make regular trips every hour and a half from 1 to 9 o'clock P. M.

Music every Sunday.

A. WATTERS,   I. WATTERS,
n16   A. WATTERS & CO.

In Sacramento, California in 1854.

the peddler is that of a man or woman with a pushcart in a crowded metropolitan ghetto fiercely competing with a thousand others for the easily available customer. But as one economist has said, these pushcart peddlers "were the faded caricatures of a once hardy, vigorous calling."

This calling had been the domain of the famous Yankee peddlers of New England, who roamed far and wide in pursuit of the far-flung customer for tinware and watches and knick-knacks. By the 1830's, when the German Jews began to arrive in greater numbers, New England factories had opened new opportunities for the Yankee youth, which turned away from peddling. German Jews stepped boldly into the gap. There was a hinterland around each city with a Jewish population, and the peddler pushed into that hinterland. It was a hard life, but immigrants could not be choosers. Starting perhaps with a little credit from a Jewish merchant in an eastern city, the peddlers would fan out, tending always towards the newly populated West. Thus the German Jews of this period were pioneers of the pack, bringing dry-goods, household wares, clothing, gadgets and trinkets to the pioneers of the land.

The poor ones lugged the packs on their backs. Those who could afford it invested in a horse and wagon. For long journeys they used the new canals and the rivers. There was loneliness and danger in this "calling," and the peddler dreamed only of when he could give it up for something better. Was there a cross-roads spot where he could pitch his pack and have the customers come to him—to a store? Was there a village in which he could locate a store and hope to expand as the village grew into a town or city? It was in these terms that the peddler spelled success. Among the 10,669 peddlers counted in the Census of 1850 many were Jews, and of the 16,594 peddlers in 1860 the majority, it is estimated, was Jewish. Most of these peddlers sooner or later became retail storekeepers, some became wholesale merchants, and a few developed into department store owners. Thus there was formed, particularly in the cities away from the eastern seaboard, the bulk of the Jewish commercial middle class.

The financial Panic of 1837 and the consequent depression that persisted, especially in the South and West, until 1843 of course had its great effect upon the Jews, particularly upon the still unsettled new immigrants. Among the people as a whole, suffering was widespread. One third of the workers were unemployed, and wages were cut 30 to 50 per cent. Craftsmen and storekeepers lost trade heavily. In 1841 the new federal bankruptcy law allowed 39,000 persons to cancel $441,000,000 of debts. There was no public relief system to feed the hungry, nor even any general charitable organizations. There were two specific results in organized Jewish life: the appearance of new philanthropic organizations, and an attempt to realize the old dream of directing Jews into agriculture.

The charity funds of the congregations and the existing Hebrew Benevolent Societies were pitifully inadequate. Among the larger Jewish populations, new groups appeared, such as the New York Hebrew Assistance Society in 1840 and the United Hebrew Beneficent Fuel Society in Philadelphia in 1841. How helpful they could be in a crisis can be judged from the fact that in New York in 1841 both the old Benevolent Society and the new Assistance Society together aided about 280 Jews with an average of $9 per person in fuel, food, clothing and cash. The more than 30 other New York relief societies that had sprung up by 1840 did no better for the non-Jewish poor. In the communities with smaller Jewish populations like Pittsburgh, Baltimore and New Orleans, no new philanthropic organizations emerged until after the depression.

The dream of agricultural colonization also found expression. While New York unemployed were demonstrating in the streets and some were breaking into flour warehouses, a number of Jews, most of whom had come from Germany in the past three years, conceived the idea of a settlement in the West, on the prairie. In the spring of 1837, a group calling itself the Association Zeire Hazon (Tender Sheep) issued an Address to the Jews asking for funds to buy land, implements, stock and other necessities. Despite the assurance that such a project would "add so much lustre to the Jewish character," there was an indifferent response. Perhaps as a by-product of this idea, however, about a dozen Jewish families established the short-lived Jewish colony of Sholam,

The Jews' Hospital when it opened in 1855 on West 28 Street, New York; later it became Mount Sinai Hospital.

in Warwarsing township, Ulster County, New York. In the winter of 1837-38, on about 500 acres in this Catskill Mountain area made accessible by the recently opened Delaware and Hudson Canal, these hardy Jews settled down to farming, supplemented by work in their own goose-quill and fur-cap factories, and by itinerant tailoring and shoemaking. But after four years, unable to pay their mortgages, all but two of the families saw their properties sold at auction in the spring of 1842—and Sholam remained only as a dim local legend.

After the depression ended in 1843, other ideas for agricultural colonization were advanced. An agent sent out by a New York group bought 160 acres in Shaumburg, Cook County, Illinois. The few Jews who went out there, however, did not like the situation and soon most of them ended up in Chicago, the new bustling town in Cook County. Another proposal by a Philadelphia merchant, for a large scale project for a Jewish state in the mid-West, never got off the paper on which it was printed. The same fate befell similar projects, small or large, in the 1850's. Lack of experience and of funds doomed them. Basically, too, in the country as a whole, it was the urban population that was increasing more rapidly than the agricultural, because the rewards of capitalist en-

Marcus Van Gelderen (1798-1871), a colonist at Sholam, Ulster County, N. Y. and "shohet" for Congregation Shearith Israel, New York.

A pointer, made in 1850 by Abraham Kayton, Jewish silversmith in Norfolk, Va., lying on a Torah scroll.

terprise were reaped more readily in the city than in the countryside.

As the Jewish population more than doubled in the 1840's, certain trends and problems appeared in Jewish life. We have already seen that the Jewish population was widely distributed into 21 states. At the same time there was a strengthening of the trend to have more than one congregation in a city. By 1850 there were 11 such cities with a total of 43 congregations. New York had 14, Philadelphia five, Cincinnati and New Orleans, four each, Albany and Baltimore, three each, and Richmond, Charleston, Cleveland, St. Louis and San Francisco, two each. The congregations were no longer multiplying on the basis of ritual differences as between Sephardic and Ashkenazic. Country or even locality of origin often became the basis for congregational life. Of the nine congregations born in New York between 1842 and 1850, three were German, three Polish, one English, one Bohemian (Czech) and one Dutch. Also beginning to make itself felt slowly in the 1840's was the new differentiation along lines of Reform Judaism, with which some of the new immigrants had had contact in Germany. One of the three new German Jewish congregations in New York was the Reform Congregation, Emanu El. In 1849 there were alto-

gether only four or five small Reform congregations in the United States.

Coupled with this decentralization of synagogue life was another, more basic, trend—towards the secularization of Jewish life. Rabbi Moshe Davis, historian of American-Jewish religious life and institutions, notes that it was in the 1840's that the process began by which "slowly the Jews were weaned away from the synagogue as their central communal institution." Jews began to feel a need for Jewish organizations other than congregations. Some of the benevolent associations already mentioned may have originated in one congregation or another, but religious affiliation was not a requirement for membership in them. In some cases, as in San Francisco, a Hebrew Benevolent Society was organized before a congregation was established. When German immigrants in 1841 organized the New Israelite Sick-Benefit and Burial Society in New York, the Preface (in Ger-

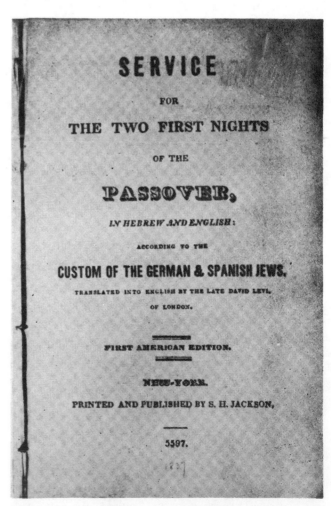

Title-page, the first Passover Haggadah printed in the United States, 1837.

man) to their Constitution and By-Laws specified that "Our society should be independent of the synagogues," and provided for the admission to membership of non-religious Jews.

Fraternal orders were another new growth in the 1840's. In 1843, refused admission by the local Odd Fellows Lodges, a group of German Jews in New York organized the Independent Order B'nai B'rith. Although the founders included a hazan and a synagogue clerk (together with two shop-keepers, two jewelers, a tailor, a shoemaker and a barber), the order was not a religious organization. Its stress was on cultural life and mutual aid. By 1850, there were ten lodges, four of them in New York with 532 members, and two each in Cincinnati, Baltimore and Philadelphia, with an additional 500 members. All conducted their proceedings and minutes in German, except Lebanon Lodge No. 9 in New York, "the first lodge in the United States working in the English language." In New York, also, an unofficial auxiliary was organized in 1846 as the Unabhängiger Orden Treuer Schwestern (Independent Order of True Sisters). Even in fraternalism, however, there was to be no monopoly. In 1849 one of the founders of B'nai B'rith helped establish the Independent Order of Free Sons of Israel (B'nai Israel). Congregational leaders and rabbis regarded these and the many later fraternal orders as competitors of the synagogue, not without justification. The sick benefits and other forms of mutual aid not provided by the congregations attracted considerable numbers of insecure immigrants to fraternal organizations. More and more the synagogue became one of many institutions in Jewish life, and the many others became increasingly important to more and more Jews.

Another feature of Jewish life in the 1840's was the beginning of the process of breaking down the localism and separatism that prevailed. Not only was there no nation-wide Jewish organization or federation of any kind, religious or secular; there were no regional or even city-wide bodies for pooling information and facing common problems. The Jewish immigrant in New York or Philadelphia knew more about the Jews in his native German or Polish town than he did about Jews in Alabama or Indiana, *if* he knew

Henry Jones (d. 1866), a founder of B'nai B'rith in 1843, from a drawing by George D. M. Peixotto.

there were Jews there. The native-born Jews and those of the earlier immigration were not much better informed.

What the absence of even elementary channels of information and communication meant can be seen from the slow, sparse, belated and ineffectual reaction of American Jews to the Damascus Affair in 1840. When a Catholic priest in Damascus, Syria, disappeared, the French consul spread the charge that Jews had killed the priest to use his blood for Passover ritual purposes. Horrible torture of scores of Jews by the Turkish authorities produced false confessions, many deaths and some "conversions" to Mohammedanism. Fifteen earlier nineteenth century ritual-murder libels in European countries had failed to arouse general interest. Since the Middle East was even then, however, the center of European big-power rivalry, much attention was focused on this atrocity when news reached European capitals and the Jews appealed to their brethren for help.

Response came first from the Jews of England, whose concern coincided with the desire of British imperial interests to challenge French domination in the area. In France a few liberal Jews joined

by their religion to make use of Christian Blood in their Unleavened Bread at Easter.

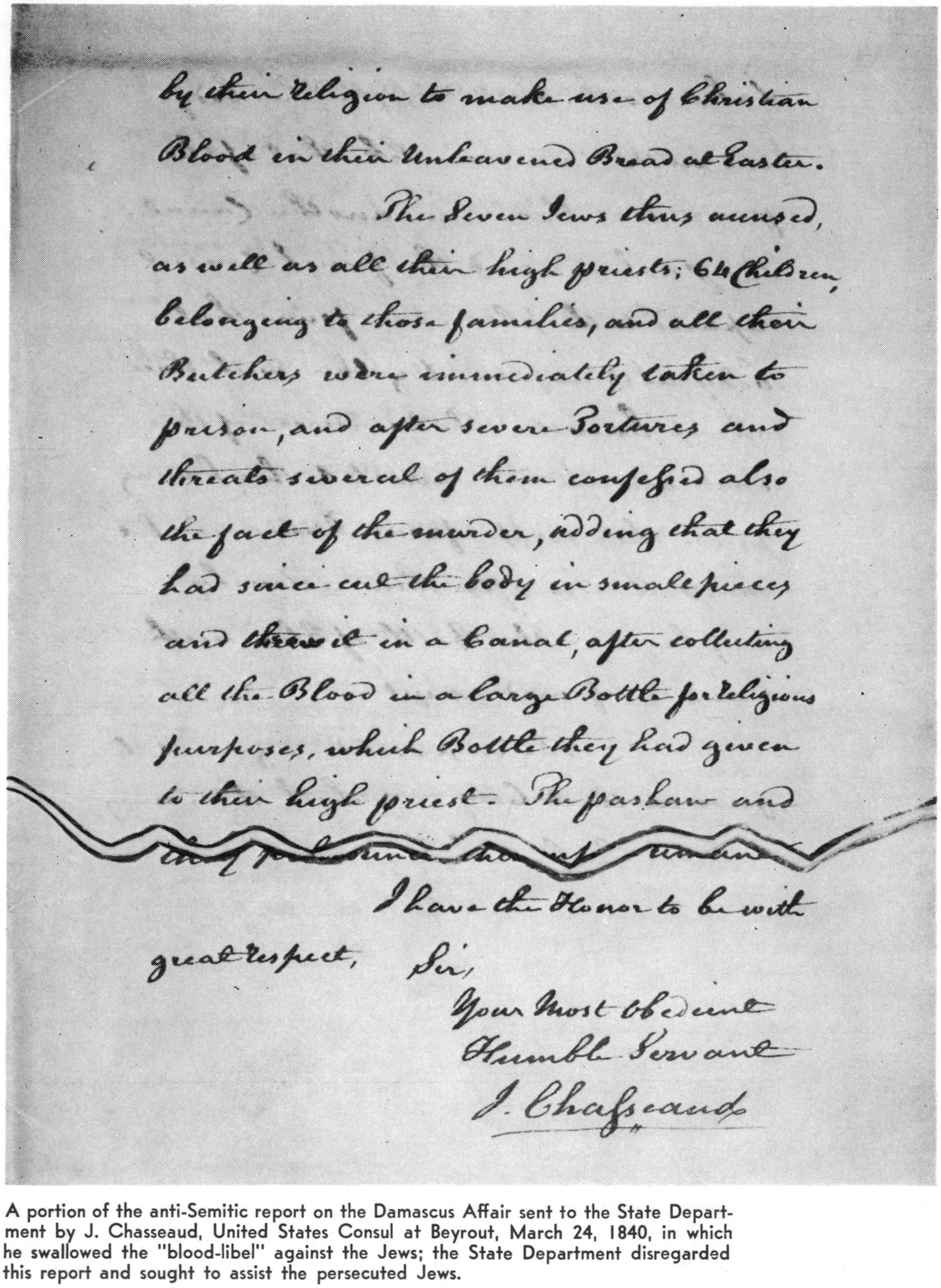

The Seven Jews thus accused, as well as all their high priests; 64 Children, belonging to those families, and all their Butchers were immediately taken to prison, and after severe Tortures and threats several of them confessed also the fact of the murder, adding that they had since cut the body in small pieces and threw it in a Canal, after collecting all the Blood in a large Bottle for religious purposes, which Bottle they had given to their high priest. The pashaw and ...

I have the Honor to be with great respect, Sir,

Your most obedient
Humble Servant
J. Chasseaud

A portion of the anti-Semitic report on the Damascus Affair sent to the State Department by J. Chasseaud, United States Consul at Beyrout, March 24, 1840, in which he swallowed the "blood-libel" against the Jews; the State Department disregarded this report and sought to assist the persecuted Jews.

the English in protest despite the involvement of the French government in the persecution. Ultimately it was British intervention, diplomatic and naval, that put a stop to the inquisition in Damascus. Meanwhile, newspapers in the United States had printed shocked reports of the outrage. The Jews here, however, were so slow to react that, before the first Jewish protest meeting was held in New York, the State Department, following the example of the British government and public opinion, had sent instructions to our diplomatic representatives in the region to render such aid to the Jews as was possible. Even these instructions arrived on the scene of distress after the matter had already been settled. Therefore the meetings held thereafter in Philadelphia, Cincinnati, Savannah, Richmond and New Haven accomplished little more than to reveal the sympathy of the Jews (and non-Jews) who attended. The whole incident pointed up the fact that lack of organization and channels of communication had prevented effective Jewish action even when the Jews sensed a menace.

While attempts at bringing congregations into one organization or even conference failed in 1841, 1846 and 1849, it was the founding of a stable Jewish press and the fraternal orders that began to provide the information and to weave the broader ties. *The Occident and American Jewish Advocate* and the B'nai B'rith both appeared in 1843.

THE OCCIDENT,

AND

AMERICAN JEWISH ADVOCATE.

A MONTHLY PERIODICAL

DEVOTED TO

THE DIFFUSION OF KNOWLEDGE

ON

Jewish Literature and Religion.

EDITED

BY ISAAC LEESER.

ללמוד וללמד לשמור ולעשות

"To learn and to teach, to observe and to do"

VOL. I.

PHILADELPHIA:
PUBLISHED AT 118 SOUTH FOURTH STREET.
5604.

Title page of the first stable Jewish monthly in the United States, 1843.

Isaac Leeser (1806-1868), traditionalist rabbi and editor.

The Occident was the creation of the Rev. Isaac Leeser, a German Jew who was *hazan* of the Philadelphia Sephardic congregation, Mikveh Israel. He edited it, wrote most of its contents, and published it until he died in 1868. By diligently obtaining and reporting news about organized Jewish life wherever it spread, *The Occident* stimulated an awareness of an American Jewish community. As a vigorous opponent of anti-Semitic prejudice and discrimination in American religious, official and public life, Leeser also made his readers conscious of a basic general problem of the Jewish population. His subscribers were in the hundreds rather than thousands, however, because *The Occident* dealt too much with matters of religious doctrine of little interest to the layman and because it was written in English at a

Israels Herold.

7. NISSAN 5609.   New-York, 30. März 1849.   No. 1.

Israels Herold,

redigirt und herausgegeben von

Isidor Busch,

erscheint jeden **Freitag** Vormittag.

Abonnement in **New-York** beim Herausgeber
419 Grand Street und in der Druckerei von
J. Mühlhäuser **237 Division Street.**
Halbjährig: Ein Dollar 50 Cents.
Vierteljährig: 75 Cents
In Vorausbezahlung an den Austräger.
Eine einzelne Nummer: 6¼ Cents.

er gab sie zunächst uns, und durch uns der ganzen übrigen Menschheit.

Jedes Wort dieser Lehre ist ewige Wahrheit; aber die göttliche Weisheit, die in Allem Einem Plane folgt, hat — indem sie diese Lehre dem Menschen gab — ihm darin nicht das fernere Streben nach Erkenntniß, das Forschen seines Genies nach diesen höchsten Wahrheiten abgeschnitten, es ihm weder unnöthig noch unmöglich gemacht. Im Gegentheile hat sie gerade dieses Forschen ihm als heilige Pflicht aufge...

in Betracht kommt. Aber das genügt Vielen nicht, sie sagen: „Die Einen werden sich nur den Anstrich der Unpartheilichkeit geben, und mit leidenschaftlichem Eifer, in bitterm Tone, der Wahrheit die Ehre zu geben betheuern, die Andern werden, statt Gründe und Beweise für ihre Meinung, nur Witz und Spott gegen die der Alten zu richten wissen."

Nun, denen werdet Ihr doch nicht leicht Glauben schenken! und wir werden bald finden, ob sie nicht bei der nächsten Rücksicht...

This first German-Jewish weekly in the United States lasted only three months in 1849.

time when the majority of literate Jews read German more than English.

Yet it was primarily in English and only occasionally in German that the Jewish press was to expand in the next half century. In fact the first venture in German collapsed in three months in 1849. Isidor Bush, a refugee from the counter-revolution in Vienna in 1848, confidently launched *Israels Herold* in New York as a weekly literary and cultural journal on a platform of social liberalism and Reform Judaism. He soon learned, however, that the audience for such a periodical was tiny. When he suspended operation, his subscribers list contained 314 persons in 31 cities in 17 states, including 175 in New York City, 25 in Cincinnati, 22 in St. Louis, 13 in Albany, and 12 in Philadelphia.

Later the same year, however, a successful weekly in English, *The Asmonean,* began to appear in New York edited by Robert Lyon, an English Jewish businessman and journalist. Addressing himself to the Jewish business and commercial elements, Lyon combined news and discussion of Jewish communal affairs with stock quotations, wholesale market reports and news of business life. He attracted considerable commercial advertising, spread his magazine into the South and West and made it flourish until his death in 1858 stopped the publication. He set many a pattern for middle class Jewish journalism.

Gradually *The Occident* and *The Asmonean,* the B'nai B'rith and the Free Sons of Israel and their successors, helped those they influenced to enlarge their horizons and begin to see American Jewish life in its nation-wide scope.

Simultaneously, the Jewish population was moving about more or less easily in the general life of the country. The constructive role of the Jewish peddler in the economy of these two decades has already been noted. Perhaps not unrelated to peddling, but worthy of specific mention is the weight that Jews began to have in the drygoods trade in the 1840's. In 1847 the New York *Drygoods Reporter* indicated that fully 25 per cent of all sales by auctioneers (wholesalers) were made to Jewish customers and that on Jewish holidays some auctioneers suspended business rather than do without this increasingly influential element.

In the movements for social reform of these decades, a few Jews became outstanding. Commander Uriah P. Levy of the United States Navy,

Masthead of the first English-Jewish weekly in the United States. 1849.

while combating anti-Semitic treatment inflicted upon him in the Navy, played a conspicuous part in the sustained agitation against the practise of flogging used in the Navy and helped abolish this brutal affront to human dignity. In rationalist and atheist circles, Charles C. C. Cohen was honored by his associates. Outstanding was the energetic and effective work of Ernestine L. Rose in several fields: the women's rights movement, the campaign for free public schools, atheist propaganda and, in the next decade, the abolitionist movement. Born the daughter of a rabbi in 1810 in Piotrkow, Poland, she had become a follower of the Utopian Socialist Robert Owen in England before coming to the United States in 1836. She at once initiated a struggle to extend to women the right to own property. Her twelve years of continual pressing of that issue was a factor in finally getting the New York State Legislature in 1848 to pass the first Married Woman's Property Act in the country. The second woman in the United States (after Frances Wright) to speak on a public platform, Ernestine Rose, by her oratorical prowess, wit, charm and physical courage in the face of rowdy male hecklers, won the designation of "Queen of the Platform."

While Ernestine Rose was working valiantly for the civic emancipation of all women, the first steps, incidentally but significantly, were being taken towards the equality of women in Jewish religious life. In his *Reminiscences,* the Rev. Isaac Mayer Wise declared that "the emancipation of the Jewish woman was begun in Albany [in 1847], by having the Jewish girls sing in the choir, and this beginning was reinforced by the introduction of family pews [in 1851]." In the Orthodox synagogue, women were segregated in a curtained balcony; the family pews of Reform Judaism brought husband and wife, and other female members of the family, into the same pew. Wise ex-

Mrs. Ernestine L. Rose (1810-1892), popular orator in the cause of women's rights, abolitionism, free-thought and public education; from a widely distributed engraving in 1857.

plained that the Congregation Anshe Emeth having bought a church for its own use, "the church-building had family pews, and the congregation resolved unanimously to retain them."

In the general cultural life of the time Jews functioned in a variety of ways. There were struggling artists and portrait painters like Frederick E. Cohen in Detroit, Theodore S. Moise in Charleston and New Orleans, and Solomon N. Carvalho in Philadelphia. In journalism there were new figures like the English Jew, Abraham Jonas, editor of *The Advocate* in Columbus, Illinois, in 1840-41, Joseph Cohn of Hamburg, editor of the semi-weekly New Orleans *Der Deutsche Courier* from 1841 on, or the American-born Gershom Kursheedt, editor of *The New Orleans Times Commercial* from 1845 to 1849. On the stage the melodramas of Jonas B. Phillips were performed in the 1830's in New York, while his brother Henry B. Phillips won a reputation as an actor.

In literature, the first book of verse by an American Jew was published in Charleston in 1833. Entitled *Fancy's Sketch Book,* it introduced the sweet small talent of Penina Moise, who for several

Self Portrait by Frederick E. Cohen, Detroit artist in the 1840's.

decades after that continued to write verse, both pious and secular, that was published in periodicals and newspapers in Boston, New York, Washington, New Orleans and Charleston. In her religious poetry she proclaimed that

> from faith my spirit borrows
> Strength its trials to endure.

Her secular poems, however, amid the sentimental and the trivial, included some vigorous topical verse on the Damascus Affair, on "The Rejection of the Jew Bill, by the House of Lords," and "To Persecuted Foreigners," urging Jews to rise, "elastic from Oppression's tread" and "Come to the homes and bosoms of the free." Her personal trials were heavy. Impoverished, she literally wore her eyes out working on fancy laces and embroideries. The last 25 of her 83 years she lived in blindness, her daily exercise the pacing of a mile a day round and round her bed.

A communal literary effort, initiated in 1845 by Isaac Leeser in Philadelphia as the Jewish Publication Society, did not last long. By 1850 it had

Self-Portrait by S. N. Carvalho (1815-1897).

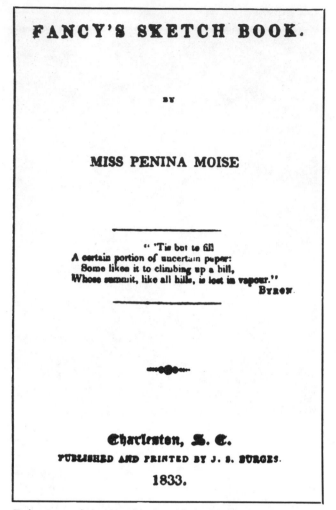

FANCY'S SKETCH BOOK.

BY

MISS PENINA MOISE

" 'Tis but to fill
A certain portion of uncertain paper:
Some likes it to climbing up a hill,
Whose summit, like all hills, is lost in vapour."
BYRON.

Charleston, S. C.
PUBLISHED AND PRINTED BY J. S. BURGES.
1833.

Title-page of the first book published by a Jewish woman in the United States, Penina Moise (1797-1880).

issued 14 small volumes of *The Jewish Miscellany,* chiefly biblical tales popularly retold, and attained 450 subscribers, but the Society disbanded when its stock was destroyed by fire in 1851. One of the volumes was reprinted for the general public in 1847 when *Hebrew Tales,* selected and translated by Hyman Hurwitz in London, became No. 1 of Spalding & Shepard's Select Library in New York.

While the Jews moved easily in these and other circles, their experience with anti-Semitism continued. In the mid-1840's, however, the Jews had a chance to compare their generally favorable situation with that of the Irish immigrant masses who, since they were being used by American employers to cut wages, became the main target of a violent anti-alien, anti-Catholic political movement calling itself the Native American Party. In 1844, it grew so strong it elected its candidate Mayor of New York and six members of

Congress. Not directly anti-Semitic, this party in 1845 even elected to Congress one of its leaders, a Jewish editor of a nativist daily, Lewis C. Levin. Yet the party agitation to require immigrants to live here for 21 years before they could be naturalized could not have added to the security of the Jews.

The nativist agitation was full of incitement and led to an outburst of violence in Philadelphia in 1844. Riots in May and July against Irish immigrants resulted in 22 dead and 94 wounded, and in the burning of two Catholic churches, a female seminary, and 230 dwellings. In a battle centered on a third church, artillery was used on both sides. The uneasiness of the Jews that such a pogrom, even if not directed against them, could take place in *this* country is reflected in a letter by Rebecca Gratz. Writing about this "attack on the Catholic Church" to her brother in Kentucky on July 12, 1844, she warned that "unless the strong arm of power is raised to sustain the provisions of the Constitution of the U.S., securing to every citizen the privilege of worshiping God according to his own conscience, America will be no longer the happy asylum of the oppressed and the secure dwelling place of religion."

No such pogrom has ever been inflicted upon the Jews in our country. Yet experience with anti-Semitism continued to worry and annoy and shape the attitudes of the Jews. A few examples are illustrative. In 1832 Philip Minis was involved in a duel in Atlanta because the epithet "Shylock" was used against him. In 1840 the German-language *Volksfreund* of Lancaster, Ohio, was conducting an anti-Semitic campaign, charging that Jews don't work, cheat Christians, cannot be good democrats and therefore ought to go back to Palestine. In the same year, Isaac Leeser found it necessary to write a series of protesting letters published in the *Philadelphia Gazette,* reprinted by him in 1841 as a volume entitled *The Claims of the Jews to an Equality of Rights.* Noting the persistence of legal discrimination against Jews in states like Massachusetts and North Carolina and to public slander of Jews in states where they did have legal equality, Leeser objected that, "being equals in law, we ought not to be pointed at with the finger of vulgar prejudice and odium as members of the Israelitish people . . ." He urged that "it is time to discard the word 'Jew' as a term of reproach . . . is the Jew more dishonest, more knavish, more cunning, than his Christian neighbour? I believe not, and I may freely challenge the proofs of the contrary."

As he and others were challenging the slanders, new malicious stereotypes were being created. With more and more Jews turning to peddling, the folk image of the oversharp Yankee peddler was extended to the Jewish peddler, but with a special edge. For a Yankee peddler to cheat fellow-Christians was one thing: for a Jew to repeat—or to be thought to have repeated—the Yankee practice was somehow, in the eyes of competitors, worse. The current image blended with an older one, and the "Jew peddler" in print and in oral lore often got to be called "Shylock."

Was this just a matter of harmless words, to be dismissed with the American saying, "Sticks and stones may break my bones, but words will never hurt me"? Some harm *was* done, political, economic, physical and psychological. In New Orleans in 1841 a Whig Jewish candidate in a state legislative election was met with a Democratic opponent's billboard containing the slogan, "Make hay whilst the sun shines! or you will swallow a Charleston Jew!" A Jewish shade-painter in 1849 complained to the *New York Sun* that he could not get work because advertisements by employers said, "No Jews wanted here." That same year in Brooklyn German immigrants "with stones, guns and clubs" attacked a Jewish funeral in East New York and, according to a press report, "wounded several persons severely." On Rosh Hashana in 1850 in Baltimore on two successive evenings many windows of the synagogue in Eden Street were smashed during the services by rowdies gathered outside, who then, "catching some of the unoffending worshippers, assaulted and beat them badly." *The Baltimore Sun* thought this was an "outrage." *The Asmonean* tried to explain it away as a political rather than a religious attack.

Incidents like these could not but make for insecurity, for fear. The measure of this may be taken from a revealing incident: early in 1848 the Rev. J. J. Lyons of Congregation Shearith Israel

Isaac Mayer Wise (1819-1900), leader of Reform Judaism, in 1850.

in New York read a tiny item in the *Tribune* about the disappearance of a Negro waiter employed in a Jewish home. Suspicious and alerted, Rev. Lyons pasted the clipping into his scrapbook, and wrote down beneath the clipping his intention "to ascertain if possible, whether it is true that such a man is missing, otherwise the motive is palpable, that of calumny; fortunately it is not near the pasover [sic] or the Blood question might be re[lated?]." Eight years after the blood-ritual libel in distant Damascus, how secure did this 35 year old American congregational leader feel if such a newspaper item could stir such apprehensions?

Yet Jews did circulate widely in American life. It was relatively easy early in 1850 for the Rev. Isaac Mayer Wise, only three and a half years out of Bohemia and now a Reform rabbi in Albany, to have New York Senator William H. Seward take him to the White House to meet and chat with President Zachary Taylor, with the Washington newspaper next morning reporting the event under the headline: "The First Rabbi to Visit a President." Rather fawningly, Wise complimented Taylor as the General who was the "hero" of the Mexican War of 1846-1848.

Among the American people there was deep opposition to the war as unjust and aggressive on our part. Outstanding writers like Emerson, Thoreau and Lowell condemned it, and political leaders like Daniel Webster, Charles Sumner and Abraham Lincoln denounced it as aggression against Mexico for the purpose of adding slave states to the Union so that the slaveowners could strengthen their control over the federal government. There may have been similar attitudes among the Jewish population, but they were not so clearly expressed. Some rabbis applauded the Government to show their "loyalty." No Jewish communal figure took a public stand in opposition. Yet hardly 50 Jews responded to the calls to enlist in the armed forces, a far smaller proportion than in the American Revolution and the

War of 1812. Perhaps Rebecca Gratz expressed the reason for this indifference when she explained, in letters to her sister-in-law in Kentucky, that she and many of her friends in Philadelphia had refused to participate in the victory celebrations. "I feel so much more sorrow & disgust, than heroism in this war," she wrote. "When we were obliged to fight for our liberty—and rights—there was motive & glory in the strife—but to invade a country and slaughter its inhabitants—to fight for boundary—or political supremacy—is altogether against my principles & feelings . . ."

In this first war of aggression by the United States against a foreign country, Jews among other Americans drew a distinction between two kinds of patriotism: that which involves blind loyalty to an administration, no matter how reactionary its policy, and that which involves enlightened loyalty to the basic democratic ideals of the American people in which love of country is fused with devotion to justice.

Abraham Lincoln, a painting in 1865 by S. N. Carvalho.

CHAPTER 7: For Union and Emancipation: The Civil War

The 1850's began with a Compromise that was supposed to settle the slavery question forever—and led into a Civil War that finally did end it. There was no compromising the irrepressible conflict between a social system based on slave labor in the South and one founded on industrial capitalism and free wage-labor in the North. The issue of 4,000,000 Negroes writhing in slavery could neither be ignored, side-tracked nor suppressed. Discontented, restless and rebellious slaves, as well as their supporters and allies, free Negro and white, in the Abolitionist movement, placed the issue ever more in the foreground as the decade advanced.

Certain economic developments were fundamental. King Cotton may have thought he was secure on his slave-based throne, ruling both the South and the federal government, when production leaped from 2,133,000 bales in 1850 to 5,387,-000 bales in 1859. But in 1859, the value of all United States industrial production reached $1,886,000,000 and thus for the first time in our history exceeded the value of all agricultural products, King Cotton included.

The increased labor force required for such production came both from the natural population growth and from immigration. From 23,191,-000 in 1850, the population climbed to 31,443,000 in 1860. Immigration surpassed all preceding levels, reaching almost 3,000,000. Fully one-third came from Germany, and it is estimated that among them were about 100,000 Jews. This influx brought the total Jewish population to about 200,000 on the eve of the Civil War, four times what it was in 1850. Among these new immigrants, arriving after 1848 under the influence of European democratic ideals, there was wide anti-slavery sentiment. From their ranks came most of the staunchest Jewish abolitionists.

The Jewish population, while growing rapidly in eastern cities like New York and Philadelphia, also spread into the western regions and even, with the Gold Rush, to the Pacific Coast. In New York the Jews multplied in number from 16,000 in 1850 to 40,000 in 1859, and Philadelphia had about half that number. By 1860 there were some 50 cities with organized Jewish communities, while there were many more cities and towns with Jews not organized in any way. The German immigration, of which the Jewish was a part, moved out into Ohio, Indiana, Illinois, Michigan and Wisconsin, and Jewish communities bloomed in these areas. Ohio flourished, with more than 6,000 Jews in Cincinnati, about 1,000 in Cleveland and smaller numbers in Akron, Columbus and Dayton. Gold-fevered California had an even larger Jewish population than Ohio. Slowest in growth was the Jewish population in the South. The economy of the slave states had little attraction for immigrants in general: in 1850 only 10%

of white immigrants lived in these states. By the eve of the Civil War, perhaps 15% of the Jews lived in the South, New Orleans being the only city with several thousand Jews.

Before turning to the main theme of the Jews and the slavery issue, it is important to note certain other developments: the anti-alien "Know-Nothing" movement, the growth of Reform Judaism, the expansion of the Jewish press, the reaction to the Swiss Treaty and Mortara affairs, and the founding of the first organization to defend Jewish democratic rights.

The "Know-Nothing" movement spurted forward in the 1850's. With the immigration tide high, employers were taking advantage of the situation to cut wages. "Pauperism increased rapidly," writes the American economic historian, Harold U. Faulkner, "and the standard of living of the working classes was pushed steadily downward as real wages declined . . . the two decades preceding the Civil War stand out as one of the most discouraging periods that the American wage earner has ever experienced." The American Party arose to spread anti-alien, anti-Catholic doctrine through secret lodges whose password was "I don't know"—hence the name, "Know-Nothing." Although directed mainly against Irish and German Catholics, this nativist propaganda affected all immigrants through its two main planks: to exclude Catholics and foreign-born from office and to require 21 year residence for naturalization. At its electoral peak in 1854, the American Party attracted some Jews whose experience with or judgment of Catholic reaction abroad clouded their understanding of the situation here. Yet the nativist bigotry characteristically spilled over into anti-Semitic utterance in Georgia, Alabama, Mississippi, Kentucky, Missouri, California and Massachusetts. A keen observer like Isidor Bush summed up the effect of the "Know-Nothing" movement upon the Jews by indicating that it intimidated them, as well as other immigrants, from active participation in public life. After 1855, however, the movement split on the issue of slavery, and faded from the political arena.

Of considerable importance in this period was the spread of Reform Judaism. Many German Jews had been under Reform influence at home

Isidor Bush (1822-1898), editor, abolitionist, and leader in B'nai B'rith.

and were ready to follow it here. The Rev. Isaac M. Wise became the master organizer of the movement. When in 1854 he left Albany for Congregation Bene Yeshurun in Cincinnati, he made that city a radiating center of Reform. The following year, the Bavarian radical Reformer, Rev. Dr. David Einhorn, came from Pesth, Hungary, to Baltimore and turned Har Sinai Congregation into an eastern center of Reform. Revision of the orthodox prayer-book was begun. The first to be published was Einhorn's *Olath Tamid* (Constant Offering). In its first form it appeared in German in Baltimore in 1856, and in completed form in New York in 1858. In 1857, *Minhag America* (American Rite), prepared by a Commission consisting of Rabbis Isidor Kalisch, Isaac Mayer Wise and Dr. Rothenheim, was issued in Cincinnati in English, German and Hebrew. The main changes made in the traditional prayer-book were the elimination of references to the coming of the Messiah, the return of the Jews to Palestine, the rebuilding of the Temple in Jerusalem and the

Title-page of first edition of "Minhag America," Cincinnati, 1857.

ספר

אבני יהושע

על פרקי אבות

מחבר בו נכבדות אמרי ספר ללמד בני יהודה אמונות אמתית
להבין סמועות באמרות סהגרות יגלה מתהאים וחתלומית, להשביע
לקוראיז סרבע סמחות חקירות במתקים אמרות מנופת מתוקם
הב מליצות התבאים ביקים , מצבירו מיצות פסוק
תורה והנבאים תמים, ובזה החזיב אני מראה אתכם
רק נסיון ממלאבת כאשר יביא בהקדמה, אמנם
אם ספרי ימצא הן בעיניכם ותקנו ממני
בכסף מלא אם ירצה הם אדיס ספר
הסני אשר ורעתי נאמהו שכל אחד
יקבל נחת רוח ויראה נפלאות
אסר יש בו בכח התורה
הקדוזה . תברתהו
אף לשיתי אני
הצעיר

יהושע פאלק בן כ"ה מרדכי הכהן ז"ל
מק"ק קארניק ול"ע בנואיארק:

נדפס פה ק"ק נואארק
אצל יוסף בן יעקב ז"ל:
בשנת **כתר** לפ"ק

NEW YORK:
PRINTED AT "JEWISH MESSENGER" OFFICE,
15 VANDEWATER STREET.
1860.

"Abne Yehoshua," a commentary on "Pirke Abot" (the Sayings of the Fathers), by Joshua Falk (1799-1864), the first learned work in Hebrew written in the United States.

restoration of the sacrificial cult, and "the lamentations over oppression and persecution and the accompanying cry for vengeance," which Wise regarded as "untrue and immoral as far as American Jews were concerned." Wise declared the aim to be to bring the prayer-book "into accord with the religious consciousness of the time and the democratic principles of the new fatherland." Einhorn, with similar deletions, added the stress on the priestly "mission" of Israel to bring light to the world. The services were of course much shortened, Wise estimating that his Sabbath service, together with a sermon, would take no more than two hours. As the German-Jewish middle class expanded in numbers and wealth, it made Reform Judaism its main religious expression.

Equally important in the Jewish life of the time was the increase of the Jewish press from two periodicals in 1850 to nine in 1861, of which two were in German. Wise in Cincinnati edited two weeklies, *The Israelite,* which he began to publish in July 1854 in an issue of 1,000 copies, and the German-language *Deborah,* launched in 1855 with 800 copies as the first Jewish woman's magazine. In the East, Einhorn edited a too ponderous German monthly, *Sinai,* in Baltimore, while in New York two weeklies, *The Jewish Messenger* in English and the *Hebrew Leader* in English and German started publication in 1857 and 1859 respectively. In San Francisco, *The Hebrew Observer* began as a German and English weekly in 1855, and *The Gleaner* came out in English in 1856. In 1860 *The Pacific Messenger* appeared in English with a one-page German supplement. The contents of all were heavily weighted with discussion of Judaism. There was also much attention to news reports of Jewish life abroad and at home, to exposure of acts and utterances discriminatory against Jews, and, in the weeklies, to serialized fiction, stories and verse. Note was also taken of general economic, political and cultural events.

Two events in the 1850's involving the equal rights of Jews led finally to the birth of a Jewish defense organization. The first was the treaty the United States negotiated with Switzerland in 1850 and ratified in 1851. In Article I, the United States government agreed that American Jews going to Switzerland would not be entitled to equal treatment with American Christians because various Swiss cantons had anti-Semitic restrictions. This official acceptance by the Federal administration of the principle of discrimination against American citizens abroad alarmed the Jews and, when their protests placed the issue before the public, aroused condemnation in a score of American newspapers. The Swiss, however, justified their discriminatory practice by pointing to the Southern theory of state's rights as parallel to cantonal rights in Switzerland. The Federal administration, dominated by the South, was ready to sacrifice the equal rights of Jews to the principle of state's rights which the slaveowners were using to protect their property. The protests of the Jews and other democratic elements, repeated through-

Deborah.

Ein Beiblatt zum „Israelite," gewidmet den Töchtern Israels.

Herausgegeben von
Bloch & Co.,
No. 43 Dritte Straße, Ecke der Sycamore.

„Es werde Licht."

Redigirt von
Isaac M. Wise,
Redacteur des „Israelite."

No. 1.   Cincinnati, den 24. August, 1855.   Erster Jahrgang.

Die Deborah.

Endlich, endlich ist sie da, die liebenswür- dige Deborah mit ihrem blendend weißen Gem... rabenschwarzen Augen...

lieblichen Klänge der Mutter, in der Deine Kindheit lallte, mit Sanftmuth und Zartheit sprechen zu den Töchtern Israels, lehren, erzählen und unterh... anmuthiger sie.

Das israelitische Weib.

Griechen und Römer widmeten den Frauen die schönsten und herrlichsten Erzeugnisse ... die schönsten und...

The first magazine for Jewish women in the United States, 1855.

out the decade, were ineffective, and the issue was not resolved until the Civil War had downed the theory of state's rights "ueber alles."

The second shocking development occurred in Italy. In 1858 Edgar Mortara Levi, a six year old Jewish boy, was torn from his parents in Bologna by the Inquisition on the ground that he had been secretly baptized by a Catholic nurse, and was taken to Rome to be brought up as a Catholic. Throughout Europe Protestants as well as Jews voiced their indignation, and even Catholic circles in Switzerland and France joined the protest. In the United States, opposition ran high. Meet- ings were held in some 17 cities, one in New York attended by 2,000, another in San Francisco by 3,000. In some cases Protestants as individuals cooperated with Jews. But efforts to persuade the President and the State Department to intervene as they had done in the Damascus Affair in 1840 failed. President James Buchanan frankly told a Jewish delegation headed by Isaac Leeser that he would not support their meritorious cause for to do so would encourage other countries to meddle in our affairs. As in the Swiss Treaty case, it was being borne in upon the Jews that issues of Jewish rights could not be separated from the fundamental problem of slavery.

PROCEEDINGS

IN RELATION TO THE

MORTARA ABDUCTION

Mass Meeting at Musical Hall,

San Francisco, California, January, 1859.

ADDRESSES

By the Hon. SOLOMON HEYDENFELDT; Rev. Drs. ECKMAN, SCOTT, PECK and HENRY; Col. E. D. BAKER; Messrs. F. P. TRACY, M. M. NOAH, and others.

Preamble and Resolutions, unanimously adopted; Letter from Rev. Dr. CUTLER; Remarks of the Press, etc., etc.

SERMON

On "RELIGIOUS INTOLERANCE" (delivered at the "Unitarian Church.")

SAN FRANCISCO:
TOWNE & BACON, PRINTERS, EXCELSIOR BOOK AND JOB OFFICE,
No. 125 Clay Street, corner of Sansome.
1859.

Title-page of a pamphlet on the Mortara Case.

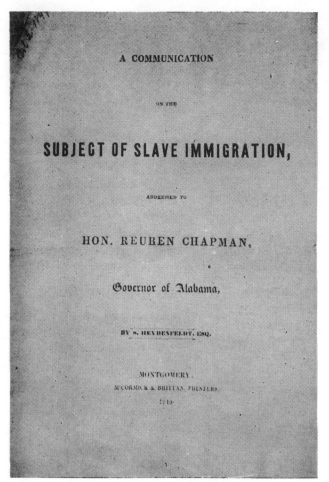

A COMMUNICATION

ON THE

SUBJECT OF SLAVE IMMIGRATION,

ADDRESSED TO

HON. REUBEN CHAPMAN,

Governor of Alabama,

BY S. HEYDENFELDT, ESQ.

MONTGOMERY,
M'CORMICK & BRITTAN, PRINTERS
1849.

Title-page of a pamphlet by Solomon Heydenfeldt (1816-1890), published in 1849 in Montgomery, Alabama, opposing importation of slaves into Alabama because of "the unproductiveness of slave labor."

Although Mortara was never returned to his parents and grew up to be a priest, the Mortara Case had one positive result in Jewish life both in France and the United States. In France in 1859 there was born the Alliance Israelite Universelle. In the United States the same year there was founded the Board of Delegates of American Israelites, with representatives from Orthodox congregations in 13 eastern and southern cities, including 11 congregations from New York. The haughty Sephardic congregations Shearith Israel in New York and Mikveh Israel in Philadelphia refused to participate, and so did the Reform groups in Cincinnati, New York, Baltimore and Charleston. Wise in Cincinnati, an opponent of abolitionism, expressed the fear that the proposed organization would take a stand on the slavery question. Nevertheless, two centuries after the first settlement, the first national Jewish repre-

sentative body was born. Its main aim was to defend the rights of Jews at home and abroad.

Turning now to the relationship of the Jews to the central issue of slavery in the 1850's, we find a revealing point of departure in the estimate made by the active abolitionists. On May 11, 1853 the American and Foreign Anti-Slavery Society convened in New York and heard its Thirteenth Annual Report. Included was an inventory of the attitude to slavery of all the religious denominations in the United States. The abolitionists concluded "that slavery has steadily increased within the pale of the Christian denominations during the last half century." The exceptions were notable, but the situation did no credit to Christian principles.

But what of the Jews? The abolitionists had a brief ten sentences on them. There was no organized Jewish attitude or opinion, they reported, because there was no central body to speak for all the Jews on any subject, even religious. The abolitionists had been informed that each Jew, as a citizen, may "choose which ever side he may deem best to promote his own interests and the welfare of his country." They assumed that the two Jewish periodicals concerned themselves only with religious matters, which was not exactly true. Significantly the abolitionists noted that "some of the Jews, who reside in slave States, have refused to have any property in man, or even to have any slaves about them." On the lengthily debated issue of whether the Bible sanctioned slavery, the Report stated that Jews "do not believe that any thing analogous to slavery, as it exists in this country, ever prevailed among the ancient Israelites." Their unnamed informant had assured them that Judaism was a religion "of purity and morality, and one which presents the strongest possible supports for civil society, *especially a government based upon principles of equality and liberty of the person!*" He added that Jews "believe that the coming of the King Messiah will be the signal for universal peace, UNIVERSAL FREEDOM, universal knowledge, and universal worship of the One Eternal."

This was the report, and on it the abolitionists made this brief and poignant comment: "The objects of so much mean prejudice and unrighteous oppression as the Jews have been for ages, surely they, it would seem, more than any other denomination, ought to be the enemies of CASTE, and the friends of UNIVERSAL FREE-DOM." How that phrase "ought to be" rang with disappointment! Abolitionists were not content to postpone emancipation to "the coming of the King Messiah." Yet this estimate of the Jews by the abolitionists, who knew more about anti-slavery work than anybody else, was sober and sound. In 1853 there was only one Jew conspicuously identified with the abolitionist movement —Ernestine L. Rose, who three years before had been fiercely heckled by pro-slavery toughs in New York when she spoke at a public meeting in support of the Wilmot Proviso to keep slavery out of the territories wrested from Mexico. Yet Mrs. Rose, isolated from organized Jewish life, had little direct influence upon it.

Between 1853 and the Civil War, however, the picture changed. The Jewish population approximately doubled, mainly because of immigration from Germany. Settling mostly in the North and West, with no such history of habituation to slavery as had affected many native-born Jews and earlier immigrants, this new mass was overwhelmingly anti-slavery in sentiment and from its depths came anti-slavery leaders. Within a few years after the abolitionist report of 1853, Jews who were to be outstanding abolitionists landed in our country. Rev. Dr. Bernhard Felsenthal came in 1854, Rev. Dr. David Einhorn in 1855, Michael Heilprin in 1856. Already here, and soon to come forward as the anti-slavery struggle sharpened, were August Bondi, who had arrived in New Orleans in 1848, and Isidor Bush, who set foot in New York in 1849. Such figures, together with Ernestine L. Rose, picked up the long unused thread of Jewish participation in anti-slavery work that went back to the end of the eighteenth and beginning of the nineteenth centuries. At that time a Solomon Bush and a Benjamin Nones in Philadelphia and a Moses Judah and a Mordecai Myers in New York had been active in the local manumission societies, the first anti-slavery organizations in the country.

What factors determined the reaction of the Jewish population to slavery? Essentially they

David Einhorn (1809-1879), a leader of Reform Judaism and abolitionist preacher, editor and writer.

were the same as those operating on the non-Jews: their place in the relations of economic production and distribution. The anonymous Jew who explained this to the abolitionists in 1853 indicated that each Jew, as a citizen, may "choose which ever side he may deem best to promote his own interests and the welfare of his country." In general the interests of Jews in the South were bound up with the slave system. Like non-Jews, Southern Jews falsely identified this system with the welfare of the United States. Jewish plantation owners like Judah P. Benjamin of Louisiana defended slavery, Benjamin becoming its outstanding apologist in the U.S. Senate in the 1850's. Jewish merchants and traders, dependent upon the slave system and King Cotton, owning slaves for business and domestic use like non-Jews, looked upon slavery with the same eyes as non-Jews. In the 1850's there was indeed extensive opposition to slavery among non-slaveowning small farmers, mechanics and artisans, but Jews in the South were but little represented in these categories. In the North too there were commer-

Know all Men by these presents, *That I Jacob Levy Junr.*

do, by these presents, for good and valuable considerations, fully and absolutely *Manumit, make Free, and set at Liberty, four* slave, named *Samuel Spyres Edwin Jackson Elizabeth Jackson and James Jackson* hereby, willing and declaring that the said *Samuel Spyres, Edwin Jackson, Elizabeth Jackson and James Jackson* shall and may, at all times hereafter, exercise, hold, and enjoy, all and singular the liberties, rights, privileges, and immunities of *an* free *men & Woman* fully to all intents and purposes, as if *they* had been born free.—And *I* do hereby, for *myself my an* Executors, Administrators, and Assigns, absolutely relinquish and release all *my* right, title, and property whatsoever, in and to the said *Samuel Edwin Elizabeth & James* as *my* slave.

IN TESTIMONY WHEREOF, _ have hereunto set _ hand and seal, the *Sixth* day of *March an* one thousand eight hundred and *seventeen*

SEALED AND DELIVERED IN }
THE PRESENCE OF }

Jacob Levy Junr.

J. Morton

The certificate by which Jacob Levy, Jr., of New York (d. 1837) freed four of his Negro slaves on March 6, 1817.

cial centers like New York, Philadelphia and Cincinnati dominated by merchants and financial interests with close economic ties to the South. These elements, including Jews among them, fought the abolitionists.

Within this general framework it is possible in proper perspective to assess the special effect upon Jewish conduct of what the abolitionists called the "mean prejudice" against Jews. For consciousness of anti-Semitic hostility is an objective force in molding Jewish attitudes. The effect of such awareness will depend upon the Jewish individual's or group's social understanding. Some for instance might fear that they would make the mean prejudice against them even meaner by expressing anti-slavery attitudes in an environment in which the dominant class is pro-slavery, and in which the Jews are dependent upon that class. In such Jewish circles a theory of accomodation to the dominant power develops: "the law is the law," and "when in the South do as the Southerners do." Since the accommodation is always uneasy, the accommodator will try to allay suspicion and guarantee a favorable impression by singing his hosanna with a little more fervor than the non-Jew exhibits.

On the other hand there were those Jews, although in the South they were few, who felt a connection between the source of the "mean prejudice" against them and the source of slave oppression. Such were moved not only to sympathy with the enslaved but, if occasion offered, to cooperation with them. A radiant example is the way in which, deep in Tuscumbia, Alabama, between 1847 and 1850, the German Jewish immigrant brothers, Joseph and Isaac Friedman, cooperated with the slave Peter Still to help him buy his own freedom. Still told the tense story to his biographer, the white Southern abolitionist Kate R. Pickard, who published it in 1856 in *The Kidnapped and the Ransomed*. We learn how these, the only Jews in town, subjected to considerable prejudice in the six years of their residence there, had impressed Peter Still as being the only white people in town likely to be sympathetic to his desire to buy himself out of slavery. Knowing his Christian owner would not allow him to buy his freedom, Still undertook to persuade the two Jews to buy him from his master with the understanding that he, Still, would then, as he earned and saved money, buy his freedom from them. How the anti-Semitic slaveowners pitied Peter Still when they learned that the horrible Jews had bought him from his kind Christian master! But the Jews were loyal to their arrangement with Still. In three years Still secured his certificate of freedom—and went North to begin to buy his family out of slavery.

When the Republican Party was born in 1854, there were Jews in at the birth and among the early builders that in 1856 rallied around the Presidential candidacy of John C. Frémont ("Free Speech, Free Press, Free Soil, Free Men, Fremont and Victory") and in 1860 put Lincoln in the White House. The Republican Party was a coalition, led by the industrialists, that aligned industrialists, some merchants, the independent farmers, a large section of the traders, storekeepers and professionals, the majority of the wage-earners and the free Negroes. While the Democratic Party

Sigismund Kaufmann (1825-1889), '48er, early socialist, Republican Party leader and abolitionist.

had developed a traditional following among the immigrant masses, including the Jews, there were Jews who made the bold break to join the new third party. Isaac Mayer Wise was so annoyed that he scolded them in *The Israelite* as "red republicans and habitual revolutionaries, who feed on excitement and delight in civil wars." But in the slave state of Maryland, David Einhorn hailed the Republican Party and backed Fremont to fight slavery, "the cancer of the Union."

Among the conspicuous Jewish Republicans were Adolph Loeb, Charles Kozminski and Abraham Kohn in Chicago, the latter a friend of Lincoln and so effective that the Democrats denounced him, to his historic credit, as "one of the blackest Republicans and Abolitionists." In Indiana there was Bernhard Felsenthal, in Missouri, Isidor Bush and Moritz Pinner, in Kentucky, Lewis N. Dembitz. Philadelphia had Moses A. Dropsie and Rev. Sabato Morais and Baltimore had not only Rev. Einhorn but Dr. Abraham B. Arnold. Moses Naar was an active Republican in Elizabeth, N. J. and Dr. Joseph Lewi in Albany,

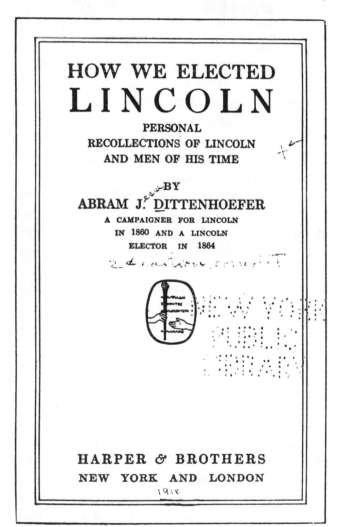

HOW WE ELECTED
LINCOLN

PERSONAL
RECOLLECTIONS OF LINCOLN
AND MEN OF HIS TIME

BY
ABRAM J. DITTENHOEFER

A CAMPAIGNER FOR LINCOLN
IN 1860 AND A LINCOLN
ELECTOR IN 1864

HARPER & BROTHERS
NEW YORK AND LONDON

Title-page of autobiographical account by Abram J. Dittenhoefer (1836-1919), early Republican leader.

August Bondi (1833-1907), '48er, abolitionist who fought with John Brown in Kansas and in the Civil War.

N. Y. Brooklyn had the German '48er and socialist, Sigismund Kaufmann. In New York there were the politically influential Jonathan Nathan and his brother Gershon, Dr. Nathan Krackowitzer, Meyer Thalmessinger, stationer and publisher, and Abram J. Dittenhoefer. Especially well known was the artist Solomon N. Carvalho, who had been a member of one of Frémont's pathfinding expeditions across the Rocky Mountains and in 1856 published a vivid account of the adventurous trip in time for the election campaign.

Hundreds of Jews followed the lead of such Republicans. Such Jews were not "Israelites with Egyptian principles," the brand that the abolitionist Senator Benjamin F. Wade of Ohio had affixed to Judah P. Benjamin after one of Benjamin's eloquent speeches in defense of slavery. Dittenhoefer was not the only Jew in the North and West who, reading Wade's telling thrust, decided that a Jew "whose ancestors were enslaved in Egypt, ought not to uphold slavery in free America, and could not do so without bringing disgrace upon himself."

Even before the Civil War, when the expanding slaveholders turned from political struggle to arms, Jews took to the field. In 1855 Southern "Border Ruffians" were pouring into Kansas Territory in an attempt to make it a slave state. Answering a call for anti-slavery settlers, August Bondi, the 21 year old veteran of '48, went to Kansas. In 1856, with two other Jews, Jacob Benjamin and a 250-pound Polish immigrant named Theodore Weiner, Bondi joined John Brown's guerrilla band and fought under him at Black Jack, Osowatomie and other engagements.

On the very eve of the Civil War, Jews were pushed into the forefront in another battle—the interpretation of the Biblical view of slavery. With Lincoln elected but not yet inaugurated into office, the outgoing Democratic President Buchanan proclaimed January 4, 1861 a National Day of Fast and Prayer. Thus the insurgent South and its northern allies sought to rally for an ideological attack on anti-slavery forces. South Carolina had already seceded when, on the day appointed, thousands of pulpits echoed with pro-slavery sermons. In New York, southern gentlemen had influenced one of the best-known rabbis in the country, Morris Jacob Raphall of B'nai Jeshurun, to preach on the Biblical view of slavery. Raphall of course added nothing new to a debate that had been waged for 160 years, one side arguing that the Bible sanctioned slavery, the other that the Bible denounced it as a sin. But here was a learned rabbi, skilled in the original Hebrew, meeting all the expectations of the southern gentlemen who had counted on his adding his Hebrew voice to the pro-slavery chorus. Hear, hear the learned Jew prove that slavery is no sin, the slavery forces chanted, as they spread the text of Raphall's sermon in newspapers, pamphlet and book throughout the land.

Jewish abolitionists were appalled. Rev. Einhorn in Baltimore published a keen refutation of Raphall in German in his monthly Sinai, which Thalmessinger in New York quickly issued as a pamphlet in an English translation. More effective was the great linguist and encyclopedist, Michael Heilprin, whose powerful denunciation, wrapped in eloquent wrath, was published in Horace Greeley's New-York Daily Tribune.

"Must the stigma of Egyptian principles," Heilprin asked, "be fastened on the people of Israel by Israelitish lips themselves?" Then he disproved Raphall's interpretation. Even in far-off Manchester, England, center of that working class anti-slavery sentiment that kept the British government from recognizing the Confederacy, Rabbi Gustav Gottheil preached two sermons on January 26 and February 2, 1861 in answer to Raphall, and then published them as a pamphlet, *Moses Versus Slavery.* Yet no Anglo-Jewish periodical here reprinted or even quoted from Heilprin's or Einhorn's rejoinders. Jews had to learn of them from the general anti-slavery press.

The slaveholders continued to organize their rebellion and finally launched the war to perpetuate the system on which was based their economic and political power and their social prestige. When the Confederates captured the federal Fort Sumter in South Carolina on April 13, 1861, Lincoln issued the call to arms to defend the Union. In the North and West the people rallied. "Stand by the Flag!" cried the *Jewish Messenger* editorially on April 26. Protect the Union, it exhorted, "which binds together . . . millions of freemen—which extends its hearty invitation to the oppressed of all nations, to come and be sheltered beneath its protecting wings."

In the Union armed forces, thousands of Jews served, leaving their dead and wounded on every major battlefield in the four long, bloody years of war. Jewish soldiers were in the Blue ranks at the battles of Bull Run and Chancellorsville, of Gettysburg, Petersburg and the Wilderness, of Vicksburg, Atlanta, Shiloh and Chickamauga—and they were present when Lee surrendered at Appomattox. Proud and anxious readers scanned the Jewish periodicals, which burgeoned with lists of casualties. It is estimated there were about 6,500 Jews in the Union Army and Navy, some 2,000 coming from New York alone. The old Midwest, with a smaller Jewish population, contributed about 3,000 Jews from Ohio, Indiana, Illinois, Michigan and Wisconsin. As an anonymous versifier wrote in "The Jew's War Song,"

From Synagogue, and home, and mart,
    To festive halls and lovers' bowers,

Part of the editorial in The Jewish Messenger that was widely commended in the general press in the North but aroused the indignation of Confederate Jews in Louisiana.

Army Jews.

The following co-religionists were either killed or wounded at the battle of Fredericksburg:

T. J. Heffernam, A, 163 N. Y., hip and arm.
Serg. F. Herrfukneckt, 7 " head.
M. Ellis, 23 N. J., hand.
Moses Steinburg, 142 Penn., legs bruised.
A. Newman, A, 72 " ankle.
Lt. H. T. Davis, 81 " arm.
J. Killenback, 4 N. J., head.
S. S. Vanuess, 15 " leg.
W. Truax, 23 " back.
J. Hirsh, 4 " "
Jacob Schmidt, 19 Penn., left arm.
Jos. Osback, 19 " wounded.
W. Jabob, 19 " left arm.
Lieut. Simpson, 19 " left leg.
Capt. Schuh, 19 " wounded.
C. M. Phillips, 16 Maine, cheek.
Lieut. S. Simpson, 99 Penn., leg.
R. Harris, 107 " thigh.
L. Brauer, wounded.
—— Wolf, 5 Penn., side.
R. Ellis, 2 " leg (slight).
S. Davidson, 186 " foot.
A. Valanstein, 105 N. Y., leg.
H. Stottler, 136 Penn., leg.

The above are at the hospital of Second Division, First Army Corps, in charge of Chas. J. Nordquish.

Franklin's Left Grand Division.

Lieut. G. L. Snyder, B, 104 N. Y., killed.
W. Lewis, B, 104 N. Y., arm.
J. Meekles, 94 " dead.
— Shupfel, D, 94 " "
G. Stancliffe, 26 " "

All the above were buried on Dec. 14, near the hospital across the river, from the battle-field.

F. Strausser, 6 Penn., hand.
J. P. Marks, 16 Maine, thigh.
C. B. Marks, 16 " arm.
C. Nunemager, 121 Penn., finger.
W. Hermeken, 12 " leg and arm.
H. Morris, 8 Penn., ankles, knee, and shoulder.
J. Hartmann, arm amputated.
P. Hemninger, 2 Del., wounded.
G. Simpson, 4 " "
Joseph Heine, 20 Mass., "
Serg. A. Rice, 20 " "
J. Morrison, 19 " "
M. Lattman, 20 " "

Part of a list in The Jewish Record, New York, of Jewish Union soldiers killed and wounded in the Battle of Fredericksburg, December 13, 1862, in which the Union forces were defeated and suffered 1,284 killed and 9,600 wounded.

The war-cry fires young Israel's heart,
  And glory robes his future hours!
His blood before saved nations! May
  The sacred wave save ours to-day.

Examples of heroism were not uncommon, and there were seven Jews among the 1,200 men awarded the Congressional Medal of Honor, the highest of decorations. One of them, Sergeant Major and Adjutant Abraham Cohn of the 6th New Hampshire Infantry, was cited "for conspicuous gallantry displayed in the battle of the Wilderness, in rallying and forming disorganized troops, under heavy fire; also for bravery and coolness in carrying orders to the advance lines under murderous fire in the battle of the Mine, July 30, 1864."

Also in the Wilderness, Leopold Karpeles, color-sergeant of Co. E of the 57th Massachusetts Infantry, "was the only color-bearer to stand his ground on that portion of the field occupied by his regiment when the fire was hottest and the slaughter greatest, and his standard was the rallying-point of a sufficient number of men to keep the enemy in check." The Medal of Honor was his reward. Karpeles himself wrote: "I participated in the engagements at Kingston, White Hall, Goldsborough, Gum Swamp, Wilderness, Spottsylvania, North Anna, Poplar Spring Church, Hatcher's Run and at Petersburg, until December 20, 1864, when our regiment was ordered on a raid, during which I fell exhausted from loss of blood from an old wound, and was paralyzed. I remained unconscious several days, and then found myself lying in a cavalry camp, from which I was sent to the hospital."

The daily life of the rank and file soldier in battle was described in a letter to his brother from the front in Bermuda Hundred, Va., sent by Myer Samuel Levy of Co. C of the 5th Pennsylvania Cavalry on June 2, 1864. "Every day, two or three times, the batteries are opened, and the other day, on our left, some of our troops made a charge on a rebel battery and took four pieces. This morning on our right, they charged on a fort of ours, and the shelling and musketry was awful, our troops falling back to the breastworks after every charge, which the rebels made with a yell, but our boys drove them back every time, they making eight charges, the shells flying all the time. . . . After a couple of hours fighting the darkie regiments were sent out from our left going around the woods, flanking the rebs and taking over two hundred prisoners, and killing a rebel colonel."

Hundreds of Jews attained officer rank in the Union Army, more than 20 as colonels in full command of regiments. The highest rank was achieved by the Hungarian Jewish '48er, Frederick Knefler, who rose from a private in the 79th Indiana Infantry to command his regiment and then was named Brevet Brigadier-General (a brevet was a nominal rank without the pay or command that comes with the real one). Colonel Edward Selig Salomon of the 82nd Illinois Infantry had a Company C, known as the Israelite Company because most of its members were Jewish.

On the home front, Jews backed the Government and the armed forces in innumerable ways —in production for the front, in financing the war, in morale-building activities. Funds to aid soldiers and soldiers' families were raised. The Jews' Hospital in New York was placed fully at

Brevet Brigadier-General Frederick Knefler (1833-1901), highest ranking Jewish officer in the Union Army.

the disposal of the wounded. Hundreds of anxious and helpful Jewish women were among those that busily sewed and rolled bandages and similar necessities for the soldiers. Many women worked with the Sanitary Commissions that were the predecessors of the Red Cross.

In the South, the Jewish population was part of the citizenry that put class and sectional interests ahead of national patriotism. Characteristically, when the Hebrew Congregation of Shreveport, La. read the *Messenger's* appeal to stand by the Union, it resolved to "scorn and repel" the call of this "black republican paper" and to rally instead to "the holy cause" of the "Southern Confederacy." About 1,300 Jews joined the armed forces of the Confederacy, many achieving distinction in combat. Jewish officers were common. In the political arena, Judah P. Benjamin held successively the posts of Attorney-General, Secretary of War and Secretary of State in the Cabinet of Confederate President Jefferson Davis. Rabbis in the South prayed for victory and slavery. Rev. M. J. Michelbacher on May 27, 1863 ended his sermon to his Richmond, Va. congregation with this

Leopold Karpeles (b. 1838), awarded the Congressional Medal of Honor for bravery at the Battle of the Wilderness, May 6, 1864, as color-sergeant of the 57th Massachusetts Infantry.

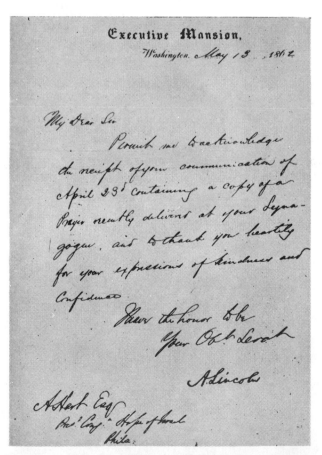

Part of letter from Myer S. Isaacs (1841-1904), editor of The Jewish Messenger, to the head of the New York Sanitary Commission, proposing that Jewish women's organizations be encouraged to take part in the war work of the Commission without discrimination.

Significantly, when New Orleans was under the occupation of the Union Army, Hirshheimer enlisted in the 92nd U.S. Colored Infantry, became a Quartermaster Sergeant and served until the end of 1865.

Fear of anti-Semitism in the south was an important factor in enforcing the "martyrdom of silence." Although anti-Semitism was widely felt in both camps, it was more extensive in the South, especially as the Confederacy began to realize the inevitability of its defeat. "The Jew Benjamin" was a convenient scapegoat readily blamed for all reverses and difficulties. Anti-Semitic agitation was extensive. In October 1861, Confederate Colonel Adolphus H. Adler was so incensed at an anti-Semitic editorial in a Richmond newspaper that he challenged the editor to a duel and thus wrung an apology from him; later Adler fled from the Confederacy to the North. In the Confederate Congress, Henry S. Foote of Tennessee argued in January 1863 that "if the present state of things were to continue, the end

prayer: "The man servants and the maid servants Thou has given unto us, that we may be merciful to them in righteousness and bear rule over them, the enemy are attempting to seduce, that they, too, may turn against us, whom Thou hast appointed over them as instructors in Thy wise dispensation. . . ."

Yet in Baltimore, the abolitionist Rev. Einhorn stood his ground until, shortly after the war began, he was forced to flee to Philadelphia to escape a secessionist mob. Shamefacedly the congregation invited him to return, on the stipulation that he avoid political discussion, but Einhorn refused to be muzzled. There were other Jews in the South who undoubtedly opposed the Confederacy. These, said Rev. Bernhard Felsenthal of Chicago on June 6, 1862, endured the "martyrdom of silence," fearing to speak out. One who did express Union sentiments in New Orleans, Julius J. Hirshheimer, was imprisoned several times.

Lincoln on May 13, 1862 acknowledged the prayers for the Union cause of the Congregation Mikveh Israel in Philadelphia.

12/27/61

THE JEWISH MESSENGER.

☞ PETITIONS for the amendment of the Acts of Congress regulating the appointment of Chaplains, have been presented by Senators Grimes, Trumbull, and Sumner, and others are in preparation in various sections of the Union. The Military Committees who have charge of the question will, we understand at an early day report the desired amendment to Congress.

The following is a copy of statement submitted by Rev. Dr. Fischell to the Committee on Military Affairs:

TO THE CHAIRMAN OF THE MILITARY COMMITTEE.

SIR, Jewish ministers being by law excluded from the office of Chaplain in the Army, the Board of Delegates of American Israelites have, at their own expense, appointed me to attend to the spiritual welfare of the Jewish soldiers in the Camps and Hospitals of the Army of the Potomac, and have, at the same time, deputed me to submit to the proper authorities the injustice inflicted by that law on the Jewish community, who cannot help viewing the same as a violation of the principle of religious equality, guaranteed to all American citizens by the Constitution. With this view, I beg

ber 10th, and under date of the 11th inst., he gives the particulars of his interview with the President, who received him with marked courtesy at a time when there were "hundreds of people anxiously awaiting their turn for two or three days." Having read the letter of the Executive Committee, President Lincoln questioned the Dr. on matters connected with the subject, saying that he fully admitted the justice of his remarks, that he believed the exclusion of Jewish Chaplains to have been altogether unintentional on the part of Congress, that this was the first time the subject had been brought under his notice, and he would take it into serious consideration. On the 13th, he received from the President, a note stating—"I find there are several particulars in which the present law in regard to Chaplains, is supposed to be deficient, all which I now design presenting to the appropriate committee of Congress. I shall try to have a new law, broad enough to cover what is desired by you in behalf of the Israelites."

From this, it will be seen that the President has manifested his interest in the question by thus promptly announcing his purpose to do what was in his power to secure the amendment of the Acts of Congress, whose

Rev. Arnold Fischel, representing the Board of Delegates of American Israelites, protested discrimination against Jewish chaplains to the Senate Military Affairs Committee and to Lincoln, who promised to change the situation.

of the war would probably find nearly all the property of the Confederacy in the hands of Jewish Shylocks." His fellow-congressmen applauded him vigorously when, a few months later, Foote declared he would seek to amend the Confederate constitution to forbid Jews to come within 12 miles of the capital. The Richmond Congregation Beth Ahabah even asked another congregation for joint action to "vindicate their character as Jews and good citizens, which has been repeatedly and grossly assailed in public prints," but nothing came of the proposal.

In the Union ranks, too, there were frequent expressions of anti-Semitism, including two notorious acts of official discrimination. These caused grave concern, but were swiftly and effectively handled. The first was the law passed by the U. S. Congress in 1861 restricting military chaplains to Christian clergymen. Tremendous protest by the Jews, through the Board of Delegates of American Israelites, the Jewish press and delegations, together with general public opinion and the intervention of Lincoln, led the next Congress to abolish the discrimination. Jewish

chaplains were then appointed. (In the Confederacy, however, although there was no discriminatory law, there were no Jewish chaplains.) The second official act occurred December 17, 1862, when General Ulysses S. Grant issued the anti-Semitic order No. 11, expelling Jews "as a class" from the Department of the Tennessee on the vicious assumption that all Jews were speculators and trading with the enemy. Prompt and loud protest and a Jewish delegation to Lincoln won immediate action. The order was rescinded on January 7, 1863. Jewish supporters of the Union were gratified with this speedy result, but pro-Confederate "copperheads" in the North, and their Jewish followers, continued to agitate the issue, demanding the resignation of Grant, the first of Lincoln's generals to win battles!

Patriotic Jews in the North sharply resisted the disruptive effects of anti-Semitism. They understood that the issue in the Civil War was not anti-Semitism, but the Union and, essentially, slavery. A bitter letter by Simon Wolf of Washington, D. C., published in November 1864 in his *New York Evening Post* by William Cullen

GENERAL ORDERS, }   HDQRS. 13TH A. C., DEPT. OF THE TENN.,
     No. 11.   }   Holly Springs, December 17, 1862.
    The Jews, as a class violating every regulation of trade established
by the Treasury Department and also department orders, are hereby
expelled from the department within twenty-four hours from the re-
ceipt of this order.
    Post commanders will see that all of this class of people be furnished
passes and required to leave, and any one returning after such notifica-
tion will be arrested and held in confinement until an opportunity oc-
curs of sending them out as prisoners, unless furnished with permit
from headquarters.
    No passes will be given these people to visit headquarters for the
purpose of making personal application for trade permits.
    By order of Maj. Gen. U. S. Grant:

                                        JNO. A. RAWLINS,
                                        Assistant Adjutant-General.

The text of the anti-Semitic General Order, No. 11.

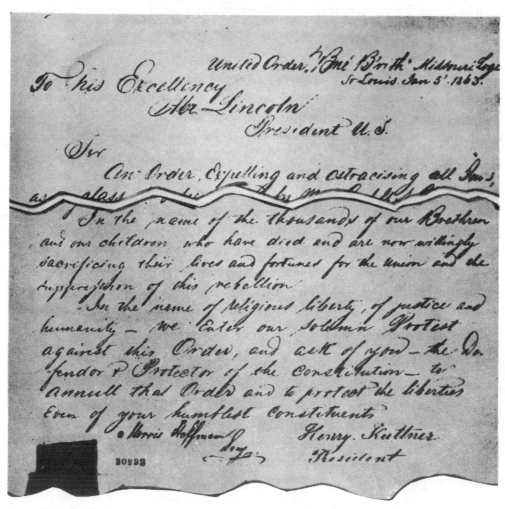

B'nai B'rith in St. Louis protested to Lincoln against Grant's Order No. 11.

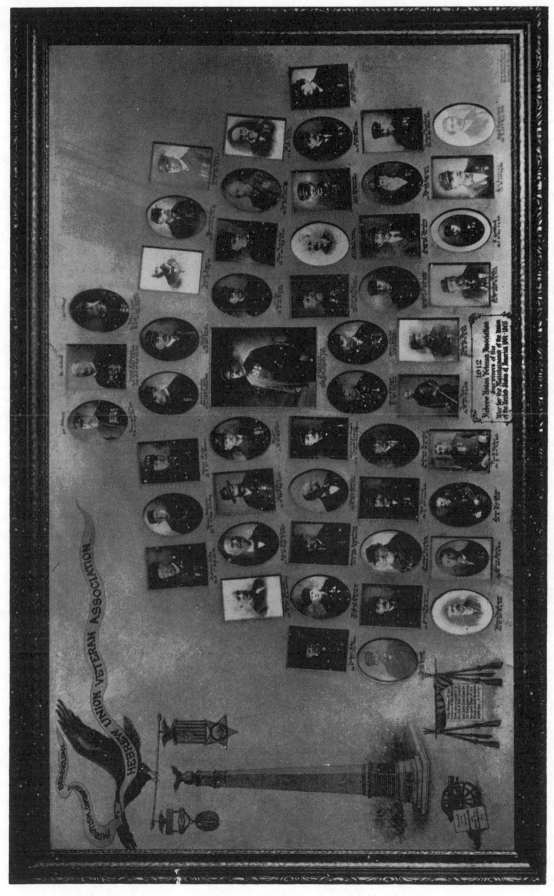

The Hebrew Union Veterans Association in 1912 mounted this panel of the pictures of 51 survivors of the Union Army.

Bryant, famous poet and editor, summed up the situation: "My heart is sick, my brain weary, my hopes dampened by these manifestations, not alone in the social, but radiating from the highest circles. . . . We have been branded and outraged for four long years, until discretion has ceased to be a virtue . . ." Then Wolf listed instances of Jewish heroism in the Union Army, of Jewish abolitionists and leading republicans, columns of facts to refute the "lie that we are cowards" and speculators and "copperheads."

From the beginning of the war there were those abolitionists who recognized that the Union could not best be preserved by ignoring the fundamental issue of slavery, as some wished to do. They saw that to rally the people fully in the North, in the border states, and even in Europe for support of the Union, a clear statement of Federal policy to abolish slavery was essential. Negro abolitionists, led by the great Frederick Douglass, were especially outspoken in pressing Lincoln to recruit Negroes into the Union Army and to proclaim the emancipation of the slaves. Lincoln hesitated before this revolutionary step, which would confiscate billions of dollars worth of private property in slaves. Finally the pressure was successful: in July 1862, the United States Congress authorized the recruitment of Negroes into the Union Army (and 186,000 Negroes enlisted); and on September 22, 1862 Lincoln announced that slaves in the rebelling states would be emancipated on January 1, 1863.

Among the Jews there were also abolitionists who had from the beginning advocated such action. For instance, Isidor Bush was a Captain on the Staff of Major-General John C. Frémont, commander of the Western Department of the Union Army when Frémont and most of his Staff, including Bush, were discharged from the army—because Frémont had on August 30, 1861 issued an order emancipating the slaves in his Department. Thus retired to civil life, Bush became an outstanding emancipationist in the border state of Missouri, pressing the issue for years in the Constitutional Convention, in which he was an influential delegate. Ending one speech in 1863, Bush challenged the white su-

premacy falsehoods common even among Union supporters, that the Negroes, if freed, "would be but one great band of idlers and vagabonds, robbers, murderers and thieves." Refuting the charges by the statistics of the census of 1860, Bush exclaimed, "I have no words for such slanders against poor human beings, so much sinned against. It is not enough that you hold them in bondage, toys of your whim and your lust, but you must charge them wit'. crimes they never committed and never dreamt of. I pray you have pity for yourselves, *not* for the Negro."

In another arena, the eloquent Ernestine L. Rose had also aroused public sentiment to move Lincoln to the act of emancipation. "Slavery being the cause of the war," she had argued again and again, "we must look to the utter extinction of slavery as the remedy. Without the entire and complete destruction of every vestige of slavery, we can have no peace." She was therefore not content with Lincoln's emancipation of the slaves in the rebelling states. She urged the Loyal Women of the Republic May 14, 1863 to press for the immediate liberation of all slaves in the border states and everywhere else in the territory of the United States. To this end, she helped to launch a petition that was ultimately signed by more than 265,000 people. As important as heroism at the battlefront was the work of such home front abolitionists, who spurred the Union to victory by helping it use its powerful black fist against the Confederacy.

The defeat of the Confederacy brought about a veritable revolution. Political power in the Federal government was transferred from the planter-class to the Northern industrialists. Slavery was abolished. Industrial capitalism would now be able to expand its economic and political rule over the entire country. The needs of expanding industry would attract millions of European immigrants. Among them would be many hundreds of thousands of Jews. The tens of thousands of Jews who had supported the cause of Union and abolition in the Civil War had helped achieve a victory that among other things made it possible for the United States to absorb the mass Jewish immigration soon to begin.

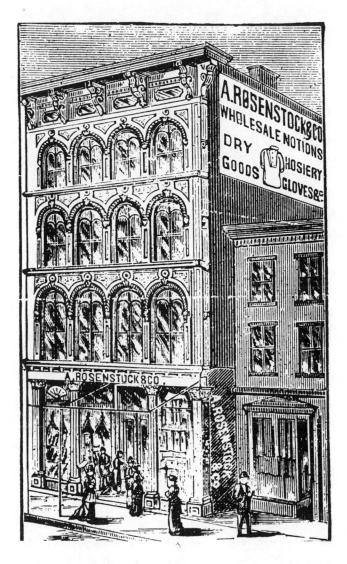

A Jewish business firm in Petersburg, Va., in the 1870's.

CHAPTER 8: The American Industrial Giant and the Jewish Middle Class

THE 15 YEARS after the end of the Civil War in 1865 marked great changes in American life. The industrialists and bankers were now the masters of the national economy and the federal government. By the energy and resourcefulness with which they used the sweat, muscle and skill of ever more workers, as well as by hook and by crook (and the crooked were brazen indeed), the rulers furiously promoted a program of economic and industrial expansion of unprecedented size.

The South presented a special problem, and Congress turned to solve it. The old slaveholding class, beaten in war and stripped of four billion dollars' worth of property in four million slaves, was down but not out. Led by the Radical Republicans, Senator Charles Sumner of Massachusetts and Representative Thaddeus

99

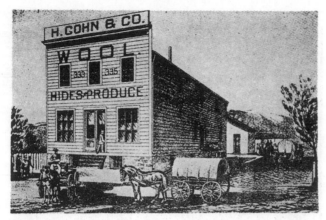

In business on State Street, Salt Lake City, Utah, in the 1870's.

Stevens of Pennsylvania, Congress passed the Reconstruction Acts of 1867-1868 and initiated the 13th, 14th and 15th Amendments to the Constitution that abolished slavery and extended citizenship and the vote to the freed slaves.

The program of Radical Reconstruction brought about great social improvements. It enfranchised the Negro people and democratized the state administration and judiciary, achieved a wider distribution of land and encouraged railroad building and manufacturing, created for the first time a free public school system and increased women's rights, and in North Carolina it eliminated from the State Constitution the last discrimination against Jews. These victories were won by the energetic struggle of the Negro people, frequently in collaboration with the democratic elements among the poorer white population of the Southern states. Together they fought for landownership and higher wages, for the right to vote, bear arms, testify in courts and serve on juries, for schooling, and for the abolition of all discriminatory laws, customs and practices based on color.

Against this democratic movement, a continual warfare was waged by the old slaveholding class and a portion of the new manufacturing and commercial middle class, some of it of recent northern origin, that rapidly emerged. Deception, fraud, the racist appeal to "white superiority," and relentless violence were the weapons of this movement to undermine the Reconstruction. From the Ku Klux Klan, born in Pulaski, Tenn., in 1866, to former Confederate General

Wade Hampton's armed Red Shirts of 1876 in South Carolina, innumerable terrorist bands hurled murderous violence against Negroes who asserted their rights to democracy and equality and against the whites who supported these rights.

There were Jews in the ranks of the active white supporters. Some were so conspicuous that in Memphis, Tenn., anti-Semitism was used in the agitation that inflamed a mob to the Riot of May 1-3, 1866, in which more than 120 Negroes were killed or injured and more than 100 Negro homes, schools and churches were burned down. In New Orleans, Morris Marks, born in Prussia and educated in Mississippi, was one of the founders of the Republican Party not long after he came to that city as a youth of 18 in 1864. The Bohemian-born Charles S. Kuh went to South Carolina from New York when the war ended, settled in the predominantly Negro city of Beaufort, and in 1868 was elected by the Negro people to the State Legislature, serving until he died in 1871.

Symbolic of this connection was the life and death of S. A. Bierfield, a Russian Jew who found his way down to Tennessee after the war. In Pulaski, birthplace of the Klan, Bierfield soon earned the reputation of a Radical "Black" Republican, and was driven from town. In Franklin, Tenn., he continued his public work for Negro equality. He employed a Negro clerk in his little drygoods store and was friendly and respectful to Negro customers. Again the Klan acted. On August 15, 1868, masked and on horseback, the Klan broke into Bierfield's store, lynched him and his clerk, and wounded another Negro, who escaped alive to tell this story of the double-lynching of a Jew and a Negro to an official investigating body.

On the other hand, throughout the South there were the hundreds of Jews who had fought in the Confederate forces. With post-war industry and commerce expanding, the Jews took their place in the ranks of the new Southern middle class. As the unreconstructed Bourbon plantation owners unfolded their campaign of fraud and terror against democracy, this middle class, including its Jewish elements, responded to the appeal of

Julius Meyer (1851-1909) of Omaha, Nebraska, an Indian trader in the 1870's, with some of his Indian friends.

"white supremacy" of the Democratic Party. In South Carolina, for example, reaction rallied to the leadership of Confederate General Wade Hampton and his terroristic "Red Shirts." Riding with these "Red Shirts" as they scourged the Negro population and its white supporters were Jewish Confederate veterans like Isaac W. Hirsch of Charleston, while the "right arm" of Hampton in his campaign for Governor in 1876 was Edwin W. Moise, a Jewish lawyer from Sumter, who was elected Adjutant-General of the State on Hampton's anti-democratic, anti-Negro ticket.

A contributing factor that tended Jews toward such activities was a rise of anti-Semitic propaganda in the South. From among thousands of Northerners who came carpet-bag in hand to settle and do business in the South, this propaganda singled out for special attack the small number of Jews who arrived with them and prospered with the others. Even today one of the foremost Southern historians, E. Merton Coulter, reveals his own anti-Semitism when he writes with characteristic exaggeration: "The end of the war saw an invasion of Jews to reap a harvest in trade; the ante-bellum Jewish peddlers . . . now settled down and opened stores.

Sticking to their business and treating the freedman as an important businessman, not eschewing to call him 'Mister,' they secured . . . a great amount of the Negro's trade. . . ." These democratic practices by the Jews merit praise rather than an "indictment" such as Coulter's.

In 1877 Reconstruction was brought to a close by the Republican Party's Great Betrayal of democracy and the Negro people. To get enough Southern votes in the Electoral College to put Rutherford B. Hayes in the White House, the Northern industrialists of the Republican Party formed an alliance with the planters and new middle class of the South in the Democratic Party. With the withdrawal of Federal troops, stationed in the South to help enforce democracy for Negro and white, the planter-middle class coalition seized full political power. Democracy in the South was laid low. By the turn of the century the Negro people and most of the poorer white population were reduced to a state of economic poverty and political rightlessness, with "white supremacy" strangling both groups. To this day the unreconstructed South is our country's No. 1 problem in economics, politics, the denial of civil rights and liberties. the debasement of education and culture. In such an atmosphere, Jewish life tended to stagnate. The Jewish population did not keep pace with the growth in the North and West, because there was nothing in the Southern way of life to attract the new Jewish immigrants who were beginning to arrive in huge waves.

This great struggle in the South was raging at a time when vast changes were taking place in the country as a whole. With the industrialists in full control of the economy and the government, the accent was on industrial expansion, especially on heavy industry. The huge profits that had been made during the Civil War, often by outrageously overcharging the Federal government for shoddy goods, were now turned to investments for the development of Big Industry. The Big Names of the period were Cornelius Vanderbilt, Andrew Carnegie, Jim Fisk, Jay Cooke, Jay Gould and J. P. Morgan, and they were joined soon by Thomas and his son Andrew Mellon, Henry C. Frick, Edward H. Harriman and John D. Rockefeller, all of whom became giants in the interrelated steel, coal, oil, railroad and manufacturing industries.

Steel production, which was basic, rocketed from 19,643 long tons in 1867 to 1,247,335 in 1880. Coal production vaulted from 29,003,000 tons in 1866 to 71,481,000 in 1880. Coal made the steam engine the lord of production, and by 1873, steam power surpassed water power as the main source of industrial energy. Railroad building leaped forward, to weld the grand spaces of continental U.S.A. into one increasingly interdependent national system of production and distribution. On May 10, 1869 the last spike, symbolically golden, was driven into the tie that joined the Central Pacific to the Union Pacific Railroad at Promontory, Utah, and a year later the first transcontinental railroad trip began, from Boston, Massachusetts to Oakland, California. From the 36,801 miles of railroad track in 1866, the figure jumped to 93,262 in 1880. The corruption and piracy that marked so much of the industrial boom was particularly flagrant, and fragrant, in the railroad field. Congress was reckless and lavish with the public domain and the public monies. In money subsidies, the rail-

roads were given $707,000,000; in land, the Federal government gave them a total of 155,000,000 acres, an area equal to that of Texas (several states granted the railroads an additional 49,-000,000 acres). When the cry of scandal and corruption around the Credit Mobilier development company could no longer be hushed, Congress took action, and two Congressmen were—censured.

On the foundation of heavy industry, manufacturing expanded and the size of the factory wage-working class doubled. By 1879, there were 253,852 manufacturing establishments with 2,-732,595 wage earners. The average size of factories was increasing. And the value of the total manufactured production had gone up from $1,885,862,000 to $5,369,579,000. For the distribution of these products on a national scale, techniques of merchandising had to be improved. The day of the socially useful country peddler ended with the railroad building era; the day of the ever larger and departmentalized store was dawning.

Industrialization was also rapidly changing the social composition as well as the location of the expanding population. The total population increased by 59 per cent between 1860 and 1880, rising from 31,443,000 to 50,262,000. But the number of factory workers in the same period grew by 109 per cent. This trend in production spurred the growth of the number of towns and cities from 392 in 1860 to 939 in 1880, while the big cities with populations over 100,000 multiplied from nine in 1860 to twenty in 1880.

Industry's need for workers and its desire for a cheap-labor supply led to the encouragement of immigration and even to organized efforts to import contract labor. From 1866 to 1880, the immigrants numbered 4,325,442, of whom 3,609,608 came from Europe and 163,322 from China. The unprecedented number of 459,803 arrived in 1873. Yet the proportion of the foreign-born in the total population *dropped* from 15 per cent in 1860 to 13.3 per cent in 1880, as immigration was slowed up twice, first by the Civil War itself and then by the economic crisis from 1873 to 1878. Nativist anti-alien, anti-immigration agitation ignored this fact.

To protect their own interests in the face of the increasing power of the manufacturers and industrialists, some of the workers organized into trade unions. Not only did the number of union members jump to 300,000 by 1870, but in this period union organization advanced from the local to the national stage, with 26 new national trade unions founded from 1864 to 1873. Furthermore, in 1866 the National Labor Union began its short but important career as the first national federation of labor. In its six years' existence, the N.L.U. pioneered in advocating solidarity with Negro workers, the rights of women, independent labor political action and international labor cooperation. The N.L.U. proclaimed "the grand, ennobling idea that the interests of labor are one," that workers should be organized without regard to "race or nationality," whether they be "Jew or Gentile, Christian or Infidel."

Most of the national trade unions, still small and weak, were wiped out by the economic crisis that began in 1873. By 1877, their number had dropped from 30 to nine, and membership from over 300,000 to some 50,000. Whatever strength the workers had lay in local and regional unions. The employers, especially in heavy industry, loosed spies, terror and violence among the workers to destroy their organizations. In the Pennsylvania coal mines, the employers framed charges of conspiracy against Irish miners, and nineteen of them were hanged on perjured evidence from 1877 to 1879. When the first nationwide strike in our history began on the railroads in July, 1877, scores of workers were killed and more scores wounded by state and federal troops. "Communist conspiracy" and "foreigners" (from England!) were the cries against the railroad strikers, to justify the murder of American workers in the eyes of the American public.

It was against this background that the history of the American Jewish population unfolded. New immigration helped swell the number of Jews to some 300,000 in 1878 and caused new cultural and organizational developments. The Jewish commercial and manufacturing middle class grew in size and strength and used its new economic prestige to consolidate its domi-

The Reformer
AND
Jewish Times.

A Journal of Progress in Religion, Literature, Science and Art.

PUBLISHED EVERY FRIDAY,
No. 62 Ann Street.
NEW YORK.

Terms $5 per Annum, 10 Cents per Copy.

M. ELLINGER, EDITOR.

FRIDAY, July 27, 1877.

LESSONS OF THE STRIKE.

The great railroad strike long since ceased to be a strike and became a revolution, a revolution of robbers, incendiaries and plunderers against law-abiding citizens and property-holders. At the beginning the railroad employees had the sympathy of the public at least, now they have aroused the anger and indignation of all intelligent people. That brakemen and firemen should have to work for less than a dollar a day is hard of course, no man can live and support a family upon such a pittance. But railroad companies, like other employers, regulate their pay-rolls according to the cost of labor; they buy labor, as they buy everything else, as cheap as they can; they are trustees of great interests and it is their duty to those whom they represent to manage their roads at the smallest possible cost; they are not charitable institutions for the support of the poor; it is no concern of theirs whether their employees can or cannot live on their wages; their duty is to pay only what they must and no more.

The beginning of an editorial on the great Railroad Strike of 1877 in The Reformer and Jewish Times, New York, in which this organ of the Jewish middle class echoes the prevailing views of the general press.

nation over organized Jewish life in all aspects, religious, fraternal, philanthropic, cultural and social. A noticeable class differentiation appeared among the Jewish people, and Jewish

ISRAELITE.

Not without a "feeling akin to pain," do we read of the great destruction of life and property, occasioned by the

RAILROAD RIOTS.

I desire to know the cause of these fearful disturbances, and I am answered only too truly in this wise: It is the monopolists and the capitalists, whose main desire is to grow rich off the working masses of this country, who are dependent upon their daily labor for their bread, and to whom every cent is an item. I allow times are exceedingly dull, and require expenses to be curtailed. This is quite right, but let it be a universal reduction; do not confine it alone to hard-working employes, who spend the best portions of their lives in the hot, broiling sun, shortening their days for a pittance, scarcely sufficient to hold body and soul together, but let those lose who can most afford it. Let presidents who receive enormous salaries for holding perfect sinecures, let their salaries be reduced; also, while the head officials of railroad corporations are enjoying themselves at sea-side resorts during the summer months, the poor, laboring employe must

"Work—work—work—
From weary chime to chime;
Work—work—work—
As prisoners work for crime!"

Although my feelings are strongly in favor of the poor, distressed, working man, still these fearful riots and disturbances have my disapproval. Neither is it manly nor just to waste wantonly so much valuable property, nor is it following the grand commandment of God to destroy the lives of their fellow-beings. It would be a far wiser policy for a committee, composed of the most intelligent of the working classes, to meet the head-officers of railroad corporations in council, and confer together, and with quiet reasoning endeavor to bring things to an amicable adjustment; this method would be far better than endeavoring to obtain their ends by harsh measures. No disturbances were apprehended here, and none have occurred.

"Minnie," the Charleston, S. C. correspondent for The American Israelite, August 10, 1877, expresses a different view of the Railroad Strike.

workers began to step into the ranks of the American labor movement. Anti-Semitism in this period began to take on a new quality: prejudice expressed itself now in action in an attempt at a widespread economic boycott by insurance companies and in public social restrictions.

The growth of the Jewish population in the post-Civil War period was slower than in the decade before the War. There was a lull. The German Jewish immigration tapered off after the unification of Germany in 1870 spurred the rapid development of German industry with its attractive opportunities for commerce and other business. From Eastern Europe, immigration

was still on a small scale. Famine and a cholera epidemic in Lithuania and Poland from 1867 to 1869, a Passover pogrom in Odessa in April, 1871, and new economic restrictions, expulsions and pogroms in Romania from 1866 to 1871 sparked some immigration of Jews from these regions. But there were only a few thousand from the Tsarist Empire and a few hundred from Romania. This was the first faint movement of what was to become, a decade later, a tide.

Of the 300,000 Jews that, according to the estimate of the Board of Delegates, were in the United States in 1878, fully one quarter, 75,000 or more, lived in New York City, the main port of entry. Very far behind, but in second place in the 1870's, was Cincinnati, followed by Philadelphia and the up-and-coming Chicago. A smaller city like Rochester, N. Y., already had over 3,000 Jews. New Jewish communities emerged in states like Maine, West Virginia, Kansas, Iowa, Arkansas, Colorado and Texas. Congregations multiplied, according to the government census, from 77 in 1860 to 189 in 1870. In 1878, the Board of Delegates counted 270 congregations with about 50,000 members. The vast majority of Jews, however, were not affiliated with congregations.

That section of the Jewish middle class which rose into the upper, but not highest, ranks of the bourgeoisie emerged into prominence and dominated Jewish life. Enriched by the war like the American bourgeoisie as a whole, this Jewish economic upper crust had its base in various pursuits. By 1878, Isaac Friedlander of California was widely known as the "Grain-King" because of his large-scale successful speculation in grain. In Pennsylvania that year two of the biggest oil-well operators were Joseph Stettheimer and David Bettman of New York (who were later forced out of the field by the piratical methods of Rockefeller). Of special importance were a number of Jewish private banking firms, a few of which are still functioning on a much enlarged scale. Before the Civil War, there were two important Jewish banking houses in New York, August Belmont and Company and Speyer and Company, both established in 1837. Belmont was the more prominent both because he was the

Rothschild agent in the United States and because, as a conspicuous backer of the Democratic Party, he was elected Chairman of the Democratic National Committee in 1860 and held the post until 1872.

During the war, a number of Jews accumulated fortunes, especially by the manufacture of clothing, that enabled them to go into banking. Thus J. and W. Seligman and Company was founded in 1862, and was very helpful to the Union in financing the war by its sale of $200,-000,000 in government bonds mostly in Germany. In 1865, Abraham Kuhn, Solomon Loeb and Samuel Wolff turned from the clothing industry to banking and formed Kuhn, Loeb and Company. In 1868, Mayer and Emanuel Lehman founded the Lehman Brothers banking establishment. There were others too, but they never achieved the eminence and stability of those mentioned.

It should be noted that even the biggest of the Jewish capitalists in the United States were not in the same class as giants like Vanderbilt or Morgan. The situation was different in European countries. There Jewish bankers, some of whose banking institutions went back to the days of feudalism, were definitely among the topmost capitalists in their countries. Therefore the Jewish bankers participated weightily in financing the development of railroad building and heavy industries in Europe, and thus got in on the ground floor of the structure of big business in these countries. In the United States, at the time the foundations of big business were being built the Jewish bankers were comparatively small and not in a position to compete with the giants in financing and controlling heavy industry. A minor exception was Kuhn, Loeb and Company, which in this period began to import German capital for the financing of railroad building in the Southwest. Thus was created the basis for Kuhn, Loeb's rise in influence to the point where, in 1900, it was the junior figure in a combine, headed by John D. Rockefeller, Edward H. Harriman, railroad magnate, and James Stillman of the National City Bank, that was almost as mighty as the House of Morgan. (This combine broke apart after the Panic of 1907.)

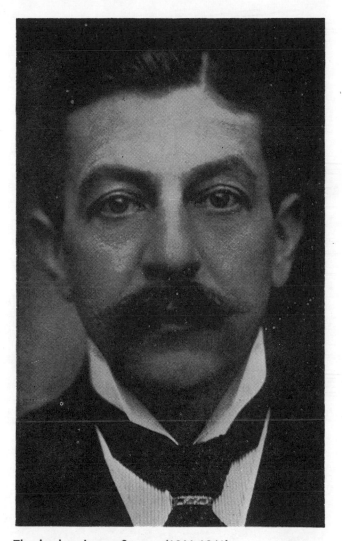

The banker James Speyer (1861-1941).

Below the thin layer of the extremely wealthy and the upper bourgeoisie, there was the large stratum of Jewish substantial merchants and manufacturers. Experience often brought over from their countries of origin had led them to fields that were also, fortunately, expanding here. Jews were particularly influential in the wholesale drygoods field, in which they were already solidly established by the 1850's. They were also important in the merchandising of jewelry, liquor, tobacco, leather and hides, and food products. But it was in the relatively new clothing industry that the Jews became most powerful, developing dominance by 1880.

The manufacture of ready-made clothing for the general capitalist market was an infant industry before the Civil War. In 1860, there were invested in the production of men's clothing only

Abraham Kuhn (1819-1892).

Solomon Loeb (1828-1903).

The Banker Mayer Lehman (1830-1897), father of Senator
Herbert H. Lehman and Irving Lehman, chief justice,
New York State Court of Appeals.

$27,200,000; and 114,800 workers in 4,014 shops manufactured clothing of which the total value was only $80,800,000. The production of women's ready-made clothing was negligible, the total value amounting to less than 10 per cent of the value of the men's clothing, or $7,181,000. During the war, the need for uniforms for the first mass army in American history had stimulated the organization of an extensive men's clothing factory system, in which Jews made a significant place for themselves from the beginning. After the war, capital flowed swiftly into this industry. By 1880, there were $79,000,000 invested in men's clothing production; and 158,249 workers, most of them German and Irish, in 6,166 shops produced $209,500,000 worth of garments. The manufacture of women's apparel still lagged far behind, totaling in value only $32,000,000. It was in this rapidly expanding new industry, in which the majority of employers were German Jews, that large numbers of new immigrant Jewish workers found a place and soon became the majority of the labor force.

With their affluence, the Jewish bourgeoisie obtained uncontested control of organized Jew-

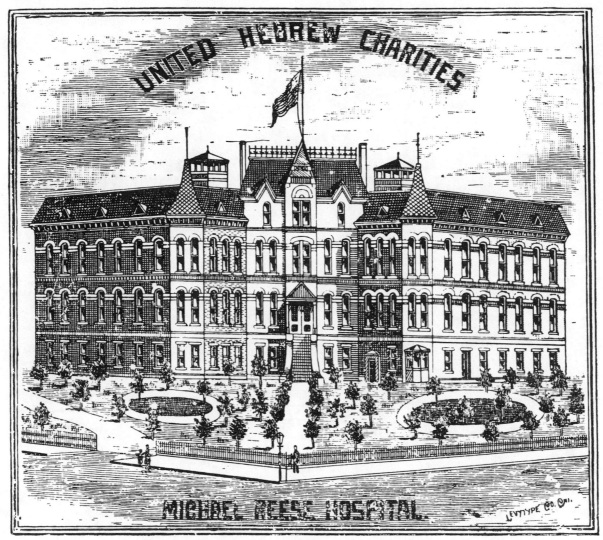

The Hospital named after Michael Reese (1817-1878), multimillionaire realtor, in Chicago. In 1881 this building had 70 beds, and was located in the then fashionable residential section of Groveland Park Avenue. Although financed by Jewish benefactions, the hospital was non-sectarian.

ish life. In congregations throughout the country, they became the officers and leaders. The well-to-do Jewish middle class showed a marked preference for Reform Judaism. Reform congregations and costly temples multiplied as Reform gained a brief ascendancy in Jewish religious life, which was retained only until the tide of East European Orthodoxy rolled in with masses of new immigrants. Reform Jewish leaders initiated efforts to create a national religious federation, and when that did not succeed, Rev. Isaac Mayer Wise of Cincinnati led 34 congregations from the South and West, convened on July 3, 1873, to form the Union of American Hebrew Congregations. Soon the few Orthodox congregations

in the Union dropped away, but within 10 years there were 128 Reform congregations in the U.A.H.C. One of the first activities of the Union was to open the Hebrew Union College on October 3, 1875, with two instructors and seventeen students ready to embark upon an eight year curriculum of religious study and training in the first stable Jewish seminary in our country.

With its newly-gained wealth, the Jewish middle class also responded in a comparatively generous but essentially inadequate way to the growing need for philanthropy. In the absence of social insurance, charity was then generally dispensed on a religious basis. Jews in hospitals, for example, enjoyed the ministrations not only

The Phoenix Club, Baltimore, founded 1886.

of doctors but of nuns who served as nurses. These would try to save the souls as well as the bodies of Jewish patients by missionary persuasion—which often interfered with the peace of mind helpful in physical cures. Now that they could afford to do so, philanthropic Jews began to build Jewish hospitals in New York, Cincinnati, Philadelphia, Chicago and elsewhere, and the donors of larger sums of course became the trustees and directors of policy in these institutions. Homes for the aged poor and for orphans also multiplied.

The needy included, however, not only the sick, the aged and the orphaned but also the able-bodied whose wages did not allow ends to meet or who were unemployed. Not only did organizations to provide some help to such persons develop rapidly, but efforts at local coordination and federation began to appear. The purpose was to centralize both the collection of funds and distribution of charity. This centralization was part of a general American effort to make the dispensation of charity more systematic and "scientific," by weeding out the "unworthy" through investigation. By 1866, then, the United Hebrew Relief Association in Chicago, founded in 1859, had 15 affiliates. In 1869, the United Hebrew Charities of Philadelphia was born. Others were stimulated by the crisis of 1873, during which Rev. Gustav Gottheil of Temple Emanu-El in New York announced in the *Tribune* that "our own poor numbered now by the thousands." The United Hebrew Charities of New York was founded in 1874 (replacing the United Hebrew Relief Association established in 1859), and the United Hebrew Charities of St. Louis in 1875. In all cases, the Jewish manufacturing and commercial bourgeoisie entrenched themselves as the directors of philanthropy, assisted by rabbinical leaders and, here and there, Jewish lawyers and doctors.

The same type of leadership consolidated its position in fraternal, social and cultural organizations that arose to fill varied needs. The B'nai

B'rith, born in 1843, had attained a membership of less than 3,000 by 1857. But after the war the order grew rapidly into a nationwide movement, with more than 23,000 members in 305 lodges by 1879. The Free Sons of Israel, born in 1849, also grew rapidly to a membership of thousands in the 1870's. Polish Jews, ill at ease in these organizations dominated by German Jews, formed their own body, Kesher Shel Barzel (Iron Band), in 1860, and in 1871 counted 1,000 members in lodges in New York and California.

The most prosperous Jews at this time also founded and built social clubs and club-houses. "Few of our citizens," *The Journal of Commerce* in New York had written editorially in 1860, "know them [the Jews] socially, and all are too willing to believe Shylock their true type." Rarely invited to the social clubs of the wealthy non-Jews, Jews who aspired to a club life for comfort and status founded institutions like the Standard Club in Chicago in 1869 or the Franklin Club in Philadelphia in 1872. These were Jewish only in their membership or at most in their cuisine.

More popular in its base and appeal, although also directed by the wealthy Jews, was another type of social and cultural organization that soon became a movement, the Young Men's Hebrew Associations. These had their predecessors in the Jewish literary societies that appeared in a few cities in the 1850's. But a very significant impetus had come from the founding on December 29, 1851 of the Young Men's Christian Association. Emphasizing evangelical preaching, temperance and criminal reform, the Christian Y's grew slowly at first, having only 60 Y's by 1865, but by 1874 they numbered 950. The Jewish Y's relatively followed the same curve. The first one appeared in Baltimore in 1854, and there were only a half dozen at the time of the Civil War. By 1874, more than 20 had been founded, but between 1874 and 1880 about 60 Young Men's Hebrew Associations were established in some 25 cities in 15 states from coast to coast and from New York to New Orleans. The Jewish Y's emphasized the cultural more than the religious, conducting lectures on current topics, social affairs, organizing Glee Clubs, orchestras, dramatic and athletic groups, and arranging classes in Hebrew language and literature, French, German and English literature, music and chess. Women were admitted to full or partial membership from 1868. In New York in 1875-76, during the crisis, the Y had an Employment Bureau, appealing to Jewish employers to give jobs to Jews.

Another feature of organized Jewish life was the burgeoning of the Jewish press, catering to the tastes, needs and interests of the middle class German Jews who supported it. Seven new English weeklies appeared in this period: in 1868, the *Jewish Sentinel* in St. Louis; in 1869, the *Reformer and Jewish Times* in New York; in 1872, the *Jewish Index* in Philadelphia, followed there by the *Jewish Record* in 1874. The same year witnessed the birth of the *Sabbath Visitor* in Cincinnati and *The Occident* in Chicago. *The American Hebrew*, which outlasted all these and survived until 1957, began publication in 1878. A monthly periodical for juveniles, *Young Israel*, began a career of three decades in New York, in 1871.

Supplementing this Jewish press in English were two German periodicals: *Zeichen der Zeit*, a Chicago monthly in 1869-1870, and *Die Wahrheit*, a St. Louis weekly beginning in 1871. In addition, German sections appeared in some of the English periodicals, such as the *Jewish Times* and *Young Israel*. German persisted among the German Jewish immigrants and there were even attempts to encourage the American born Jewish youth to study it. The adults used German both in their economic and cultural relations with non-Jewish Germans, among whom they often found it advantageous to live and work. German was also the official language in which proceedings were conducted and minutes kept in many of the Reform congregations and in organizations like the B'nai B'rith. In 1875, for instance, the Detroit Reform congregation Beth El ordered its rabbi to preach only in German, although four years before that English had replaced German as the language of instruction in the Beth El Religious School. Among the youth, whose primary language of play and learning was English, German found no real base.

Dr. Abraham Jacobi (1830-1919).

Flushed with its new and spreading control of organized Jewish life, the Jewish bourgeoisie after the Civil War became aware, however, that a class differentiation had developed among the Jewish population. The number of Jewish wage-

workers had been continually increasing. Furthermore, some of these workers had begun to take their first tentative, feeble steps in the ranks of the American labor movement. "The Labor Question" was confronting Jewish employers like all others, as *The Jewish Messenger* indicated in its editorial on that subject on May 10, 1867. Facing nationwide trade union organizational growth, then still in its infancy, the editor wailed that "capital is, practically, at the mercy of labor." Pious in its dedication to "philanthropy," but blinded by the interests of the employers, whose viewpoint it reflected, the *Messenger* denounced the rising demand for the eight-hour working day as "most outrageous and unjustifiable." Callously the editorial protested: "Sixteen hours daily upon an ignorant man's hands! It is a deliberate wrong for society to permit such a dangerous waste of time."

It was in 1850 that the first signs of activity by Jews in the American labor movement had appeared in the New York journeymen tailors' strike that summer. Jews were among the strikers as well as among the employers, and one of these workers was arrested for picketing. In the German-American labor movement, Jews appeared in 1852 in the Arbeiter-Bund in Philadelphia, Cincinnati and Louisville. The same year, Sigismund Kaufmann, a German-Jewish "48'er" and then a utopian socialist, was editor of the *Turn-Zeitung*, organ of the Turner-Bund, a league of German-American gymnastic, cultural and fraternal societies. Kaufmann thus published the political essays of Joseph Weydemeyer, the first Marxist to work and write in the United States, as well as a major book by Frederick Engels, Marx's close collaborator. Late in 1853 there arrived Dr. Abraham Jacobi, one of the eleven members of the Communist League tried in Prussia on a charge of conspiring to overthrow the government. One of four acquitted, Dr. Jacobi promptly helped Weydemeyer set the record clear against the detractors of Marx and the defendants. (While his contact with the labor movement did not extend beyond the 1870's, Dr. Jacobi achieved high eminence as a socially-minded medical man and as the acknowledged founder of the science of child care, pediatrics.) In 1857, when the first Communist Club in the United States was formed in New York, Fritz Jacobi (no relation to Dr. Jacobi) and Max Cohnheim were members and Jacobi was the first secretary of the group. The Club disbanded when most members enlisted in the Union Army, Cohnheim becoming an artillery captain and Jacobi a first lieutenant of infantry before he was killed in battle in 1862.

After the Civil War, Jews appeared more numerously and actively in the general labor movement. When the second Congress of the National Labor Union opened in August 1867, one of the 71 delegates was Jacob G. Selig of the Chicago Cigar Makers' Union. There were hundreds of Jewish cigar makers, many of them belonging to the Union, some becoming local officers in cities like Norfolk, Va., Cincinnati, St. Louis, Troy, N. Y. and New York. Jewish capmakers and shoemakers were also observable in the unions of their crafts, and in the leadership. In the 1870's, conspicuous numbers of Jewish

Adolph Strasser (1844-1939), president of the Cigar Makers' International Union of America, 1877-1891.

THE HAT, CAP AND FUR TRADE REVIEW.

The Capmakers' Strike.

THE cap trade in this city has been in a state of ferment during the past few weeks, owing to certain difficulties that have arisen between the work-people and their employers, which finally culminated in a general strike and lockout.

Under the title, "The Lesson Taught by the Capmakers' Strike," we have given our own opinion in this matter, and shall, therefore, in this portion of our journal content ourselves with briefly narrating the chief points of interest that occurred during the history of the strike.

The total number of persons out of work varied between 1,500 and 2,000, including both sexes, the women being principally Irish, while the men mostly were German Jews. The first to strike were the employees of M. J. Willis & Co. The following are the principal manufacturing establishments from which the strikers turned out:

Marks Brothers & Co., Greene Street, 53 hands; J. L. Phillips & Co., Greene Streets, 76 hands; Marks & Lasky, Greene Street, 40 hands; Schwartz Brothers & Co., Greene Street, 53 hands; Isidor & Hein, South Fifth Avenue, 75 hands; S. Korn & Brother, South Fifth Avenue, 100 hands; Marks Brothers & Thompson, South Fifth Avenue, 150 hands; Rosenbaum & Peterson, South Fifth Avenue, 25 hands; Charles Foxe's Sons, South Fifth Avenue, 150 hands; Julius Sarner & Brother, Greene Street, 50 hands; Rothstein, Broome Street, 40 hands; Markevitch & Petch, Spring Street, 40 hands; Roll & Meyering, Grand Street, 20 hands; Limburger Brothers & Co., Broome Street, 25 hands; S. Wolfe, South Fifth Avenue, 75 hands; and R. W. Willis & Co., South Fifth Avenue, 50 hands.

The story of the capmakers runs somewhat as follows: They

Part of the story on the capmakers' strike in the trade journal, February, 1874.

workers took part dramatically in two important strikes. In the first one, which began in New York on January 29, 1874, the capmakers, desperate because of repeated wage-cuts, disregarded the theory that an economic crisis is not a time for strikes and went out on a general strike involving 1,500 to 2,000 workers, the majority of them German Jews. Since the main employers were also Jewish, this strike assumed in part the form of a struggle within the Jewish community. Headquarters for the Jewish, Irish and other striking men and women were, interestingly enough, in B'nai B'rith's Covenant Hall on Orchard Street. The leader of the strike and secretary of the Central Union of Capmakers was M. Weiner. Militant picketing and support from capmakers in other cities won an increase of 15 per cent after six weeks of struggle.

Not so successful were the hundreds of Jewish workers who were among the 11,000 to 15,000 cigar makers in New York that waged the great strike from October 15, 1877 to February 3, 1878. The day to day leadership of this bitter fight was given by a German-Hungarian Jew,

Adolph Strasser, president of the Cigarmakers' International Union. Strasser was a masterful trade union organizer as well as a political figure, having become national secretary of the Social Democratic Party of North America in 1874. Aiding Strasser effectively in the leadership was the 27-year-old Samuel Gompers, president of Local 144, which had initiated the strike. The employers, including the Jews among them, worked mightily to break the strike, shipping work out of town, using scabs, threatening to import Chinese contract labor, instigating police attacks and arrests, and "red-baiting" Strasser as "an avowed German Communist." Among the strikers, the press noted "a few Polish Jews." Finally the employers, who owned many of the tenements in which the cigarmakers both lived and worked, resorted to evicting 1,300 striking families in the dead of winter. The strike was lost, but Gompers recorded in his autobiography that "it was a wonderful fight. . . . we learned the fundamentals and techniques which assured success later." Drawn into the struggle by the suffering and heroism of the workers were a number of Jewish doctors, lawyers and landlords, who were among those that offered varied help to the strikers.

The class differentiation in the Jewish population was also expressing itself in ways other than the economic struggle between worker and employer. The character of the East European immigration was just beginning to make itself felt. These immigrants differed sharply from the well-to-do German Jewish Reform element that dominated organized Jewish life. Their religion was severely Orthodox, their language was Yiddish, their background was poverty and they tended to swell the ranks of the workers here. Differences of religion and language frequently sharpened the class conflict and the bitterness.

East European orthodox congregations multiplied. By 1872, there were 29 of them in New York City (the first, established in 1852, was alone for some time). In the years immediately thereafter, such congregations, often more than one in a city, developed in Boston, Rochester, Philadelphia, Baltimore, Chicago and out to the West Coast.

The Russian, Polish, Lithuanian and Romanian new immigrants also began to establish the kind of organization that was to mushroom when the big tide came, the *landsmanshaft,* a mutual aid society based on the city of origin. In 1864, the *Bialistoker Intershtitsung Farein* (Bialistok Mutual Aid Society) had been chartered in New York. By 1877, there were a half dozen others in New York alone, and they began to emerge in other cities. The new immigrants built their own parallel religious and secular organizations undoubtedly because the middle class German and native American Jews regarded the newcomers with a chilly snobbishness summed up in a letter that one Isaac Hart wrote from Detroit to Isaac Leeser early in 1867: "The Polish Minhag I do not so object to as the mixing with its worshippers."

In addition to Orthodoxy, the new immigration brought with it an element influenced by the Haskalah (Enlightenment) in Eastern Europe. This movement of the Jewish middle class in Europe challenged feudal traditionalism in Jewish life and practice. While the upper circles of the Haskalah ended in full cultural assimilation, the bulk of the movement created a literature in Hebrew and in Yiddish. On the basis of the Haskalah, the Golden Age of Yiddish literature was just coming into being, beginning in the 1860's. The "Grandfather" of that literature, Mendele Mocher Seforim (Shalom Jacob Abramovich, 1836-1917), had already turned from writing in Hebrew for the intellectuals to writing in Yiddish for the masses. *Dos Kleine Mentshele* (The Little Fellow) in 1864 and *Fishke der Krummer* (Fishke the Cripple) in 1869 described with tenderness and indignation the life of the Jewish poor. *Di Taxe* (The Meat Tax) in 1869 attacked the bosses and tax-suckers of the *Kahal* (Jewish community) so fiercely that Mendele had to move from Berdichev to Zhitomir. In 1873 he returned to the attack with *Di Klatche* (The Nag), contrasting the Jewish masses with the Jewish philanthropists and "benefactors," and in 1878 he described the plight of the Jewish people, dreaming and suffering, in *The Travels of Benjamin the Third.*

Jewish intellectuals among the immigrants, with a background of the Haskalah and the new

Yiddish literature, found here an atmosphere encouraging to the development of a Jewish press. In English and German, Jewish journalism was flourishing. The new immigrants could be attracted, however, only by a press in Yiddish and, to a lesser extent, in Hebrew. The beginnings of such a press occurred in the 1870's.

The first Yiddish periodical was not even printed but lithographed because there was no Yiddish typesetter available. On March 1, 1870 there appeared the first number of the weekly, *Di Idishe Zeitung,* with the English name, *The New York Hebrew Times,* and the grandiose description, "A Weekly Paper of Politics, Religion, History, Science and Art." The editor was J. K. Buchner, a Russian-Polish Jew who had already had editorial experience in Yiddish in Stuttgart. Only a couple of copies are extant, but issues were noted as late as 1877.

In August, 1870, there was published the first printed Yiddish periodical, *Di Post,* edited in New York by Zvi Hirsh (Henry) Gersoni, a Maskil (an Enlightened one) from Vilna, but this weekly lasted only a half year. The publisher was Zvi Hirsh Bernstein, a Polish Jew from Suwalki province, who on June 11, 1871 also issued the first Hebrew weekly in the United States, *Ha-Zofeh ba-Erets ha-Hadasha* (Watchman in the New Land), edited in New York by Mordecai Jalomstein, also from Suwalki. This journal

The first issue, June 11, 1871, of the first Hebrew weekly published in the United States.

lasted until 1876. Before puting out *Ha-Zofeh,* Bernstein had launched on a brief career of 13 weeks a multi-lingual venture, *Hebrew News,* in English, Yiddish, Hebrew and German. This

The first issue of the first Yiddish daily in the United States and in the world, Friday, April 6, 1883.

Title-page of the first collection of Hebrew poems, with translation into Yiddish, by Jacob Zebi Sobel (1831-1913).

first issue came out in 32 pages on April 5, 1871, to back the candidacy for a minor local office in the spring elections of a Jewish Tammany aspirant, Jacob Cohen.

In 1872 a new publisher came on the scene, Kasriel Zvi Sarasohn, from Suwalki. His first venture, *New Yorker Idishe Zeitung*, lasted only four or five months as a weekly, but his second took root. In 1874, with Jalomstein as editor, Sarasohn issued the *Yiddishes Gazetten* (Jewish Gazette), which lasted for more than 50 years.

By 1877 there were enough Yiddish-speaking Jews in Chicago for Nachman Baer Ettelsohn, a Polish Jew, and S. L. Marcus of Alabama to edit and publish the weekly *Israelitishe Presse* in the hope that the eagerness for news of the Russo-Turkish war would attract readers. In 1880, however, the enterprise was transferred to New York,

where it died after four years of competition with Sarasohn.

Another attempt to challenge Sarasohn's monopoly was made in the summer of 1878, when the printer Moses Topolowsky began the publication of the weekly, *Judishe Volks Zeitung,* edited by Gustave Landau. This was the best edited and most progressive Yiddish periodical of the time, but in the spring of 1880 it was sold to—Sarasohn, whose *Yiddishe Gazetten,* Orthodox in religion and conservative in politics, was the only Yiddish newspaper available when the big migration of Yiddish-speaking Jews from Eastern Europe started.

Significantly, it was in a newspaper that the first Yiddish poem written here was published. In the *Yiddishes Gazetten* of July 28, August 4 and 19, 1876 there appeared, in rather crude verses, the poem by Jacob Zebi Sobel entitled "Di Drei Hoipt Prinzipen der Torah." Sobel, a Maskil from Kovno in Lithuania who had left Russia after enduring the Odessa pogrom of April 9, 1871, defined the three principles of the Torah as the avoidance of superstition, tolerance and humanism, and the abolition of poverty. These he illustrated in terms of his experience in the pogrom, his wanderings in Romania, Galicia, Germany and England, and his observations as a new arrival in New York. The following year, Sobel issued a small book, first of its kind, containing a long poem in Hebrew, *Shir Zahav likhvod Yisrael hazaken* (A Golden Song in Honor of Israel the Old), and its translation into Yiddish, as *Yisroel der Alte* (Israel the Old). Sobel lived to be 82 in 1913, but wrote no more. A decade was to pass after 1877 before the new immigration brought forth new poets and new audiences.

Always in the background and sometimes pushing into the foreground was the factor of anti-Semitism. New features began to appear in the quality of this anti-Semitism. Early in 1867, the fact that fire insurance companies had been discriminating subtly against small Jewish merchants was brought out into the open by *The Israelite* in Cincinnati and *The Jewish Messenger* in New York. Leading New York insurance companies, it was shown, had issued a "Special

Circular" instructing agents not to insure Jews. An energetic protest movement was soon under way, involving meetings, boycotts, cancellation of policies and public discussion in Cincinnati, Indianapolis, St. Louis, Louisville, Chicago, Memphis, Cleveland, Evansville and Ligonier, Ind., New Haven, Quincy, Ill., Philadelphia, New York, Baltimore, Richmond and Petersburg, Va., Nashville and other cities. This was the most widespread movement so far conducted by American Jews in defense against anti-Semitism. The majority of the general newspapers that commented on the situation, it is true, opposed

to it. A committee was appointed to consult with the insurance companies, and a circular was issued asking each of them whether they approved of the proscriptive movement. To this a large number of replies were received, all of them written in respectful terms except those from the Home and Metropolitan companies. Others did not reply, and it was consequently concluded that they endorsed the action of the Underwriters' Agency. The committee who had the matter in charge recently made a report to a large meeting of Jewish merchants, who assembled in the synagogue on Nineteenth street in New York, and they offered the following preamble and resolutions, which were unanimously adopted:

Whereas, Unjust discriminations have been adopted by certain insurance companies between citizens professing the Jewish religion and those of other denominations;

And whereas, This course is calculated to deepen prejudices unworthy the age and country; therefore

Resolved, That duty and self respect alike demand that we, as Israelites, should cease all connection with such institutions.

Resolved, That the following insurance companies — the Merchants', Croton, Exchange, Firemen's, American Exchange, Howard, National, St. Nicholas, International, Humboldt, Indemnity, Lafayette, Arctic, Commercial, Corn Exchange, Commerce, Fulton, New Amsterdam, United States, St. Mark's, Hanover, Niagara, Connecticut, Long Island, Montauk (of Brooklyn, Jersey City, Enterprise, Firemen's Trust, Peter Cooper, Washington and North River Companies—having failed to reply to the circular of the committee, they recommend that until satisfactory replies are received, our co-religionists do not insure in either of these companies.

Resolved, That the Jewish citizens throughout the United States be requested not to insure in the Home or Metropolitan Companies until the insulting letters sent to the committee be retracted; and finally,

Resolved, That the proceedings of the meeting be published in pamphlet form for distribution throughout the United States.

The Jews say that the dishonesty of one or two persons, even if proved, is no reason why the whole body of Hebrew citizens should be proscribed, and they denounce the action of these insurance companies as nothing more nor less than an attempt at persecution, and as utterly unworthy of the present age and country. It is an un

From a report in the Philadelphia "Sunday Dispatch," April 21, 1867, of how Jews organized to oppose the efforts of insurance companies to deny fire insurance to Jews. The "Dispatch" condemned the action of the companies.

The banker Joseph Seligman (1819-1880).

the discrimination, but a minority, including widely read newspapers like the New York *Herald*, supported discrimination with stock argumentation about the cheating Jew.

In a couple of months, discussion of this insurance issue died out, and undoubtedly some of the companies retreated under pressure. But anti-Semitic prejudices continued to be cultivated and spread. Defending the Jews against the cry, "The Jews Have It," (that is, all the wealth), the Los Angeles *Daily News* in 1869 pointed out that it was the images of Shylock and Fagin that "feed fat the old unfounded prejudice against the Jews." Confused currency reformers began to use Jews as their symbol of the "money power," with August Belmont, American agent of the Rothschilds, as their favorite target. Wrathful workers protesting the frame-up and execution of Pennsylvania coal miners, placed responsibility not only on the coal barons but on London Jewish bankers! Utterances and incidents become too numerous to cite. The "comic" magazine added visual form to the standard image, and the Jew with "hook-nose" and thick accent became a familiar type on many a printed page.

One incident, however, attracted national attention because it involved a prominent Jewish

A SENSATION AT SARATOGA.

June 19, 1877 — *N Y Times*

NEW RULES FOR THE GRAND UNION.

NO JEWS TO BE ADMITTED—MR. SELIGMAN, THE BANKER, AND HIS FAMILY SENT AWAY—HIS LETTER TO MR. HILTON—GATHERING OF MR. SELIGMAN'S FRIENDS—AN INDIGNATION MEETING TO BE HELD.

On Wednesday last Joseph Seligman, the well-known banker of this City, and member of the syndicate to place the Government loan, visited Saratoga with his wife and family. For 10 years past he has spent the Summer at the Grand Union Hotel. His family entered the parlors, and Mr. Seligman went to the manager to make arrangements for rooms. That gentleman seemed somewhat confused, and said: "Mr. Seligman, I am required to inform you that Mr. Hilton has given instructions that no Israelites shall be permitted in future to stop at this hotel."

Mr. Seligman was so astonished that for some time he could make no reply. Then he said: "Do you mean to tell me that you will not entertain Jewish people?" "That is our orders, Sir," was the reply.

Before leaving the banker asked the reason why Jews were thus persecuted. Said he, "Are they dirty, do they misbehave themselves, or have they refused to pay their bills?"

"Oh, no," replied the manager, "there is no fault to be found in that respect. The reason is simply this: Business at the hotel was not good last season, and we had a large number of Jews here. Mr. Hilton came to the conclusion that Christians did not like their company, and for that reason shunned the hotel. He resolved to run the Union on a different principle this season, and gave us instructions to admit no Jew." Personally he [the manager] was very sorry, inasmuch as Mr. Seligman had patronized the hotel for so many years, but the order was imperative.

Mr. Seligman felt outraged and returned to New

In this letter Mr. Seligman commented upon the lack of sagacity shown by Mr. Hilton, the insult to the Jewish people, and said that if he did not consider Jews worthy to enter his hotel it would be wise for him to send a circular to all Jews not to make purchases at his Broadway stores. He thought the Jewish people would appreciate this point, and in conclusion gave his opinion that whatever might be the ability of Mr. Hilton to superintend a dry-goods store he was deficient in the necessary training to conduct a hotel. The language was severe and the good points in the letter were warmly applauded by those present.

Mr. Lauterback said that the Jews of this City and country could not afford to let this matter rest. In this century, when the proscription of the

The New York Times reports the discrimination against Joseph Seligman.

RACE PREJUDICE.

JUDGE HILTON probably perceives that he has made a serious mistake, although there is no reason to doubt his statement that the Grand Union Hotel at Saratoga did not decline to receive Mr. SELIGMAN because he was of the Hebrew religious faith. But whatever explanation may be offered, the action illustrates and confirms a prejudice which is simply monstrous. Judge HILTON said to a reporter of the *Times* that there was no religious question involved in any degree, and that the affair was simply "a question of what class of guests is wanted at a hotel." But what class of guests is excluded? Israelites, Hebrews, Jews. Not disorderly or drunken persons, or those who in any way violate the ordinary social proprieties of hotels, of whatever faith, or race, or nativity, but simply Jews, Hebrews, Israelites. Now as they are all mainly of one religious faith, and as few except of their race hold their faith, the exclusion is, in the first place, practically a religious exclusion. We do not suppose, however, that Judge HILTON views the subject from the religious point. His view is strictly commercial. His reasoning is that, right or wrong, there is a prejudice against Jews; that they are clannish among themselves and disagreeable to others; and as he has learned by experience that the kind of guests which he desires at his hotel will not come to it if Jews come, Jews must not be admitted.

Under the law he can not make this discrimination. Any proper, orderly, responsible guest who presents himself at a public inn must be entertained if there be accommodation. He can not be turned away because he is bald or ~~~~~~~~~~~~~~~~~~~~~~ lord, he can not do what he pleases.

Quite beyond all this, however, it is a great moral and social wrong to stigmatize an entire class against which a wretched prejudice already exists. There are undoubtedly disagreeable Hebrews or Jews, as there are disagreeable people of all other races, but undoubtedly, also, in every age and country there are Jews who have been masters in every sphere. To exclude Jews as Jews is as monstrous as to exclude English as English or Californians as Californians. Judge HILTON volunteers a distinction between "SELIGMAN Jews" and a superior class of Hebrews. But that is a purely arbitrary discrimination of his own, which he has no lawful authority to impose upon those who seek accommodation at his inn. If what is called "vulgarity" is to exclude, the rule must be enforced against a great many other guests than those known as Jews, while to exclude Jews as a class because of vulgarity is preposterous. The action of Judge HILTON has had at least the good effect of showing how sincere and universal is the protest against the indulgence of a race prejudice against white skins. We beg to remind the protestants that a race prejudice against black skins is quite as despicable.

Harper's Weekly, July 7, 1877, editorially condemns the discrimination against "Seligman Jews."

banker. On June 13, 1877, Joseph Seligman and his family were denied accommodations at A. T. Stewart's Grand Union Hotel in fashionable Saratoga, N. Y. Only the previous year, as part of the celebration of the Centenary of American Independence, Moses Ezekiel's Statue to Religious Liberty had been erected in Fairmount Park, Philadelphia, by the B'nai B'rith. Yet Judge Henry Hilton, who had inherited the Hotel from the Stewart estate, had given instructions that "no Israelites shall be permitted." Again there was extensive controversy in the press about the qualities of the Jews, and again there was much criticism of the discrimination.

The fact was that economically successful Jews were trying to exercise their democratic right to climb the social ladder together with the other newly rich, while those already on the upper rungs sought to keep the newcomers out. The excluded fought back. A boycott of A. T. Stewart's New York department store led to its being sold to John Wanamaker. Jews also promptly purchased several leading hotels in Saratoga itself. The discussion of the Seligman Affair died out, but not the practice of discrimination. A couple of years later, the promoters seeking to develop Coney Island in New York into a swank summer resort announced that "we do not like the Jews as a class" and do not want them at Coney Island.

Both in Jewish and general circles, the issue continued to be discussed. In 1881, Nina Morais wrote on "Jewish Ostracism in America" in the *North American Review*. Emma Lazarus pointed out in *The Century* in 1883 that "within recent years, Jews have been 'boycotted' at not a few places of public resort; in our schools and colleges, even in our scientific universities, Jewish scholars are frequently subjected to annoyance on account of their race. The word 'Jew' is in constant use, even among so-called refined Christians, as a term of opprobrium, and is employed as a verb, to denote the meanest tricks." In 1887, Alice Hyneman Rhine described "Race Prejudice at Summer Resorts." Some Saratoga hotels in 1890 still carried placards, "No Jews or Dogs Admitted Here." Thus, just as the great immigration was beginning, anti-Semitism was becoming more vocal and active. The new immigrants were to learn that, in the United States, the fight for democracy required, among other things, continual struggle against the encroachment of anti-alienism and its specific form of anti-Semitism in business, employment, housing, and cultural and social life.

"The Storm," by E. M. Lilien (1874-1925), an illustration to the German
edition of Morris Rosenfeld's "Lieder des Ghetto."

CHAPTER 9: "Tempest-tost" through The "Golden Door"

In the last twenty years of the nineteenth century, a profound change took place in the American Jewish population, a change that lasted at least until the immigration gates clanged to a close in 1924. A sudden but long sustained spurt in size transformed the quality of the Jewish community. In 1878 there were 300,000 Jews in the United States; in 1895 there were 300,000 Jews in New York City alone, with two-thirds of them packed, "head-on-head," into the steep tenements of a few blocks on the lower East Side, between Houston and Division Streets, east of the Bowery. With 586,000 Jews entering the country between 1881 and 1900, the Jewish population passed the million mark in 1900, when the total population was almost 76,000,000. Yet the Jews were but a small part of the immigrant tide, only 6½% of the almost 9,000,000 that came in

those years, forerunners of the still bigger migration of the next period.

In the Jewish community the change was one of body, face, tone of voice, heart and soul. With regard to class and social composition, the number of shop and factory workers grew so quickly that by the turn of the century they outnumbered all the Jewish commercial, manufacturing and professional middle classes put together. In language, folkways and secular culture, the change was to Yiddish and the East European tradition. In religious culture, the weight swung to the East European tight Orthodoxy. In political outlook, the broad stress was insistently on social justice, the working class accent was on socialism, with the key of zionism beginning to be heard, in the minor.

Like all the immigrants, the Jews came seek-

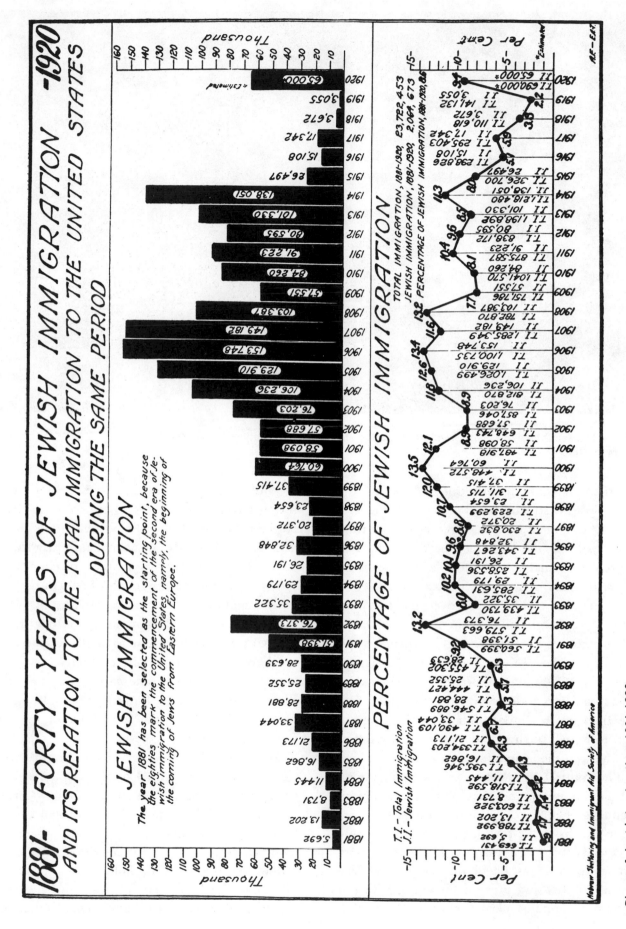

Chart of Jewish immigration, 1881-1920.

Castle Garden, the New York immigrant station, from an oil painting by Andrew Melrose, 1885.

ing the opportunity, if not the gold, fabled to be lying in the streets. They came, in the great phrase of Emma Lazarus, "yearning to breathe free," panting for an atmosphere in which the church bells on Easter Sunday did not ring out the wild news of a possible pogrom, incited or condoned by a tyrannical government. To the pull of economic advancement exerted on all Europeans by the dramatically expanding production in the United States, the Russian pogroms of 1879 and 1881 (and how often thereafter!) added a unique and decisive push. Only the Irish had a similar spur of national oppression to propel them to our shores, if poverty and famine were not enough.

The contrast between the social framework of the Old Country and that of the New was tremendous. The Tsarist Empire, from which came three-fourths of the Jewish immigrants, was ruled by the fist of "the autocrat of all the Russias." The autocracy was based on the ruling classes of the nobility and great landowners, with even the rising capitalist class excluded from a share

in political power. No capitalist-democratic revolution having taken place, there were no democratic forms through which the people might express their needs, no democratic rights, no civil liberties. There was a fusion of church and state, with one official established church. All other religions were severely handicapped. Economically, industrial capitalism was developing belatedly and slowly, and agriculture was backward, often almost primitive. Pretty much the same situation, with some variations, existed in the Austro-Hungarian Empire and in Romania, from which most of the remainder of the East European Jews were coming.

As for the Jews in the Tsarist Empire, they were the most persecuted of all peoples in what justly came to be known as the Tsarist "prison of nations." There were heavy official restrictions on where they could live and move, on landownership, on the occupations they could follow, on the right to hold public office, on their use of educational facilities and the practice of professions, on religious equality, on the use of Yiddish, in the theater and journalism and in official life, on the right to enjoy life, limb and property without the lowering threat of pogroms.

After the troublesome, anxious and tedious voyage over thousands of miles of land and ocean, the immigrants landed in a country in which the basic social framework was strikingly different. Here was a democratic republic with a huge white male electorate, and a deep-rooted and continually reasserted tradition of democratic ideals, rights and civil liberties. Political power was unmistakably in the hands of the ruling class of ever growing industrial, financial and commercial giants. But the active exercise of democratic rights by the electorate could and sometimes did act as a brake on the use of this political power, and exacted concessions and reforms for the benefit of the people. Industrially, the United States was leading the world, forging rapidly ahead of England in the 1890's. Agriculture was technically advanced, and productivity, aided by machinery on ever larger farm units, was continually expanding. As for relation of church and state, there was a higher degree of separation than existed anywhere else at the time, and no official church. There was also in the churches a liberal social tradition that went back to the American Revolutionary, abolitionist and other reform movements. Before the law, Jews were generally entitled to all civil rights and liberties, although Sunday laws and practices like New Testament readings in the public schools were discriminatory. This general American framework, both dimly and romantically perceived, was the great magnet for all the immigrants.

Within this frame, these two decades were marked by growth, ferment and turbulence. Heavy industry multiplied. Steel production leaped from 1,588,000 tons in 1881 to 10,188,000 tons in 1900. Coal production more than tripled, to 270,000,000 tons, and railroad mileage almost doubled, to 193,000. Manufacturing of consumers' goods also multiplied: the 254,000 factories and other productive establishments in 1879 jumped to 512,000, and the number of wage-workers doubled. The value of the clothing and personal furnishings produced in 1879 was $344,-000,000; in 1900, it was $794,000,000.

The wealth was staggering, and the wealthy made of its consumption a spectacle that was conspicuous, ostentatious and obnoxious. This was indeed "The Gilded Age." The 1890 Census revealed that the top one per cent had a bigger total income than the lowest 50% of the population; that of twelve million families in the United States, 5,500,000 had no property. Henry George's *Progress and Poverty* went into edition after edition from 1879 because it was a study of the great new social fact, "increase of want with increase of wealth." In 1888, Edward Bellamy's *Looking Backward,* a Utopian socialist picture of life without exploitation and poverty in the year 2,000, began a sale that reached a million copies and Bellamy Clubs mushroomed all over the land. President Grover Cleveland, in his December 3, 1888 Message to Congress, pointed to the trusts and monopolies, "while the citizen . . . is trampled to death beneath an iron heel." Mark Twain in 1899 summed it all up in his famous story, "The Man that Corrupted Hadleyburg," with its mordant picture of how wealth can corrupt human character.

Two economic depressions, from 1883 to 1885 and from 1893 to 1897, ravaged and lacerated the workers and the little business people dependent upon them. The bottom quaked and rose, but could not unhorse the small but mighty top. A "Great Upheaval" of labor organizations fighting for the eight-hour day brought the strength of the unions to a million in 1886. Then came the Haymarket Affair, the frame-up of eight and the hanging of four, and the top cracked down with all its red-baiting, alien-baiting might to smash the workers' organizations. It was not until 1900 that trade union membership, with the Knights of Labor wrecked and the American Federation of Labor not yet strong, reached one million again. Labor struggles were put down by armies, private, state and federal. The Homestead, Pa., steel strike in June 1892 was broken by armed Pinkerton private police and state troops. The next month, Federal troops crushed a silver miners' strike in Coeur d'Alene, Idaho. In 1894, the Pullman and railroad workers strike

A Jewish worker, at the turn of the century, by Jacob Epstein (1880-1959).

of 100,000 was put down by Federal troops and injunctions. The same year, when "General" Jacob Coxey led an army of unemployed workers in the depth of the crisis to Washington for relief, the tidy police arrested the leaders— for walking on the Capitol grass. Shortly after the depression ended, the jingoes in business and government launched the war to conquer Spain's island possessions in the Caribbean and the Pacific. With all this foreground, the immigrants intermeshed.

The Jewish immigration shared many qualities with the general European immigration, but also had its own specific features. More conspicuously than any any other immigrant group except the Irish, the Jews were able to strike economic roots here by making a living, no matter how poor a one at first, and remained as permanent residents. While about one third of all the European immigrants arriving between 1880 and the first World War went back home, and in some groups the percentage was as high as two-thirds, among the Jews the disappointed road back was taken by less than one-tenth. The desire of Irish and Jewish immigrants to stay, even

when sharpened by the dread of returning to persecution by British landlordism or Tsarist tyranny, is not enough to explain this permanence. Decisive was the ability to find work. In this respect the Irish and Jews each had a special advantage that lessened the effect of anti-Irish and anti-Semitic hostilities.

The Irish could speak English, and many a door to a job opened to them, even though their brogue became the butt of unfriendly mockery. The Jews, on the other hand, had the advantage of coming from urban backgrounds with urban occupations which turned out to be useful in the branches of manufacture that were then expanding.

The vast majority of other European immigrants were of peasant background, coming to a land that was booming industrially but that did not need more farmers. The Census of 1890 had in fact pronounced the end of the frontier, and native farmers were being driven from marginal land by bankruptcy or lured to the city by the hope of "high" factory wages. The East and South European peasant could get work mainly from those who would hire his peasant brawn as low-paid, back-breaking "unskilled" labor in heavy construction jobs (like road-building or ditch-digging), or in the heavy "semi-skilled" work in the steel, mining, or, later, meat packing industries. No wonder millions of such immigrants could not stand it and went home!

The Jews from the Tsarist Empire, however, because of Tsarist restrictions had developed as an urban people, living in towns and cities in the Pale (fence) of Settlement, a huge area in 15 provinces of western and southwestern Russia from the Baltic to the Black Seas. From 1870, it was in this area, especially in the northern part, that Russian capitalism developed. Jews were quickly drawn into this process, so that the Russian census of 1897 showed more Jewish artisans, journeymen, apprentices and factory workers than tradesmen. Although there were Jews in 60 different kinds of occupations, they were concentrated in six industries: clothing, metal-work, wood-work, building, textile, and tobacco, with more in the clothing than in all the others combined.

When Jews with such backgrounds came to the United States, they found that these light industries were also rapidly expanding, especially in the great metropolitan ports of entry, New York, Philadelphia, Boston and for a time Baltimore. Therefore a unique development took place: while most European immigrants of peasant background were involved in tremendous occupational changes on arrival, the Jews instead showed a remarkable continuity. Conditions of Jewish life in the Old Country merged with conditions of light industrial development in the New to create this unusual continuity. Thus a study of 135,000 East European Jews in New York City in 1890 revealed that three quarters of those gainfully employed were workers and craftsmen, 78% of them in the garment industry, and less than one fourth were tradesmen, including the conspicuous pushcart peddlers and the custom peddlers who trudged the steep stairs of the tenements. Next to the garment makers were the building trades workers, cigarmakers, wood-workers and metal-workers.

Another factor which both contributed to and was reinforced by the permanence of Jewish immigrants was the family character of this migration. Either families came over as a unit, or the bread-winner came first and then sent for wife and children. The Jews brought over a greater proportion of children than any other immigrant group.

Complex indeed was the problem of mastering

Jewish working girls returning home, by Jacob Epstein.

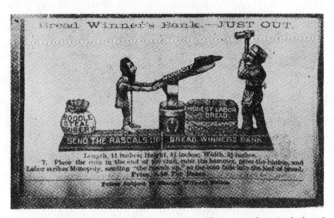

An anti-Semitic gadget, 1887. This mechanical bank presents an old Jew holding the club of "Monopoly" across an anvil so that the worker cannot get his "Honest Labor Bread." When a coin is put in the bank, the worker's hammer strikes "Monopoly" and sends the Jew head over heels!

the new ways of life faced by immigrants still psychologically and culturally rooted in ways not only old but vastly contrasting. Yet the task was greatly complicated by the fact that, as Dr. John Higham noted in *Strangers in the Land,* "the new immigrants had the very bad luck to arrive in America en masse at a time when nativism was already running at full tilt . . ." In the long history of nativism in our country, a turning point had been reached with the Haymarket Affair in 1886. The ruling circles led in ascribing all wickedness to immigrants. *The New York Times* of April 25, 1886 was certain that the eight-hour day movement was "un-American" and that "labor disturbances are brought about by foreigners." Yet immigrants continued to be admitted because dominant business elements were torn between the usefulness of immigrant labor and its rebelliousness.

The newcomers often faced hostility, mockery, contempt, violence, job, wage, residential and social discrimination, and restrictive legislation, first on a local and then on a federal level. The Italian immigration, double the size of the Jewish, met the most extensive hostility, with the Jewish not far behind. Three events in 1891 were representative. In New Orleans, eleven Italians were lynched, with business leaders and the local press applauding and the officialdom indifferent. In Millville, N. J., the Philadelphia *Public Ledger and Daily Transcript* reported on September 19, 1891 that hundreds of glass-works tending boys struck for a wage-increase and for the dismissal of Jewish tending boys. Strikers "ran through the [railroad] cars waving their sticks and clubs in search of the Jews. Finally three were found, and immediately the cry was raised, 'kill them.' " But railroad men saved them. In Washington, a law was passed extending and tightening immigration regulations and providing for the first time for the deportation of foreign-born.

The anti-alienism, of which anti-Semitism was a prominent part, developed as a confused and misleading attempt to cope with real problems. The nation's economic expansion was accompanied by intense group and individual competition, economic and social displacement, insecurity and distress. Among the displaced and exploited there emerged the nationalistic tendency to "blame the immigrant." The Jews, among whom a middle class was working itself up most rapidly and conspicuously, were mistaken to be the cause of what was really produced by social processes of capitalist development over which the Jews had no control and to which they were themselves subject. The "Shylock stereotype," Dr. Higham observes, "assumed a new potency," and began to take on the form of the menacing "international bankers" conspiring to dominate the Gentile world. New England intellectuals of the old merchant aristocracy like Henry Adams and Henry Cabot Lodge began to regard the Jew as the symbol of the hated plutocracy that was displacing their class from positions of economic and political power and social prestige. Leaders of debt-ridden farmers in the West and South violated the democratic tenets of their radical Populist movement by likewise holding up the Jewish banker, embodied often by Rothschild, as their main enemy. An Associated Press despatch from the

Populist convention in St. Louis, July 22, 1896, noted "the extraordinary hatred of the Jewish race" manifest there and in all the hotels where delegates gathered. The Populists endorsed the "silver-coinage" advocate, William Jennings Bryan, who had won the Democratic nomination for President with his magniloquent oration ending, "you shall not crucify mankind upon a cross of gold." In his campaign, as *The Jewish Voice* of St. Louis pointed out, Bryan used "the name of Rothschild promiscuously" as the embodiment of the "gold standard" and the cause of the current industrial depression. Of more immediate impact upon the Jewish masses was the anti-Semitism that appeared among other immigrant groups, with whom Jews in the big cities lived in closer contact. Themselves the victims of anti-alien hostility, Irish and German workers in urban slums caricatured the nativist "blame the immigrant" by their own version, "blame the other immigrant." Much of the street violence endured by Jews was at the hands, fists and stones of such immigrant workers. Of course, neither intellectual, agrarian nor proletarian solved any of their real problems by looking down the blind-alley of anti-Semitism for the cause. In fact, social solutions were hindered by anti-Semitism and anti-alienism, and only those benefited who were content with the situation that created the social problems.

The Jewish middle-class, both the native born elements and those of the earlier German-Jewish immigration, was aware of this rising nativism and anti-Semitism. In a dilemma between fears for their own none-too-secure status and sympathy for the immigrants, these Jews at first tried in vain to discourage the immigration. Others rose to the need of helping the immigrants through groups like the Hebrew Emigrant Aid Society in New York, founded in December, 1881. Distinguished for the respect, understanding and genuine concern he revealed for the newcomers was its Secretary, the Polish-born revolutionary 1848'er, Abolitionist and encyclopedic scholar, Michael Heilprin. Unfortunately he was a rarity among the too many who, generously busying themselves with helping the immigrants, openly showed an irritating condescension to people

AMBROSAVAGE 1-2

GOSH...EIGHTEEN, HUH? WHEN I WAS EIGHTEEN I WAS GOING TO SEE THE WORLD...

...BOY, THAT WAS OVER TWENTY YEARS AGO...

SEND IN THE NEXT APPLICANT, PLEASE...

YES, SIR...

HOTEL AMERICA

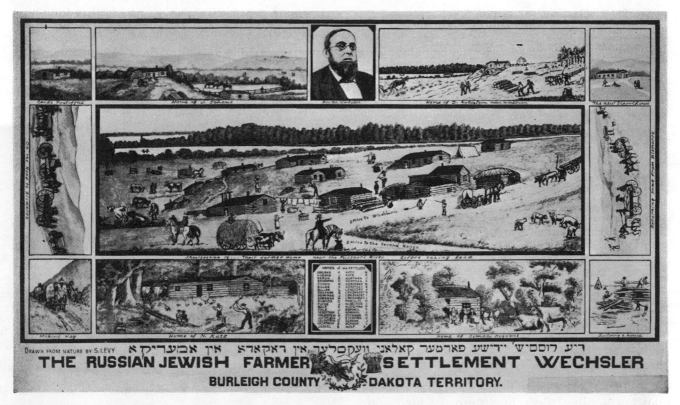

A memento of a vain attempt in the 1880's to establish a Jewish agricultural colony in the West long before the Dakotas became States of the Union.

whose different habits, garb, and very poverty were taken as evidence of inferiority. Even their language, Yiddish, was contemptuously dismissed as a "jargon" by those ignorant of the literary masterpieces already written in it by Mendele Mocher Seforim, and by the younger Sholem Aleichem and I. L. Peretz, some of whose finest writings, now known as classics, were even then being published in these last decades of the century. The fact that many Yiddish-speaking Jews themselves used the Yiddish word, "Zhargon," meaning "vernacular," to distinguish the language from Hebrew, did not alter the deprecating scorn contained in the description of Yiddish as "a jargon" by German- and English-speaking Jews—and by the non-Jews who borrowed the term from them.

Fearful that anti-Semitism would increase because of the concentration of Jews in the huge ports of entry—where of course the majority of all the immigrants, non-Jewish as well as Jewish, tended to settle—some of the immigrant aid societies made feeble efforts to ship Jews out of the big metropolitan areas. Quantitatively the

results were negligible, mainly because the basic trend in the country was the movement from rural into urban areas and from small cities into bigger ones. Nevertheless one result was that the map of Jewish settlement became dotted with handfuls of Jews in innumerable small places.

Timid efforts were also made to found agricultural colonies. Some Jewish immigrants had dreams of redeeming the Jews by tilling the soil. Daring but generally pathetic attempts were made in 1882 to establish such colonies in Louisiana, South Dakota, Oregon and New Jersey, but only those in New Jersey, at Vineland, Rosenhayn and Carmel, lasted more than a few years, some dying in the year of their birth. Failures were also the result in the next few years of attempts in Arkansas, Kansas, and North Dakota. Yet the dream persisted, and in 1891, *The Peddler,* the very popular song written by Eliakum Zunser, the newly arrived Old Country versifier and minstrel, was being sung with words that included: "Could I but gaze afar and see the happier days ahead, when the peddler will become a farmer and Jews will live united in

DER PEDLER

The music to the famous song by Eliakum Zunser (1836-1913).

peace and joy!" This became the theme-song of the Jewish Alliance, founded that year, with 37 branches hoping to get Jews onto the land. The Baron de Hirsch Fund, incorporated in New York in 1891 with $2,400,000, cooperated with the Alliance to establish the colony in Woodbine, N. J., the most enduring of all these efforts. Yet even that, ten years after its establishment in 1891, was in decline, as was a smaller independent colony in Michigan. The reasons were obvious: agricultural inexperience, insufficient financing, and the fundamental trend of United States agriculture, which was driving even experienced native-born farmers off the land into the cities.

It was not into the small towns and the farms that the overwhelming majority of immigrant Jews crowded. Like peasants from Italy and the Slavic lands, they sought work and a place to live in the economically expanding metropolitan regions. The justified fear of hostility underlined the safety as well as the convenience of living among those who spoke your language and shared your old ways of life. Poverty drove them into the poorest sections of the city, and the slum and the unwalled ghetto resulted. Each great city soon had its "Little Jewry," "Little Italy," "Little Greece"—little areas dense with struggling, aspiring immigrant life. On the East Sides of New York, Philadelphia and other cities, Jews

lived in foul, lightless, tuberculosis-breeding tenements. They worked in dank, dark and grimy sweatshops. The cruel pathos of this privation was summed up memorably in *Mein Ingele* (My Little Son), a poem by Morris Rosenfeld that was on the lips of the East Side for many years after it was published late in the 1880's. Rosenfeld, himself a recently arrived young garment sweatshop worker, sang of the son he rarely saw when "he's wide awake and bright" but only "sound asleep" and "late at night." In Aaron Kramer's translation:

> The time-clock drags me off at dawn,
> at night it lets me go.
> I hardly know my flesh and blood;
> his eyes I hardly know . . .

Yet from these tenements and sweatshops rising high, as Rosenfeld vividly expressed it, at the "corner of Pain and Anguish" on the East Sides, there came not only lament but protest. There was not only bewilderment but the striving, individually and as a group, to escape from or to end the misery. Hard-pressed parents, despite the impulse of deep poverty to send their children to work, often seized opportunities for free public education for them, even before schooling became compulsory, as it did in Chicago, for example, in 1891 or in New York in 1904. There the basis was laid for that large number of inquiring intellectuals that later made themselves felt in the arts, in the natural and social sciences,

Morris Rosenfeld (1862-1923), sketched by Jacob Epstein, 1901, to show his relation to the shop-workers.

in public life, welfare fields and the professions.

The immigrants, coming in such large numbers and settling in compact urban masses, brought organizations with them and established others here to meet their needs. The religious swelled the existing Orthodox congregations and swiftly founded many new ones using the East European forms of organization, worship and customs. These soon outnumbered all other congregations. In New York, the Russian-Jewish congregations united in 1888 to import from Vilna the Rabbi Jacob Joseph, who served as their "Chief Rabbi" until he died in 1902. Orthodoxy flourished. Having in 1886 opened their first intermediate institution, the Yeshiva Etz Haim in New York, the Orthodox Russians Jews in 1896 founded their first real seminary, the Rabbi Yitzhok Elhanan Theological Seminary (since 1928, Yeshiva College). In 1900, Rabbi Joseph organized the Beth Sefer Yeshiva, marking the beginning of the Jewish elementary all-day school movement (after his death, the Yeshiva was renamed for Rabbi Jacob Joseph). At the same time other branches of Judaism were organizing themselves. In 1889, the Central Conference of American Rabbis was founded, with about 100 reform rabbis joining, and in 1894 it issued the Union Prayer Book. Another religious movement, protecting traditional Judaism from the extremes of Reform but still sharply distinguishing itself from Orthodoxy, especially the East European type, was Conservative Judaism. To prepare rabbis to "Americanize" the new Russian Jewish immigrants and combat the inroads of secularism among them, Conservative Judaism in 1887 dedicated the Jewish Theological Seminary of America, in New York, with Sabato Morais at its head, and in 1897 opened Gratz College in Philadelphia as the first Jewish teachers' college in the United States.

Serving a different need were the many hundreds of *landsmanshaften,* free loan and other kinds of mutual aid societies. Chicago, with a Jewish population of about 75,000, had 14 free loan societies in 1896 for Russian Jews alone. In New York, between 1883 and 1900 there were founded 147 *landsmanshaften* that were still extant in the 1930's, and there were many others

An old-fashioned "heder," in which East Side boys obtained their rudimentary Hebrew schooling, drawn by Jacob Epstein.

that had shorter lives. Almost everybody belonged to a *landsmanshaft,* both for its material values (sick benefits, cemetery and burial services) and for the warmth it generated among people from the same Old Country town, continuing old ties, refreshing old memories, exchanging news about those left behind and sometimes helping bring them over. The *landsmanshaft* was an all-class organization to which worker, trader and employer belonged together, with workers predominating because of their greater numbers in the community. A more selective organization, with largely lower middle class and middle class membership, was the "Lodge" of new fraternal orders with East European membership, of which the stablest was the Independent Order Brith Abraham, born in 1887. Many of these orders had women's auxiliaries or lodges.

More dynamic than any of these religious or fraternal associations were the labor organizations that emerged out of the desperate struggle against the sweatshop. Jewish workers as individuals, it has been seen, had taken part in the American labor and trade union movement since 1850, and they continued to do so in ever larger numbers. But for about a half century from 1880 a new development unfolded: there emerged and grew rapidly a specific Jewish labor movement, which was always affiliated with and part of the general American labor movement,

Jews of all ages reading in the Aguilar Free Library, New York, 1895.

but which was also a distinguishable section of it, with its own mood, spirit and method. This Jewish labor movement was organized not on the basis of religion, of Judaism. In fact, Jewish employers were not above traducing Judaism for their gain. They compelled pious workers to accept lower pay and worse conditions in their shops, for the privilege of not working on the Sabbath. The Orthodox Yiddish press, moreover, sided with the employers against strikers. Therefore, from the beginning and for too long a time, the leadership of the labor movement was crudely and harmfully anti-religious, flaunting a simplified atheism, derived from the principles of the Anarchist trend in labor thought, that repelled workers who were religious. The distinct Jewish labor movement was necessary because the majority of the Jewish workers were now Yiddish-speaking immigrants who could be organized only in their own language. While German- or English-speaking Jews could function in existing organizations, those who spoke Yiddish had to build their own, making always sure, however, to develop ties with the other organizations.

The first steps in the early 1880's were feeble,

faltering and unsteady, as are all first steps. But those who took them gained experience, learned lessons and developed leadership. Russian-speaking intellectuals, realizing that they could reach the Jewish workers only in Yiddish, began to study and use Yiddish. Abraham Cahan is reported to have stepped forth as the first Yiddish labor lecturer in 1882, and became one of the pioneers of the Jewish labor movement. After a number of local unions had been born in the heat of sudden strikes and then died in infancy, an organizing center was created in New York in 1885 called Der Idisher Arbeter Farein, or the Jewish Workingmen's Union. Within a year it set up 14 unions with 3,000 members not only in the garment trades but for grocery clerks, barbers, compositors, tinsmiths and peddlers; issued the first Yiddish labor leaflet, written by Jacob Schoen on the eight hour day; brought Jewish workers into the first May Day demonstration ever held, on May 1, 1886 in Union Square, New York, and into the fifth Labor Day parade in New York in 1886. Yet by mid-1887 the nationwide hysteria induced by ruling business circles after the Haymarket Affair, and internal theoretical controversies between socialist and anarchist elements led to the collapse of the organization. More enduring was the first Yiddish labor and socialist-oriented weekly in the United States, *Di Nu Yorker Idishe Folkszeitung*, which the Arbeter Farein had helped to publish on June 25, 1886, and which in 1888 became a stimulus to the birth of a permanent organizing center for Jewish trade unions, the United Hebrew Trades of Greater New York and Vicinity. Noteworthy at this time also was the influence of Jewish trade union and socialist activities in London. It was there that scores of East European Jews who later came to the United

To prepare to become workers, Jewish boys went to the new Hebrew Technical School in New York; a classroom workshop in 1895.

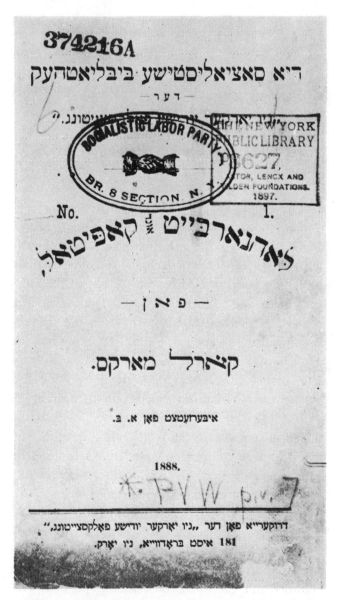

Title-page of Abba Braslavsky's translation into Yiddish of "Wage-Labor and Capital" by Karl Marx, published in New York, 1888. Note the stamp of the Yiddish Branch 8 of the Socialistic Labor Party.

States took their first steps in the Jewish labor movement. The *Arbeiter Freind*, published monthly in London in the summer of 1885 and then as a weekly at the end of 1886, also had its readers in the United States. Its editor, Philip Krantz, and its most renowned contributor, Morris Winchevsky, became prominent in the American Jewish labor movement when they came over in the 1890's.

As was the case with all the earlier organizational attempts, it was socialists that brought into being the United Hebrew Trades. In the spring of 1888, the *Folkszeitung* published serially a Yiddish translation of Karl Marx's pamphlet, *Wage-Labor and Capital*. Here Marx, for the first time in economic science, presented the theory of surplus value, explained the process by which the capitalist exploited the worker by appropriating this surplus value, and pointed out that the worker can protect himself against an increased rate of exploitation only by building trade unions. Having studied this translation, the young workers of Branch 8 of the Socialist Labor Party, a Yiddish-speaking branch meeting on New York's lower East Side, bought 800 copies of the pamphlet reprint and decided to launch the organization of Jewish trade unions. With the cooperation of Branch 17, a Russian-speaking Jewish branch of the S. L. P., of the experienced German socialists of the United German Trades, and of the small Actors,' Choristers,'

Rabbi Emil G. Hirsch (1851-1923), of the Sinai Temple, Chicago, from a portrait in the Temple by Louis Betts.

and Compositors' unions, the founding conference was held October 9, 1888, the 24 year old shirtmaker, Leo Bandes, presiding. The following week, the 23 year old Bernard Weinstein and the 18 year old shirtmaker Morris Hilkovitch (later Hillquit) brought in a draft program modeled closely on the socialistic program of the Central Labor Union of New York, the largest city labor federation in the country. Their understanding sharpened by *Wage-Labor and Capital,* the founders of the United Hebrew Trades modified sentences or even words so as more fully to express their socialist consciousness. There emerged a ringing statement of principles calling for "the struggle against united and organized capital . . . for the purpose of mutual protection against the oppression of capitalism," declaring that "with the accumulation or concentration of capital in a few hands, so-called political freedom becomes no more than an empty phrase," that "there can be no peace between capital and labor under the present social system," that "the working class is destined to change the existing unjust system into a new order founded on justice, freedom and the solidarity of all the workers of the world," and therefore

"every worker . . . must renounce all ties with any political capitalist party . . ." Then came the immediate demands, among which were the eight-hour day, equal pay for equal work for women, the abolition of child labor, payment in cash not goods, and sanitary inspection of all shops. Reflecting the inability of the Socialist Labor Party to distinguish between the program appropriate for a political party and that of a trade union, this statement seems too advanced politically for a trade union center. The apparent insistence on a socialist outlook as a condition for membership in the United Hebrew Trades tended to isolate it from non-socialist and especially from Orthodox Jewish workers, who were repelled by the flamboyant atheism of the Jewish socialists of the time. Nevertheless, the zeal and energy of the founders and the needs of the militant workers meshed; by March 1890, there were 22 unions with 6,000 members in the United Hebrew Trades, and Jewish workers in other cities were beginning to take note, Philadelphia founding a U. H. T. in 1891 and Chicago in 1896.

The plight of the workers stirred the conscience of other Jewish groups. The flame of social justice in the rabbinate flared out in the Pittsburgh Platform of Reform Judaism in 1885, which declared it a "duty" to solve, "on the basis of justice and righteousness, the problems presented by the contrasts and evils of the present organization of society." And Rabbi Emil G. Hirsch of Sinai Temple in Chicago, author of this plank, observing the condition of Jewish workers, exclaimed in horror in a sermon in 1891, "They work from sixteen to eighteen hours a day at a mere pittance . . . Jew is enslaving Jew," and on the eve of Yom Kippur in 1894 he solemnly exhorted his well-to-do congregation: "Sweatshops are the expedient of hell . . . Ye Jewish merchants . . . Do . . . your duty to stamp out this barbarous system." Yet it was neither merchants and employers nor latter-day prophets like Hirsch—and he was not unique—who stamped out the barbarous sweatshop. That end was achieved mainly by the unceasing struggle for several decades by the gaunt and sweated workers themselves, who of course welcomed the sympathy and aid of all who were inspired to give it.

With the strike then the only instrument available to the workers, they resorted to it frequently. Typical of the larger strikes in the garment industry, in which the bulk of the Jewish working-class was employed, was the 13 week struggle of 4,000 New York cloakmakers in the spring and summer of 1890. Locked out by the big employers, mostly Jewish, because the union was growing and had taken part in the May Day demonstration, the union struck back vigorously under the leadership of Joseph Barondess. With the moral backing of the trade union movement and of some middle class liberal groups, the workers held out despite deprivation, and finally won the main demands: recognition of the union and a closed shop. *Die Arbeiter Zeitung*, the new Yiddish weekly organ of the Socialist Labor Party, on August 1, 1890 applauded "these poor, starved, emaciated Jewish workers" on "this great triumph," which was seen as "the best proof that the Jews of America . . . do not consider themselves God's chosen people; they come forward as workers, as members and allies of the American working class." In the same issue, Morris Rosenfeld had "A Zieger-Lied" (A Victory Song), "dedicated to all Jewish cloakmakers in New York," which ended: "Go and sing it in the streets for the enslaved masses! Sing, and show all the classes that the Jew is a fighter!" On August 2, the *Workmen's Advocate*, English organ of the S. L. P., concluded that "these immigrants from lands of despotism have set an example of courage and valor . . . which many a labor organization of American born workers would do well to follow."

Yet stubborn vigor and bright social idealism were not enough to ensure steady growth for Jewish trade unionism. If the end of the century found the movement in a critical condition, there were two reason. First was the economic crisis of four long years from 1893. When a Jew in New York was horrified "to see people walking about who have not eaten for days," and when in Chicago thousands subsisted by eating in two Jewish community People's Soup Kitchens, only the biggest unions could survive. But

Samuel Gompers (1850-1924) in 1886, when he was elected President of the American Federation of Labor.

a greater drain than the depression was the persistent tendency to turn the unions into arenas for unnecessary political strife between anarchists and socialists. Conflicts which should have been contained within anarchist and socialist groups were disastrously injected into the unions. For a time there were even rival unions, anarchist-led and socialist-led. Then in 1895, in the middle of the crisis, the Socialist Labor Party made its supreme blunder. Daniel DeLeon, a West Indian Jew and Columbia University lecturer who had become the dominant and often high-handed leader of that party, followed a professedly Marxist policy that was even then criticized by Marxists here and abroad. This S. L. P. leadership ordered all S.L.P. members to leave the Knights of Labor and the American Federation of labor on the ground that these unions were not socialist, and founded the Socialist Trades and Labor Alliance in December 1895. The harmful "pure and simple" trade unionism of Samuel Gompers was thus countered by the equally harmful "pure and simple" socialism of the sectarian DeLeon. Thus self-isolated, the Alliance soon withered, and the United Hebrew Trades, which had been one of the founders of the Alliance, was in grave danger.

Hannah G. Solomon (1858-1942), for many years President of the National Council of Jewish Women, as she appeared in 1903.

A sharp opposition to DeLeon's policy had grown up, especially among the Jewish socialists. This opposition, including such figures as Hillquit, the famous editor and journalist. Morris Winchevsky, recently arrived from London, Louis Miller, Meyer London, Isaac A. Hourwich and M. Zametkin, headed towards a breakaway from the Socialist Labor Party. One far-reaching result was the publication, by a group including some of those mentioned above, of the *Jewish Daily Forward*, on April 22, 1897, edited by Cahan until August, by Miller until 1902, and then by Cahan again until his death in 1951. To complete the break with DeLeonism, this group and the *Forward* swung over in August 1897 to the newly born movement led by Eugene V. Debs, the Social Democracy, and then in 1901 to the new Socialist Party. The debilitated trade unions were to be rebuilt and many new ones were to be built, with the *Forward* helping greatly in the organization of the Jewish masses. At the same time, while shunning sectarianism, the *Forward* developed its own characteristic

weakness: in tight situations, it would opportunistically and timidly hold the workers back from the sharpest struggle, demobilize them, and disillusion them. From the beginning, the *Forward* was a mixed blessing.

Besides the working-class organizations. others sprouted, too many even to list. Some need to be mentioned. The National Council of Jewish Women, growing out of the Chicago World's Fair Congress of Jewish Women in 1893. had sections in 11 cities and a membership of 1,300 within a year, and by 1900 had 37 sections in 20 states and the District of Columbia, as well as two in Canada. With Mrs. Hannah G. Solomon as president and Miss Sadie American as executive secretary, the Council promoted a program of "religion, philanthropy and education. of studying the "history, literature and customs of the Jews," of aiding Sabbath-schools and "the work of social reform," and of opposing all religious persecution. Later it became largely a service organization with strong liberal tendencies.

Service was from the beginning the purpose of the Educational Alliance, founded in 1889 by New York's "uptown" Jews to aid the new immigrants. Hitting its stride in 1893, it aimed to be "of an Americanizing, educational, social and humanizing character." Despite the contempt implied in the idea that the East European Jews needed "humanizing," the Alliance immediately

The Educational Alliance in New York, 1895.

became a popular center on the East Side. Youth and adult flocked to learn English, to attend lectures, cultural programs in all the arts, games, and social affairs. In 1900 Surprise Lake Camp began to offer East Side youngsters a rare taste of green country. The Alliance helped many thousands of adults to understand the new country, and while it did that for the youth too, it also helped the youth appreciate the old heritage of the adults.

Much less conspicuous and influential at the time than the labor movement was the infant Zionist movement. From about 1884, *Hoveve Zion* (Love of Zion) groups, consisting mostly of Orthodox East European Jews who followed the example set in Odessa in 1880, began to appear in New York, Boston, Philadelphia, Baltimore and, in 1896, in Chicago. In 1885 a *Shovei Zion* (Returners to Zion) group was formed in Baltimore and in 1890 one in New York. In 1893 a *Hebras Zion* (Zion Association) appeared in Baltimore. After the publication of Theodore Herzl's *The Jewish State* in Vienna in February 1896, the first response here came in Chicago through Chicago Zionist Organization No. 1, its leaders including Max Shulman, Harris and Bernard Horwich and Léon Zolotkoff, a Yiddish journalist who was later a delegate to the Basle Congress. Daughters of Zion clubs appeared in New York and Baltimore. In Philadelphia, *Ohave Zion* (Lovers of Zion), was organized, and in 1898, a Yiddish annual, *Zion's Friend,* was edited by Herman Krieger. A spurt came after the first World Zionist Congress, in Basle, August 29-31, 1897. In November, 13 Zionist groups formed the Federation of New York Zionists, and on July 4, 1898 the Federation of American Zionists was established with 100 affiliated societies from 14 cities on the eastern seaboard and Troy, Syracuse and Chicago. Professor Richard J. H. Gottheil was president, Rev. Stephen S. Wise was secretary, and of the ten vice-presidents, seven were rabbis (four Orthodox, two Conservative, one Reform). Significantly, the membership consisted generally of East European, lower middle class, Yiddish-speaking immigrants, but the leadership was middle and upper middle class, and American born or at least English-speaking. By

The Federation of American Zionists chartered the Friends of Zion Society in Philadelphia in 1902.

1900 there were 8,000 members in organizations affiliated with the Federation.

Opposition to Zionism was extensive among middle class Jews influenced by Reform, and among organized Jewish workers led by socialists. In the Pittsburgh Platform of 1885, Reform had declared, "we consider ourselves no longer a nation but a religious community." Therefore in 1897, the Central Conference of American Rabbis resolved "that we totally disapprove of any attempt for the establishment of a Jewish State" as casting doubt upon the patriotism of Jews wherever they live and interfering with the mission of Judaism to spread "peace, justice and love in the human race." The B'nai B'rith followed this position. It was reaffirmed by the Reform laymen of the Union of American Hebrew Congregations in 1899 with the proclamation, "American is our Zion," which made a slogan of a view that originated in the first Charleston Reform movement.

Among the workers, the objection to Zionism was not connected with fears of charges of dual loyalty or visions of a unique Jewish spiritual mission. The middle class nationalism of the Zionists was countered by a simplified working class cosmopolitanism that was mistaken for internationalism. Neither the American nor the international socialist movement had yet developed a mature approach to the national question as a whole and the Jewish question in particular, which would properly relate the internationalism of the working class with the national rights of

Front-page cartoon in "Die Arbeiter Zeitung," February 27, 1898, calling on Uncle Sam to cool off. With the cartoon came verses by G. Lempert, to be sung to the tune of "Yankee Doodle."

nations, peoples and ethnic minorities. Even the Negro question, so fundamental and urgent in American history, was not seen by the Socialist Labor Party or later by the Socialist Party as a specific question and was crudely reduced to a class question, to be solved as a byproduct of the class struggle. Similarly the Jewish question was viewed simply, too simply, as a class question. Class conscious Jewish workers rejected Zionism as a movement of another and hostile class. Zionist employers who sweated Jewish workers, and those Zionist rabbis who were indifferent to the Jewish masses' cry for social justice here, sharpened the hostility of Jewish workers to Zionism. All major events, it may be said, were seen in contrasting ways: the frame-up in France of Captain Alfred Dreyfus as a traitor turned some European Jews like Herzl and some American Jewish middle class elements to Zionism, but the same Dreyfus case confirmed Jewish socialist-minded workers, who had no illusions about the inconsistency of middle class democracy, in their conviction that only under socialism could anti-Semitism be eliminated.

Even more complex was the division among the Jewish population on the Spanish-American War of conquest of Puerto Rico, Cuba and the Philippines. Jewish banking, manufacturing and commercial interests lined up behind the dominant non-Jewish business forces that launched the war. The Anglo-Jewish and Yiddish press repeated the general demagogic slogan of "Cuba Libre" (Free Cuba) and "Remember the Maine!" But to bring the issue home to Jews, they added, "Remember 1492!"—the Spanish Inquisition and the expulsion from Spain! More than 4,000 Jews enlisted in the State Volunteers and the regular army, and in Chicago a group of Zionists began to drill, hoping to be enrolled as a Zionist company. There was some opposition to the war even in the middle class, expressing itself in the Anti-Imperialist League, in which there were also active Jewish liberals like Dr. Solomon Solis-Cohen in Philadelphia, Felix Adler in New York and Sigmund Zeisler in Chicago (one of the four lawyers who had boldly defended the Haymarket martyrs in court). The ranks of advanced labor, however, were generally united against the war, but a split occurred among the Jewish workers. *Die Arbeiter Zeitung* and *Die Abend Blatt,* weekly and daily Yiddish organs of the Socialist Labor Party, edited by

Felix Adler (1851-1933), founder of the Ethical Culture movement.

Sigmund Zeisler (1860-1931).

Emma Lazarus (1849-1887) in 1872.

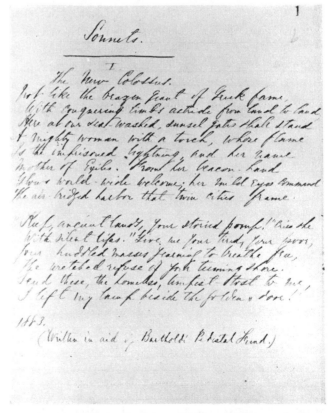

"The New Colossus," in the handwriting of Emma Lazarus. Written in 1883 to help raise funds to build the pedestal for the Statue of Liberty, the sonnet was later embossed on a plaque on the pedestal.

Philip Krantz, courageously followed DeLeon in opposing the war. But although Debs and the Social Democracy of America were also against the war, the unofficial Yiddish organ of that movement, the *Jewish Daily Forward*, capitulated to the pressure of the Jewish middle class and supported the war from the beginning, proclaiming it a people's war for the Americans as a whole and for the Jews a war of retribution for the expulsion from Spain four centuries ago. While the New York authorities banned the May Day parade of the S. L. P., they encouraged a pro-war May Day parade staged by the *Forward*. Thus the *Forward* began a practice, in critical situations, of subordinating the national interests of the American people and workers as well as the interests of the Jewish masses to the class needs of the imperialists.

Among the achievements of the immigrants,

perhaps the most enduring was the cultural ferment they inspired. The country as a whole and all sections of the Jewish population were affected. Most notable of the writers in English was Emma Lazarus. She might have died unremembered, the sheltered daughter of a wealthy family with her literary talent pettily dissipated by a placid life, had not her interest in Jewish life and all her consciousness been suddenly deepened and quickened by news of and then contact with the refugees from the Tsarist pogroms. She stepped out firmly into the arena of public controversy, writing polemics against anti-Semites, urging understanding as well as aid of the immigrant, advocating a kind of Zionism in which not American but East European Jews would settle in Palestine, connecting the social principles of the Hebrew prophets with "the fathers of modern socialism," whom she proudly identified as Jews like Ferdinand Lasalle and Karl Marx. In 1882 she published a heroic verse drama composed a few years before, *The Dance to Death;* dealing with the persecution of Jewish Germany in 1349, the play gained timeliness from the current Russian pogroms. "An Epistle to the Hebrews" roused the readers of *The American Hebrew* during the winter of 1882-83. Her spirited Jewish poetry she challengingly entitled *Songs of a Semite.* She gloried in "the glorious Maccabean rage," and sang of Bar Kochba, "the last Warrior Jew" who led "the weak, the wronged, the miserable" into battle "for freedom." She nobly articulated the meaning of the United States as a land of refuge for "the tempest-tost" when in 1883 she wrote "The New Colossus" in aid of the Fund to build the pedestal for Bartholdi's Statue of Liberty—to which the sonnet is now affixed in bronze. When cancer wore her out in 1887 in her thirty-ninth year, she was widely mourned not only among English-speaking Jews, but by Robert Browning and John Greenleaf Whittier, by Harriet Beecher Stowe and Walt Whitman.

Among the Yiddish-speaking Jews, however, she was but little known in her own lifetime. The new immigrants, especially the workers, created their own vigorous secular cultural life, in a militant journalism, a mass theater, and a body of poetry and narrative prose of high literary quality and social depth. Pre-eminent are the four proletarian Yiddish poets who won world renown in other languages as well as wherever Yiddish was spoken, and who literally inspired their own and succeeding generations of Jewish workers and all who were close to them. First on the scene was Morris Rosenfeld (1862-1923); settling in New York in 1886 he worked as an operator and presser in a garment sweatshop. His were the first poems of life in the shop. He sang of work, of exhaustion, of poverty, of protest. "So wild is the roar of machines in the sweatshop, I often forget I'm alive—in that din!" Bending over the heavy pressing-iron, "I am a tear-drop millionaire," he wrote, "and weep upon my hoard." His consolation was that he could let the world know. As he said in "My Little Boy" (in Kramer's translation),

And yet these trials were not in vain.
The cries I hurled
Across the world

Made known, to all, a worker's pain. Rosenfeld crossed the language barrier. The songs that were on the lips of thousands of Jewish workers attracted the notice of Professor Leo Wiener of Harvard, who translated *Dos Liederbuch* as *Songs from the Ghetto* in 1898 and launched it on a world career of translation into German, Czech, Polish, Russian, Japanese and other languages. Rosenfeld's picture of the "worker's pain" was an indictment; it stirred the conscience as well as the sense of beauty. Significantly, his later work—nature and personal lyrics and nationalist poems (he was a delegate to the World Zionist Congress in 1900)—, although esthetically as good as his proletarian poems, never attracted the attention quite properly lavished upon the latter.

David Edelstadt (1866-1892) was angrier and more rousing. Injured in a Kiev pogrom in 1880, he came here in 1882 and was working in a garment shop, writing in Russian and thinking more of Russian affairs than of American, when the Haymarket frame-up "Americanized" him. He plunged into the defense of the Haymarket men, was arrested for his work but not deterred. He turned to writing Yiddish poetry. In the first of six poems on the Haymarket men, "Who Were They?", he exclaimed (in Max Rosenfeld's translation):

They carried in their breasts the scarlet flame
Of Truth, sweet radiance that freedom casts.
They bid us speak in Truth's unsullied name,
And summoned us to men's unfinished tasks.

Edelstadt was published mainly in the anarchist Yiddish press, but his poems were read widely. He summoned and roused and cried "Vacht Oif" (Wake Up): "How long, o how long, will you keep on as slaves and carry the shameful chain?" He called to battle. "In Kamf" became a workers' hymn. In Kramer's translation:

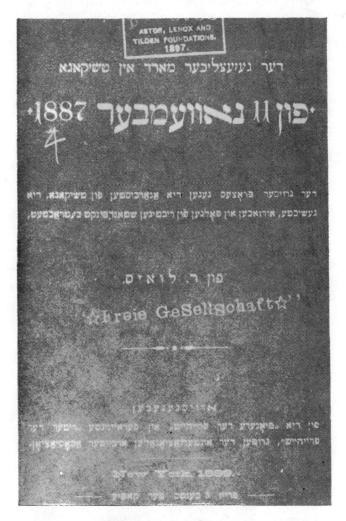

Title-page of a Yiddish pamphlet on the Haymarket Affair, issued by Jewish anarchist groups in New York, 1889, entitled (in translation), "The Legal Murder in Chicago of 11 November 1887." It was in this pamphlet that David Edelstadt's poem, "Who Were They?," was first printed.

Joseph Bovshover (1872-1915) in 1897 in New York.

We're hated and damned and driven,
we're hounded from shore unto shore,
and all for the love we have given
to those who are hungry and poor.

Also stirring and demanding was the work of Joseph Bovshover (1872-1915), who arrived in New York in 1891 and went to work in a fur shop. In a creative period of only a few years before his life was clouded by mental illness, Bovshover made dulling eyes shine. In 1892, in "Zum Vint" (To the Wind), he wrote, as translated by Kramer:

And if you find the blood is frozen,
awake it, as you wake the sea;
and make it seethe, and make it angry,
and wake the flame of liberty!

Not so closely connected with the labor movement as was Edelstadt, Bovshover nevertheless expressed his real intimacy with the workers in a profound image in "Zu Meine Brider" (To My Brothers): "I am the violin, you are the strings; you alone can awake the music in me." Always he sought to expand the horizon of the

Morris Winchevsky (1856-1932).

song. In "A Bezim un a Ker" (A Broom and a Sweep), in Kramer's translation, he blew loudly:

Enough! I will not sow again
For idle hands to reap!
I never will bow low again.
A broom, and watch me sweep!

In "A Kamf Gezang" (A Battle Song), he blared: "Unfurl the flags in red, strike up a march and get under way!" It was the editor writing poetry, just as it was the poet who wrote flaming editorials and eloquent articles.

In addition to these and many lesser poets, there were the writers of prose, usually for the periodical press. In the best of them there is a wealth of realistic portrayal of immigrant Jewish life. Outstanding were Zalmen Libin (1872-1955) and Leon Kobrin (1872-1946), both of whom arrived in 1892. Libin wrote innumerable sketches and stories of the workers' life in the shops and tenements. Kobrin, who became an artist in the short story form, broadened his range to include the conflict between the immigrants and their American-born or English-speaking children, as well as the contrast between

people. "Lift up your eyes," he appealed to them in "A Gezang Zum Folk" (A Song to the People) in 1895-1896. "Long enough have you been the robbed! Long enough have you been the cheated! Take hold of the treasures that are your heritage, take hold of the fruit of your labor!"

The eldest of the four, but the last to settle here, was Morris Winchevsky (1856-1932), who during his own life came to be known as the "grandfather of Jewish socialism." When he arrived in 1894 he was already widely known in Yiddish-speaking labor circles not only for his ten years of work as a Yiddish labor editor in London, but especially for his songs of struggle, the first in Yiddish. Widely reprinted in Yiddish labor journals here, they were already on the lips of many a shop worker. His literary instrument was like the bugle and the drum, his rhythm was the tempo of the march. The workers' steps quickened and lengthened as they sang Winchevsky's

Z. Libin (1872-1955), from a drawing by Bernard Gussow (1881-1957), in 1901.

the material benefits gained by many immigrants and their cultural and spiritual confusion.

A cultural force that reached more deeply among the immigrant masses than poetry or bel-letristic prose was the Yiddish theater, for which not even literacy was required. It was in the theater that the immigrant masses, almost totally without secular schooling, found both entertainment and education of a sort. They were naive and enthusiastic. They came to have both a good cry and a loud laugh. They swerved from the sentimental to the boisterous in a flash. Nothing was too melodramatic for their taste. Conscious of their lowly status, they swelled with national pride in response to scenes of ancient Jewish prowess. The actor was central—and devotees of particular stars competed in public exhibition of their ardor.

Beginning early in the 1880's, with a visiting company from London, this theater grew rapidly in popularity. By 1887 there were six Yiddish companies performing in New York, and road companies had gone as far as Chicago. In general

Leon Kobrin (1872-1946).

"At the Yiddish Theater," drawn by Jacob Epstein, 1901.

Abraham Goldfaden (1840-1908), from a bust by Aaron Goodelman.

a comedian for the display of whose 'stunts' the action was frequently and arbitrarily suspended." The themes ran from low comedy about immigrant life to stilted "operettas" on Bible stories, but included current matters of headline interest like Hurwitch's *The Heroes of Homestead,* about the Homestead, Pa. steel strike in 1892, *Cuba, or General Maceo's Heroism,* 1897, and *Captain Dreyfus,* 1898 (in which year the last play competed with another of the same name by Shomer). But a new and healthier element was brought into the Yiddish theater when Jacob Gordin (1853-1909) came to New York in 1891. Introducing realism in plot and especially in character portrayal, Gordin did not drive the "shund" from the stage-market-place, but he did challenge it with plays like *Der Idisher Kenig Lear* (1892), *Mirele Efros* (1898), and *Gott, Mentsh un Teivel* (1900), in which Jacob P. Adler, David Kessler, Kenny Liptzin, Bertha Kalisch and others won acting fame. Although the locale of these three plays was in Europe, they dealt with themes sharply meaningful in immigrant life.

the Yiddish theater was still in its infancy. Its father, Abraham Goldfaden (1840-1908), had developed it in Eastern Europe in the 1870's with a copious output ranging from *genre* comedies of Jewish life to "operettas" on Jewish historical themes, in which as in *Sulamith, Bar Kochba,* and *Doctor Almosado* there was a real folk spirit, with songs that virtually became folk songs. Commercial theater producers here, however, preferred to exploit the popular vulgarity ("shund" in Yiddish) of the main box-office hit-writers like Joseph Lateiner (1853-1935), "Professor" M. Hurwitch (1844-1910), M. Zeifert (1851-1922) and N. M. Shaikevitch (Shomer; c. 1846-1905) who flooded the stage with almost 300 plays among them. As Nathaniel Buchwald described them in the *Cambridge History of American Literature,* they were compounded of "the most preposterous plots, a few songs of the salacious and sentimental pseudo-nationalistic kind, [and]

Nathaniel Buchwald (1890-1956), drama critic and journalist.

Jacob Gordin (1853-1909), from a drawing by Bernard Gussow in 1901.

Albert A. Michelson (1852-1931), physicist and winner of the Nobel Prize.

Bertha Kalisch (d. 1939), a star of the Yiddish theater.

The first two treated the breaking up of families in which children turn away from parents. The third showed the consequences of the senseless scramble for money. In theme as well as in form, Gordin developed followers who carried on his fight for a popular theater of higher standards. Libin and Kobrin were the most prominent among these in the 1890's, with David Pinski (1872-1959) joining them the next decade.

Outside the metropolitan immigrant "ghettoes," as the East Sides soon got to be called by all observers, Jews were participating in the vast variety of American life despite anti-Semitism. In academic life, a score of Jewish scholars held university posts: Thus in 1890 the 27 year old Dr. Cyrus Adler was promoted to the rank of associate professor of Semitics at Johns Hopkins (in 1892 he became librarian of the Smithsonian Institute in Washington); in 1891 the 29 year old Edwin R. A. Seligman, of the banking family, became professor of political economy at

Adolph S. Ochs (1858-1935) as he appeared in 1896 when he purchased "The New York Times."

Columbia; and in 1892 Albert A. Michelson became head of the physics department of the new University of Chicago, having already for five years conducted the great experiments with light for which he later won the Nobel Prize in 1907. Political eminence was being attained by Jews in many ways, as diversely as in the appointment of Oscar S. Straus as Minister to Turkey in 1887 by President Cleveland and again in 1898 by President William McKinley, in the election in 1894 of Adolph H. J. Sutro as Mayor of San Francisco (in which he was reputed to own one-tenth of all the real estate), or, across the continent, in the election of Samuel Rosenberg to the Common Council of Portland, Maine, in 1898. In general American journalism, Jewish activity was common; in 1896 the *New York Times,* on the brink of bankruptcy, was bought by Adolph S. Ochs and convered into a profitable and famous newspaper by 1900. In the theater, David Belasco (1854-1931) and the brothers Frohman (Charles, 1860-1905, and Daniel, 1850-1940) were well on the way to conspicuous careers, Belasco as play-

wright, all three as managers and producers. In the opera, Oscar Hammerstein (1847-1919) had in 1892 opened the Manhattan Opera House, rivaling the Metropolitan, which started in 1883. In music, Leopold Damrosch (1832-1885) was the conductor of the Symphony Society of New York, and when he died he was replaced by his son Walter (1862-1951). Fanny Bloomfield Zeisler, our country's leading woman pianist, at 30 appeared with Paderewski as the first two instrumentalists to give concerts at the Music Hall in the Chicago World's Fair in 1893. In the field of literature, Abraham Cahan's *Yekl,* a novel in English about immigrant life, published in 1896, won the praise of William Dean Howells, and in 1898 Mary Antin's *From Polotsk to Boston,* with an introduction by Israel Zangwill, stimulated wide interest, paving the way for her famous *The Promised Land* in 1912.

In this period, too, the first stable communal Jewish publishing house was founded with the organization in 1888 of the Jewish Publication Society of America. By 1900 it had issued 32 volumes, among which were Heinrich Graetz's *History of the Jews,* in five volumes, 1891-1895, the

Fanny Bloomfield-Zeisler (1863-1927), an outstanding concert pianist at the turn of the century.

young Israel Zangwill's *Children of the Ghetto* in 1892, *Dreamers of the Ghetto,* 1898, and *Ghetto Tragedies,* 1899, and the first volume of the *American Jewish Year Book,* 1899. At about this time there also emerged an American Jewish historical consciousness and the beginning of the writing of American Jewish history. The first in the field was Isaac Markens' *The Hebrews in America* in 1888. In June 1892, only eight years after the birth of the American Historical Association, the American Jewish Historical Society was founded, in part because of the 400th anniversary celebration of Columbus' discovery of America, in part because misrepresentation of American Jewish history was becoming a matter of concern. In December 1891, the *North American Review,* the most influential magazine in the country, had had an article charging that Jews had not taken part in the Civil War. With rampant anti-Semitism in Russia, Germany and France finding imitators in the United States, Simon Wolf, who as far back as the days of the Civil War had been trying to keep the American Jewish record straight, set to work on a full-panoplied defense. This finally appeared in 1895 as his large-scale pioneer compendium, *The*

Jacob Hirschorn (1829-1906) of Providence, R. I. playing pinochle with his wife in the Nineties.

American Jew as Patriot, Soldier and Citizen. In 1893, Max J. Kohler's edition of *The Settlement of the Jews in North America* by an Irish liberal judge, Charles P. Daly, was published. In 1894 the first history of the Jews of an American city appeared: *The Jews of Philadelphia* by Rev. Henry Samuel Morais.

As the century turned, the Jews it seemed, were "everywhere," especially in the East Side "ghettoes."

The Jewish Worker, an illustration by E. M. Lilien (1874-1925) to Morris Rosenfeld's "Songs of Labor" in his Berlin edition, 1903, of his "Songs of the Ghetto."

CHAPTER 10: The New Century
and the New Labor Heroism

Never before or since have so many Jews come into the United States as arrived between 1900 and 1914. Never have so many Jews come in so few years into any one country as came to our ports then. Yet the Jews were only a small fraction of the high immigration tide; of the 13,500,000 entering from 1900 to 1914, only 1,450,000 were Jews, while the Italians had double that number. The Jewish population multiplied from about one million in 1900 to three million in 1914, with the working class element continuing to swell.

Three forces impelled Jews to emigrate to this country from the Tsarist empire in numbers that reached the peak of 482,000 from 1904 to 1908. First was the Russian industrial and agricultural crisis of 1903-1904. Second was the reactionary terror, loosed by the government after it had crushed the 1905 Revolution, which brought thousands of Jews with revolutionary experience into the American Jewish population, where they created a special ferment. Third was the pogrom wave, manipulated by the government to divert attention from the crisis, from the cause of

Judah Leib Magnes (1877-1948).   Oscar S. Straus (1850-1926).   Jacob H. Schiff (1847-1920).

the revolution and from the military defeat by Japan.

Terrible indeed was the toll of the pogrom wave. It began in Kishinev at Easter, 1903, when 47 Jews were killed, 437 injured, and 1,500 homes and stores pillaged in three days. Deterred perhaps by Russian, European and American protests, the Tsarist government desisted, but in 1905, disturbed by war and revolution, it turned to the pogrom again. The list is long even if we include only those in which murder of Jews was extensive: 15 killed in Zhitomir, 10 in Troyanov, 50 in Byalistok, 10 in Kerch, 29 again in Kishinev. The worst came the week beginning October 18, 1905 (old Russian calendar—November 1 in our calendar), during which pogroms raged in six hundred towns, in some 50 of which Jews were murdered. In Odessa alone more than 300 Jews were slaughtered and thousands wounded. After a lull, a pogrom in Syedletz on August 28, 1906 killed 30 Jews. The economic ruin was incalculable.

Indignation in the United States was widespread and intense not only among Jews but in the general community. After the first Kishinev pogrom, at least 80 newspapers in 28 states and the District of Columbia published denunciatory editorials. Sermons by Christian clergymen and protest meetings were common. President Theodore Roosevelt vainly tried to transmit to the Tsar a B'nai B'rith petition signed by 12,544.

More than a million dollars was collected for pogrom orphan relief. But it was the 1905 pogroms that fully loosed the torrent of wrath and sorrow in the United States. On October 7, the Jewish workers in New York—unionists, socialists, labor Zionists, Bundists, fraternalists — marched 30,000 strong, according to *The New York Times,* in "protest against Russian atrocities." Then came, however, the stunning reports of the second Kishinev pogrom and the Odessa massacre. The entire Jewish population was shaken. On the initiative of the Jewish Socialist-Revolutionaries, a conference was held on the East Side of New York on November 6, attended by socialists, Zionists, conservatives, Orthodox and atheists. Out of this emerged the Jewish Defense Association, headed by Rabbi Judah L. Magnes, to organize protest action and raise funds. In Philadelphia on November 29, in a heavy rain 18,000 Jews trudged in a "march of sorrow." But the great demonstration took place on December 4 in New York, called by the Jewish Defense Association. Led by Grand Marshal Joseph Barondess and Magnes, 125,000 Jews, said the *Times,* paraded from Rutgers Square to Union Square, garbed in black or wearing black arm-bands, bands playing funeral music and cantors and boy choirs chanting prayers, carrying black flags, American flags and flags with the Star of David. From Williamsburg, 20,000 had walked across the new bridge to join the parade;

30,000 women were in the line of march; "hundreds of thousands" crowded the sidewalks to watch the solemn procession. When the parade reached Grace Church on Broadway at Eleventh Street, the pastor was standing on the church porch, bareheaded and in his vestments, while the church bells pealed in sorrowful sympathy. At Union Square, resolutions called upon our Government and others to intervene to stop the pogroms.

These Russian pogroms had ramified effects. Some, like Joseph Barondess, turned from Socialism to Zionism as the solution to the Jewish question in Eastern Europe. Another result was the American Jewish Committee, a select group of 50, which was formed in 1906. While it expressed the views and methods of the Jewish plutocracy, its declared aim was acceptable to all Jews: "to prevent infringement of the civil and religious rights of Jews, and to alleviate the consequences of persecution." That year, too, President Roosevelt, moved by the public revulsion at the Russian atrocities, by his own policy of gunboat-and-dollar diplomacy against Russia in the Far East, and by his own practical eagerness to win votes for the Republican Party, appointed the wealthy merchant, diplomat and philanthropist, Oscar S. Straus, as Secretary of the Department of Commerce and Labor. "I want to show Russia and some other countries," Roosevelt told Straus, "what we think of the Jews in this country." Thus for the first time a Jew attained cabinet rank in the United States. The sympathy revealed in all these actions and demonstrations encouraged East European Jewish immigration, which properly regarded the United States as the bright haven from persecution.

Within the country, industrial progress surged on, but social progress was barely beginning to toddle. Economic power was concentrated in ever fewer but bigger and more grasping hands. Yet at the bottom poverty was so widespread as to arouse in the middle classes not only sympathy for the masses but also fears for the stability of the prevailing social system. Bold activity by the workers in the trade union and political arena spurred the middle classes into a movement for political and social reform. This anti-monopoly

crusade won some concessions, mainly on a municipal and state level. The period has been over-enthusiastically labeled The Progressive Era, but the basis of economic monopoly and its dominance in government were untouched.

The United States Steel Corporation, born in 1901 as the first billion dollar combine in the world, integrated 11 steel, mining and shipping companies with a capital of $1,400,000,000 into one economic empire, with J. P. Morgan in full control. That year more than 35% of the farmers in the land were already tenants and did not own the fields they tilled. In a book simply named *Poverty*, Robert Hunter in 1904 revealed that "in fairly prosperous years" of the total population of 80,000,000, some 10,000,000 lived in poverty, "underfed, under-clothed, and poorly housed," with 4,000,000 of them public paupers. Moreover, he found 2,000,000 workingmen unemployed four to six months a year. "Among the Jews," he noted, "distress and poverty are widespread." Yet the *World Almanac* of 1902 had listed 4,000 American millionaires, of whom over 120 were Jews.

Ten years later, a committee of the House of Representatives headed by Arsene P. Pujo, with Samuel Untermeyer of New York as chief examiner, began an investigation of financial and industrial concentration. Reporting in 1913, the Pujo Committee presented an elaborate picture of monopoly control. The six "most active agents" in the process of monopolization were three Morgan units (Morgan & Co., the First National and the National City banks of New York), two Boston firms (Lee, Higginson and Kidder, Peabody), and Kuhn, Loeb & Co., of which the best known partner was Jacob H. Schiff. The Morgan network included 341 directorships in 112 corporations with a total capital of $22,245,000,000. In such company, Kuhn, Loeb was small, holding leading directorships in only eight banks, nine railroads (including the Pennsylvania, Union Pacific, Southern Pacific, and Baltimore & Ohio), and industrial outfits like American Telephone and Telegraph, Western Union, and Westinghouse Electric. Tied in, incidentally, with the National City Bank was the biggest Jewish-owned industrial enterprise,

Meyer Guggenheim (1828-1905) and his seven sons, left to right: Benjamin (1865-1912), Murry (1858-1939), Isaac (1854-1922), Daniel (1856-1930), Solomon R. (1861-1949), Simon (1867-1941) and William (1868-1941).

the American Smelting & Refining Company, which was taken over in 1901 by the Guggenheim brothers (Daniel, John S. and five others), and built in less than two decades from a leading copper combine into an international operation with nitrate fields in Chile, tin mines in Bolivia and rubber plantations and diamond fields in the Belgian Congo.

Summing it up in 1912, the successful presidential candidate Woodrow Wilson declared in a campaign speech later reprinted in *The New Freedom*: "The masters of the government of the United States are the combined capitalists and manufacturers of the United States, the big bankers, the big manufacturers, the big masters of commerce, the heads of railroad corporations and of steamship companies." Wilson saw that "American enterprise is not free" and has been replaced by "a great economic system which is heartless" and moves in an "un-American set of conditions." But all was not yet bigness, and the little Jewish immigrants, crowding up along the bottoms of sections of the economy not yet monopolized, found ways of getting a toehold. They fought fiercely and successfully to remain and to advance.

Throughout the country, American workers, Jews conspicuously among them, turned to organization and harsh struggle. Harassed by the economic crises of 1903, 1907-08, 1910-11 and 1913-14, they sought to protect and if possible improve their working and living conditions. Employers, especially the big ones, were ruthless. The National Association of Manufacturers, in the crisis year of 1903, issued its open-shop "Declaration of Labor Principles," opposing labor organization and advocating individual bargaining between a worker and his employer. Equality was parodied and democracy reduced to the "right" of Joe Worker individually and personally to "bargain" with J. P. Morgan. The industrial magnates manipulated the courts to get injunctions against strikers, to deny the right of free speech, to try to frame-up labor leaders like Charles Moyer, William D. Haywood and George Pettibone of the Western Federation of Miners and the Industrial Workers of the World. Violence by vigilantes and soldiers was turned on the most stubborn workers. In a 16 month struggle for the eight-hour day in Colorado, 42 workers were killed, 112 wounded, 1,345 arrested and 773 deported in 1903-04. Ten years later in Ludlow, Colorado, during a strike of the United Mine workers against a Rockefeller enterprise, company thugs and National Guardsmen set fire to strikers' tents and shot and killed five men, two women and 13 children.

Only organization, collective bargaining, soli-

Lillian D. Wald (1867-1940), social work pioneer.

darity and co-operation could help the workers and they turned in this direction. The trade unions grew in size and number. The A. F. of L. rose from 548,000 members in 1900 to 2,021,000 in 1914, which was still, however, only about three-quarters of the total union membership. Strikes were common, often large-scale and prolonged. Those led or stimulated by the I. W. W. were militant. Whatever its sectarian weaknesses, the I. W. W., formed in 1905, "spectacularly centered attention," as Foster Rhea Dulles noted in *Labor in America* in 1947, "on the desperate needs of vast numbers of unskilled workers." And among the Jews, even skilled workers, impatient with certain garment union leaders, were attracted by the militancy of the I.W.W. The gains the workers made were chiefly in reduction of hours. In unionized and skilled trades, hours were cut from 54.4 in 1890 to 48.9 in 1914; this reduction helped cut the hours of unorganized and unskilled labor from 62.2 to 55.6 hours a week. Increases in wages, however, while won by strug-

gle and organization, "were swallowed up by commensurate increases in the cost of living," as shown in the studies of Professor Paul H. Douglas, *Real Wages in the United States, 1890-1926.*

Other sections of the underprivileged masses were also under sharp attack. The Negro people suffered especially. These were the years in which, by terror and unjust legislation, the rulers of the South tore from the Negroes all the rights and opportunities they had won during Reconstruction and imposed brazen disfranchisement and rigid segregation upon them. In 1900, at least 104 Negroes were lynched, and by 1914 the number of victims of murderous mobs had reached 1,079. "Race riots," which were very much like pogroms, worried immigrant Jews, who assumed they had witnessed the last of such terrors when they had emigrated. In August, 1900 there was a "race riot" right in New York! The most serious was the Atlanta Massacre in September, 1906, during which ten Negroes, including two women, were killed and 60 seriously injured, while two whites lost their lives and ten were wounded. But the one that got national and somewhat remorseful attention occurred in August, 1908 in Springfield, Ill., which prided itself upon being the home town of Lincoln. The irony of a "race riot" in Springfield punctured the democratic conscience.

One consequence was the founding of the National Association for the Advancement of Colored People. Already in 1905 the Niagara Movement of Negro intellectuals and business men had been founded, under the inspiration of Dr. W.E.B. Du Bois, that new insistent voice of the Negro people calling for full equality. After the Springfield affair, the Socialist, William English Walling, sparked activity with the radical, Mary White Ovington, and the liberal Democrat, Dr. Henry Moskowitz, that led to the merger of the Niagara Movement into the N.A.A.C.P. Among the 49 persons who signed the call for the conference held on Lincoln's Birthday, 1909, there were six Negro leaders, several socialists, and four prominent Jews: Rabbi Emil G. Hirsch of Chicago, Dr. Henry Moskowitz, a figure in Mayor John P. Mitchell's administration in New York, Rabbi Stephen S. Wise, and Miss Lillian

An anti-Semitic cartoon by Harrison Cady, in the center-spread of "Life," May 12, 1910, entitled "The Surrender of New York Town."

D. Wald of the Henry Street Settlement on the East Side of New York. Soon thereafter, Professor Joel Elias Spingarn became one of the national leaders of the N. A. A. C. P., holding various offices, including those of Treasurer and President, for more than 25 years, until his death in 1939.

Next only to the Negro people, the immigrant masses became favorite targets of those who, by spreading nativism, were consciously or blindly averting the attention of some of the discontented from real problems and real solutions. The racist theme became dominant in anti-alien nativist propaganda. "White Supremacy" theories that had been directed against Negroes and Asians were now turned against Italians and Jews. Nativism surged in the South and West as well as on the northeastern seaboard, where these immigrants were heavily concentrated. The Jews faced not only social exclusion but active discrimination in employment. Petty violence in the form of public name-calling, beard-pulling and hoodlum roughing-up antics was not uncom-

mon. Serious violence erupted on July 30, 1902. As tens of thousands of Jews were taking part in the funeral of Rabbi Jacob Joseph on the East Side of New York, workmen in the R. H. Hoe and Co. printing machinery plant barraged the mourners with stones and scrap metal. When the Jews fought back, the police zestfully attacked the funeral procession, doing more damage than the original assailants. The resulting official investigation into anti-Semitism in the police force led the Brooklyn *Standard Union* to conclude editorially that "this riot may result in better treatment of the Jews. If it does the suffering and loss will not have been in vain."

Some ten years later, however, the Jews had to endure a much greater ordeal, the frame-up of Leo Frank in Atlanta, Georgia, in an atmosphere of intense and shrill anti-Semitic propaganda. Frank, superintendent of a small pencil factory, was accused of the rape and murder of Mary Phagan, a 13 year old worker in the plant. Sentenced to death after a sensationalized trial that ended August 21, 1913, Frank became the focus

A left-wing comment on the lynching of Leo Frank: cartoon by Robert Minor on the cover of "The Masses," August, 1915, entitled, "In Georgia. The Southern Gentleman Demonstrates His Superiority."

of a nation-wide campaign by Jews and other supporters of justice. At the same time, Jews here learned with horror that the Tsarist government had indicted a Jewish worker, Mendel Beilis, on a charge of ritual murder in Kiev. On October 10, 1913, Frank was to be executed, but a postponement was won. In Kiev on October 28, 1913, a jury made up mainly of peasants rejected the frame-up and acquitted Mendel Beilis. The movement to free Frank spread; a second and third time the date of execution was postponed. On the eve of the fourth date, June 21, 1915, the Governor of Georgia commuted the sentence to life imprisonment. On August 17 came the final horror: an armed band took Frank from prison, drove him to Marietta,

Georgia, Mary Phagan's home town, and lynched him. No attempt was made to bring the lynchers to trial. Thus frame-up and lynch law, which had so often hit Negroes, Indians, Italians, and labor organizers, struck directly at a Jew in a case in which anti-Semitism was blatantly involved.

Yet these developments were taking place in a period generally called the "Progressive Era." As has been noted, the struggles and organization of the workers did spur a reform movement among the middle classes. Reforms were achieved in many municipal and state governments, in the unfolding of labor and social legislation, in the development of democratic forms of mass participation in politics and in the size of the electorate by state woman suffrage laws. By 1915, 25 states had laws limiting the working day and 35 had workmen's compensation laws. By 1912, 38 states had child labor laws, and Massachusetts became the first state to pass a minimum wage law, with eight states following its example in 1913. By 1914, eleven states had woman suffrage and Illinois allowed women to vote for President. In 1913, the Sixteenth and Seventeenth amendments to the United States Constitution went into effect: the first authorized federal income taxes, formerly considered socialistic, and the second provided for election of United States Senators not by the state legislatures but by direct popular vote. To give the electorate a chance to initiate legislation by popular referendum, several states, beginning with Oregon in 1902, adopted initiative and referendum laws. To limit the absolute power of political bosses in selecting candidates, direct primary laws were introduced, starting with Wisconsin in 1903.

At the base of these and other reforms was the upward pressure of actively organized workers, who realized that not only trade union but political activity was important. In 1901, when the Socialist Party was established with a membership of some 10,000, about 300 socialists were elected to local office. By 1912, not only had the dues-paying party membership grown to 125,826, but 1,039 Socialists were elected officials in 36 states. There were 56 Mayors, over 300 Aldermen, one Congressman, several state legislators,

and a host of local officers. In 1914, 31 socialists were elected to the legislatures of 13 states. In 1912, despite the reform platforms of Theodore Roosevelt and Woodrow Wilson, the socialist Debs got 900,000 votes, 6% of the total. This general socialist surge fused with the new militancy sparked by Jewish refugees from the defeated Russian Revolution to turn the Jewish masses into a stronghold of socialist activity. Debs had no more loyal base anywhere than among the Jewish workers.

The major critique of society by working class socialism stimulated less basic but intense criticism by middle class elements whose conscience was affronted by ostentatious civic corruption as their security was threatened by the expanding trusts. In 1901, when Lincoln Steffens became editor of *McClure's Magazine,* he began a journalistic crusade for the exposure of social rot. He was soon joined by magazines like *Collier's, Munsey's, Everybody's, Cosmopolitan,* the *Independent,* and the *American Magazine.* While Thomas W. Lawson exposed the Money Trust (1902), Ida M. Tarbell the Oil Trust (1903), Charles Edward Russell the Beef Trust (1905), Ray Stannard Baker the railroads and David Graham Phillips the Senate (1906), and Burton J. Hendrick the Life Insurance operators, Steffens himself concentrated on the muckraking exposure of the ties between business, the underworld, and the system of political power. *In Shame of the Cities* in 1904 and *The Struggle for Self-Government* in 1906 he brilliantly bared the corruption on the municipal and state levels. In 1910, in describing "It," or "the Sovereign Political Power of Organized Business" in *Everybody's Magazine,* Steffens shrewdly observed that, because of anti-Semitism among the biggest financiers, the Jewish bankers were excluded from "It," the "sovereign political power." (The muckrakers as a whole, incidentally, were very sympathetic to the immigrant Jewish masses, especially to the militant workers, and did much to create a friendly opinion of them.)

The very conspicuousness of wealth underlined what Jacob H. Hollander, a Jewish professor of economics at Johns Hopkins University, called "the needlessness of poverty" in *The Abolition of*

Jewish girls working in the canning factory at the agricultural settlement at Norma,
N. J. in 1907.

Poverty in 1914. "The very forces which increase the national product and enlarge the social surplus, if left to themselves," Hollander wrote, "breed conditions of want. . . . Now, in our own day, the conquest of poverty looms up as an economic possibility, definitely within our reach—if only society desire it sufficiently and will pay enough to achieve it." As remedies, Hollander advocated collective bargaining through unions, unemployment insurance, and social insurance for the sick and aged. Nevertheless Hollander ended futilely as an advisor to Republican presidents, including Harding.

A stream of socially realistic and critical literature merged with the flood of journalistic exposure. The first radical or proletarian novel of the century was *By Bread Alone* by a Chicago Jewish socialist, Isaac Kahn Friedman, published by McClure, Phillips and Company in 1901. "A solidly realized novel of contemporary life," it deals with conditions in a steel-town, including a bloody strike based on the one in Homestead; the Jewish theme is marginal, but there is much insight into immigrant life. "By a neat and not unrelated coincidence," the book was issued the year the Steel Trust was born. The same year, in his novel *The Octopus,* Frank Norris showed the wheat-growers in the toils of the Southern Pacific Railroad, and in *The Pit* (1903) he followed them into the den of the grain speculators in Chicago. In *The Jungle* (1906), the socialist Upton Sinclair combined a picture of the exploitation of Bohemian immigrant workers in the Chicago stockyards with such a vivid depiction of the disease-breeding filth of the meatpacking industry that the American gorge rose in defense of its own health and stomach. Congress had to pass meat inspection and pure food and drug acts. Another socialist, Jack London, in *The Iron Heel* (1908) dramatically predicted that the capitalist oligarchy would use force to prevent Socialists from taking office and power once they are elected. During these years, also, Theodore Dreiser began those studies in social realism in which he deeply and enduringly probed the effect of the social system on morals, human relations and human character, in novels like *Sister Carrie* (1900), *Jennie Gerhardt* (1911), *The Financier* (1912) and *The Titan* (1914).

The exposure by journalists and novelists of the deep immorality of our society was accompanied by spiritual disquiet in part of the religious leadership of the nation. The Christian Socialist Fellowship, founded in 1906 and openly supporting the Socialist Party, numbered about 300 clergymen in 1908. The Methodist Federation for Social Service was founded in 1907, the year in which Walter Rauschenbusch wrote *Christianity and the Social Crisis,* calling for the revival of the social gospel. In 1908, the General Conference of the Methodists promulgated "The Social Creed of the Churches." Among the Jews also the theme of social justice became ever louder in religious circles. "Between 1910 and 1915," concluded one student of this subject, "social justice became almost an obsession with the rabbis. The pulpit spoke of it incessantly. The Jewish periodicals were filled with it." This interest was expressed also in the Central Conference of American Rabbis (Reform) through the Committee on Synagogue and Labor, 1910, the Committee on Synagogue and Industrial Relations, 1913, and most effectively through the Committee on Social Justice created in 1914.

It was this gathering head of social steam, rising from the active discontent of the working class and the fears of the middle classes, that pressed the gauge of "Progressivism" upward. In 1901, with Tom L. Johnson as Mayor of Cleveland and Robert M. LaFollette as Governor of Wisconsin, reform gained momentum. By 1912, municipal reform movements and administrations were widespread, and eight states (New York, New Jersey, North Carolina, Michigan, Iowa, Wisconsin, Texas and California) were in the progressive camp. In 1901, also, Theodore Roosevelt had stepped into the White House, making the loud noises for reform that both expressed and intensified the middle classes' sentiments for reform. He denounced "malefactors of great wealth" and won a reputation as a "trust-buster" at a time when the trusts were in fact growing unprecedentedly during his administrations, 1901-1909. Of progressive accomplishment

United States Supreme Court Justice Louis D. Brandeis (1856-1941).

there was pathetically little: Roosevelt fought private plundering of natural resources and railroad rebates to favored customers; he secured the enactment of the meat-inspection, pure food and workmen's compensation laws; he persuaded the coal operators to arbitrate the coal strike, and appointed Oliver Wendell Holmes to the Supreme Court, in which he became the Great Dissenter. Roosevelt was nevertheless, as Professor Eric F. Goldman says, "progressivism incarnate" for the vast majority of reformers because, as Professor Richard Hofstadter has discerned, "the Progressive mind was easy to please." The progressive who was hard to please, a Lincoln Steffens, decided at this time that what was needed was not social reform but social revolution.

Easy or hard to please, the people of progressive views had a multiple choice in the 1912 presidential election. A new light of reform had appeared

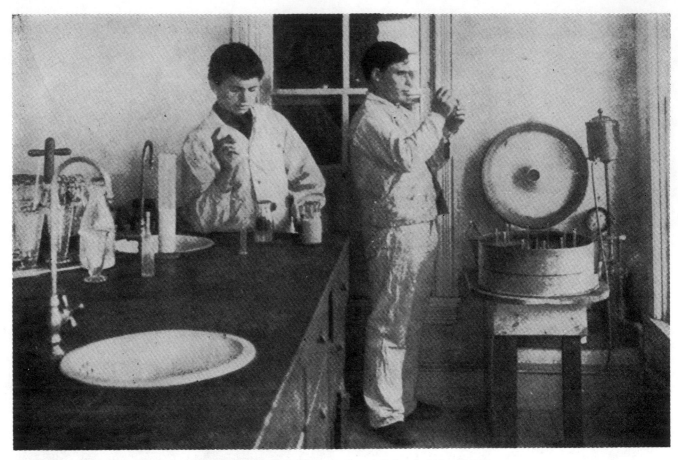

Students in the laboratory at the Baron De Hirsch Agricultural School, Woodbine, N. J., in 1907.

in Gov. Woodrow Wilson of New Jersey. In the summer of 1912, Wilson met Louis D. Brandeis, already known as "the people's lawyer" because of his anti-monopoly position. "And it was Brandeis," in the judgment of Professor Arthur S. Link, Wilson biographer, "who clarified Wilson's thought and led him to believe the most vital question confronting the American people was preservation of economic freedom in the United States." Progressive opinion rallied to Wilson's slogan of the New Freedom and to his anti-monopoly program. Theodore Roosevelt having seceded from the Republicans and founded the Progressive Party, there was a three-cornered race (in New York, Oscar S. Straus ran as candidate for Governor on Roosevelt's ticket). The popular vote was: for the progressive Democrat, Wilson, 6,293,019; for the Progressive, Roosevelt, 4,119,507; for the conservative Republican, President William Howard Taft, 3,484,956; for the Socialist, Debs, 901,873. As Professor Link

remarks, "the country was now overwhelmingly progressive in temper," and "all major parties suffered a relative and absolute decline in 1912, because about half a million disgruntled progressives voted for Debs." A people groping for political progress in a country in which, as Brandeis wrote in 1913, a few "bankers bestride as masters America's business world"—such was the essential character of the United States during this period when the Jewish population was being tripled.

The Jewish masses contributed to, and were also heartened by, the general "progressive temper." Of course they had brought with them a hatred of tyranny, and a dream of democratic and even socialist ideals. There took place a two-sided process of reacting to American reality: disappointment in the bald contrast between democratic ideals and their limited application under business domination, and encouragement in finding the people actively engaged in the struggle to realize and even expand these ideals.

The bulk of the Jewish population consisted of wage-workers, most of them slaving away in sweatshops. Dependent upon the economic life of these wage-workers was a large body of small traders, many of them the smallest of the small: selling from pushcarts, from box-like sidewalk stands, or in tiny stores and cellars. From this mass, driven by necessity, there grew mass organization and mass struggle, on a new scale.

These were the years in which Jewish workers built their *national* trade union, fraternal and political organizations. In the case of the unions, the structures raised were at first small shells; mass membership was not won until they led the great strikes that marked the heroic period of the American Jewish labor movement from 1909 to 1914. Yet the effort to establish a national trade union was the necessary next step that flowed from the workers' experience in organizing local unions and city-wide federations. The growing concentration of Jews in the various branches of the garment industry made this the most important arena for Jewish working class organization. Thus in 1900 there was founded the International Ladies Garment Workers' Union, in

---

CONSTITUTION OF THE INTERNATIONAL LADIES' GARMENT WORKERS' UNION.

PREAMBLE.

Recognizing the urgent necessity of unity among the several branches of workers engaged in the manufacture of ladies' garments, if it is desired to effectively resist the united efforts of the employers to reduce the workers to the condition of obedient wage-slaves ready to work for a pittance, we have organized the INTERNATIONAL LADIES' GARMENT WORKERS' UNION. It is intended to bring together all workers, regardless of race, nationality, creed or sex, employed in the manufacture of cloaks, suits, skirts, ladies' waists, tailor-made gowns, dresses, etc., so as to present a solid front in cases where the workers of one branch of this great industry are trying to better their condition by demanding living wages or reasonable hours of labor.

Preamble to the Constituton of the I.L.G.W.U., 1902.

קאָנסטיטוציאָן

— פון די —

יוניטעד קלאָטה-העט אונד קעפ מייקערס

אָף נאָרטה   אַמעריקא

פעראייניגט מיט די

אמעריקאַן פעדערײשאָן אָף לייבאָר.

צרגאָניזירט מאַרטש 20טען, 1901.

Title-page of the Constitution of the United Cloth-Hat and Cap Makers of North America, 1901.

1901 the United Cloth Hat and Cap Makers of North America, and in 1904 the International Association of Fur Workers of the United States and Canada. The fur union, failing to organize the Jewish furriers in New York, collapsed and a new one did not replace it until after a major strike in 1912. The cap makers, with 1,200 members in six cities at the time of the birth of the union, included only part of the Jews in the headgear industry: in Newark there were 1,300 Jewish hatters, who had finally been admitted in 1900 to the United Hatters of North America, after having been excluded for a decade by an arti-Semitic policy. The men's garment workers were still kept from effective organization by the bureaucracy of the United Garment Workers'

Union and it took the gigantic struggles of 1910 to 1914 to create a new and effective union.

The most significant of these unions at this time was the I. L. G. W. U. At its birth at the convention of June 3, 1900, there were only 2,310 members represented in the seven locals in New York, Brownsville in Brooklyn, Philadelphia, Baltimore and Newark. The militant mood of the workers was expressed in the winning of 158 out of the 189 local strikes conducted in the first two years. By 1904, there were 5,400 members in 66 locals in 27 cities. Growth was slow because of the cautious policy, patterned on the American Federation of Labor's example, thus described by Louis Levine, historian of that period of the union's development: "There was a definite desire to restrain the workers from striking often. Organization and preparation were the main slogans. High dues were advocated as a means of building up a strong treasury. A system of sick-and-death, strike and out-of-work benefits was recommended to the local unions. Boycotts were advocated and used. But above all, faith was pinned to the union label." When masses finally did join the union it was because this policy gave way to one of mass struggle.

The membership was also socialist-minded. Although President Gompers of the A. F. L. had declared in 1901 that "socialism . . . has no place in a trade union," the I.L.G.W.U. ignored this dictate. The 1902 convention refused to listen to a non-socialist assemblyman and amended the union constitution to bar Democratic or Republican office-holders from addressing future conventions. In 1903, the convention congratulated the Socialist Party on its support of trade unionism (in contrast to the Socialist Labor Party attitude) and recommended the study of the socialist movement to all union members. The 1904 convention resolved "to permit the discussion of socialism" at the conventions themselves. So pervasive was this socialist sentiment that conservative leaders of the union had to appeal to it to win support for their proposals. Thus at the 1905 convention, in a resolution for a union label campaign, they felt impelled to glorify the useful but hardly revolutionary union label as "the best means of emancipation of the working classes from the oppression of capitalism."

Aiding the trade union movement was the first national labor fraternal organization, the Workmen's Circle (*Arbeiter Ring*), founded September 4, 1900. At that time there were twelve Jewish fraternal bodies in the country, but their membership was largely middle class. The innumerable *landsmanshaften*, which had mutual aid features, were all-class in composition, including many workers, but the leadership and social outlook were generally of the middle-class. Class-conscious workers wanted their very own mutual aid organization.

The need was urgent. In the total absence of any forms of social insurance, the catastrophe of unemployment or family illness was cushioned for the worker only by private charity. At the first meeting of the National Conference of Jewish Charities, held in Chicago in 1900, there was discussion of the problems of poverty, slum housing, tuberculosis, desertion of families, and vocational training. Undoubtedly "Jewish Charity" was beginning to win public recognition as a leader in the field of private American charity. Yet the workers were humiliated by and resented the inevitable condescension of the "benevolent" and the "philanthropic." In the Workmen's Circle the worker kept his self-respect because he was participating in a program of self-help with fellow-workers. The order grew by leaps from a membership of 300 in 1900 to 48,000 in 546 branches in 1915. At this time it was larger than the B'nai B'rith (40,000), and was outstripped only by the Independent Order Brith Abraham (192,000), the Order of Brith Abraham (72,000), and the Independent Order Brith Sholom (50,000).

In its first ten years, the Workmen's Circle paid out in benefits to its members $263,867. In the crisis year of 1908, when the United Hebrew Charities had to shut their doors because they could not meet the needs of the needy, the Workmen's Circle paid out $35,211 in sick benefits and $4,025 in special monies to consumptive members. The ravage of this "workers' disease" was intense. In 1909, of the 61 members who died, 14 were victims of consumption and pneumonia.

A group of founders of the Workmen's Circle, left to right, top to bottom: M. Schwartz, S. Becker, L. Kelman, M. Goldreich, D. Gingold, L. Kozlin, A. Goldsmith, H. Lasker.

The original building in 1899 of the National Jewish Hospital at Denver, Colorado.

On February 12, 1910, the Workmen's Circle opened, at Liberty, N. Y., its sanitarium for the tubercular, the second in the United States, the National Jewish Hospital at Denver, founded in 1899 by B'nai B'rith having been the first.

For the Workmen's Circle, mutual aid was for the present, but only socialism would do as a future. *Mir Kemfen Gegen Krankheit, Fri-Zeitigen Toit, un Capitalismus* (We Fight Against Sickness, Premature Death, and Capitalism) was inscribed on the cover of the Report to the Fifth Convention in 1905. Until 1920, the constitution pledged the members to vote only for socialist candidates. The intense cultural life of the branches, with lectures, readings, singing, dramatizations and recitations, was steeped in the Yiddish literature of social protest and socialist idealism.

Socialist thinking was the main force at the time in organizing both the Jewish trade union and labor fraternal movement. The political organization of socialists, therefore, also expanded. Stimulus and recruits for socialism came often from the East European Jewish socialist movement, which in 1897 had given birth to the Algemeiner Idisher Arbeterbund in Lita, Poilen un Rusland (General Jewish Labor Federation of Lithuania, Poland and Russia), known as the "Bund." In 1900, a branch was formed in New York, consisting of immigrant Russian Bundists and their supporters. By 1904 there were enough branches to hold a convention and found the Friends of the Bund, whose main interest was the support of Bund activities in the old coun-

tries. In the meantime, Yiddish-speaking members of the Socialist Party, like those of the Socialist Labor Party before them, had been holding occasional conferences since 1902. By 1907 there emerged a Yiddish Agitation Bureau to issue propaganda and to direct socialist activity in the trade unions. Bundist refugees from the defeated Russian Revolution of 1905 promoted the desire for a separate federation, such as the Finns and Letts had established here. The 1910 decision of the Socialist Party to accept affiliation of such foreign-language federations led to the birth of six more bodies by 1912, including the Jewish Socialist Federation, founded in Paterson, N. J. on May 20, 1912. In 1913, since the *Forward* did not adequately publicize Federation activities, it began to issue the *Yiddish Sozialist* as a weekly. By 1915, the Federation had about 5,000 members in 90 branches in 21 states and the District of Columbia (22 in New York, 10 in Massachusetts, 9 each in New Jersey and Connecticut, 7 in Ohio, 6 in Pennsylvania, etc.). At the same time, many English-speaking Jews were active in the general organization of the S. P., among them such national leaders as Morris Hillquit, Victor Berger and Meyer London.

Another trend was born in the ranks of labor in 1903 when the first Labor Zionist group was formed in New York. But as David Wertheim, national secretary of the movement in 1942, observed in his article in the *Universal Jewish Encyclopedia*, labor Zionism met "strong resistance on the part of the Jewish workers, who were largely influenced by the anti-nationalist socialism which, at that time, dominated the Jewish labor movement." To class conscious Jewish workers fighting bitterly against the Jewish sweatshop employers, the idea that the workers could take a stand alongside their employers on a platform of Zionism flew in the face of immediate reality. Zionism was seen as a diversion from grim struggles on hand and a confusing dilution of class consciousness. In March, 1906, a New York conference of Yiddish-speaking socialists therefore refused to seat delegates sent by the just formed Jewish Socialist-Territorialist Labor Party.

Nevertheless the labor Zionist movement grew

Victor L. Berger (1860-1929), the first socialist elected to Congress, 1911-1915.

Morris Hillquit (1869-1933).

Meyer London (1871-1926).

slowly and modestly in both its wings, the Jewish Socialist Labor Party Poale Zion, founded December, 1905, and the Socialist-Territorialists (who did not insist on Palestine only as the site for a Jewish homeland). By 1915 the first had 3,500 members in 72 branches and the second 3,000 in 43 branches. In 1912, moreover, the labor Zionists had formed their own fraternal

Hayim Greenberg (1889-1953), Labor Zionist leader.

order, the Jewish National Workers Alliance of America. There were 95 branches with 5,000 members by 1915, not only with the mutual aid benefits they had formerly found in the Workmen's Circle but with a Zionist cultural program. Yet *Der Idisher Kemfer,* the labor Zionist weekly organ, begun in 1906 with Kalman Marmor as the first editor, ceased publication in 1911 and was not revived until 1917.

Labor Zionist work had three aspects: to interest workers in Zionism, in aid to and in personal emigration to Palestine; to advance a labor platform for Palestine within the general Zionist movement; to take some part in the American labor movement. The Poale Zion supported Eugene V. Debs and other socialist candidates, while many labor Zionists as individuals were active in trade unions and in the general branches of the Socialist Party. Labor Zionists preferred to join these branches rather than Yiddish-speaking branches where the anti-Zionist feeling was strong. In sum, the labor Zionists laid no more than a foundation of their movement before the first World War.

Among the Jewish population and in the eyes of the general public, these Zionist developments were heavily overshadowed by the desperate and dramatic mass trade union struggles that have led to the designation of the five years preceding the First World War as the "heroic period" in

The Executive Committee of Waist Makers Local 25, I.L.G.W.U. in 1910, shortly after it led the great shirt-waist makers' strike of 1909-1910. Third from the left in the top row is Clara Lemlich; Morris Winchevsky, accountant for the local, is seated in the ornate chair.

the Jewish labor movement. There was sheer rebellion in the shops by some 200,000 workers, facing unbearably long hours of toil in filthy surroundings, subject to the indignities of arrogant foremen and bosses, and hearbreakingly trying to provide a decent living for their families on miserably low wages. Unions that were hardly more than skeletons after the crisis years of 1907-09 took on solid flesh as they led masses of workers in unyielding struggle in New York, Chicago, Philadelphia, Boston, Baltimore, Cleveland and other cities. For the first time. the Jewish unions had mass memberships, which could enforce the contracts won in battle, consolidate the gains, and prepare for new advances. In New York, the United Hebrew Trades had 61 unions with 65,000 members in 1910; in 1914, there were 104 unions with 250,000 members. In the garment trades, the unions increased their membership by 68 per cent between 1910 and 1913, gaining 66,000 members (while the A. F. of L. as a whole grew by 28 per cent, with only the

miners' union approaching the garment workers with a 60 per cent growth).

Jewish workers struck in a variety of trades as the Jewish neighborhoods buzzed and bubbled with news of organization, demands, picket lines and victories. The tinsmiths, the laundry workers, the retail clerks struck and won. The dollmakers, their lungs clogging with the sawdust they had to breathe, won a bitter strike to compel employers to put in exhausts to clear the air. Jewish butchers were getting $12 to $18 a month with room and board in the home of the boss; a strike won them $12 to $18 a week, and the precious right to live where they pleased. The Jewish bakers, lowest of the low, sweated 18 hours a day six days a week for $8 to $11; a seven week strike won a 10-hour day with wages $12 to $16 a week—and yeast-like the union grew. Yet these were only the little struggles. The big ones were in the garment trades.

First to erupt, literally, were the ladies' shirtwaistmakers. Young women, 16 to 25, were work ing 56 hours a week for low wages made still lower by charges for electricity used at the machines, for chairs and lockers in the unsanitary shops. The union had 100 members and a treasury of $4 when the organizing drive began in July 1909. But the workers were ripe for action. When the eloquent little Clara Lemlich interrupted a packed meeting at Cooper Union in New York on November 22 with her passionate call for general strike, what followed was an avalanche. "The Uprising of the 20,000" was what a sympathetic press named the high-tension struggle. Most of the strikers were Jewish immigrants, with a couple of thousand Italian. Mass picketing, demonstrations and parades maintained workers' solidarity and evoked the sympathy of middle class elements like the Women's Trade Union League and Rabbi Stephen S. Wise. Violence was used against the workers. By December 25, 723 strikers had been arrested and 19 sent to the workhouse, but neither terrorism, hunger nor cold could break the strike. When it ended on February 15, 1910, more than 300 of the 500 struck firms settled on the union's terms of a 52 hour week, wage increases, and union recognition. Local 25 of the I.L.G.W.U. emerged with a membership of 10,000. The entire American trade union movement applauded the gallant shirtwaist-makers.

A chain reaction began. The New York cloakmakers had been preparing for a general strike against conditions so backward that half the workers still had to lug their own sewing machines on their backs into the shops. In April, 1910, the New York Joint Board of Cloak and Skirt Makers Unions began to publish *Di Neie Post* to promote organization for the strike. Workers flocked to the union. The secret strike ballot on July 2 and 3 registered 18,771 for striking, 615 against. More than 50,000 workers left 1,500 shops at the call of the special red-paper strike issue of *Di Neie Post* on July 7. This was the biggest strike New York had seen. Week after week the workers' determination and enthusiasm remained high, although the mass picketing was often met by police clubs and the violence of the bosses' special guards. Late in August the employers tried to break the strike by winning a

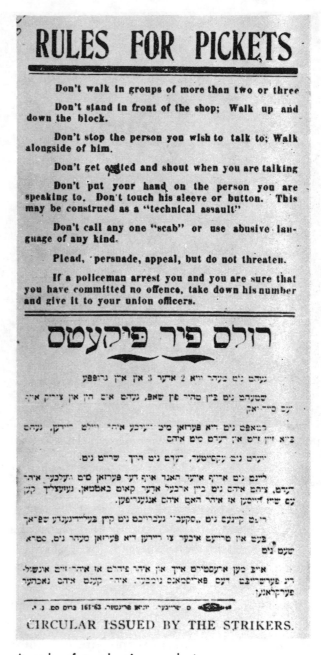

CIRCULAR ISSUED BY THE STRIKERS.

A code of good union conduct.

court injunction described by the *New York Times* as "the strongest decision ever handed down against labor."

When the manufacturers on September 2 offered a compromise with important concessions, the Strike Committee yielded, and with the support of only 200 hastily assembled shop chairmen, accepted the Protocol of Peace, the first collective bargaining agreement in the industry. The workers had won a 50 hour week, ten legal holidays, free electricity for the machines, weekly pay in cash, no home work, limitations on over-

The painting by Philip Reisman depicting the shirt-waist makers' strike, commisisoned by the Emma Lazarus Federation of Women's Clubs for the Tercentenary of Jewish Settlement, 1954. Clara Lemlich is shown at Cooper Union administering the "Jewish oath"; Samuel Gompers is next to her.

time, a joint board of sanitary control, a committee on grievances and compulsory arbitration, and price settlements to be made by negotiation in each shop. One point hitherto considered crucial was missing: the closed shop. Instead Louis D. Brandeis as mediator had secured agreement on the "preferential union shop," which allowed the employer to retain scabs and hire non-union members provided they then joined the union. Although the manufacturers terminated the Protocol in 1915, the greatest of the victories was not affected: the union emerged with vast strength. By January 1912, the New York Joint Board had over 50,000 members, and 1,796 out of 1,829 shops were under contract.

Three weeks after the Protocol of Peace was signed in New York, a wage cut in Chicago sparked a strike that soon involved 40,000 men's garment workers, mostly Jewish, but with large numbers of Italians, Poles, Lithuanians and Czechs. The violence against the workers was intense: seven were killed and 374 arrested. More

demoralizing were the misleading policies of the national leaders of the United Garment Workers, headed by the conservative bureaucrat, Thomas E. Rickert, who made every effort to drive the strikers back to work with no agreement and no union recognition. A partial victory was won by the 8,000 workers of Hart, Schaffner and Marx, who consented to arbitration on January 14, 1911; they were awarded a 10 per cent wage rise, a 54-hour week, time and a half for overtime, a grievance machinery and an arbitration apparatus. But the other 30,000 workers were finally ordered back to work by Rickert on February 3, gaining nothing but the experience of treachery among their national leaders. Although no powerful union came out of this strike, there did appear figures like Sidney Hillman, Frank Rosenblum, Sam Levin, and Bessie Abramowitz (later Mrs. Hillman) who three years later led in the founding of a new mass union in the men's garment industry.

In New York, the Jewish workers were still

The scene of the Triangle Fire, March 25, 1911.

Bessie Abramovitz (later Mrs. Sidney Hillman), when she was a leader in Local 152, United Garment Workers of America.

aglow with their victories of 1910 when a new nightmare burst upon them. The Triangle Waist Company, employing over 700 in its factory on Washington Place, had been a center of the shirtwaist makers' strike in 1909. Harris and Blanck, the owners, kept the factory doors locked during working hours; the demands of the union for fire escapes were ignored. Thus when fire struck on Saturday, March 25, 1911 the workers were sealed in and charred bodies piled up inside the immovable doors. The only exits were the windows, ten stories high, from which many jumped flaming to their death. The dead alone numbered 143, most of them Jewish girls and young women. Numb with horror, the Jews sat out their week of mourning. When on April 5 the union organized a funeral procession, 50,000 marched silently in the rain, hushed in the ominous unity of grief and hatred. When Yehoash, whose poem on March 28 was the first to appear, challenged the "Priests of Mammon" to deny their guilt, the people echoed his cry. Their mood was pro-

The Call to the funeral procession for the victims of the Triangle Fire.

foundly expressed by Morris Rosenfeld in his organ-toned poem of lamentation, "The Red Terror." He exclaimed (in literal prose translation): "Drape yourself in black, you Golden Land! Too deep your crime, too horrible your shame, Too deaf your conscience, too blind your law, Too hellish your 'care,' too bloody your net, Your net, which catches your poor—The time will come! . . . Your time will come! . . ." (In poem, play, story and novel, the theme recurred down to the 1940's, lighting up in its glare a corner of the life the immigrant Jewish masses once led.)

The decisive strike struggles continued. The fur-workers were the next to rally. Although the national union had folded, the United Hebrew Trades had by the spring of 1912 established three locals with 3,000 of the 10,000 workers in the field. By a vote of 2,135 to 364, the workers launched a general strike in New York on June

20, involving 8,500 men and women, three-fourths of them Jewish. A month later, when 1,000 German workers came out, the strike was solid. Thugs hired by the employers accentuated the violence. Over 800 strikers were arrested, 54 getting workhouse sentences, while 215 were seriously injured by the clubs and knives of the thugs. Finally on September 8, a two-year agreement was signed, including a cut in the workweek from 56 to 49 hours, ten legal holidays, time and a half for overtime in the busy season, a joint sanitary committee, and wages to be paid weekly in cash. This victory and the organization of the bulk of the furriers into New York unions paved the way for the revival of the national union in the industry, which was chartered by the A. F. of L. July 1, 1913.

Still unorganized, and therefore suffering the worst conditions in the clothing trades, were the men's garment workers, among whom there were tens of thousands of Jews. Spurred on by the struggles all around them, the workers practically forced the indifferent leaders of the United Garment Workers to move into action. Aided by the United Hebrew Trades, a recruiting campaign in the fall of 1912 swelled the union. Balloting in December showed 35,786 for a general strike and 2,322 against it. On December 30, when the strike began in New York, 75,000 turned out and in a week there were more than 100,000 on strike, 35,000 of them women. Soon supporting general strikes broke out in Philadelphia, Buffalo and Rochester. Next to the majority of Jews, there were many thousands of Italians and smaller numbers of Poles, Russians, Lithuanians, Hungarians, Greeks, Germans, Czechs and others. The strike was a triumph of labor solidarity.

When the united and determined workers rejected an agreement containing petty concessions, President Rickert of the United Garment Workers repeated his Chicago performance of 1910, but without the same success. Disregarding the strike leadership and the workers, Rickert brazenly signed an agreement with the employers which one local union aptly labeled as "treacherous . . . a shame and an insult." At that point the *Jewish Daily Forward*, which with its circulation of over 130,000 had been a powerful factor in building the union and supporting the strike, suddenly came out in favor of Rickert's agreement. Incensed at this not unusual reversal, thousands of strikers on March 1, 1913 streamed in wrath to the Forward Building and smashed its windows. The employers learned the lesson, and on March 12 signed an agreement that included union recognition, a 52 hour week by 1914 and wage increases.

No agreement, however, could be reached between the militant workers in the union and its domineering President Rickert. When in October 1914 his machine at the Nashville convention refused to seat the delegates that actually represented a majority of the membership, the excluded delegates held a separate conference. There they laid plans for the convention in December at which the Amalgamated Clothing Workers of America was born, with an initial membership of 38,000—which more than doubled in three years. The Preamble to the Constitution of the new Union reflected some of the socialist principles of the leadership and sections of the membership. "A constant and unceasing struggle is being waged," declared the Preamble, between the class owning the means of production and "the class that possess nothing but its labor power." In the light of recent developments, "the working class must accept the principles of Industrial Unionism or it is doomed to impotence." Further, "the education of the working class is most essential" to achieve the aim of "a universal working class organization, united along the entire line of the class struggle, economically and politically." This organization, "built upon the solid rock of clear knowledge and class consciousness will put the organized working class in actual control of the system of production, and the working class will then be ready to take possession of it." This ideal that the workers should and will possess the world was tremendously widespread among the Jewish masses, and was perhaps the single most important moral force among the 3,000,000 Jews in the United States in 1914.

This Jewish population was very elaborately but loosely organized. In 1900, a summary of

Sidney Hillman (1887-1946), portrayed by the Jewish sculptor, Jo Davidson.

Jewish organizational life in the *American Jewish Year Book* took stock of 791 congregations, 415 educational and 593 philanthropic organizations. It was then estimated that four-fifths of the 200,000 Jewish families in the land were not members of congregations, although many unsynagogued Jews paid for the opportunity to attend the special High Holiday services. However, three-fourths of the educational organizations were attached to congregations. The center of organized Jewish life was nevertheless moving further and further away from the synagogue. As the Jewish population virtually tripled, secular organizations mushroomed and fanned out. By 1915, the *American Jewish Year Book* listed 67 national organizations with thousands of lodges, chapters, and branches throughout the land. The largest were the fraternal orders; 17 of them had a total membership of 507,870. Masses of Jews were also to be found in the vast network of *landsmanshaften*. In some of these, there was the beginning of centralization. Thus in 1908 there were founded the American Federation of Polish Jews and the Federation of Romanian Jews. The latter, although reflecting the smallest stream in the East European immigration tide, had 40,000 members in 50 branches. At the other end of the scale was the select American Jewish Committee, which, with its 105 members chosen primarily for wealth and public position, presumed to be the spokesman for the American Jews as a whole and was too often accepted as such by general public opinion.

One new organizational form bloomed briefly, the New York Kehilla (Organized Jewish Community). A scandalous incident crystallized the gathering sentiment for such an organization. When General Theodore Bingham, New York City Police Commissioner, charged in the *North American Review* of September, 1908 that half the criminals in New York were Jewish, the Jews were alarmed at the slander. The charge was easily proved false, and Bingham apologized, retracted and later resigned. But out of the agitation grew the New York Kehilla, with a Constituent Assembly in February, 1909 of 222 organizations (74 synagogues, 42 mutual benefit societies, 40 fraternal lodges, and various Zionist, literary and philanthropic groups). The professed ideal was to have a body that would democratically represent all trends in Jewish life. In actuality, the Executive Committee of the Kehilla was restricted to the New York members of the American Jewish Committee! The plutocracy had in fact succeeded in harnessing, at least temporarily, an active but small part of the bulk of Jewish organizations, for the 222 affiliates were only a minor fraction of the 3,500 Jewish organizations in New York. Rent by dissension over religious, class and communal issues, the Kehilla virtually ceased to function during the war and went out of existence when its main guiding spirit, the actively liberal rabbi, Judah L. Magnes, went to Palestine in 1922. (A similar attempt in Philadelphia, begun in 1911, lasted only until the war began). Yet the Kehilla rendered useful service: through its Bureau of Education (1910) it sought to systematize Jewish Education; through its Bureau of Social Morals (1912) it so effectively combatted Jewish juvenile delinquency and Jewish participation in gangsterism and the white slave traffic that it won the praise of Mayor William J. Gaynor; through its Bureau of Industry it acted as mediator and arbitrator when Jewish workers confronted Jewish employers in labor disputes; and through its Bureau of Philanthropic Research it sought to bring new social work techniques into Jewish philanthropy. The Kehilla had least success when it attempted, in the hope that Jews who paid for *kosher* products actually got them, to regulate and enforce the dietary laws upon the various business interests involved.

Organizational growth was both expressed in and spurred by the expansion of the Jewish press in Yiddish, English, Hebrew and other languages. In 1900 there were the following periodicals: in Yiddish, six dailies, eight weeklies, and one monthly; in English, 22 weeklies and four monthlies; in Hebrew, one weekly. By 1915, the picture was more ample: in Yiddish, nine dailies, 15 weeklies, four monthlies; in English, 27 weeklies, 38 monthlies, three bi-monthlies and five quarterlies and two Hebrew monthlies, one German monthly and one weekly in Ladino. But the number of periodicals tells only part of the story, for the most significant feature was not the increase in their number but in their total circulation. The greatest spurt was still in the Yiddish press: in 1912, for instance, the total circulation of the Yiddish press in New York was 360,123; in 1915 it was 525,690 and still going up. In 1914, among the Yiddish dailies there were three with over 100,000 circulation: the *Forward,* 174,699; the *Varheit,* 108,000; the *Morgen Jurnal,* 106,258.

Another aspect of Jewish life which began to get special attention in all camps was Jewish education. With general schooling having become compulsory in the public school system, Jewish education had become marginal. There was the Sunday school for Reform Jews; the old-fashioned, often primitive *heder* in which the sons of Orthodox new immigrants were crudely taught the Hebrew prayers and parts of the Bible, and prepared for *bar mitzvah;* and the somewhat more modern communal Talmud Torah for the teaching of Hebrew and Judaism. A New York report made to the Kehilla revealed that in 1909 only 41,000 out of 170,000 children

Chaim Zhitlovsky (1865-1943).

Boris Thomashevsky (1866-1939), star of the Yiddish stage.

Joseph Schlossberg.

of school age were getting any kind of Jewish education, and a similar report in Philadelphia two years later presented a comparable picture. As a result of the communal alarm that resulted, Dr. Samson Benderly, the director of the Bureau of Jewish Education of the Kehilla in New York, was able to exert a national influence by pioneering in directing the attention of religious elements to improving teaching methods and personnel, to modernizing buildings, curriculum and texts, and to broadening the scope of Jewish education.

At the same time, and as part of the general communal ferment, there developed a trend for secular Jewish education in the ranks of labor Zionists and the radicalized Jewish workers. The first expression was a National-Radical School founded December 10, 1910 on the East Side in New York; similar schools soon appeared in Chicago and elsewhere. The first national conference of these institutions, held in New York, April 18-21, 1914, resolved that Yiddish and Hebrew have equal status in these schools, and that Judaism be approached affirmatively from the historical and cultural viewpoint. Conflict between Yiddishists and Hebraists led to the formation of two separate schools in Chicago and spurred a movement for Yiddish schools. Thus in 1913 the first Sholem Aleichem Folkshule was founded in New York. Later the Workmen's Circle, which had been conducting children's Sunday Schools in English since 1900, interested

itself in Yiddish secular education. The radical Jewish workers' opposition to Zionism was reflected in this movement. An important influence in moving the Workmen's Circle in the direction of socialist Yiddish schools was Dr. Chaim Zhitlovsky, who has been described as "the outstanding theoretician of Jewish nationalism in the camp of socialism" by C. Bezalel Sherman, the labor Zionist sociologist. At its convention in 1916, the Workmen's Circle resolved to found socialist Yiddish schools to rival the religious Talmud Torahs and the labor Zionist schools.

Another expanding cultural force was the Yiddish theater, which, on the crest of the immigration tide, reached a broader audience than any other Yiddish medium, attracting even the illiterate. Unlike the general American theater public, the Jewish audience was highly organized, filling the four playhouses in New York from Monday to Thursday on the basis of the benefit system, by which the innumerable Jewish societies bought blocks of seats at reduced prices to aid their own causes. Only on week-ends did the box-office depend on the unorganized theater-goer. The bulk of the repertory consciously catered to the most primitive tastes, and even into some of the best plays, as Hutchins Hapgood remarked in 1902 in *The Spirit of the Ghetto*, "grotesque humor, popular songs, vaudeville tricks are inserted everywhere." Yet amid the flood of crude melodrama, bombastic musical-historical spectacles and general vulgarity (*shund* in Yiddish), the more consciously artistic plays of Jacob Gordin, Leon Kobrin and David Pinski began to create their own devoted following. The realism and social idealism surging through the European theatre were prime influences on this better type of Yiddish drama.

Gordin continued to be the leader of this movement until he died in 1909, and even after that his plays, having become a part of the repertory, exerted their influence. In this specific period, his *Kreutzer Sonata,* dealing with Bohemianism and the emancipation of women, was staged in 1902 (in English translation in 1904 and 1906), and his *Dementia Americana,* a cutting exposé of the real-estate business, in 1908. Leon Kobrin became more and more prominent, with realistic plays on American themes like *The Lost Garden of Eden* (1902) and *American Prosperity* (1905), followed later by *Enemies* (1912), *Breach of Promise* and the very popular *Yankel Boile* (1913), and *Magic* (1914). The new dramatic light of the time was David Pinski. with *The Mother* (1904), *Yankel the Blacksmith* (a hit in 1909), *The Family Zvi* (1910; written in 1905 after the Kishinev pogrom had swung Pinski from Bundism toward Zionism, the play shows the hero under the same impact turning from assimilationism to the Torah), *The Treasure* (1911, a comedy composed in 1906, which like Mark Twain's *The Man That Corrupted Hadleyburg,* depicted how money can corrupt an entire community) and *Each With His God* (1912).

In addition to such plays by dramatists living in the United States, the Yiddish theater also performed many by the outstanding Yiddish writers of Europe and by the most prominent European dramatists, past and present. Thus Sholem Asch, Sholem Aleichem and I. L. Peretz began to attract an American audience. Asch had many plays produced: *Messianic Times* (1906), *The God of Vengeance* and *With the Stream* (1907), *The Fellow-Countryman* (1911) and *Our Faith* (1914). Sholem Aleichem had three plays staged in 1907, *The Outcast, Jewish Daughters* and *Stempeniu.* And Peretz, whose *Stories and Pictures,* translated into Eng-

lish by Helena Frank of London, had been issued by the Jewish Publication Society in 1906, had two plays on the Yiddish stage: *The Sisters* (1906) and *Der Nisoyon* (The Trial or Temptation), in 1908.

The European drama was excellently represented, even though too often by crudely adapted and translated versions of Shakespeare, Ibsen, Strindberg, Echegarray, Ostrovsky, Gorky, Hauptman, Sardou, Zola, Moliere, Maeterlinck, Zangwill, Tolstoy, Goethe, Andreyev, Bjornsen and Brieux. The playgoer who was interested felt he had access to the best of the classical and advanced modern drama.

Not only the play but the player was often the major attraction. Influenced by the American practice, the star system developed and the actor became the thing. Jacob Adler and Boris Thomashefsky, David Kessler and Zelig Mogulescu, Bertha Kalisch and Madame Kannie Liptzin, Leon Blank and Bessie Thomashefsky, all had their partisans and their claques, who spiritedly cheered their own and derided others' favorites, before, during and after performances. There was nothing staid and little of decorum in this Yiddish theater. To audiences so hungry that they gulped plays almost without tasting them, it brought color, music and slapstick humor, trite fancy and winged imagination, pride of Jewish identity and sensitivity to anti-Semitism, sentiment and sentimentality, life as it is, measured by life as it could and should be.

Outside the theater, working class poets and prose writers who had appeared at the end of the last century still held their sway with work which was ever close to the lives of the masses, consoling, educating and inspiring them to struggle. The heroic period of workers' struggles found its life-size image in the continued work of the poets Rosenfeld and Winchevsky and in the prose sketches and stories of Kobrin, Libin, and the more recently arrived Abraham Reisin. But new trends also appeared.

Yehoash (Solomon Bloomgarden), who arose and attained his peak in this period, brought not only unusual variety of theme but a new emphasis on and an exceptional achievement in poetic artistry. At the same time, he maintained his so-

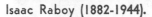

Isaac Raboy (1882-1944).

The Yiddish poet Yehoash (Solomon Bloomgarden; 1871-1927), portrayed by Aaron Goodelman.

Abraham Reisin (1872-1953).

cial sense, his social conscience. From his first appearances in 1901 in the *Forward* and the socialist literary and political monthly, *Di Zukunft* (The Future), Yehoash was hailed as a new star in the Yiddish literary firmament. His *Collected Poems* and his translation of Longfellow's *Hiawatha* into Yiddish, published in 1907, established his popularity and his prestige. Although his *Dos Neie Lied* (The New Song) had urged the Jewish masses protesting the Tsarist pogroms under the black flag of lamentation to turn to the red banner of class-struggle, Yehoash did not go in that direction; already a Zionist, he became a religious nationalist. In 1910 there began to appear his major work, the translation of the Bible into Yiddish in a style that purified and enriched the Yiddish language itself. In another volume of poems and prose-poems in 1913, *In Zun un Nebel* (Through Mist and Sunshine), he continued to express his love of nature, his lyricism and his social sense in varied forms rare in Yiddish literature.

While Yehoash was wedding superior artistry to the social theme, a rebellion was brewing among a number of new writers who, calling themselves The Young, had no literary or other creed in common except a hostility to certain existing situations. "When we arrived on the scene," wrote one of them, Reuben Eisland, "Yiddish literature was in the service of ideas and movements, social and national." The Young, who were mostly in their late twenties on the eve of the First World War, rebelled against the classic Yiddish writers of Europe and against the older generation of American Yiddish writers, whose stress was on realism and social protest. In a series of fugitive periodicals and anthologies (*Di Yugend*—The Youth—1907; *Troimen un Virklichkeit*—Dreams and Reality—1909; *Literatur*, 1910; *Shriften*—Writings—1912, etc.; *Di Neie Haim*—The New Home—1914; *Fun Mentsh zu Mentsh*—From Man to Man—1914), and in their individual volumes, a score of new creative talents appeared, seeking new themes and new forms. Most of them turned away from the life of the laboring masses in the East Sides and the ghettoes with their sweatshops and strikes and tenement squalor and the endless struggle for a better life—and found individualism, mysticism, impressionism, eroticism, moodiness, loneliness, all wrapped up in the theory of "art for art's sake." Menahem Boraisha, who adhered to The Young when he came to the United States after the War had begun in Europe, noted at the time that many of them were "lost," were "children with blind eyes looking for the moon." They reacted against the vulgarity and materialism of the new Jewish middle class, which was moving out of the East Side to the fancier regions of Harlem and the Bronx in New York, but these aesthetes had no new values or new experiences to serve them as an anchor. One of the leading "aesthetes," Zischa Landau, expressed a characteristic mood of futility and pessimism in his poem in *Shriften* in 1914.

Yet part of The Young developed a trend to-

Moishe Leib Halpern (1886-1932).   Moishe Nadir (1885-1943).   H. Leivick (1882-1962).

ward a new Realism. Some went outside the swarming East Sides to discover other features of American life, geographically and socially. Thus Isaac Raboy, in *Herr Goldenbarg,* a novella published in 1914, described the life of a Jewish farmer in North Dakota. Another realist was Joseph Opatoshu, whose first book, *Fun Nu Yorker Ghetto* (About the New York Ghetto) appeared in 1913. Forty years later, in a retrospective view, Opatoshu declared that then "Yiddish literature ceased to be an educational tool and became an end in itself. It assumed artistic standards," and began to advance "linguistically and formally," far beyond the skill even of a "fine poet" like Morris Rosenfeld. When H. Leivick, having escaped from Siberia, to which he had been sentenced for life, arrived in New York at the end of 1913, he too moved in the circle of The Young. As time passed, moreover, many of The Young, under pressure of inexorable events in the 1920's and 1930's, responded and reflected the life about them in their work. Those more sensitive to the needs of the people, like Moishe Leib Halpern, Moishe Nadir, Leivick and Raboy, developed new ties with the struggling and class-conscious Jewish workers. In addition to those already mentioned, The Young whose careers stood out as they unfolded during and after the War included David Ignatov, Haim (Henry)

Rosenblatt, Joseph Rolnick, I. J. Schwartz and Mani Leib. As a whole, The Young added immeasurably to the style and quality of Yiddish literature, and to the shaping and enriching of the Yiddish language itself as a literary instrument.

Another development, decidedly minor at this time, was the effort to plant the seed of Hebrew culture. From the 1880's there had been attempts to organize societies in New York and Chicago for the promotion of Hebrew, to establish a publishing house and to issue periodicals. The trickle of Hebraists arriving from Eastern Europe after 1900 led to new modest attempts, which were spurred when Reuben Brainin came over in 1910. In 1913, with the founding of Histadruth Ivrith (National Organization for Hebrew Culture), of which Brainin was president, there was a spurt forward. By 1915, this group had 19 affiliates in seven cities. The attempt to publish a daily newspaper, *Ha-Yom* (The Day), in 1913 promptly collapsed, but two monthlies appeared the same year and held on: *Ha-Toren* (The Mast), issued by Ahiever (The Hebrew Brotherhood) and *Ha-Tehiyah* (The Renaissance). The tiny audience was fed by two sources, the Zionist movement and the new method of teaching Hebrew in Hebrew that the more modern religious schools were beginning to use.

Reuben Brainin (1862-1939).   Max Weber (1881-1961).   Dr. Solomon Schechter (1850-1916), from a painting by C. Mielziner, 1916.

In the religious field, the important new development was the rise of Conservative Judaism as an organized force. Conservatism's "initial character as a movement of protest against the radicalism of 'Reform Judaism,'" was modified in this period, according to Rabbi Ben Zion Bokser, and Conservatism "became the party of the Center, having to fight for its survival on two fronts," against Reform and against Orthodoxy. The towering figure of Conservative Judaism was Dr. Solomon Schechter, who was brought in from England in 1902 to head the Jewish Theological Seminary of America. Born in Romania, trained both in the East European *yeshivas* and in German universities, he was a lecturer at Cambridge University and the renowned discoverer of the Genizah manuscripts at Cairo. Dr. Schechter had the background, prestige and organizational talent to advance this fight on two fronts in Judaism, while in his political and economic views he was a liberal. In 1913, he organized the United Synagogue of America with 23 Conservative congregations affiliated. Addressing the founding conference, Dr. Schechter stressed that to conserve traditional Judaism, it was necessary "to introduce the English sermon, and adopt scientific methods in our seminaries, in our training rabbis and schoolmasters, for our synagogues and Talmud Torahs, and bring order and decorum in our synagogues."

The organization's statement of purpose accepted the validity of the Talmud, rejected by Reform, as "the historical exposition of Torah," reaffirmed traditional Sabbath observance and the dietary laws, on which Reform had compromised, continued the use of the traditional liturgy with prayers in Hebrew in contrast to Reform's stress on the vernacular, and supported Zionism in the face of opposition by Reform and the Orthodox Agudas Israel. Although in 1915 Reform as organized in the Union of American Hebrew Congregations outnumbered the Conservative congregations by eight to one, Conservatism began systematically to close the gap as it developed a rich base among the rapidly growing middle class of East European origin.

As for the participaton of Jews in the general life of our country, there was hardly an aspect in which they were not represented. Jews were in all the arts, sciences and professions, in many of the crafts and industries, in every field of financial and commercial transaction, and in a good many spheres of public life. Anti-Semitic restrictions hindered but did not stop this development. *Who's Who in America* in 1905 listed 199 Jews of eminence (102 of them native-born): 32 in the legal profession, 21 each in the theater and literature, 20 each in medicine and education, 18 bankers and merchants, 15 in the rabbinate, 12 in journalism, 11 in the graphic arts, and

Abraham Walkowitz (1880-1965).   Congressman Adolph J. Sabath   Senator Isidor Rayner (1850-1912).
(1866-1952), elected to House
of Representatives 24 times.

others in chemistry, music, legislative office, the armed forces, and so on. The ability and energy of the Jews dovetailed with the basic democratic features of American society to enable them to expand the use of their skills and talents. To outline the relation of Jews to many of these areas of creativity would require monographs and special studies, most of which have not yet been made. The barest sketch of fields as diverse as art and politcs may be suggestive.

In art, many of the Jews entering the field in this new century achieved eminence. Jacob Epstein, born in 1880 on the East Side of New York, used his talented pencil to record sensitively the Jewish life all around him. "There is no nature in the sweatshop," he said, "and yet it is there and in the crowded street that my love and my imagination call me." His drawings really illuminated Hapgood's *The Spirit of the Ghetto;* Epstein cultivated this vein for several years before he left to settle in England. Born in the same year as Epstein but in Siberia, Abraham Walkowitz had arrived on the East Side as a child. He too contributed much to the rich gallery of East Side types and life.

The main excitement in the art world, however, was being caused by the beginnings of modernism. Here too Jews were conspicuous. The key advocate of modern art was Alfred Stieglitz,

himself a master photographer. At his gallery at 291 Fifth Avenue, Stieglitz from 1905 introduced the best European modern art and presented the works of American painters inspired by the new vision, including the controversial paintings of a figure like Max Weber. Born in Bialystok, Weber came to New York in 1891 at the age of ten, obtained his art training at Pratt Institute, went to France to complete his studies and returned in 1908 steeped in the new influences of Matisse, Cezanne, Rousseau, African idols and El Greco. In Weber's one man exhibition at Stieglitz's in 1910, one critic saw only "travesties of the human form" and another was much annoyed by "grotesqueries," but a third found "architectural solidities like those of old mural paintings." A distinguished career was being launched.

The big demonstration in behalf of modern art, however, took place in 1913 under the auspices of the Association of American Painters and Sculptors, of which Jo Davidson and Jerome Myers were members. Opening for a month at the 69th Regiment Armory in New York on February 17, the International Exhibition of Modern Art not only had many Jews represented among the artists of Europe but also about 20 in the American Room, among them Walkowitz, Epstein, Maurice Becker and William Zorach.

In the political arena, Jews were attaining

Governor Moses Alexander of Idaho (1853-1932).

Governor Simon Bamberger of Utah (1847-1926).

elective office at many levels. In the House of Representatives between 1900 and 1914 there were 11 Jews at various periods, six of them from New York, two from Illinois, and one each from Maryland, Louisiana and California; most of them were elected for more than one term. In the 1914 elections to the House, five Jews won: in New York, Meyer London (Socialist) and Isaac Siegel (Republican), in Atlantic City, N. J., Isaac Bachrach (Republican), in Chicago, Adolph J. Sabath for his fifth term (Democrat), and in San Francisco, Julius Kahn for his thirteenth term (Republican). In the United States Senate for this period, the Jews were Joseph Simon of Oregon, 1898-1903, Isidor Rayner of Maryland, 1907-1912, and Simon Guggenheim of Colorado, 1907-1913. In the 1914 elections, one Jew was also elected as Governor: Moses Alexander in Idaho, which had only a couple of thousand Jews. Alexander had already been Mayor of Chillicothe, Mo. before coming to Boise, where he also served as Mayor from 1897-1899 and 1901-1903. Success in business while operating a chain of clothing stores and local politics paved his

way to the Governor's office. Jews were more likely to win political office, especially in Congress and State Legislatures, in areas where there was a sizable Jewish population, if only because the political bosses were already well aware of the need to win support from immigrant groups by offering them certain "plums." However, the cases of Moses Alexander, of Simon Bamberger, elected Governor of Utah in 1916, and several others indicate that in Western states, where Jews had grown with the local communities almost from pioneering days, they advanced politically not because of the "Jewish vote" but because they were generally integrated into the community. It was a Victor Rosewater, born in Omaha, Nebraska, who became Chairman of the Republican National Committee in 1912.

It was bright opportunity and shining security that had attracted the masses of immigrants. The Jews were pursuing these aims stubbornly. They fought boldly as individuals and as a group to realize the new possibilities they found. They had made considerable headway in many directions when the World War began.

Dear Sir:

　　The Jewish League of American Patriots, organized several weeks ago by nearly all of the Yiddish and Jewish-English dailies and weeklies of New York, has decided to form a committee of 100 of prominent Jews of New York City, representative of all classes, for the purpose of aiding and extending the work of the League.

　　The chief purpose of the League will be to undertake the systematic mobilization of the forces of the Jewish race with the view of placing them at the disposal of our country.

The Jewish League of American Patriots was formed March 25, 1917, before war was declared.

CHAPTER 11: War, Revolution, Reaction and Prosperity

WHEN RIVALRY among the big European powers erupted into war late in July, 1914, millions of Jews in the United States, like other European immigrants, were personally and emotionally involved from the beginning. Among the thirteen million Jews in the world in 1914, nine and one-half million lived in the warring states, with hundreds of thousands in the armies of both camps.

What was the war about? With the smoke of battle came the fog of propaganda to hide the real stakes. But in a moment of post-war candor, President Woodrow Wilson defined the character of the war in his speech in St. Louis on September 5, 1919: "This war was a commercial and industrial war. It was not a political war. . . . Under the League plan, the financial leadership will be ours, the industrial supremacy will be ours, the commercial advantage will be ours and the other countries of the world will look to us, and shall I say, are looking to us, for leadership and direction."

But it was to be 32 months before the United States entered the war on April 6, 1917. In 1914, our country was in an economic depression and was still a debtor nation, since European investments here outweighed United States investments in Europe. Our ruling circles brought the country out of the depression and turned it into a creditor nation by selling war materials both to the Allies and the Central Powers until the ties with the Allies became supreme. Among the Jews, despite the economic prosperity, there was mass personal anxiety. While the attention of most Americans was fixed on the Western Front and the German rape of Belgium, the feelings of most Jewish Americans, although not indifferent to Belgium, were concentrated on the Eastern Front. For there the huge Jewish populations, including so many kin, friends and brethren of American Jews, were in the very center of the carnage. Financial aid was the least that could be given to these war-ravaged Jews, and it was speedily forthcoming.

Although there was unanimity of sentiment for a huge relief effort, its organizational expression was determined by class and religious divisions. The first to respond was the Central Committee for the Relief of Jews Suffering Through the War, founded on October 4, 1914 under the auspices of the Union of Orthodox Jewish Congregations; with Leon Kamaiky, owner of the daily

Louis Marshall (1856-1929).

Felix M. Warburg (1871-1937).

Yiddishe Tageblatt of New York as chairman, $1,500,000 were raised by mid-July, 1917. The wealthier Reform Jewish element organized the American Jewish Relief Committee on October 25, 1914, headed by Louis Marshall, chairman of the American Jewish Committee; by July, 1917, with 39 national organizations participating, it had collected $6,000,000. Both groups, to facilitate the distribution of funds, established the American Jewish Joint Distribution Committee on November 27, 1914, with Felix M. Warburg, the banker, as chairman. Socialist-minded and class-conscious Jewish workers at first contributed through the Workmen's Circle. Then in August, 1915 they formed the Jewish People's Relief Committee under the chairmanship of Meyer London, Socialist Congressman from New York's East Side; by July, 1917, it had turned over to the Joint Distribution Committee $800,-000, collected in the shops in innumerable small sums.

These Committees, operating through local groups in about 1,500 Jewish communities throughout the land, continued their work right through the war and even after it. Since then, overseas aid has been a major concern of American Jewish organized life. By July, 1919, the J. D. C. had allocated more than $22,000,000, of which $17,000,000 went to the Jews of Eastern Europe and about $4,000,000 to the Jews of Palestine and the Middle East. More than $10,-000,000 was assigned in the year 1918-1919, a peak not surpassed until 1944. The masses were thoroughly involved in this huge effort, especially the workers. For example, 62,000 members of the I.L.G.W.U. in New York, including non-Jews, donated $140,000, the proceeds of their volunteering to work on Washington's Birthday in 1918. Other unions followed suit, such as the New York furriers' union, which set aside March 29, 1919 as a day of work for Russian-Jewish relief.

While there was Jewish unity on overseas relief, there was diversity on other issues. Like the general population, the Jews wanted the United States to stay out of the war and be neutral. But although neutral in deed and policy, the Jewish population was partisan in sympathy and opinion. Hatred of Russian tsarism was universal among the American Jews. The great bulk of middle and lower middle class Jews and even sections of the Jewish working class, whose attitude to the war was based only on anti-tsarism, thus became "pro-German." (Irish-Americans likewise expressed their hatred of British oppression of Ireland by being "pro-German.") To be against tsarism and not pro-German required a consistent anti-imperialist neutrality found only in the firm socialists.

International socialist congresses in 1907 and 1912 had foretold that the big powers would go to war to redivide their colonial possessions and reshuffle spheres of economic influence, and resolved that it would be the duty of all socialists to oppose the war when it began and to arouse the masses for "the overthrow of capitalist class rule."

Yet when the war came, the majority of the socialist leaders in the belligerent states yielded to the ruling classes in their own countries, and supported the war on each side. In each warring country except Serbia and Italy, only minorities among the socialists held fast to the anti-war position, the largest and later the most influential of these being the Bolsheviks in Russia.

Although disconcerted and disillusioned by the failure of the European socialists to live up to their anti-war resolutions, the majority of the American socialist movement maintained an anti-imperialist neutrality position. Among the Jewish socialists, however, the situation was more complicated. Some were pro-German not only because they were anti-tsarist but because they had also been brought up in veneration of the German Social-Democratic party. Thus Abraham Cahan had on December 10, 1914 written in the *Jewish Daily Forward* that he was "convinced that in the interests of general progress and for Jews specifically a Russian defeat would be fortunate . . . that it would be fortunate for all of Europe and for the whole Jewish population if Germany would take all of Poland and also Lithuania from Russia." Such anti-tsarist "pro-German" sentiment was almost universal in the Yiddish press (the *Varheit* was the main exception) and widespread in the Anglo-Jewish press.

The Zionist movement showed the same pattern. Except for a few outstanding leaders like N. Syrkin, most Zionists were pro-German. Officially they were for neutrality, as the Poale Zionists declared at the Rochester Convention in December, 1914 and the Federation of American Zionists at its Boston Convention in June, 1915. The Provisional Executive Committee for Zionist Affairs, however, formed in August, 1914 with Louis D. Brandeis as chairman, was pro-Ally. Yet most Zionists were pro-German for "Zionist" reasons: a German conquest of Poland and Romania would free the Jews there, they thought, and a victorious Turkey, allied to Germany, would then agree to Palestine's becoming a Jewish province. The German government, eager for Zionist support, promised in November, 1916 to create a Jewish democratic central council to govern Jewish communities in territories conquered by Germany—and the Zionists rejoiced. To combat this orientation, the British stepped up their efforts to woo the Jews and finally issued the Balfour Declaration of November, 1917. British motives were defined in a Foreign Office memorandum sent to the Russian Foreign Minister on March 13, 1916: "It is clear that by utilizing the Zionist idea, important political results could be realized. One of the results would be the conversion of the Jewish elements in the East, the U.S.A. and other places, to the use of the Allies; elements whose attitude is at present rather antagonistic to the Allies."

Generally, the peace sentiments of American Jews remained strong. Various classes used various means to express this desire for peace. Jewish trade unions in New York and Chicago staged protest meetings on August 8, 1914, sent peace memorials to Wilson and organized outdoor rallies later that month with the slogan: "Starve the war and feed America," to protest shipments of food abroad that were forcing prices up at home, Jewish working women paraded for peace down Fifth Avenue in New York on Saturday, August 29.

Stimulated by this groundswell, middle class groups passed resolutions for peace at their conventions: for example, the Union of American Hebrew Congregations in January, 1915; the New York Kehilla in May, 1915; the Independent Order of Brith Abraham in June, 1915; the Federation of Galician and Bukowinian Jews and the Central Conference of American Rabbis in the spring, 1916. On November 4, 1915, however, President Wilson, affected by the rise of anti-German opinion that followed the sinking of the *Lusitania* by a German submarine, with the loss of 1,198 passengers, including 124 Americans, reversed his position of unarmed neutrality and came out for "preparedness." He swept with him on this road to war the conservative Yiddish press, some rabbinical organizations and the Jewish fraternal orders, with the exception of the Workmen's Circle. The resistance of the Jewish labor and socialist groups stiffened at this time, in part because of the socialist conference held in Zimmerwald, Switzerland, early in September, 1915. There anti-war socialists from eleven countries, including the Jewish Bund, condemned the pro-war socialists and advanced a minimal program of "no annexations"

and "self-determination of peoples." The *Forward* criticized this conference, but supporting the lead of Zimmerwald were the Jewish Socialist Federation, the Workmen's Circle and like-minded elements in the unions, as well as the *Idishe Arbeter Velt* in Chicago.

The neutrality and peace sentiments of the Jews registered in the presidential election of November, 1916 by a swing to Wilson. Like most other Americans, the Jews believed that Wilson had not only kept us out of war but would continue to do so. Therefore, as Professor Lawrence H. Fuchs reports, Wilson "became the first Democratic Presidential candidate to crash the Republican hold over the Jews in half a century." In addition, thousands of Jews voted Socialist; the New York East Side re-elected Meyer London to Congress.

After the elections, with our economy completely geared to the Allied war needs, our ruling circles accelerated their effort to drag the country into war. When Wilson broke diplomatic relations with Germany on February 3, 1917 following its resumption of submarine warfare, Jewish workers increased their anti-war protest. The 60,000 members of the Workmen's Circle were rallied to resist the war drive. The Jewish Socialist Federation and the Poale Zion issued anti-war manifestoes. The Current Events Committee of the Waistmakers Local 25 of the I.L.G.W.U. distributed a leaflet opposing entry into a war "conducted only for imperialistic purposes." On February 11, a convention called by the National Workmen's Committee for Jewish Rights, representing 190 organizations with a half million members, resolved to oppose the war and sent Morris Winchevsky to speak for it on a mass delegation to Washington. A conference on March 11, sponsored by the Jewish Socialist Federation, was attended by delegations from the Workmen's Circle, the United Hebrew Trades, the I.L.G.W.U., the Amalgamated Clothing Workers and other unions. They resolved that "If our efforts should not have the desired success and war does break out, we shall do everything possible to bring about an immediate peace, to oppose the war and the war policy of our government . . ." Although this was the view

Congressman Julius Kahn (1861-1924), who served 12 terms in the House of Representatives.

of the majority of organized Jewish labor, the majority of the general labor movement was moving in the opposite direction. A conference of American Federation of Labor and railroad unions on March 12 pledged unconditional support of the government's policy. Conspicuously absent were the United Mine Workers, the Typographical Union, the Western Federation of Miners, the Journeymen Barbers and the I.L.G.W.U.

That same day, March 12, 1917, the event occurred in Russia that cleared away the last big obstacle to United States entry into the war and instantly changed the "pro-German" sentiments of the Jews. No matter how much it had beaten the drum of a "war for democracy," the American war propaganda machine had not been convincing so long as that dubious democrat, the Tsar, was one of the Allies. The beginning of the Russian Revolution, and his abdication on March 15, changed all that. For various reasons, all classes in American life hailed this revolution with unprecedented unanimity. But the jubila-

tion of the Jews, most of whom had known tsarism at first hand, was boundless. Overnight "pro-German" sentiment was replaced by a pro-Ally tide that engulfed the Jewish middle and lower middle class and sections of the working class. Yiddish newspapers like the *Tog,* the *Varheit,* the *Morgen Jurnal* and the *Tageblatt* in New York and the *Yiddisher Record* in Chicago proclaimed their readiness for war. On March 25, 1917, pro-war Jewish newspaper editors and publishers formed the Jewish League of American Patriots, with Samuel Untermeyer as president, to place "the forces of the Jewish race" at "the disposal of our country."

Pro-war hysteria was so high that in California Warren K. Billings and Tom Mooney, labor leaders, were falsely convicted of bombing a "Preparedness Parade" in San Francisco on July 22, 1916. Late in 1916 Billings was sentenced to life imprisonment, and on February 24, 1917, Mooney was sentenced to hang on May 17. Jewish working class organizations as well as many middle class liberal Jews joined in the nationwide and international protest to stop the execution. Late in 1917, two other defendants, Mrs. Mooney and Israel Weinberg, a member of the Executive Board of the Jitney Operators' Union, were acquitted after a chief prosecution witness was exposed as a perjurer and a suborner of perjury. A Presidential commission, headed by Secretary of Labor William B. Wilson and Harvard Law Professor Felix Frankfurter, reported that "the verdict against Mooney was discredited," but a new trial was denied. In 1918, his sentence was commuted to life imprisonment; Mooney and Billings were not released until 1939.

The desire for peace, however, did not down. In these "last critical days" there arose from "the great mass of citizenry . . . such an outpouring of peace sentiment" that Professor Arthur S. Link, after studying the evidence, concluded "that even as late as April 1, 1917 the majority of people were still firmly for peace." Nevertheless, the next day Wilson asked Congress to declare war against Germany. In the debate, Senator George W. Norris warned that "we are about to put a dollar sign on the American flag," since our bankers had lent over two billion dollars to the Allies and trade with them had jumped from $825,000,000 in 1914 to three and one-quarter billion in 1916. But war was declared on Good Friday, April 6, the vote in the Senate being 82 to 6, and in the House 373 to 50. Of the five Jewish Congressmen, only the Socialist Meyer London voted against the war, declaring, "No! I shall not kill! I shall not vote to kill!"

Immediately there were declarations of support for the war from many Jewish circles. All the fraternal orders except the Workmen's Circle, all the rabbinical organizations and the Federation of American Zionists promptly put themselves on record. Rabbi Stephen S. Wise dropped his pacifism and, as he reports in his autobiography, literally draped his pulpit with the American flag. The Poale Zionists on April 26 rallied 3,000 to Cooper Union in New York, where they hailed the war as advancing "the principles of democracy and free nationality" and hoped they would be applied to Jewish claims to Palestine. In Congress, when Democrats heading the Military Affairs Committee hesitated to press Wilson's Conscription Bill, the Jewish Congressman from San Francisco, the Republican Julius Kahn, took charge of the unpopular bill and "managed" it through enactment on May 18, 1917—with Meyer London among those voting against it. Meanwhile on May 14 the League of Jewish Patriots had urged enlistment upon the 20,000 that crowded Seward Park on the East Side of New York. Pro-war circles exploited the threat of anti-Semitism to win loud support from nervous and insecure immigrants. "Let us act as natives, not as foreigners," appealed the pro-war Socialist, M. Baranov, in the *Forward* on June 12, and ten days later Louis E. Miller echoed that view in his *Vochenshrift,* arguing that Jews and immigrants have "less right to engage" in anti-war activity "than the native-born."

To be sure, the Jews did not lag behind in bearing the burdens of war. By enlistment and conscription, over 200,000 Jews served in the armed forces, 3,500 dying and 12,000 suffering wounds for ideals that Wilson later mocked with the harsh truth that they like others had bled in a "commercial and industrial war."

Mrs. Florence Prag Kahn (1868-1948), who was elected to fill her husband's seat in Congress and served from 1925 to 1937.

More than 9,000 Jews were officers, and 1,132 were awarded decorations and citations. Three won the Congressional Medal of Honor and 147 the Distinguished Service Medals and Crosses. Anti-Semites jeered that Jews were mostly in the Quartermaster department, but in fact they were disproportionately high in the infantry, the most dangerous arm of the service, and under-represented in the "safe" Quartermaster outfits. Like all immigrants, Jews showed a higher percentage in the armed forces than the native population. The foreign-born constituted about 18 per cent of the Army, more than their share of the total population, because among immigrants there was a higher percentage of young men than among the native-born. Jews, moreover, being city residents working in light industries, had less claim to deferment than did farmers or those in essential industries.

To service the Jews in army camps there was created in September, 1917 the Jewish Welfare Board, officially endorsed by the Government and backed by 14 Jewish national rabbinical, fraternal, women's and cultural organizations. Doing the same kind of work that the Salvation Army, Y.M.C.A. and the Knights of Columbus did for Protestants and Catholics in uniform, the J.W.B. soon had a couple of hundred trained workers in these camps, as well as over 100 branches in Jewish communities throughout the country.

There was also, however, much opposition to the war. Rabbis like Judah L. Magnes in New York and Abraham Cronbach in Cincinnati spoke out as pacifists. Anarchists like Alexander Berkman and Emma Goldman organized the No Conscription League. But the most extensive center of war-resistance was in the Jewish labor movement, led as it was by socialists. At the St. Louis Convention of the Socialist Party that opened April 7, 1917, the overwhelming majority denounced the war "as a crime against the people of the United States and against the nations of the world" and pledged "its unalterable opposition to the war." A referendum of the membership recorded more than seven to one against the war. From April to June this membership grew from 67,788 to 81,172 despite minor defections of pro-war elements.

For a time this St. Louis resolution had a large influence on Jewish labor organizations. The Workmen's Circle, the Jewish Socialist Federation, the Jewish unions and even many Poale Zionists supported this stand. (Most of the latter, of course, were later won over to the war by the Balfour Declaration, but a minority split with the Zionists and became anti-war socialists.) Several conventions expressed this anti-war position, the first being that of the Capmakers, May 1-10, 1917. On May Day, Jacob Panken, a socialist lawyer who six months later was elected a New York municipal court judge, addressed the convention. "On with the fight against war," he cried, to loud applause, "on with the fight against an expeditionary force to Europe; on with the fight against conscription . . ."

That same month the Workmen's Circle convention endorsed the St. Louis resolution with only four opposing votes. In June, 1917 *The Fur Worker*, organ of the International Fur Workers' Union, concluded an editorial on the approaching convention by pointing out that

"now is the time to demonstrate . . . that you have courage enough in a time of oppression and reaction to speak out against militarism, against the domination of those who would conquer the world . . ."

Oppression and reaction were really in the saddle. Wilson himself had on April 1 privately foretold that, come the war, "the spirit of ruthless brutality will enter into the very fibre of our national life, infecting Congress, the courts, the policeman on the beat, the man in the street." Congress passed the Espionage Act in June, 1917. Under it, the distinguished historians, Charles A. and Mary R. Beard, have noted, "not a single first-class German spy or revolutionary workingman was caught and convicted of an overt act designed to give direct aid or comfort to the enemy." But in August, 1917 the act was used to ban a dozen radical publications from the mails. In October, Congress passed the Trading With the Enemy Act, requiring foreign language newspapers to file translations of all materials on the war or foreign affairs. At this point Cahan and the Forward Association capitulated and abandoned the St. Louis resolution; but out in Chicago Kalman Marmor of the Yiddish *Daily World* resourcefully found ways of getting his anti-war point across to his alert readership.

The Federal Bureau of Investigation enrolled more than 200,000 volunteers into what became an irresponsible network of private snoopers. The courts summarily packed hundreds of war-resisters, conscientious objectors and radicals off to prison. In one case, Federal Judge Kenesaw Mountain Landis in Chicago in April, 1918 sentenced 93 I.W.W. men, several of them Jews, to a total of 801½ years in prison; when their counsel said the case would be appealed, the Judge added fines totaling $2,570,000. The Metropolitan Opera and symphony orchestras stopped playing German music; and sauerkraut was renamed Liberty Cabbage.

Many were intimidated, but the peace forces could not be silenced. At the end of May, 1917 there was formed the People's Council for Democracy and Terms of Peace. Among the organizers were Jewish figures like Benjamin Schlesinger, president of the I.L.G.W.U., Joseph Schloss-

דער פאָר־אַרבייטער 2

דער פאָר־אַרבייטער

אַ צוויי־וועכענטליכע טרייד־צייטונג.
ערשיינט יערען 1טען און 3טען ריינסטאָן אין מאָנט.

אַרויסגענעבען פון די
אינטערניישאָנאל פאָר וואָירקערס יוניאָן אָף יונייטעד סטייטס און קענעדע.

אַלבערט וו. מילער, דזשענעראל פרעזידענט.
אַנדרין וועניאם, סעק.־טרעזשורער און עדיטאָר.
מאַרריס קוישמאָן, מענעדזשער פון אידישען דעפּאַרטמענט.

אָפיס : 9 דזשעקסאָן עוועניו, לאָנג איילאַנד סיטי, נ. י.
סובסקריפּשאָן פּרייז : יעהרליך 50 סענט.   איינצעלנע קאָפּיע 5 סענט.

אונזער קאָנווענשאָן און איהרע אויפגאַבען

זעהר פיעל פון אונז קוקען מיט אַ געוויסער נלייכגילטינקייט אויף די מעהרסטע
קאָנווענשאָנס וואָס ווערען געהאַלטען.

די עקאָנאָמישע באדינגונגען פאָר צעהנדליגער יאָהרען פון דעם אַמעריקאָנער אַר־
בייטער קלאַס שטערען אין געפאַהר צו ווערען אָבנעוויסט און אייסגעריסען מיט'ן
וואָרצעל. די שטעלונג פון די פיהרער פון די אַמעריקאָנער אַרבייטער מאַסען אין דער
פראַגע פון קריעג און סופּאָרט פאָר מיליטאַריסטישע אַוואַנטיורעס איז אַזוי, אַז זיי
שפּיעלען איינפאַך אַריין אין די הענד פון די וועלט פערשלינגער. און אונזערע
אַרבייטער מאַסען שווייגען, אַזוי ווי זיי וואָלטען געווען זייטיגע אין דער גאַנצער
אַנגעלעגענהייט, ניט פערשטעהענדיג אַז דאָס גראָבט מען אַ גרוב פאָר זיי אין וועלכען
מען וועט פערשיטען און בעגראָבען אַלעם וואָס זיי האָבען אייסגעקעמפט אין פאָר
וועלכע זיי האָבען בעצאָהלט גרויסע אָפּפערס.

עס איז אמת, אַז עס פאָדערט זיך פיעל בי דער יעצטיגער צייט, ווען
מען קראַטישעט אויפצוהענגען אַ שלאָם אויף יעדענס מייל, וואָס עס יועט וואָנען
צו פּראָטעסטירען, און אייך פערפאָקען אונטער אַ פערריגעלטען שלאָס יעדען איינעם
וואָס וועט זיך וואָגען געגענצושטעלען די פערזוכע פון בערייבען די אַרבייטער מאַסען
פון זייערע פראָכט.

אונזערע דעלעגאַטען, זייענדיג פערזאַמעלט אין קאָנווענשאָן צו פערהאַנדלען
פראַגען פון וואָהל און וועה אין בעסטען פאָר די אינטערעסען פון טויזענדער אַרבייטער פאַ־
מיליעם, וועלכע זיינען אַ גליעד פון דער גאַנצער אַרבייטערשאַפט אין וועלכע יועלען
אייך דירעקט אין אינדירעקט ליידען פון די אַטאַקעס וואָס ווערען געמאַכט אויף די
אַרבייטער אָרגאַניזאַציאָנען אין רעבטע, איז זייער הייליגע פּפליכט צו פּראָטעסטירען
געגען די אַלע פערזוכע און ארויסזאָגען אַזוי שאַרף אין שטאַרק זייער שטעלונג, אַז
זייערע אָרגאַניזאַציאָנען זאָלען בעקומען מוטה צו נאָכבאָלגען זייער ביישפּיעל אין

מיט דעם שטערען די פייגד פון אָרגאַניזירטע אַרבייט אין זייערע רעאַקציאָנערע אין
פינסטערע פלענער.

יעצט, פריינדע דעלעגאַטען איז די צייט צו דעמאָנסטרירען דעם פאַקט, אַז ניט
נאָר זיינען מיר העלדען צו פאַסען רעזאָלוציאָנען, אינטערשטיצענדיג די בעזיעגונג
פאָר אינדוסטריעלע דעמאָקראַטי, אין רוהיגע צייטען, ווען יעדען איינעם איז ער־
לויבט צו אָגיטירען אין פערדינגען די ראדיקאַלסטע און רעוואָלוציאָנערסטע אידעען,
נאָר אַז אויך אין די צייטען פון אונטערדריקונג אין רעאַקציאָן האָט איהר געגוג מיטה
צו פּראָטעסטירען געגען מיליטאַריזם, געגען דער הערשאַפט פון די ווערט פערשלי־
נערס און שטאָהן פאָר פולען דעמאָקראַטיזם אין פּאַליטישען אין אינדוסטריעלען
לעבען.

Editorial in The Fur Worker, June 1, 1917, calling upon convention delegates
to resist the war program.

Rose Schneiderman, Women's Trade Union League leader.

berg, secretary of the Amalgamated Clothing Workers, P. Geliebter of the Workmen's Circle, Max Pine, secretary-treasurer of the United Hebrew Trades of New York, Rose Schneiderman, I.L.G.W.U. organizer, Jacob Panken, Morris Hillquit, Alexander Trachtenberg and Rabbi Judah L. Magnes, chairman of the Jewish Kehilla of New York. In Chicago, Boston and Philadelphia similar Councils appeared. The New York Council, headed by Panken, had 284 affiliates, including 93 unions. At a national convention in September, 1917, more than 40 of 350 delegates represented Jewish organizations. To combat this peace movement, the pro-war socialists founded, in August, 1917, the Jewish Socialist League of America, in which Poale Zionists were conspicuous.

The peace temper of the Jewish masses and the influence upon them of the Russian revolution were shown in the November, 1917 municipal elections. In New York Morris Hillquit headed the Socialist ticket as candidate for Mayor. His backers included the I.L.G.W.U., the Amal-

gamated Clothing Workers, the U.H.T., the Workmen's Circle, the Poale Zion, the Jewish National Workers' Alliance—as well as the Progressive Irish League and the Negro Independent Political Council of Harlem. His campaign dynamically related local issues to the main problem of the war. Alarmed by the popular idea that a vote for Hillquit was a vote for peace, the Jewish plutocracy and its supporters reacted with the threat that a large Jewish vote for the socialists would provoke anti-Semitism. Jacob H. Schiff, Oscar S. Straus, Adolph Lewisohn, Daniel Guggenheim, Henry Morgenthau and Louis Marshall were among those who signed huge paid advertisements in the Yiddish press warning the voter against Hillquit.

Yet even by a Tammany count Hillquit got 145,332 votes, almost nosing out John Purroy Mitchell for second place (155,497), and carried 12 assembly districts with heavy Jewish population (Tammany later reorganized these districts to avoid such democratic disasters). More important, ten socialists were elected to the State Assembly, seven to the City Board of Aldermen,

Benjamin Schlesinger (1876-1932), a leader of the International Ladies' Garment Workers' Union.

and one to a judgeship. Meantime, in Rochester, N. Y., three Jewish socialists had been elected: an alderman, a supervisor, and a constable. And while Hillquit polled 22 per cent of the total vote in New York, the Chicago socialists attained one-third.

The day after these elections the Bolshevik Revolution began on November 7, 1917. The universal acclaim that had greeted the March revolution ended abruptly. It was one thing for the Tsar to be overthrown; it was quite another for the rule of landlords and capitalists to be replaced by the rule of workers and peasants. The social instinct of American reaction responded with an immediate wholesale propaganda attack on the new Soviet government.

How misinformed the American people were became a matter of public record when Walter Lippmann and Charles Merz (now editor of the *New York Times*) made a study of the way the *Times* had reported the *news* about the Bolshevik government in the first 1,000 days after November 7, 1917. Published as a supplement to the

Jacob Panken, labor lawyer and New York City municipal court judge.

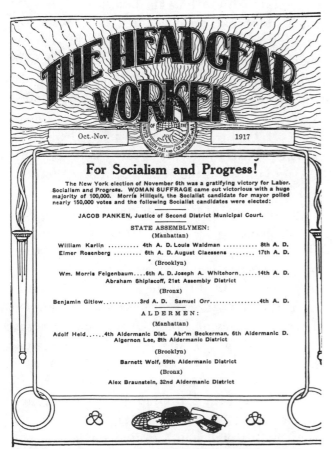

A Union newspaper reports socialist victories in the November, 1917 New York City elections.

New Republic on August 4, 1920, "A Test of the News" concluded that those who relied upon the *Times* had been totally misinformed about the *facts* of Soviet life for those 1,000 days, when basic attitudes and opinions were being shaped.

Part of the Yiddish press similarly reacted on the basis of its social class prejudices. Thus on November 9, 1917, the orthodox *Morgen Jurnal* already declared dogmatically that the Bolsheviks "have brought Russia closer to slavery and barbarism than at any time since the Romanov dynasty was destroyed." And the liberal *Tog*, on June 29, 1918 insisted that "once and for all an end must be made of the Bolsheviks." Yet the instincts of the Jewish masses, like those of millions of American workers, led them to perceive what was inspiringly new behind the tainted "news." In his doctoral dissertation on the Yiddish press of that day, Joseph Rappaport ended a close study with the observation that "the Leninists of Russia came to be looked upon in 1918 as the hope of the world for Socialism. . . . Sympathy for the Bolsheviks mounted in the succeeding months as Leninist efforts to stabilize conditions appeared to be the only alternative to chaos and a Rightist reaction." The *Forward* was then loudly pro-Bolshevik.

Simultaneously, however, ever larger sections of the socialist leadership began to capitulate to the government pressure to support the war. The glitter of Wilson's Fourteen Points of January 8, 1918 was taken as real socialist gold. When the drive for the Third Liberty Loan began in April, 1918, it was endorsed by the seven socialist aldermen in New York, just elected on a peace platform, as well as by Judge Jacob Panken and Congressman Meyer London. In Chicago on May Day, 1918, London rejoiced that Wilson had "adopted the substance of the international Socialist program." On May 10-12, 1918, the Jewish Socialist Federation held a national conference at which a majority repudiated the St. Louis resolution and took a pro-war stand by a vote of 25 to 19. This position was soon endorsed by the leadership of the Workmen's Circle, the U.H.T., the I.L.G.W.U., the Amalgamated Clothing Workers and other organizations. The unions not only bought Liberty Bonds with union funds but conducted a drive on the East Side that boosted the sale from $200,000 in the Second Liberty Loan to $12,000,000 in the Third.

Wilson, in the meantime, had so far failed to realize that he had "adopted the substance of the international Socialist program" that on August 3, 1918 he announced the United States would take part in Allied military intervention against the Soviet government. Wilson was applauded as a "liberator" in middle class Jewish organs like the *Morgen Jurnal,* the *Tog,* the *Varheit,* the *Yiddishe Tageblatt,* and the *American Hebrew,* while left wing Jews and even some supporters of the war fought this new move. The press incitement against such opposition led to hoodlum attacks. The New York Y.M.H.A. *Bulletin* of October, 1918 called upon its young charges to "break up that street meeting where Bolshevik doctrine is preached."

While there was disunity among the Jews on American policy and on the nature of the Bolshevik government, there was unity in deep horror at the pogroms in Eastern Europe in which thousands of Jews were being murdered in Poland, Galicia, Romania and most extensively in the Ukraine. In New York 8,000 Jewish workers gathered at Madison Square Garden on December 12, 1918 to "demand that civilized nations take steps to check the pogroms in Galicia and Poland," and on May 21, 1919 tens of thousands of Jews conducted a half-day protest strike against pogroms there and in the Ukraine. They were gratified to learn that in the Ukraine on August 22, 1919, 67 pogrom agitators were sentenced to death in Kiev.

Activity here in behalf of the Jews of Europe had two additional ends: to influence the peace treaties to guarantee formal legal rights for Jews in new states emerging from the war, and to promote recognition of Jewish claims in Palestine.

For these ends an American Jewish Congress convened in Philadelphia from December 15 to 18, 1918. Initiative for this movement had been taken by the Zionists from 1914, but there had been strenuous opposition from the Jewish plutocracy, which was quite content to have the public believe that the American Jewish Committee represented all the Jews in the country. Despite much indecision, organized Jewish workers participated in the Congress movement through the National Workmen's Committee on Jewish Rights in the Countries at War and in Romania, representing altogether 350,000 workers (founded April 15, 1915, and composed soon thereafter of the U.H.T., the Workmen's Circle, the Jewish Socialist Federation, the Poale Zion, Socialist Territorialists and the Jewish National Workers' Alliance).

On June 19, 1917, about 335,000 Jews voted for 300 delegates, an unprecedented event in Jewish life. Tactical differences had delayed the Congress, but when it did open, after the Armistice, on December 18, 1918, these 300 delegates plus 100 elected by national organizations, constituted the most representative body of Jews ever assembled in our country. All classes, religious groupings and social philosophies were there.

Two major decisions were reached. One was to cooperate with European Jewish delegations in presenting to the Paris Peace Conference a "Jewish Bill of Rights," calling for equal civil, political, religious and national rights in the new and enlarged states being formed out of the defeated Central Powers. The second was to cooperate with the World Zionist Organization so that "the Peace Conference might recognize the aspirations and historic claims of the Jewish people in regard to Palestine" as defined in the Balfour Declaration, and to ask that Britain assume the mandate over Palestine. A delegation of nine was elected: Judge Julian W. Mack, chairman, Joseph Barondess, Harry Cutler, Jacob de Haas, Rabbi Bernard Louis Levinthal, Louis Marshall, Nachman Syrkin, Morris Winchevsky and Rabbi Stephen S. Wise, with Bernard G. Richards as Secretary. Marshall of the American Jewish Committee and Winchevsky, representing socialist labor, were the only non-Zionists.

In Paris the delegation worked effectively, outstanding as lobbyists being Marshall, Mack and Wise. Woodrow Wilson was a powerful ally. The outcome was strikingly successful: in the Versailles Peace Treaty of June 28, 1919, Poland agreed to equal civil, political, religious and national rights for minorities, including the Jews, and similar clauses were written into the peace treaties with Austria, Yugoslavia, Czechoslovakia, Bulgaria and Romania. The League of Nations became the guarantor of this provision, as of all others in the Treaties. The fact that neither Poland nor Romania abided by it, and that the League did not enforce it, the American Jewish Congress could neither anticipate nor prevent. The second aim of the Congress was realized on April 24, 1920, when at San Remo the Peace Treaty with Turkey recognized Britain as the mandatory power over Palestine. Therefore when the American Jewish Congress reconvened to hear its delegation's report on May 30-31, 1920, gratification was high. But unity came to an end here. Marshall and the American Jewish Committee had at the first Congress exacted a pledge that it would be only a temporary body with a specified task. Now Marshall invoked this promise and the Congress dissolved. Immediately thereafter, however, the Zionist delegations convened to plan a permanent organization, which was finally established in 1922.

When the Armistice was signed, November 11, 1918, there was rejoicing in the land. Then came the bitter aftermath. The economic lords of our country were at the peak of their strength. Europe was now heavily indebted to them. War profiteering, subsequent official investigation revealed, had been rampant; even ordinary war profits had been enormous. Real wages, however, had declined and, as the economic historian, Professor Harold U. Faulkner, declared: "the immediate effect of the war appeared detrimental to labor."

Yet these rulers were haunted by a new form of their ancient fear of labor organized and the people aroused, which they saw embodied in the new Russian government. The Siberian Expeditionary Force, it was hoped, would help overthrow that government, but what about the eyes in our own country that had turned towards the East with curiosity, hope or even enthusiasm? And what about those who had taken literally the propaganda that they had been fighting for democracy and now wanted the fruits of victory? In answer, American reactionaries loosed against the American people an attack on all fronts. The conservative Frederick Lewis Allen described the result as "an era of lawless and disorderly defense of law and order, of unconstitutional defense of the Constitution, of suspicion and civil conflict—in a very literal sense, a reign of terror."

The targets of the terror were not new: the worker organized or trying to organize, the Negro, the foreign-born, the Jew. But these traditional strands of American reaction were fused by a new element: the International Red Scare and the cry of Bolshevik. Unions, aliens, Jews were all considered "Bolshevik." They and their defenders must be smashed, imprisoned, terrorized, deported.

Those who suffered most were the Negro people, who simply wanted elementary democratic rights. Southern trees rocked with the "strange fruit" of 239 reported lynched, some of them in army uniforms, from 1919 to 1922. Race riots swept the land in the summer of 1919: in Washington, D. C., Knoxville, Tenn., Tulsa, Okla., Longview, Tex., Omaha, Nebr., Elaine, Ark., and worst of all in Chicago. The Ku Klux Klan by 1924 claimed a membership of 4,500,000

From New York Times, Sat

SAYS MASS OF JEWS OPPOSE BOLSHEVIKI

Louis Marshall, Head of American Jewish Committee, Replies to Dr. Simons.

EAST SIDE NOT A HOTBED

Statement Calls Testimony to the Contrary Before Senate Committee "Ridiculous."

Louis Marshall, President of the American Jewish Committee, has given out a statement taking issue with the testimony of Dr George S. Simons [...]-Committee [...] quota to our military and [...] than any other part of our population.

"Let me also refer to the casualty lists to establish the fact that the Jews of this country not only served, but that they were brave and heroic, and were prepared to make the supreme sacrifice for America because they love it. Let me also refer to the list of citations for exceptional heroism, to the men who fought in the Argonne Forest, to those who constituted a part of the lost Battalion, and who participated in every movement of our troops. You will find among them east side Jews in large numbers.

"It is difficult to understand the motive behind this attempt to arouse unworthy passions. Attack Bolshevism as much as you please, and the Jews of America are with you.' But what justification is there for charging the Jews with Bolshevism, when in reality there is a smaller percentage of them who can truthfully be so denominated than there is in any other section of the American people? I might illustrate this point by referring to the recently published list of I. W. W.'s who are awaiting deportation, the vast majority of whom are non-Jews."

The American Jewish Committee reacts to a smear of the Jews, The New York Times, February 15, 1919.

and held dominant political positions in Ohio, Indiana, Arkansas, Oklahoma, Texas, California and Oregon.

Of course this racism spilled over into the mounting hostility to the immigrant masses. Racist theories of Anglo-Saxon superiority merged with anti-Bolshevik hysteria. The chairman of the Senate Committee on Immigration, Thomas R. Hardwick, "proposed restricting immigration as a means of keeping out Bolshevism." The result was the Immigration Law of 1920. Its preamble baldly accepted the unscientific premise of Anglo-Saxon supremacy. The law itself encouraged "Anglo-Saxon" immigration from Central and Northern Europe, and discouraged immigration from Southern and Eastern Europe, specifically Italian and Jewish. A quota system was devised that would annually admit three per cent of the number of immigrants from any country already here in 1910.

Upon Jewish immigration the effect was drastic. Average annual immigration from 1904 to 1914 had been over 100,000. In 1921, just before the law went into operation, Jewish immigrants numbered 119,036. In 1922, the total dropped to 53,524. But even that was considered too much. Therefore in 1924 the quotas were cut from three to two percent, and the base year was set back from 1910 to 1890. This new formula slashed Jewish immigration by more than 75 per cent, so that in 1925 it was only 10,292, a figure around which it hovered until the late 1930's. Jewish organizations had led all other immigrant groups in their determined efforts to resist immigration restrictions, but all of them together could not stem the tide.

Even before the passage of the immigration law, but as part of the new pattern of reaction, Jews were being subjected to new levels of anti-Semitic attack that sought to identify them with Bolshevism. In 1919 a Senate committee, headed by Lee S. Overman of North Carolina, inspired by the fable that the Kaiser and Lenin had conspired to establish the Bolsheviks in power, began public hearings on the relation between "German brewers and Bolshevik propaganda" in the United States! At widely-publicized hearings there was planted in the minds of millions, in garish color, the bewhiskered image of the free-loving, bomb-throwing, church-burning Bolsheviks.

From this governmental platform there was also proclaimed the "Jew-Bolshevik" link. A Dr. George S. Simons testified on February 13, 1919 that the Bolsheviks were Jews and that the conspiracy to overthrow the tsar was hatched in New York's lower East Side. The "defense" offered by the American Jewish Committee was characteristic. Its statement appeared in the *New York Times* on February 15 under the headline, "Says Mass of Jews Oppose Bolsheviki," followed by the subhead: "East Side Not a Hotbed." President Louis Marshall, who issued the statement, did not assert the democratic principle that Jews had as much right as anybody else to be Bolsheviks or communists. Instead he argued that Jews were patriotic and loved law and order like everybody else. Then Marshall, presuming to speak for all Jews and not only his Committee, declared, "Attack Bolshevism as much as you please and the Jews of America are with you." Ironically, Marshall himself was described as "a Bolshevik orator" on June 5, 1920 by Henry Ford's Dearborn Publishing Company.

Having weakened the public mind by this propaganda barrage, our government late in 1919 began mass raids in a hunt for "alien radicals" to be deported. This marauding was ordered by U.S. Attorney General A. Mitchell Palmer and executed under the direction of his Special Assistant J. Edgar Hoover. On November 7, 1919, second anniversary of the Soviet revolution, raids netted 452 arrests in 11 cities. The big putsch came New Year's Day, 1920, when 2,758 were arrested in 33 cities. The raids continued until 10,000 had been wantonly arrested, and despite much protest 300 were actually deported. Protests were loud, even if unheeded. One of the most resounding was made by Francis Fisher Kane, United States Attorney in Philadelphia, who resigned his post on January 12, 1920 with a public letter to Palmer and President Wilson. "Is it necessary," Kane asked Palmer, "to protect our American workingmen . . . from the influence of a handful of Russians and Russian Jews?"

While these mass arrests were making the sky crimson with injustice, Socialist Congressman Victor Berger of Milwaukee was denied his seat in the House on January 11, 1920, five Socialist New York State Assemblymen, a couple of them Jewish, had their seats challenged on January 7 and were finally excluded in April, 1920, and on May 5, there began the frame-up of Sacco and Vanzetti. It was in this fateful year that Henry Ford began his campaign of unbridled anti-Semitism.

The International Red Scare was at the bottom of this development too. Ford was converted to militant anti-Semitism by Boris Brasol, an agent of the tsar's secret police who had been involved

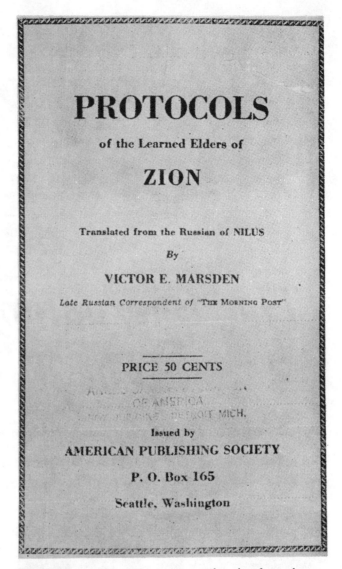

PROTOCOLS

of the Learned Elders of

ZION

Translated from the Russian of NILUS

By

VICTOR E. MARSDEN

Late Russian Correspondent of "The Morning Post"

PRICE 50 CENTS

OF AMERICA
DETROIT MICH.

Issued by

AMERICAN PUBLISHING SOCIETY

P. O. Box 165

Seattle, Washington

Circulating anti-Semitic propaganda, the forged "Protocols."

in the Mendel Beilis blood-libel case. Now a refugee employed here by the United States Secret Service, Brasol had the forged *Protocols of the Elders of Zion* translated into English and placed in the Secret Service files as a document to "explain the Russian Revolution." Then Brasol got the *Protocols* to Ford, who was promptly convinced that this "international Jewish conspiracy" was the cause of all the ills of the world. Thus from May, 1920, for over seven years, Ford's weekly, *The Dearborn Independent,* poured an uninterrupted stream of uninhibited and venomous anti-Semitism into millions of American homes.

This was the first large-scale, unified, nationwide anti-Semitic drive in American history. Dis-

The Ford International Weekly
THE DEARBORN INDEPENDENT

| By the Year One Dollar | Dearborn, Michigan, May 22, 1920 | Single Copy Five Cents |

The International Jew:
The World's Problem

Henry Ford's anti-Semitic campaign was conducted through this weekly for seven years.

tributed throughout the land by an apparatus that included the far-flung network of Ford deal-

ers, the *Dearborn Independent* swelled all the rivulets and quickened all the stagnant little pools of anti-Semitism that had accumulated all over the country on the basis of many sporadic local instances. Ford's drive began on the eve of the economic crisis of 18 months in 1920-21, when there were 4,750,000 unemployed, wages dropped, and 20,000 businesses failed, all providing rich soil for the growth of suspicion and hatred among the confused and perplexed. The International Red Scare had spawned the myth of the International Jewish Banker paradoxically linked to the International Jewish Bolshevik. The mysterious and interlocked Jews were said to be at the bottom of everything evil. Discrimination against Jews in employment, housing, social contacts and admission to colleges sharpened.

Ford's campaign here was so successful that on February 8, 1923, the *New York Times* reported Ford had expanded his interest to anti-Semitism abroad and was financing the newcomer, Hitler. A protest movement, however, had begun to mount in 1920, rapidly involving not only all of Jewish organized life but also many non-Jews. Headed by President Wilson, 119 distinguished

William Fox (1879-1952), movie magnate.

••• THE NEW YORK TIMES,

ISSUE A PROTEST ON ANTI-SEMITISM

A Notable Document Signed by Distinguished Americans, Led by President, Put on Record.

WHOLLY OF CHRISTIAN ORIGIN

Originated by John Spargo, Leaders of Thought Readily Signed It, Some of Them Adding Personal Comment.

BENNINGTON, Vt., Jan. 16.—A protest against anti-Semitic propaganda in the United States, bearing the signatures of President Wilson, William H. Taft, Cardinal O'Connell and 116 other prominent known men and women of this nation, single citizen himself, acting upon his own initiative and responsibility, and without consultation with anybody," he said, "wrote the brief protest and invited other distinguished citizens, non-Jews like himself, to sign it. All the work connected with the protest and all the expense involved, therefore, represent the contribution of an individual citizen to the defense of American ideals. Neither directly nor indirectly did any person of Jewish ancestry or faith, or any Jewish organization, contribute as much as a postage stamp to the cost of the undertaking."

President Wilson's Opinion.

So far as the President's signature is concerned, it was learned that when the protest was submitted to Mr. Wilson by its originator there was no thought in his mind that the President would himself desire to sign the document. At most the originator believed and hoped that Mr. Wilson might send some word of sympathetic approval of the protest. The President, however, preferred to sign the document and personally requested that his name be attached. President Wilson wrote:

ator Beveridge and John Spargo, the Socialist.

Following is the text of their protest, with the full list of signatures:

The undersigned, citizens of Gentile birth and Christian faith, view with profound regret and disapproval the appearance in this country of what is apparently an organized campaign of anti-Semitism, conducted in close conformity to and co-operation with similar campaigns in Europe. We regret exceedingly the publication of a number of books, pamphlets and newspaper articles designed to foster distrust and suspicion of our fellow-citizens of Jewish ancestry and faith—distrust and suspicion of their loyalty and their patriotism.

These publications, to which wide circulation is being given, are thus introducing into our national political life a new and dangerous spirit, one that is wholly at variance with our traditions and ideals and subversive of our system of government. American citizenship and American democracy are thus challenged and menaced. We protest against this organized campaign of prejudice and hatred, not only because of its manifest injustice to those against whom it is directed, but also, and especially, because we are concerned that it is wholly incompatible loyal intelligent opinion—the clergy and laity of all Christian churches, publicists, teachers, editors and statesmen—to strike at this un-American and un-Christian agitation.

Signed:

WOODROW WILSON.
WILLIAM HOWARD TAFT.
WILLIAM CARDINAL O'CONNELL.
LYMAN ABBOTT.
    Editor The Outlook.
JANE ADDAMS, *Social Worker.*
JOHN G. AGAR, *Lawyer.*
NEWTON D. BAKER,
    Secretary of War.
RAY STANNARD BAKER, *Author.*
CHARLES A. BEARD,
    Author and Educator.
JAMES M. BECK, *Lawyer.*
BERNARD I. BELL,
    President St. Stephen's College.
ARTHUR E. BESTOR,
    President Chautauqua Institution.
ALBERT J. BEVERIDGE,
    Former U. S. Senator.
W. E. B. DUBOIS,
    Editor The Crisis.
MABEL T. BOARDMAN,
    Commissioner D. of C.
EVANGELINE BOOTH,
    Commander Salvation Army.
BENJAMIN BREWSTER,
    Bishop of Maine.
CHAUNCEY B. BREWSTER,
    Bishop of Connecticut.
JEFFREY R. BRACKETT.

Democratic American opinion condemns the anti-Semitic movement, January 16, 1921.

non-Jews on January 16, 1921 issued a statement defending the Jews. On another level, the film magnate, William Fox, compelled Ford to stop a scheduled smear of him by threatening Ford with a news-reel campaign in all Fox theaters demonstrating that Ford cars get into more accidents than any others. Decisive, however, was the mass boycott of Ford cars, which led to a great slump in the sale of the Model T, especially in the East. Finally, on June 30, 1927 Ford addressed an apology to Louis Marshall as head of the American Jewish Committee asking forgiveness and promising to stop circulation of the "exploded fictions," "gross forgeries" and other slanders against the Jews. Yet he did not do so, for *The International Jew,* a compilation of vicious anti-Semitic articles in the *Dearborn Independent,* has continued to circulate, both here and abroad.

The bulk of the Jewish population, as part of the working class, suffered from still another phase of the post-war reaction: the direct attack

Check of the Amalgamated Clothing Workers of America for the Steel Strikers.

The Amalgamated Clothing Workers of America contribute $100,000 to the steel strikers, November 8, 1919.

on the labor movement. During the war, despite Gompers' and the other A. F. of L. leaders' support of the war, the workers had fought against the bounding cost of living. Thus there were more strikes (4,233) in 1917 than in any preceding year, and A. F. of L. membership rose from 2,072,702 in 1916 to 2,726,478 in 1918. After the Armistice there was an upsurge of labor action. By 1920, A. F. of L. membership had leaped to 4,078,740. From 1919 to 1922, about 10,000,000 workers went on strike. In 1919 more than 4,160,000 struck, with 411,000 coal miners led by John L. Lewis and, most important, because the steel industry was an open-shop fortress, 367,000 steel workers led by William Z. Foster.

On their own scale, the Jewish workers were also active. The war boom had enabled them to improve their conditions, especially by reducing the hours of work. By 1919 the Amalgamated Clothing Workers, the I.L.G.W.U., and the fur and headgear workers had won the 44-hour week in many garment centers. The Jewish workers particularly saw the significance of the steel strike, the first major effort to unionize the giant among monopolies. Of the total of $418,141 in contributions received by the strike committee, $20,000 came from the International Fur Workers' Union, $60,000 from the I.L.G.W.U., and

$100,000 from the Amalgamated, the last being up to that time "the largest gift of its kind ever made by any union in this country."

In 1920 the big employers, having broken the steel strike, counter-attacked with the American Plan, which, as Professor Selig Perlman and Philip A. Taft note, "purported to abolish the 'un-American' closed shop but as in previous open shop crusades, the destruction of unionism was the real objective." This offensive was effective. Instead of facing the open-shoppers squarely, the A.F.L. Executive Council was diverted by the Red Scare. At the very depth of the economic crisis, on February 23, 1921, the Council called a meeting of union officials "to combat the problems arising from unemployment, reaction and Bolshevism." The A.F.L. lost more than one million members, declining by 30 per cent from its 1920 peak to 2,865,979 in 1924. In the Jewish field, the employers, being much smaller, had no such successes. The New York cloakmakers won a general strike of 55,000 that began on November 14, 1921 and lasted nine hard weeks. In the summer of 1922, the men's clothing workers won a two-week strike of 40,000. But in the next few years the international Red Scare and anti-Bolshevism descended upon the Jewish labor movement and blighted it.

While the Red Scare was siphoned into the

ranks of the workers in general by the leadership of the A.F.L., it was brought into the ranks of the Jewish workers by the leaders of the Socialist Party. Since the consequences directly affected every aspect of Jewish working class life, economic, political, cultural and social, and therefore indirectly influenced the entire Jewish population, it is necessary to examine the bitter struggle that ensued.

In the Socialist Party, the split, which had deepened on the issue of the war, reached the breaking point in 1919. The fundamental differences had to do primarily with foreign affairs, but also with domestic issues like the workers' living conditions and rights. Decisive was the attitude to the Russian Bolshevik Revolution and the first socialist state it had established, and to the newly-born Communist International. Beginning in May, 1919 the National Executive Committee, led by Morris Hillquit, began to expel entire state, city and foreign-language socialist federations. From a membership of 108,504 in 1919, the party fell to 26,766 in 1920. (Yet that year, Debs, Presidential candidate on the socialist ticket, polled 915,302 votes, pulling especially well in Jewish working-class areas.)

In the Jewish Socialist Federation the process by which the left majority turned its back on the entrenched leadership lasted until September, 1921. By that time the communist movement, having survived the Palmer Raids and the police persecution, was ready to found the Workers (later the Communist) Party. The left Jewish Federation took part in the first convention of the Workers Party opening December 23, 1921, with the Left Poale Zion represented by fraternal delegates. Immediately thereafter the Jewish Federation set to work to publish a daily newspaper despite very limited resources. Under the editorship of the brilliant and influential Olgin, and with a body of writers that included the venerable Winchevsky, the first issue of the *Freiheit* appeared on April 2, 1922. Although some of its writers like Zivion (B. Hoffman) after about a year or so reverted from the Freiheit to the *Forward*, there quickly rallied around the *Freiheit* the left-wing Yiddish-speaking workers, communist and non-communist. In 1925, when,

out of a Workers Party membership of 16,325, the Jewish Federation had only 1,447, the *Freiheit* circulation was several times that number. The *Jewish Daily Forward,* in which socialist content was steadily draining away, at that time, however, had a circulation of over 150,000.

Now the right-wing socialists who had not hesitated to expel tens of thousands from the S.P. were also in the leadership of the large Jewish unions and the Workmen's Circle, and carried their war against the left-wing into these organizations. The struggle was sharpest in the garment industry. It was civil war in the ranks of Jewish labor, and only the main enemy, the organized employers, benefited. Even anti-communist labor writers have conceded that the right-wing socialist office-holders were callous, ruthless and dictatorial in their attacks on the *majorities* that followed the left, and that the "successes" of the right wing prostrated the unions and drove workers' conditions down. Thus Joel Seidman, one such writer, observed that "the failure of some of the old union leaders to solve these industrial problems provided an opportunity for an opposition group to win support from the dissatisfied and restless masses. . . . The policy of mass expulsions and revocations of charters followed by the I.L.G.W.U. national leadership, far from having the desired effect, instead solidified large sections of the rank and file behind left leadership. . . . The movement that the Communists led won wide support in union ranks partly because, unlike the I.W.W., it long opposed dual unionism."

The expulsions mentioned by Seidman were no trifling matters. They began on a small scale in 1923 in New York and Chicago. But in 1925, about 30,000 were expelled in June when the elected leaderships of Local 2, 9 and 22 were removed, the offices of two locals were seized and the third, Local 22, held on to its office only by mounting a continual emergency membership guard. Their jobs, shop conditions and the very union at stake, the workers rallied to a Joint Action Committee of the three locals, 40,000 coming to a Yankee Stadium meeting on July 10 and 30,000 responding to a call for a work stoppage on August 10, 1925. As the anti-communist Benjamin Stolberg admitted in his history of the union in 1944, "obviously the vast majority of the workers were with the left wing and not with the International. But that didn't seem to faze Morris Sigman," president of the International. At first, Sigman retreated and the expulsions were rescinded. But "Sigman's power rested," Stolberg coolly remarked, "on the rotten borough system. . . . A small local of a few hundred buttonhole makers, for instance, had five delegates on the Joint Board and so did the huge dressmakers Local 22 . . . the small unions had a disproportionately large number of delegates in the national conventions. Since most of them were mainly right-wing, they made up a Sigman majority in the conventions."

Finally the right wing saw its "opportunity," towards the end of a long and faction-ridden strike of 40,000 cloakmakers that had begun on July 1, 1926. On December 9, two days before the signing of a compromise agreement covering about one third of the workers, the United Hebrew Trades, according to Morris C. Feinstone, a leading figure in this action, "took the initiative. It sent out a call to all affiliated unions and internationals and to the American Federation of Labor inviting delegates to convene and discuss the organization of a counter-movement against the Communist penetration of the trade union movement." On December 13, Sigman removed the officers of the New York Joint Board conducting the strike, settled the strike over the heads of the locals and the Joint Board, liquidated the existing locals—and then invited the members individually to re-register with the International or else lose their jobs in union shops. In reply, 18,000 workers rallied at Madison Square Garden on December 18 to fight such bureaucratic tactics. But on December 21 the conference called by the U.H.T. was held with 500 delegates and Feinstone as secretary. Feinstone concluded his account thus: "They organized a Committee for the Preservation of Trade Unions. . . . Its success was enormous, since the whole labor movement co-operated with it. Great numbers of communists were driven from cover and forced to start opposition unions." And then the same right wingers denounced the expelled as "dual

unionists" for organizing to protect their very livelihoods!

It was not the bureaucrats but the workers, including those not expelled, who suffered. For, as another anti-communist labor writer, Melech Epstein, summed it up in 1953, "The right had won the battle, but the union lay wrecked." The left wing, led by communists, made many errors of judgment and policy, stemming from the general sectarianism and revolutionary romanticism of the communists. They failed to study the specific political and industrial conditions in the United States. They disregarded major objective differences between American industrial and class relations and the situation in Russia, although one can understand that Russia, as the first socialist state, inevitably would have an inspiring influence on workers everywhere. There was confusion of political and trade union aims, a heritage of Daniel De Leon's old theory, and sometimes interference by political leaders in the internal life of the unions. Main responsibility for the disasters nevertheless lay with the right wing socialist bureaucrats and the A.F.L. leadership that spurred them on to fight the expressed will of the membership.

In the headgear and men's clothing trades the fight was not so intense, although attacks against left workers were not uncommon. Sidney Hillman, president of the Amalgamated Clothing Workers, was not part of the *Jewish Daily Forward* group which led the attacks, nor was his independent union subject to A.F.L. pressure. On general issues, furthermore, the A.C.W. often took positions supported by the left wing. Although there were occasional expulsions and suspensions of officers, Hillman, perhaps learning from the I.L.G.W.U. debacle, rejected mass expulsions.

It was only in the furriers' union that the workers defeated the right wing. Mass expulsions by socialist officials were ineffective because the left-led Joint Board and locals had organized the trade so thoroughly that employers could hire workers only through the left-led locals. Ben Gold, militant and resourceful himself, was surrounded by a more homogeneous leadership than existed in other garment trades. This left leader-

Furriers conducting mass picketing in the 1926 New York general strike.

ship defeated the coalition of A.F.L. and social-ist machines by uniting the workers and dividing the coalition, which had in vain resorted to gang-sterism and the aid of the police against the left. The victors were the united workers—as their improved union conditions demonstrated.

Ben Gold, leader of the furriers' union.

All along the line the Jewish trade union movement was weakened. When the economic crisis struck in 1929, unionism, except for the furriers, was low indeed. Again it was from the left that there came the initiative, clarity and courage to lead the workers to defend them-selves against the worst immediate ravages of the crisis.

In the Jewish labor fraternal movement there occurred a parallel development. This was inter-related with the strife in the unions, since many union members also belonged to the Workmen's Circle. But other inner tensions also played their part in the developing split: the conflict with the Old Guard, the clash with the "assimila-tors" who opposed the Yiddish children's schools, the hostility to the dominance of the organiza-tion's leadership by the *Forward,* with its sharp-ening anti-Sovietism.

There was, however, one significant factor that might have saved the situation had it con-tinued to operate: the Workmen's Circle had from its origin explicitly declared that it would be non-partisan with regard to the labor politics of its members, and would encompass and support them all (socialist, socialist-laborite, anarchist, etc.) without discrimination. The National Executive Committee of the Workmen's Circle, however, abandoned this cardinal tenet when it joined the fight against the left wing. The 1921 convention thus refused to support communist periodicals by a vote of 59 to 56. At the May, 1922 convention, another decisive difference came to the fore. There was unanimity on a resolution that the United States and other powers recognize the Soviet Union. But there was harsh debate on a proposal to call upon the Soviet government to "allow full freedom to all socialist parties in Russia" and to "free the socialist political prisoners," the vote being 100 to 49 for the resolution. Finally, by 111 to 26 the convention condemned the "methods" of the newly-born *Freiheit* and the Jewish Section of the Workers' Party, which had been bluntly critical of the Workmen's Circle leadership.

The conflict sharpened. At the 1925 convention, the vote was 834 to 171 to invoke disciplinary measures against the left. For organizing the League of Progressive Branches of the Workmen's Circle, the N.E.C. dissolved 64 branches (which were later reinstated), began to reorganize others, to remove left-wingers elected to city committees, and in general to provoke a split. The left-wingers gave up the League but continued to work for their program. Unfortunately, there was much heated, abusive recrimination on both sides, characteristic of such factional strife.

The N.E.C. also struck at the children's Yiddish *shules* (schools), promoted for ten years chiefly by the left-wingers. Early in 1926, the N.E.C. withdrew financial support from 18 of the 24 schools in New York. Reorganized as the Non-Partisan Yiddish Workers' Children's Schools, the left Yiddish educational movement grew by 1929 to 57 schools with almost 3,000 pupils in New York, Philadelphia, Chicago, Boston, Detroit and Los Angeles, while the Workmen's Circle and other Yiddish schools in 1928 had 3,600 pupils in 52 schools in New York City.

Meanwhile the Workmen's Circle was losing membership, dropping from 84,791 in 1925 to 71,482 in 1929. Proposals by the left wing for peace on the basis of an all-inclusive Workmen's Circle were ignored by the right-wing National Executive Committee. Finally the left-wingers allowed themselves to be provoked. At a conference on October 11-13, 1929, delegates from 108 branches and 22 minority groups issued a call for secession. When the N.E.C. succeeded in influencing the Independent Workmen's Circle to reject the proposed affiliation of the seceders, the latter felt compelled to found a new organization. On March 30, 1930, delegates from 157 branches of the Workmen's Circle and Independent Workmen's Circle and of 13 minority groups decided to organize the International Workers' Order, and elected Rubin Saltzman as General Secretary. The Jewish Section of the I.W.O. was established in July, 1933, with Saltzman as National Secretary.

Another phase of Jewish life vitally affected during this period was its relationship to Zionism and Palestine. With the Balfour Declaration there began a long-range process of realignment of all forces, including anti-Zionists and non-Zionists, to the reality of the Jewish community in Palestine. Not only did Zionist organization temporarily grow in size (150,000 members in 1917; 173,000 in 1920; 237,000 in 1921; but 120,-000 in 1927), but it grew more significantly in influence as it developed a united front with non-Zionists who wished to aid in building the Jewish community in Palestine.

There were two areas in which opposition to Zionism had for two decades been traditional. The first was in Reform Judaism, with its upper middle class following and its plutocratic leadership, which was anti-Zionist, with such notable exceptions as Bernhard Felsenthal of Chicago, Max Heller of New Orleans, Stephen S. Wise of New York and a few others. Reform proclaimed "America as our Zion," and wanted no other, fearing that Zionist clamor for another homeland would raise the question of "dual loyalty" about all Jews. And since "100 per centism" had spread during and after the war, and "loyalty" was therefore a touchy issue, Reform was alarmed when the Balfour Declaration gave the Zionists their big impetus.

The second center of opposition was in the Jewish class-conscious workers and their socialist-oriented, anti-imperialist leadership. Here there were two lines of criticism. The first was that Zionist nationalism, even in Poale (labor) Zionism, diverted the workers from the class struggle here, including the fight against anti-Semitism in this country, and diluted the loyalty of the workers to the labor movement and its socialist aims. The second criticism made was that the Zionist alliance with Great Britain, whose imperialist ends in the Middle East were transparent, placed them in opposition to the historically progressive tide of anti-imperialism rising in the Middle East.

While hostility to Zionism loosened very slowly in the Reform and Jewish labor movements, a favorable attitude to Palestine itself began to appear after the Balfour Declaration. Among wealthy and Reform Jews, change was evident in the resolution adopted by the American Jewish Committee at a special meeting on April 28, 1918. Guided by Louis Marshall, the meeting resolved "to aid in the realization of the Balfour Declaration" for the benefit of that minority of Jews that would settle in Palestine, and "to cooperate . . . to establish in Palestine a center for Judaism . . . and for the rehabilitation of the land." True, the Central Conference of American Rabbis in 1919 opposed the Balfour Declaration and declared that American Jews "do not seek for Israel any national homeland," and in 1922 prominent Reform rabbis fought the resolution in the United States Congress supporting the Declaration and the British Mandate (which Congress passed unanimously on September 14). Yet more and more Reform rabbis and laymen gave aid to Palestine until in 1935 the C.C.A.R. reversed its position. Chaim Weizmann, eager to get the financial aid of rich American Jews, in January, 1924 won over their spokesmen, Louis Marshall, Felix Warburg and Cyrus Adler, to his plan to expand the Jewish Agency for Palestine by giving them equal representation. However, the death of Marshall in September, 1929, shortly after the final arrangements, and Lord Passfield's British White Paper of October, 1930, virtually suspending Jewish immigration into Palestine because of the Arab riots of 1929, disrupted the plan, and the Jewish Agency soon reverted to being an arm of the World Zionist Organization. Helpful in reorienting the rich Jews was the support given the Mandate by imperialist powers in the League of Nations in 1922 as well as by the U.S. Congress. This factor had quite the opposite effect upon the anti-imperialist Jewish workers, who were suspicious of the League of Nations and opposed to the reactionary Congress.

Yet among the workers, too, the distinction between Palestine and Zionism began to be drawn early but gingerly. That the A.F.L. Convention on November 30, 1917 endorsed Jewish aspirations "for a national homeland in Palestine" was more impressive to the general public than to Jewish labor, which regarded the A.F.L. as conservative politically. The Independent Workmen's Circle, however, at its convention on December 20, 1917, resolved to advocate a Jewish state in Palestine and urged that conditions favorable to labor be created there. A New York City Jewish labor congress from January 16 to 19, 1919, called by the Jewish Socialist Federation, agreed to favor in Palestine a republic in which all nationalities have equal rights, but since Jews were a weak minority there it was urged that their rights be protected by international guarantees. Yet, as Joseph Schlossberg, Socialist, Zionist, and secretary-treasurer of the Amalgamated Clothing Workers, has said, "in the early Twenties, anti-Palestine feeling was dominant among the Jewish laboring masses in America."

In 1923, nevertheless, the Histadrut (General Federation of Labor in Palestine, founded in 1920) appealed to the United Hebrew Trades and Zionist labor leaders for support. The right-wing Jewish Socialist Farband (Alliance) opposed the Histadrut invitation to send a labor delegation to Palestine. The Zionists, however, did launch the *Geverkshaften Campaign* to collect funds from Jewish trade unionists, and raised $51,000. In 1924 the United Hebrew Trades of New York gathered $55,000 for the Histadrut and since then the Campaign has expanded so that over a 30-year period it has averaged more than a million dollars per year. Poale Zion, of course, was an important force in this activity, as well as in doing what the general Zionists neglected, initiating a youth movement that

Louis Lipsky (1876-1963), Zionist.

started to train a few agricultural settlers for pioneering in Palestine.

Inside the Zionist movement, two vital developments occurred. The first was the Pittsburgh Program, adopted at the June, 1918 convention of the Zionist Organization of America, which had in 1917 replaced the Federation of American Zionists. This program was drafted by Louis D. Brandeis, who had remained as the "silent leader" after he had been sworn in as a United States Supreme Court judge on June 5, 1916 and had had to yield the reins of office to his followers, Federal Judge Julian W. Mack and Rabbi Stephen S. Wise. The Program called for: 1) "political and civil equality irrespective of race, sex, or faith of all the inhabitants of the land," 2) "ownership and control by the whole people of the land, of all natural resources and of all public utilities," 3) the leasing of all land on conditions that "will insure the fullest opportunity for development and continuity of possession," 4) "the cooperative principle . . . so far as feasible in the organization of all agricultural, industrial, commercial, and financial undertakings," and 5) "free public instruction" in "all grades." The liberal, almost socialistic, air of

the Program—which reflected both the sentiments of the Jewish people and the personal anti-monopoly views of Brandeis—was displeasing to the conservative European Zionist leadership.

This rift grew into the second development, the conflict with Chaim Weizmann and the European Zionist leadership that led to defeat of the Brandeis forces at the Cleveland Convention of the Z.O.A. in June, 1921. Brandeis simply wished to establish a homeland in Palestine for those Jews who needed to go there; therefore he wanted to concentrate on stimulating investments and collecting funds specifically for this end. He was much less concerned than the Europeans and some American veteran Zionists with Hebraism, with agitation to awake Jewish nationalism and with Zionistic education. He opposed particularly the "commingling of funds" raised for Palestine with those to be used for the promotion of cultural nationalism. The Brandeis leadership was repudiated by a vote of 153 to 71. The majority, led by Louis Lipsky, reflected not only the principles of the Weizmann

Rabbi Hillel Silver (1893-1963) of Cleveland, Ohio, Zionist leader and liberal Republican.

forces but also habits of thought and feeling of the East European Jews who made up the bulk of the Zionist support. Immediately after this defeat, not only did Brandeis resign as Honorary President, but so did 37 officers, including Mack, Wise, Frankfurter, Abba Hillel Silver, Nathan Straus and Benjamin V. Cohen. The breach was not fully healed until 1930. Meantime Zionist work, chiefly fund-raising and propaganda for its political ideal, continued, although much hindered by the absence of the Brandeis style of planning and methodical operation. From 1921 to 1929, about $10,000,000 were turned over to the *Keren Hayesod* (Palestine Foundation Fund), 55 per cent of the total gathered throughout the world. Ford's campaign of anti-Semitism may have turned many Jews to an interest in Zionism; yet the membership in 1927 was 50,000 less than in 1920. Nevertheless, social idealism and self-sacrifice characterized tens of thousands for whom the Zionist movement became a way of life.

Shaping such developments in the labor and Zionist spheres were changes in the social composition of the Jewish population. These shifts were determined by two factors: the cutting down of immigration, which led to the stabilization of the Jewish community and growth in influence of English-speaking and native-born Jews, and the boom period in the American economy, which led to the expansion of the Jewish middle and lower middle class.

In 1920, shop and factory workers made up the majority of Jews gainfully employed, at least in big cities with large Jewish populations. Part of this proletariat, however, and a large section of its children, responding to the "American dream" of rising out of the working class, took advantage of available opportunities and began to work their way up into business and professional categories. The boom helped some leave the shops and become small storekeepers. Other workers became contractors or small employers in their own trades. In heavy industry it was impossible for the steel worker or miner to go into the steel or mining business for himself; for the Jewish garment, food or similar worker who was thrifty and ambitious, it was relatively

Henrietta Szold (1860-1945), founder of Hadassah, the womens' Zionist organization.

easy to go into business for himself on a small scale until he expanded or failed—and the rate of bankruptcies was very high indeed. The clothing industry, for instance, was undergoing a phenomenal expansion, especially in women's apparel. From a little over two billion dollars worth of clothing produced in 1916, the figure jumped to almost four and a half billion in 1929.

Another booming area was in real estate speculation and building construction. In 1925 alone there was six billion dollars worth of building done in the United States, one billion dollars of it in New York City. There emerged a considerable number of Jewish builders, realtors, and landlords in the large cities. Jews were heavily involved in the wildcat Florida land speculation, which collapsed in the summer of 1925 when anti-Semitic manipulators, in trying to fleece the Jews, ruined Jewish and non-Jewish speculators alike. The damage was compounded by the hurricane of September 18, 1926, which took over 700 lives and caused about $100,000,000 property damage. Yet Jews stayed on to build up a fast-growing community in Miami of which this real estate was the foundation.

Still another road to advancement was through

Julia Richman (1855-1912), educator.

higher education into the professions, which were also expanding swiftly. In the Old Countries, legal quota systems had excluded thousands of Jews from the *gymnasium* and university and therefore from the professions. This frustration caused a thirst for higher education and professional careers. The absence of such formal barriers in the United States encouraged Jews to snatch at the unprecedented opportunities for higher education. Shop workers themselves did not find this path easy, although many eagerly used the available evening school facilities. As often as possible, however, shop workers steered their children away from following them into the shops to share the low wages, poor working conditions and the demoralizing slack periods in the seasonal trades. By scrimping for a few years, parents could thus redirect their children because of the availability of higher education in the big cities, especially New York, which had

half the Jewish population of the country. There, uniquely, workers' sons and daughters could get higher education free, and children of the middle class who preferred to pay tuition could still live inexpensively at home while attending the private colleges in the city. Thus a study for the academic year 1918-1919 showed about 15,000 Jewish students in 106 colleges in or near large Jewish population centers; of these about half were enrolled in nine colleges in New York City. It is an index to the growth of the middle class that while 2,046 went to the free colleges, C.C.N.Y. and Hunter, 4,007 went to New York University and Columbia.

In comparison with the general population, the proportion of Jews in college was greater. A 1916 estimate indicated that 2.1 boys and 1.1 girls went to college out of every 1,000 persons in the country, while among the Jews it was 3.6 boys and .4 girls out of every 1,000 Jews. The disproportion has increased. The reasons are threefold: 1) the Jewish tradition of respect for learning; 2) their ready access to educational facilities as a group that is overwhelmingly urban and increasingly middle-class; 3) their awareness of anti-Semitic discrimination in employment, which turns many Jews to the self-employment of the "free professions." Thus the 1918-1919 study revealed that Jews in professional courses were concentrated much more than non-Jews in medicine, dentistry and pharmacy (36.5 per cent together), in commerce and finance (accounting; 23.1 per cent), and in law (14.7 per cent), while Jews were very much under-represented in engineering and education, which are not generally professions of self-employment. The number of Jewish physicians in 10 big cities who were graduated from 1916 to 1930 was 5,128.

With the number of Jews in these intellectual pursuits growing, there came an increase in the quality of their contribution. Many achieved eminence in their fields. In 1922 a listing brought to light about 1,500 "Jews of prominence" in the United States outside rabbinical and Jewish communal work. There were 483 Jews prominent as writers (275), editors (73), journalists (58), newspaper and book publishers (37), dramatists (27), and so forth. There were 435 Jews eminent in other arts, including 180 artists, 105 composers, conductors and teachers of music, 87 in theatrical work as actors, directors, producers and managers, and 30 in the new field of film. There were about 150 prominent Jewish physicians and surgeons, 150 in the legal profession, 208 in science, from anthropology to zoology. Jewish representatives in Congress multiplied from five and six in 1916 and 1918 to ten and eleven after 1920. Significantly, of these 1,500 Jews, 578 were born in the United States, about 400 in Slavic countries, and about 200 in Central and Western Europe. So soon after their arrival in large numbers, East European Jews, having mastered various aspects of American life, were rivalling the prestige positions of the German Jews and the native-born Jews of German-Jewish parentage.

While there was this steady shift of the Jewish population towards the middle class, there was also a growth in the total Jewish population, although the rate of growth declined. From 1907 to 1917, it had almost doubled, from 1,777,000 to 3,389,000, but from 1917 to 1927 the Jewish population increased only 25 per cent, to 4,228,000. For the United States as a whole, population rose only 14.9 per cent from 1910 to 1920 and 16.1 per cent from 1920 to 1930.

These four and a quarter million Jews were very elaborately organized. A detailed study made by Harry S. Linfield in 1927 brought to light 17,238 Jewish organizations, not including Jewish branches of general organizations. There were 3,118 congregations (18 per cent of the total), and 7,138 local organizations directly affiliated with these congregations, making 60 per cent of all Jewish organizations revolving on this religious axis. Of the congregations themselves, however, only 56 per cent were served by rabbis (1,751 in number). In comparison, there were already 1,400 social workers in the National Conference of Jewish Social Service.

Philanthropic organizations were of two kinds: the economic that provided benefits for its own membership, and the social that raised funds to help others. There were 4,238 economic-philanthropic groups, of which 58 per cent were not affiliated with congregations. For economic self-help, the trend was away from the congregation.

Thus, of 2,367 mutual benefit societies, 94 per cent were not connected with congregations. The 10 fraternal benefit orders had a total membership of 282,504, of which 90,000 belonged to the Workmen's Circle, the largest of all. The second type, social-philanthropic groups, numbered 2,895, two-thirds of them women's societies. Of the total, 65 per cent were affiliated with congregations, and 56 per cent were women's clubs in congregations. (Women had become the most active workers in congregational endeavors.) Also in this social-philanthropic category were 206 Sections of the National Council of Jewish Women with 50,000 members; the national *landsmanshaften* like the Federation of Polish Jews with 50,000 members, the Federation of Hungarian Jews with 35,000, and the United Romanian Jews with 16,000; and 24 Jewish country clubs and 145 city clubs for wealthy Jews faced with social discrimination in club life.

A special kind of philanthropic work was done by 12 national Zionist societies with about 120,000 members; about 10 per cent were in three youth organizations, Young Judea, Junior Hadassah, and Young Poale Zion. The women's Zionist society, Hadassah, had 285 chapters and 232 junior groups. In the year ending September 30, 1927, the recently organized United Palestine Appeal collected $3,257,881. An even larger sum, $4,838,592, was spent in 1927 by the Joint Distribution Committee, which concentrated on aiding Jews in Eastern Europe, although almost 10 per cent of its overseas allotment went to Palestine. Almost half this sum was used by the American Jewish Joint Agricultural Corporation (Agro-Joint), established in 1924 to cooperate with the Soviet Russian government in settling thousands of Jewish families on the land. For a similar purpose, the left-wing, Yiddish-speaking Association for Colonization of Jews in the Soviet Union (ICOR) also collected funds, but on a much more modest scale.

Jewish youth were served both by organizations and by educational institutions. There were 912 organizations, only 401 connected with congregations. In 139 colleges there were 502 Jewish student groups, 80 per cent of them fraternities; 44 were Menorah Societies stressing Jewish

The Pacific Hebrew Orphan Asylum, in 1916. Sponsored by the B'nai B'rith, it housed 89 boys and 98 girls that year.

cultural interests, and five were chapters of Hillel, founded by B'nai B'rith in 1923. The Jewish educational network was ramified. There were 249,409 pupils in 2,192 Jewish elementary schools in 1927. Of these, 44 per cent were attending Sabbath or Sunday schools, 1.48 per cent (3,697)

Two tents on desert land near Los Angeles in 1913 marked the beginning of the tuberculosis hospital, City of Hope, which treats patients of all creeds and nationalities.

The City of Hope National Medical Center at Duarte, California, as it is today.

were in 12 full-time Jewish parochial schools, and the remainder in week-day afternoon schools. The education was overwhelmingly religious. Almost 80 per cent of the pupils attended congregational schools, whose main aim as a rule was to prepare the boys for *bar-mitzvah*. Most of the others went to Talmud Torahs, where a more rounded education in religion and Hebrew studies was the objective. Only in 59 communities with Yiddish schools was the curriculum secular. There were also 605 pupils in three Jewish secondary schools in New York, which grafted a Jewish curriculum to the regular high school course, 575 students in five rabbinical seminaries, and 2,405 in 19 Jewish teachers training schools.

Among philanthropic organizations, there were 1,020 concerned with the care of dependent children, the handicapped, widowed, sick, delinquent and aged. They maintained 44 orphan homes, 43 homes for the aged, and 25 day nurseries. There were also 61 Jewish hospitals, sanatoria and convalescent homes in 25 cities in 17 states, 25 in New York City with a bed capacity of over 5,000, half the total. The biggest hospitals were Mount Sinai and Montefiore in New York, with bed capacities of 635 and 600 respectively, and Michael Reese in Chicago, with 565.

Organizations of a special kind were the American Jewish Committee and American Jewish Congress. The former in 1927 had 189 "corporate members" who decided policy, and 1,908 persons who contributed $5 or more (sustaining members), in 264 cities in 46 states; there were 16 national organizations affiliated. The Ameri-

"La Vara," Ladino weekly published in New York.

can Jewish Congress had chapters or committees in 100 communities, and 32 affiliated national organizations, which included 12 insurance-paying fraternal orders, six Zionist organizations, three *landsmanshaften,* two congregational federations, two rabbinical seminaries and a rabbinical association, a woman's organization and a college society. Finally, for coordinating philanthropic work, in 1927 there were 42 city federations, New York having two, one of them in Brooklyn. These federations integrated the work of Jewish philanthropies only. In addition, Jews were known as active contributors to general philanthropic funds such as the Community Chests, and also attained renown for munificence bestowed on innumerable causes and institutions.

The Jewish population, then, was highly organized and thus constituted a community. At the same time there was vast diversity of interest and much division along class, political, social, religious and cultural lines.

A great unifying factor within the Jewish population was the Jewish press, which also, however, reflected the diversity of views within the Jewish community. The number of periodicals (daily, weekly, monthly, and so forth) in Yiddish, English, Hebrew and Ladino grew steadily, almost doubling from 57 in 1917 to 111 in 1927, but there was a drop to 95 in 1928. In circulation, the Yiddish press was dominant, with the causes for the later decline, however, accumulating. In 1916, the five Yiddish dailies had a circulation of 537,982, with the *Jewish Daily Forward* having 198,982; in 1922, the circulation of nine Yiddish dailies was 452,569, and of 13 weeklies, 185,496; in 1927, seven dailies circulated about 414,000 copies, but the figure declined to six dailies and 372,000 copies in 1928. The proportion of Yiddish periodicals in the Jewish press sank from 51 per cent in 1917 to 37 per cent in 1927, and to 22 per cent in 1928; in absolute figures the decline was from 29 in 1917 to 21 in 1928. This trend reflected the fact that more and more Jews were using English as their vernacular in personal relations and their cultural life. It is true that in the 1920 census a majority of the Jewish popu-

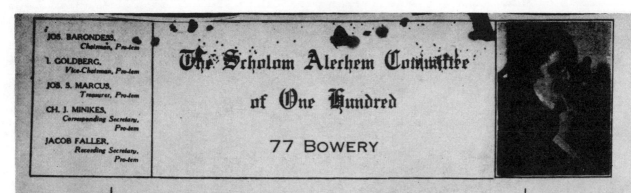

When Sholem Aleichem was stranded in Copenhagen because of the First World War, Jewish cultural leaders brought him to the United States.

lation, over 2,000,000 persons, gave Yiddish as their mother tongue. This was almost 23 per cent higher than in 1910, but since the Jewish population had almost doubled in that decade, proportionately there was actually a decline. There were four reasons for this. The choking off of the major stream of Jewish immigration dried up the main source of the replenishment of the Yiddish-speaking element. The pressure of the nativist theory of Anglo-Saxon superiority over all immigrant cultures merged with the Ford-activated anti-Semitic wave to spread among Jews the fear that the use of Yidish would harm their economic, social and cultural status. To this apprehension, the well-established *Yahudim* of Ger-

man background contributed by their derision of Yiddish. Third was the normal, desirable mastery of English common to children attending a compulsory school system. Finally, the *Jewish Daily Forward,* dominant among the Yiddish-speaking, actively promoted its theory of assimilation, and hindered those seeking to build the educational and other institutions needed to develop Yiddish culture.

There were various responses to this trend away from Yiddish, some trying to stem and others only to ride the tide. Merely a curiosity was the attempt to print Yiddish as transliterated into English, one such anthology, *Modern Yiddish Poetry,* edited by Samuel J. Imber, appear-

When Sholem Aleichem died in The Bronx, New York, on May 13, 1916, his funeral was one of the greatest in the history of the city. Above is a part of the procession at Kelly Street and Prospect Avenue.

ing in 1927. More significant though not enduring was the effort to develop a bi-lingual press,
with Yiddish and English in one periodical. In
1928 there were eight such weeklies, one monthly
and one daily. More lasting was the growth of

the Jewish press in English, with 62 periodicals
appearing in 1928. Of the 43 weeklies and 11
monthlies, several had substantial circulations:
The Sentinel and *Reform Advocate* in Chicago,
39,500 and 30,000 respectively, the *Jewish Advo-*

cate in Boston with 27,000, *New Palestine* with 23,725, the *American Hebrew* and *Jewish Tribune* of New York with 19,864 and 17,728 respectively. (The only Hebrew weekly, *Hadoar*, had 5,703, and the Ladino weekly, *La Vara*, 16,500.) Of the English monthlies, *Young Israel* led with 138,148 and the *B'nai B'rith Magazine* had 66,898.

In literature and the theater there were also important developments in the post-war decade. In Yiddish there were new trends, new themes and some peaks of achievement. Simultaneously there came to the fore a body of Jewish literature, including drama, in English. During the war, all three Yiddish classic writers had died: Peretz in 1915, Sholem Aleichem in 1916, Mendele Mocher Seforim in 1917. An epoch ended with them. Because of the war-havoc, many East European Yiddish writers settled in the United States, increasing its prominence as a Jewish literary center; outstanding among these reinforcements were Sholem Asch, Abraham Reisen and Peretz Hirschbein. Here, while they continued to deal with the European Jewish theme, they also turned

Joseph Opatoshu (1897-1954), Yiddish novelist.

creatively to the American scene, both Jewish and general. The "ghetto" ceased to be the main theme of Yiddish writing.

An upsurge of creativity was evident in all literary forms, poetry, fiction and the drama. There was a great moral and intellectual ferment in Jewish cultural life that preceded by a decade the similar development in the Thirties in the country as a whole. All the post-war immigrating Jewish intellectuals had been touched by the revolutions in Eastern Europe and they brought over new ideas, attitudes and moods. The sudden impressive burgeoning of the new Yiddish literature in the Soviet Union in the Twenties also acted as a goad on the American Jewish cultural scene. A grand, many-faceted chapter was being created not only in American-Yiddish writing but in the Yiddish literature of the world. As there appeared the fresh and challenging works of such leading figures as Asch, Halpern, Leivick, Nadir, Opatoshu, Pinski, Raboy and Reisin there was excitement in the air. This was veritably a renaissance, and would be looked back upon as another Golden Age.

Pre-eminent as a poet of the period until his

Peretz Hirschbein (1880-1948), Yiddish dramatist.

Sholem Asch (1880-1957).

death in 1932 was Moishe Leib Halpern, the turbulent and impassioned. While the *In Sich* group (Jacob Glatstein, A. Leyeles, N. B. Minkoff and others) made introspection the aim of poetry, Halpern was exhibiting his prodigious talent and craftsmanship in poetry vibrant with social pathos. Although he had no clear direction, Halpern was suffused with a class feeling for the oppressed. The rich and the hypocrite he derided in parody, in satire that was broad and hoarsely mocking. For a time, feeling the impact of the radical Jewish workers, he turned from Labor Zionism to the communist movement. Together with the brilliant fellow-poet, Moishe Nadir, Halpern was on the staff of the *Freiheit* from 1922 to 1924. A new enthusiastic audience heartened him as he declaimed his proletarian poems to them: "The Jewish Blacksmith," "Salute" (on the lynching of a Negro), or "Sacco-Vanzetti." In 1924, his second volume, *Di Goldene Pave* (The Golden Peacock—his first, in 1919, was *In New York*), revealed a new power

in expressing the pangs and ideals of the masses. After he broke away from the *Freiheit,* he slid into despair and emptiness, from which he occasionally emitted flashes of hope. His was a restless, brooding but tender spirit.

In the novel and drama, Yiddish writers were achieving recognition not only from readers of Yiddish but from a growing audience for English translations. Outstanding were Sholem Asch, Joseph Opatoshu and David Pinski. Pinski's realism was popular. Huebsch published translations of the drama, *The Treasure,* in 1915, *Three Plays* in 1918, and *Ten Plays* in 1920, while Brentano issued a collection of stories, *Temptations,* in 1920. Pinski was at his best in this period in his novels of American Jewish life, *Arnold Levenberg* (English translation 1928) and *The Generations of Noah Eden* (Yiddish, 1929, English, 1931). The latter is a family saga of three generations stemming from Lithuania in the 1880's. Pinski stressed the Jewish-cultural decline accompanying the material successes of the children and grandchildren. In the loosening of family ties and the abandonment of old religious values, Pinski saw the disintegration of the Jewish people.

Joseph Opatoshu's horizons were broader. The post-war savagery against the Negro people moved him to write many stories and novella on the subject, a collection of them, *Rasse* (Race), being issued in Warsaw in 1923 after appearing in American periodicals, while his long story, "Lynching," was published in Hebrew in New York in 1920. His major work of this period was the trilogy (*Alein,* 1920, *In Poilishe Velder,* 1921, *The Year 1863,* 1926) on Polish Jewish life of the past century. The first Yiddish writer to undertake a large-scale Jewish historical novel, Opatoshu depicted intimately the various trends of Polish Jewry from 1830 down through the century, including Hassidism in decay (Polish Hassidic rabbis banned the book!), the rise of Haskalah and a middle class, the participation of Jews in the 1863 uprising.

But most prominent was Sholem Asch, a novelist in the European grand manner, prolific in output, rich in characterization, varied in setting, fertile in situation and brimful of vitality.

Maurice Schwartz (1888-1960) in Sholem Asch's "Kiddush Hashem" at the Yiddish Art Theater, 1928-1929.

After a visit in 1910, he settled in the United States in 1914, becoming a citizen in 1920. As early as 1911, he had written about American Jewish life in *Der Landsman,* a three-act comedy, and the novella *America* (translated into English, 1918). He continued to write about Jewish life in Europe and Palestine, publishing *Mottke Gonef* in 1917 (translated as *Mottke the Thief* the same year), picturing with realism and mysticism combined the Warsaw Jewish underworld. But some of the most moving works of his long career described American Jewish life and were written when he was closest to the mass of struggling, hard-working Jewish immigrants. (In 1920 he supported Debs for President.) *Uncle Moses* (1916; English, 1920) showed the class conflict breaking through the patriarchal hold Uncle

Moses had on his *landsleit*-workers in his Bowery sweatshop. In *Chaim Lederer's Return* the setting has changed from the Bowery to Broadway, but the retired boss, Lederer, disgusted by the newly rich Jews among whom he moves, decides to return to the socialist ideals of his youth and go back to the shop. In *Electric Chair* (1923; in English, 1938, as *Judge Not*), Asch evaluated the life of an American banker, a Jew, trapped in a mesh of unhappiness and corruption that put him in the death house.

To the same period belong works as different as the novel *Mother,* about life in the old country and in New York Bohemia, and the plays, *Koiln,* about non-Jewish miners in Arizona, and *Rev. Dr. Silver,* the tragedy of a successful midwestern rabbi who loses both wife and faith. Si-

Rudolph Schildkraut (1862-1930), actor on the Yiddish and English stages and in films.

multaneously, early works appeared in English translation: his mordant, controversial play, *God of Vengeance,* in 1918, and in 1926 *Kiddush Ha-Shem,* a masterly novella on the slaughter of the Jews during the 1648 Ukrainian uprising against Polish oppression.

The Yiddish theater in this period witnessed an artistic upsurge and continued to attract large audiences. In 1928, there were 24 Yiddish theaters, 11 in New York City, four in Chicago, two in Philadelphia, and one each in Newark, Boston, Baltimore, Cleveland, Detroit, St. Louis and Los Angeles. In most New York theaters, vulgar melodramas and stale operettas were dominant. Occasionally Jacob Adler, David Kessler or Boris Thomashefsky produced a play of higher quality, but intelligent theater-goers wanted more. In 1918 a decade of high achievement began. When Maurice Schwartz on October 16 successfully produced Peretz Hirschbein's comedy *In a Far-vorfen Vinkel* (In An Out-of-the-Way Corner),

he inaugurated the Yiddish Art Theater movement. Jacob Ben Ami followed in 1919 with The New Yiddish Theater; in 1925 there appeared Our Theater and Rudolf Schildkraut's Theater; in 1926 Ben Ami and Jacob Mestel opened The New Yiddish Art Theater. The most important, lasting beyond the decade, was Schwartz's Yiddish Art Theater.

The repertory was vast. In the first five seasons, Schwartz produced more than 50 Yiddish plays, and more than 30 translations from the major European dramatists, including Ibsen, Tolstoy, Andreyev, Sudermann, Schnitzler, Strindberg, Gorky, Gogol, Molière, Toller, Rolland, Lope de Vega and Chekhov. Mainstays of the Yiddish repertory were Jacob Gordin, Sholem Aleichem (with the 17-week run of *Tevye der Milhiger* Schwartz initiated his vivid gallery of Sholem Aleichem types), Asch, Ossip Dymov, Pinski, Hirschbein and Leivick. The other art theaters also drew upon the work of these authors. Leivick's symbolic verse-drama, *Der Goilem* (The Golem), published in 1921, was produced in New York in English in 1929 and in Yiddish in 1931 (in Russia it was staged in Hebrew in 1924.) But the plays by Leivick that aroused enthusiasm were *Shmattes* (Rags, 1921), *Andersh* (Different, 1922), *Bettler* (Beggars, 1923), *Shop* (1926) and *Kaitn* (Chains, 1929), in which critical realism outweighed the mysticism and pessimism that later dominated him.

David Pinski, who was also a Labor Zionist editor, had successes on the Yiddish stage that carried over into English. His *Der Shtummer Meshiach* (The Mute Messiah) about the Inquisition, was produced by Ben Ami in 1918 and in English the same year. One of the finest Yiddish comedies, *Der Oitser* (The Treasure), depicting what happens in a Jewish town when an idiot, finding gold coins, involves the town in a treasure hunt, was produced by Schwartz in 1919 and by the new Theater Guild in 1920. A satire on the business world, *Der Letster Sach-hakel* (In the Last Analysis), was played in Our Theater in 1924-25 and in English in 1927. And *Der Aibiker Id* (The Eternal Jew), a historical play composed in 1906, was performed in English in 1929. Also popular on the Yiddish stage were

Jacob Ben Ami, actor and director on the Yiddish and English stages.

Ludwig Satz (1891-1944), a comic star of the Yiddish theater, in "My Wife's Lover," by Bader Semhoff.

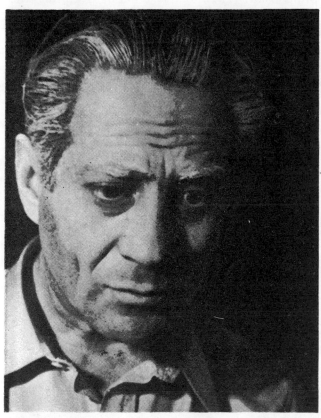

Joseph Bulov, star of the Yiddish and English stages, in a Yiddish production of Arthur Miller's "Death of a Salesman."

Paul Muni, whose early training was on the Yiddish stage, became one of the great actors in the general American theater and film. Above he is shown in Maxwell Anderson's "Key Largo."

Celia Adler, a star of the Yiddish stage,
from a head by Aaron Goodelman.

Pinski's many dramas exploring the ways and meaning of love.

A new note was struck by Peretz Hirschbein with his plays of Jewish folk life and folk-lore, which were lyrical, bucolic and full of the charm of simplicity. The plots were often common-place—*In a Farvorfen Vinkel* dealing with love between a boy and girl whose parents are enemies, and *Dem Schmied's Techter* (The Blacksmith's Daughters) with the romantic simple rivalries of twin sisters—but the atmosphere was warm, tender and folkish. Very popular were *Di Puste Kretchma* (The Haunted Inn) and *Griene Felder* (Green Fields), produced by Ben Ami in 1919, which also found their way into English.

The Twenties marked the high point of Yiddish theater art, and at the center was Schwartz's Art Theater. Schwartz was producer, director and invariably the star. Its repertory was of a high

quality, socially motivated and broadly humanistic. The acting corps included first rate talent like Ludwig Satz, Samuel Goldinberg, Joseph Bulov, Jacob Ben Ami, Muni Weisenfreund (Paul Muni), Celia Adler, Isidor Kashier, Bertha Gerstin, Hannah Appel, Mark Schweid, Abraham Teitelbaum, Bina Abramovitch, Boaz Young, Lazar Fried, Anatol Vinogradoff and Noah Nachbush. Even at its height, though, the Yiddish Art Theater had a structural weakness: it was based upon the enterprise, will and sometimes whim of one man, Maurice Schwartz. There was no stable theater, no ensemble, no organization, no responsible social base to cushion its financial difficulties.

While the art theater movement was flourishing, furthermore, there began a new trend. Neither the Yiddish Art Theater nor the other art theaters had any guiding principle except that their plays should be in the realm of literature and not just vulgar entertainment. With the founding of the *Freiheit* in 1922, however, there began to crystallize a demand for a specifically proletarian Jewish culture. The stimulus was

Bina Abramovitch (1865-1953), pioneer
and veteran of the Yiddish stage.

provided by revolutionary class consciousness and international solidarity with the Soviet Union, which served as inspiration and model. Around the *Freiheit* there grew a vibrant movement for workers' culture in music, literature and the theater. The Yunger Arbeter Shreiber Farein (Young Worker Writers Society) was founded in 1924, workers' choruses established the Idishen Musicalishen Arbeter Farband (Jewish Music Workers Alliance) in 1925, and a conference in December, 1925 created the Arbeter Teater Farband (Workers' Theater Alliance—Artef), which that very month organized the Freiheit Dramatic Studio with 19 students and Jacob Mestel as director. The first to mature was the theater movement, and in the Thirties the Artef contributed significantly not only to the Yiddish but to the general American theater.

Parallel with these developments in Yiddish, there was a blooming of English-Jewish literature: works about Jews written by Jews in English. The forces had been gathering slowly but definitely. Since the death of Emma Lazarus in 1887, a quarter century elapsed before an enduring English-Jewish work appeared. *The Promised Land,* autobiography of Mary Antin, published in 1912, reprinted more than 30 times, is still in print 45 years later as a classic of "Americanization" literature. In a tone of ecstatic gratefulness, she traced her rise from a Jewish girl of Polotzk in the Russian Pale of Settlement, excellently described in the first half, to an American young woman who knows deeply "what a real thing is this American freedom," and who at Barnard College "learned at least to think in English without an accent." She was indifferent to Jewish life thereafter, somehow having lost her people while she was finding herself in this, the promised land.

After the war there came into view a distinct stream of English-Jewish writing of merit and sometimes of distinction. In poetry, the Jewish theme emerged, usually as one among many, in the work of Alter Brody (*A Family Album,* 1918), Babette Deutsch (*Banners,* 1919—on the Russian Revolution), Arthur Guiterman, Elias Lieberman, James Oppenheim, the Zionist Jessie E. Sampter, Jean Starr Untermeyer (*Growing Pains,*

Molly Picon, Yiddish musical comedy star, in "Hello, Molly."

Jessie Sampter (1883-1938), poet.

Louis Untermeyer, poet and poetry anthologist.

Jean Starr Untermeyer, poet.

Samuel Ornitz (1890-1957), novelist and screen--writer.

Abraham Cahan (1860-1951), novelist and editor of The Jewish Daily Forward.

Ludwig Lewisohn (1882-1955), novelist and literary historian.

Moss Hart (1904-1961), playwright.

George S. Kaufman (1889-1961), Hart's collaborator.

Two of the four Marx Brothers, Groucho and Chico (1891-1961).

1918) and Louis Untermeyer (*Roast Leviathan*, 1923).

In fiction, the achievement was considerable, with Abraham Cahan, Anzia Yezierska, Ludwig Lewisohn and Samuel Ornitz producing notable books. Cahan's *The Rise of David Levinsky* met with both acclaim and trepidation in 1917. Cahan unfolded the material rise, "Americanization," and cumulative spiritual hollowness of Levinsky as he forges ahead in the garment industry. We have a full-length, life-like, probing portrait of

what *The Nation* reviewer called "that type of Jew who raises the gorge of all decent human beings." But since Levinsky was presented neither in the context of the at least equally common rise and decay of non-Jews in the business world, nor in the context of those Jews who, while they may not be "rising," are rich in spiritual life and values, the book pointed up a problem central to American Jewish writing: what effect does a Levinsky have upon the popular concept of American Jews, which is continually being dis-

Al Jolson (1888-1950) in "The Jazz Singer," which established the success of the talking film.

torted by anti-Semitic stereotypes? Concern about this problem was expressed at the time often in general reviews of the book and once even in the *Jewish Daily Forward.* All writers dealing in English with national groups subjected to discrimination face the complex task of fulfilling their communal responsibility to tell the truth in its full social context lest partial truths harm the group involved.

In a different vein from that of Cahan was the writing of Anzia Yezierska, who won a warm reception for her somewhat sentimental novels of immigrant Jews' wretchedness, *Hungry Hearts* (1920), *Salome of the Tenements* (1922) and *Bread Givers* (1925). Harsh disappointment also molded the more influential work of Ludwig Lewisohn. An indifference to Jewish life traditional in his German middle class parents was transformed by his experience with anti-Semitic

exclusiveness in the teaching profession into an impassioned Jewish consciousness first expressed in his autobiography, *Upstream* (1922) and its sequel, *Midchannel* (1929). A visit to Palestine turned him into a zealous Zionist. In 1928, in *The Island Within,* Lewisohn combined the staple theme of sexual unhappiness, treated in his many novels of marital life, with a fanatical Jewishness that even his eulogist, Rev. Dr. Felix A. Levy, refers to as "a special (or is it specious) type of orthodoxy."

On the English stage, dramatists as important as Sidney Howard, S. N. Behrman, George S. Kaufman and Elmer L. Rice were Jewish, but except for Rice they rarely made a Jewish character, setting or theme central in their plays. Rice's *Street Scene,* for which he won the Pulitzer Prize in 1929, was the only significant play of this period that can be called English-Jewish

Fannie Brice (Fannie Borach, 1891-1951), musical comedy and film star.

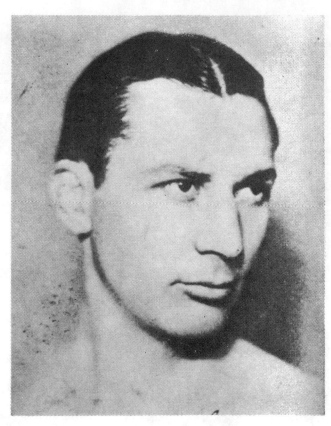

Benny Leonard (1896-1947), lightweight world boxing champion, 1917-1924.

George Gershwin (1898-1937), composer.

Louis B. Mayer (1885-1957), film magnate.

The Warners Brothers, left to right: Harry M. (1881-1958), Jack, Sam, Dave (not in the film business) and Abe.

theater, although there are other examples, like Milton H. Gropper and Max Siegel's *We Americans,* dealing with the "Americanization" of a Jewish family (1928), and Bella and Samuel Spewack's *Poppa* (1929), showing a Jew in political life.

On stage, furthermore, Jews had made their way into the foreground of popular success as first-rate entertainers and song writers in vaudeville, musical comedy and film. As comedians

Marcus Loew (1870-1927) at the age of 36.

they ranged from Weber and Fields, George Jessel and Ed Wynn to the Marx Brothers. At the top in "show business" where Eddie Cantor in a host of "shows" like *The Ziegfeld Follies* and *Kid Boots,* and Al Jolson, who made his mark in "black-face" (a style now vanishing as public taste, affected by the growing assertion of equality by the Negro people, turns away from a form that wounds their sensibilities) and whose *The Jazz Singer* in 1927 established the success of the talking movies. Right alongside these at the top were Belle Baker, Fannie Brice and Sophie Tucker. Setting Americans a-singing were composers like Irving Berlin, Sigmund Romberg, Jerome Kern (whose *Show Boat* was launched in 1928), and George Gershwin. The latter was out in front with such musical comedy hits as *George White's Scandals,* 1920-1924, *Lady Be Good,* 1924, *Strike Up the Band,* 1927, *Show Girl,* 1929, *Girl Crazy,* 1930 and the Pulitzer Prize winner, *Of Thee I Sing,* 1931, while he was writing notable music in the jazz idiom in *Rhapsody in Blue,* 1924, *Concerto in F,* 1925, *An American in Paris,* 1928, culminating in 1935 in his folk-opera, *Porgy and Bess,* which, despite its one-sided view of Negro life, has become an American classic.

Connected with the popular spectacle was also the prowess of two Jewish world boxing champions, Benny Leonard, who held the lightweight crown, 1917-1924, and Battling Levinsky, light heavyweight king, 1916-1920.

Adolf Zukor, head of Paramount Pictures Corporation.

For Jews to participate in sports at all, especially professionally, was to break with centuries of Old Country Jewish tradition. To the East European immigrant generations an athlete was in an alien and suspect tradition—a "bummer" or bum. To the Jewish youth, athletic prowess was a supreme sign of "Americanization." On the big city diamonds and school yard courts, myriads of Jewish boys avidly mastered American games like baseball and basketball, some becoming school and college stars and a few maturing into professionals. A Johnny Kling (Kline, 1875-1947) for example, born in Kansas City, was a catcher for the Chicago Cubs, 1901-1911. But it was the spotlit glamor of a Benny

Leonard that naturalized the Jew in the tough world of sports in general and of the ring in particular—in which Jews won no fewer than 22 world championships. Later Jews were to take the road to achievement from the 1930's to the present in football (a Sid Luckman), baseball (a Hank Greenberg and an Al Rosen), basketball (a Nat Holman), tennis (a Dick Savitt), track, swimming and the Olympic sports.

Jews were likewise prominent in the film industry, which attained new heights of prosperity after World War I, but the Jewish theme was even more systematically avoided. From infancy, when its status, financially and culturally, was low, the industry had been built by a number of Jewish furriers, nickelodeon operators and jewelers who started when capital requirements were small and built up a huge structure. The well-known names include Marcus Loew, Nicholas Schenk, Louis B. Mayer, Adolph Zukor, Samuel Goldfish (later Goldwyn), William Fox, Jesse Lasky, and the Warner Brothers, Abe, Sam and Harry. They dominated the field in the Twenties. So profitable did the industry become, however, that the Morgan and Rockefeller banks moved into it when the crash came in 1929 and gained full control; original Jewish financial interests are now important only in Loew's and Warner's.

For the Jews the post-war decade had been a period of numerical growth at a reduced rate, of the rise of a centralized, nationwide, anti-Semitic movement, of strife in the ranks of labor, of organizational and institutional expansion, of cultural development and diversification. The economic crash and its consequences brought new problems and new trends in the attempt to solve them.

A portion of an anti-Nazi demonstration in Chicago, May 10, 1933, the day the Nazis were burning books written by Jews, liberals, democrats and social revolutionaries.

CHAPTER 12: The Fateful Decades: 1930-1950

MORE FATEFUL PERHAPS than any in human history were the decades 1930-1950. A world in crisis produced the menace of world fascism. World War II in triumphant unity reaffirmed the four freedoms—of speech and worship, from want and fear—though at an awesome price. New whirlwinds of freedom stormed up from the heaving colonial world. Atomic energy harnessed for war bred new terrors. World peace became the only alternative to world annihilation. Not nations, not peoples, not states were at stake, but the world itself.

For the Jews, the choices often came in their most acute form, and the price exacted was catastrophic. The six million dead, victims of Nazism, were two-thirds of the Jews of Europe, and more than one-third of all the Jews in the world.

Amid the human ashes of the crematoria there rose high that enduring symbol of resistance to Nazism, the Warsaw Ghetto Uprising. The ashes and the symbol finally fashioned the understanding that led the democratic, anti-imperialist and socialist forces of the world to help the Jews establish the State of Israel—and then defend it against aggression. Upon the Jews in the United States these events wrought a profound transformation.

The first decade began in deep economic crisis and ended in the anti-fascist World War II, but there were also great struggles for recovery and broad movements for peace through collective security. Hitlerism advanced like lava on its appeasing neighbors, scorching the working class movements, Jews and democracy itself, and giv-

The "Hunger Marchers" in Washington, D. C. on December 6, 1932. On the steps of
the Capitol, Herbert Benjamin (A) and David Levinson (B) talking to the police before
they were permitted to enter the Capitol to present their program.

ing transatlantic encouragement to native American reaction. But the democratic resistance
formed itself on many fronts and beat back the
recurrent charge of fascism. The infant New
Deal was pushed by the needy and impatient
masses onto the path of social reform as they
rallied around Franklin D. Roosevelt and helped
make him the great figure he became. In these
struggles, sharing all the problems of the Ameri-

can people but especially alarmed by Hitlerism
abroad and the anti-Semitic wave in our own
country, the Jews distinguished themselves.

In 1930, unemployment and hunger wracked
the American people. The workers had no
cushion of government relief or social insurance.
President Herbert Hoover was indifferent. William Green and his fellow chiefs of the American
Federation of Labor were impotent, merely ap-

pealing to the workers as Americans proudly to refuse the "dole" that workers in Britain had won. Initiative in the fight for relief therefore came from militant and left forces. The Trade Union Unity League call for demonstrations of the unemployed brought more than a million workers onto the streets in a dozen cities on March 6, 1930. In New York alone, where Israel Amter was one of the leaders imprisoned for this action and thousands of other Jews took part, about 100,000 turned out. The Unemployed Councils rapidly became a mass organization in 46 states and Puerto Rico, with large numbers of Jews among its active members and Herbert Benjamin and Sam Wiseman among its top leaders, while the smaller, Socialist-led National Unemployment League was headed by David Lasser and also included many other Jewish workers. Louis Weinstock, a leader of the largely Jewish New York painters' union, was the head of the A.F.L. Committee for Unemployment Insurance and Relief which, despite denunciation by William Green, won support from 3,000 locals, 35

Joseph Baskin (1880-1952), general secretary, The Workmen's Circle, 1916-1952.

city Central Labor Unions, six state federations and five internationals. Jewish women were active in Women's Councils leading consumer struggles.

Jews were also active in the nation-wide hunger marches to Washington that brought 1,800 persons there on December 7, 1931 and 3,000 on December 6, 1932. Jews were among the thousands of unemployed auto workers who marched on Ford's River Rouge plant on March 7, 1932, and among the four shot to death by the police that day was 16-year-old Joseph Bussell, a Jewish member of the Young Communist League. Hundreds of Jewish war veterans were in the ranks of the Bonus March when the Workers' Ex-Servicemen's League brought almost 20,000 veterans to Washington in the summer of 1932, with Emanuel Levin as one of the main organizers.

The Jewish charitable agencies tottered under the weight of mass privation, which no private benevolence could begin to meet. Increased anti-Semitic discrimination in employment stimulated the birth of communal Jewish employment agen-

Rubin Saltzman (1890-1959), general secretary, Jewish Section, International Workers' Order and then of the Jewish People's Fraternal Order, 1930-1954.

Julius L. Meier (1874-1937), Governor of Oregon, 1930-1934.

Henry Horner (1878-1940), Governor of Illinois, 1933-1940.

Arthur Seligman (1873-1933), Governor of New Mexico, 1931-1933.

Herbert H. Lehman (1879-1963), Governor of New York State, 1933-1943, Unite States Senator, 1950-1956.

cies, but efforts to induce Jewish employers to hire Jews were hindered by the general job scarcity. The 70,000 members of the Workmen's Circle in the early 1930's learned again that the resources of that organization were no match for an economic crisis, and had to turn to struggle for public relief and social insurance. More energetic in this respect was the new International Workers' Order. The Jewish Section, which founded the Order, grew from 5,000 in 1930 to 51,000 members by 1939, while the I.W.O. as a whole was expanding into a multi-nationality organization of 15 sections with 161,624 members.

Amid these massive struggles the electoral will of "the forgotten man" placed Roosevelt in the White House. Jewish voters were overwhelmingly for Roosevelt, although many thousands voted for minority party candidates, Norman Thomas the Socialist (backed by Rabbi Stephen S. Wise) and William Z. Foster the Communist. (In his next three candidacies, Roosevelt's program won the votes of most of the minority party supporters, too.) Elected to Congress in the first Roosevelt landslide were ten Jews, eight of them Democrats. Of the four Jews who were Governors in 1933, Julius L. Meier of Oregon was a progressive Independent, and three were Democrats: Arthur Seligman of New Mexico, Henry Horner of Illinois and Herbert H. Lehman of New York.

Driven by want and heartened by Roosevelt's moderate encouragement of unionism, the workers began the greatest wave of activity in their history. Millions were in motion. From 1934 to 1936, about 3,397,000 unionists were involved in great strikes, including the San Francisco General Strike of 1934; in these, after 20 workers were killed in action, important concessions were won. The drive to organize the unorganized rolled on. In September, 1933, the A.F.L. had only 2,127,000 members, the lowest number since 1916, and the total union membership was 2,-857,000. By 1940, the total was 8,944,000, of which the A.F.L. had 4,247,000 and the Congress of Industrial Organizations, born in 1937, had 3,625,000. The biggest gains were in heavy industry, in which very few Jews were employed. But new unions were also being established in the

Benjamin Nathan Cardozo (1870-1938), Justice of the United States Supreme Court, 1932-1938.

white collar and professional fields, where there were large numbers of Jews.

Responding to the "American dream" to rise to a higher class, many tens of thousands of Jews, children of sweatshop and factory workers, strove to rise. Using the educational and other opportunities uniquely available in the metropolitan centers in which Jews were concentrated, they had made their way into professional and white collar pursuits. When the crisis threatened their status, many fought back. Where their parents had built socialist unions, this new generation organized progressive, anti-fascist unions, or infused new militancy into old unions like the Teachers'. The first to move were the Jewish social workers in New York; in 1931, when they faced a wage cut, they transformed the Association of Federation Workers into a union for the staffs of Jewish agencies, to the consternation of many Jewish philanthropists. In 1933, unions emerged for artists, for architects, engineers, chemists and technicians, and for newspapermen. In 1935 there were born the Interne Council of Greater New York, the Pharmacists Union, the

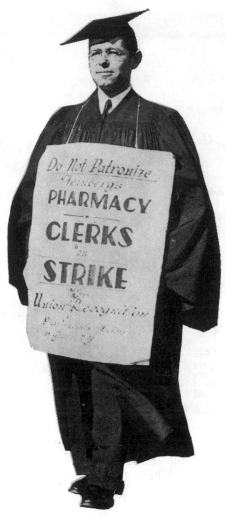

A clerk picketing Feinberg's Pharmacy in The Bronx, New York, in a strike in 1934 for union recognition and improvement of working conditions.

Psychologists League and the Lawyers Security League of New York City. In 1937 the state, county and municipal workers, the office and professional (publishing house) and the federal workers organized. In all these movements there were thousands of Jews and they were heavily represented in the leadership.

A dynamic force in the organizing drives both inside and outside the C.I.O. were the communists. Foster Rhea Dulles in *Labor in America* observed that John L. Lewis, leader of the C.I.O., "did not hesitate to draw upon their experience and skill in building up the C.I.O." In this period, the Communist Party multiplied from 14,-000 in 1932 to its peak of 75,000 in 1938, while the Young Communist League grew from 3,000 in 1933 to 22,000 in 1939. Many Jews were attracted to this movement by its socialist per-

spective, its militancy in fighting for the improvement of the conditions of the masses and especially by its uncompromising stand against fascism, racism and anti-Semitism. Large numbers were influenced by its program without affiliating with the Party itself.

Hitlerism soon loomed as the great enemy. Backed by German Big Business and the Prussian big landowners, Adolph Hitler came to power on January 30, 1933 and launched his program of terrorism for the workers, Jews and democratic masses of Germany, and of conquest and war for the world. Although the left had been signaling the danger for months. there was at first incredulity and indecision in the Jewish community. Had not 29 leading and wealthy Jews of Germany sent a message in October, 1932 to Rabbi Stephen S. Wise assuring him that "Hitler will never come to power"? Wise did not believe this assurance, but others did and were disarmed even after it had proved hollow. The *Jewish Daily Forward,* its vision distorted by bitter anti-communism, carried a Berlin report from Jacob Lestschinsky, published

Rabbi Stephen S. Wise (1874-1949).

Part of the anti-Nazi demonstration in New York, May 10, 1933, under the auspices of the American Jewish Congress, to protest the Nazi burning of "un-German" books.

February 16, 1933, that Goebbels had ordered an end to pogroms and that Hitlerism, now that it was in power, would "have to become well-behaved." Even on March 6 this newspaper speculated editorially that the Hitler-Von Papen regime would "now give up a significant part of its hooligan and terroristic tactics."

The Jewish population, however, soon revealed its eagerness to do something against Hitlerism. Yet the plutocracy around the American Jewish Committee sought to prevent any demonstrative anti-nazi actions. Why, it was argued, such deeds would stir Hitler to anti-Semitic acts and endanger the Jews of Germany! Organizations like the B'nai B'rith were virtually paralyzed by this approach, and bestirred themselves mainly, as did the American Jewish Committee, with vain programs of research and publication to prove that Jews were not in fact, as Hitler charged, international bankers and communists. With tragic futility, both the Jewish plutocracy and the Jewish right-wing social democracy sought to divert Hitler from the Jews by demonstrating that Jews too could be anti-communist. Inevitably these groups frustrated their intention of fighting Hitlerism with maximum effectiveness.

Decisive in rallying the huge Jewish middle class to anti-nazi activity was the American Jewish Congress. The first big action consisted of mass meetings in a score of cities on March 27, 1933. In New York, Madison Square Garden was packed. Rabbi Wise had been subjected to enormous pressure from the State Department and the German Embassy in Washington to cancel the plan, but, backed by Brandeis, he refused. Hundreds of thousands took part in these meetings. Once in motion, the people wanted to keep going. Hitler had announced there would be a burning of the books (Jewish, communist, democratic, liberal) on May 10. The government in Washington, although called upon to speak out, was mum. "We went ahead," wrote Wise, "pressed forward by the Jewish masses who could

B. Charney Vladeck (1886-1938).

not be expected to understand such silence." The Congress organized a great street parade in New York on May 10 to protest this infamy; the police estimated there were 100,000 marchers, and 250,000 took part altogether, representing all shades of anti-Nazi opinion. In Chicago, the marchers numbered 50,000; in Philadelphia, 20,-000; in Detroit, 10,000. Such activity among the Jewish masses aroused non-Jews also to join the protest.

Meanwhile on April 1, 1933 a movement had been started to boycott German goods and services. Conceived by the versatile Yiddish journalist, Abraham Coralnick of the *Day,* and initiated by the Jewish War Veterans, the boycott was pushed vigorously by the Non-Sectarian Anti-Nazi League, headed by the prominent lawyer, Samuel Untermeyer. The American Jewish Committee and the B'nai B'rith sharply condemned the action as provocative. Dr. Joseph Tenenbaum, chairman of the Executive Committee of the American Jewish Congress, ur-

gently promoted the boycott, despite Wise's hesitation. Finally, the Congress on August 20, 1933 officially backed it and put great energy into the campaign. The first big achievement was the resolution favoring the boycott passed by the A.F.L. convention on October 13. In time, the boycott involved a mass movement not only of consumers but of trade unionists, who refused to work on materials imported from Germany.

The records of this period abound in movements and campaigns in which Jews played their full and often distinguished part. Jews were strongly represented in a general movement that was launched on September 29, 1933 at the founding convention of the American League against War and Fascism (changed in November, 1937 to American League for Peace and Democracy). Initiated by the left, this movement at its height embraced about 4,000,000 Americans and became the central organized force fighting for an international program of collective security against fascist aggression. One action that became a worldwide symbol was the climax of a demonstration on July 26, 1935 of some 4,500 persons on the dock alongside the German liner *Bremen,* when one daring soul ripped the Nazi swastika flag from its staff and tossed it into the Hudson River. Magistrate Louis B. Brodsky expressed the deepest feelings of all anti-Nazis when he released five of six persons arrested at the demonstration with the remark from the bench that the swastika was "similar to the black flag of piracy." The fact that, because the German Ambassador protested, Secretary of State Cordell Hull apologized officially for the incident, could not undo the resounding deed.

Powerful in their effect on public opinion were certain nation-wide campaigns even when they had only partial success. In 1936 widespread opposition was mobilized against United States participation in the Berlin Olympics, and against the sending of delegations to the Heidelberg University 550th anniversary celebration. In New York the officials of the City College, attended by thousands of Jewish students, had a black border placed around the Heidelberg flag hanging in the Great Hall, mourning the death of academic freedom. When Goettingen Uni-

Samuel Levinger (1917-1937), a member of the Lincoln Battalion, who was wounded at Jarama and killed at Belchite.

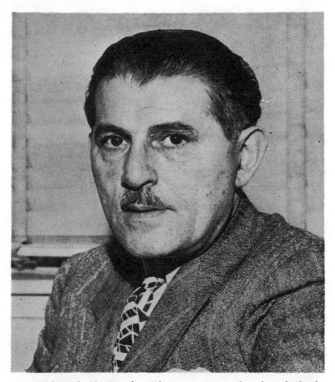

Dr. Edward K. Barsky, the surgeon who headed the Medical Unit that served the Abraham Lincoln Battalion in Spain.

versity invited foreign delegations to its 250th anniversary exercises in 1937 there was also extensive protest and boycott.

If in the country as a whole there was a prime necessity for anti-fascist unity in action, the need was even more compelling among the Jewish people. Yet class and factional differences stood in the way of such unity. Not only in the Jewish plutocracy or in the heterogeneous middle classes but even among the Jewish trade unionists and socialists there were those who could not subordinate their fear of communism to the immediate pressing need for coordinated action against fascism. The anti-Nazi coordinating center for trade unions and Jewish fraternal organizations exclusive of the left was the Jewish Labor Committee, founded in 1934 under the leadership of B. Charney Vladeck, manager of the *Forward*.

Mass sentiment for anti-fascist unity, however, was too great to be entirely thwarted. Thus in 1936, after the American Jewish Congress had refused to admit representatives of left groups like the Jewish Section of the I.W.O., there was formed the Jewish People's Committee against Fascism and Anti-Semitism. When the institut-

ing of "ghetto benches" in Polish schools in 1937 was followed by a pogrom wave, and even the American Jewish Congress contented itself with the quiet submission of a memorandum to the State Department, the Jewish People's Committee brought almost 1,000 delegates representing over 400,000 Jews to Washington for a national conference on November 19-20, 1937 that thundered its protest against anti-Semitism in Poland.

The left acted as a gadfly pricking other sections of the population into awareness and activity. Hitler was systematically carrying out his time-table of conquest, fully exploiting the appeasers in the foreign offices of Great Britain, France and the United States which, sharing Hitler's anti-communism, made concession after concession to him in the hope that he would turn his assault primarily against the Soviet Union. Franco's uprising against the democratic Spanish government on July 17, 1936, backed by Hitler and Mussolini, became a major test of strength between the forces of aggression and appeasement and those of collective security to quarantine the aggressor. While the Western Big Three followed a cynical policy of "non-intervention" that

Joe Hecht of the Lincoln Battalion took part in the Battle of the Ebro; in 1942 he enlisted in the United States Army, and was killed in action in 1945 at Saarlautern, Germany.

left Spanish democracy to fight all alone against the fascist aggressors, the anti-fascist forces of the world rallied to its defense. Part of this aid to Spain came in the form of the International Brigades, with some 30,000 men arriving in Spain from 54 countries (including Palestine) to fight Franco and Hitlerism. From the United States came the Abraham Lincoln Battalion, formed on January 6, 1937. About 3,000 Americans volunteered, and half of them died in Spain. There were many hundreds of Jews, perhaps a third of the total, in this heroic Lincoln Battalion, as well as very many Jewish doctors and nurses in the no less heroic medical units. These Jews went to Spain for a variety of reasons, all of them essentially anti-fascist. One level of consciousness was expressed by a boy who wrote home to his mother while convalescing from a thigh wound: "I took up arms against the persecutors of my people—the Jews—and my class, the oppressed. I am fighting against those who establish an inquisition like that of their ideological ancestors several centuries ago, in Spain."

Hitler's program of terroristic anti-Semitism in-

side Germany, with his proclaimed goal of the extermination of the Jews, had also quickened the native anti-Semitic movements in Poland, Lithuania, Romania and Hungary. Tens of thousands of Jews sought escape by emigration. With the doors of the United States barely ajar because of the 1924 anti-immigration law, only 11,-343 Jews were admitted in the three years, 1933 to 1935. Palestine became the main refuge, with 134,540 Jews arriving there in those three years, a number larger than the total of 122,600 that had come to Palestine in the entire period from the Balfour Declaration in 1917 to 1932. In the United States, aid to refugees became the main interest of the Jewish community in the Thirties. The Joint Distribution Committee spent more than $20,000,000 from 1933 to 1939. In 1934, the Coordinating Committee for Jewish Refugees was established (reorganized in 1939 as the National Refugee Service, which in 1946 merged into the United Service for New Americans). Active in refugee work was HIAS (Hebrew Immigrant Aid Society), the National Council of

Louise Waterman Wise (Mrs. Stephen S. Wise, d. 1947), head of the Women's Division, American Jewish Congress.

Israel Zangwill (1864-1926), from a painting by Leopold Pilichowski.

Jewish Women, the Women's Division of the American Jewish Congress, special groups like the German Jewish Children's Aid and the Emergency Committee in Aid of Displaced Foreign Scholars, and many *landsmanshaften*.

The impact of Hitlerism and the flight to Palestine produced an ideological transformation in the entire Jewish population here. There was a general upsurge of Jewish identification, expressing itself in many forms, in all trends of Jewish life, from right to left. Membership in Zionist groups, which had been 150,000 in 1930, reached 400,000 in 1940. Large numbers who had been casually indifferent to Jewish life, or who had assumed that the Jewish question would be solved simply as a marginal by-product of general radical solutions to social problems, were turned by Hitlerism to specific concern with Jewish af-

fairs. The theory of the "melting pot," which Zangwill had dramatized in his famous work by that name, was now thoroughly discredited. "Americanization" as a process of pressure to obliterate or "melt down" all immigrant group cultural characteristics and identity was now widely rejected by liberal Americans, native as well as foreign-born. What the cult of Anglo-Saxon superiority had tried to impose by compulsion was made impossible by anti-Semitism rampant. On various levels, the religious, the cultural, the political or even the purely financial, a great number of Jews were won back for the fight for Jewish survival.

While the main stimulus to this revival and deepening of Jewish consciousness came from Hitlerism abroad, another powerful impetus came from resurgent anti-Semitism in the United

Circulars, stickers, handbills—these anonymous drops of poison give graphically the gist of millions of words of anti-Semitic propaganda put out in this country. The round sticker, above, is interesting because "*the* communism" indicates that it was not "made in America."

Examples of anti-Semitic propaganda, fused with "red-baiting" and Soviet-baiting, that were circulated in the United States in the 1930's.

States. The soil that Henry Ford had fertilized in the prosperous Twenties was ready for the plow in the depression Thirties. The Jews were falsely blamed for all the unemployment, poverty, misery and even war dangers, thus diverting millions of suffering people from the search for the real causes of these afflictions in the social relations and the political power structure of our society. Between 1933 and 1939 there were 114 anti-Semitic organizations formed, and 77 of them were still active in 1940. Towards the end of the decade the radio-priest, Charles E. Coughlin, was reaching an audience of ten million with his anti-Semitic propaganda from Detroit, and the strong-arm men of the Coughlinite "Christian Front" organization were roaming the streets of New York peddling his magazine, *Social Justice,* which used the forged Protocols of the Elders of Zion as a guide. Demagogically, Coughlin named his organization the National Union for Social Justice, thus seeking, by an appeal to the profound need of the disinherited masses for social justice, to pervert that need to ends the very opposite of social justice. In addition the German-American Bund, the Silver Shirts and the Black Legion were among the organizations that added the storm-troop flavor to their anti-Semitism. New York City had 26 of these anti-Semitic outfits (17 of them units of the Hitlerite Bund), Chicago had 18 and Los Angeles seven. Hoodlum violence was added to demagogy. And in 1936 a bacteriologist for the Detroit Board of Health was even approached by the Black Legion with a proposition "to breed typhoid germs to infect milk sold to Jews"; he was fired for failure to report the proposal.

The propaganda was vicious, and reflected all the social tensions caused by the economic crisis. "Jews have the jobs you ought to have," unemployed workers were told. "Jews will take away the jobs you have," was whispered to workers unsure in their employment. "Jews will drive you out of business by unfair competition," was what the worried retailer heard. The Coughlins also exploited two contradictory anti-Semitic stereotypes: the "Jew-banker" and the "Jew-communist." When the New Deal was attacked from the right as "socialistic" and "communistic," it

Julius Rosenwald (1862-1932), merchant prince (Sears, Roebuck & Co.) who in 1917 established the Rosenwald Fund to aid Negro education in the South, which spent more than $100,000,000 for that purpose in 15 Southern states.

was labeled the "Jew Deal" and Roosevelt's real name was solemnly declared to be "Rosenfeld." Jews employed in the many New Deal agencies were among the favorite targets of this anti-Semitism.

In combating this tide, many Jewish organizations were involved, as well as general democratic groups. Conspicuous were the Jewish War Veterans, the American Jewish Congress and the Jewish People's Committee. The Veterans took on the task of defending Jews against the storm-troop tactics of the Nazi Bund and the "Christian Front." The American Jewish Congress sought to help the American people understand that anti-Semitism, like fascism as a whole, was a blow to American democracy. The Jewish People's Committee emphasized also the economic

Joseph R. Brodsky (1889-1947), civil rights lawyer.

and social roots of anti-Semitism, pointing out that only stable peace and prosperity could deprive the propagandist of the favorable soil for his evil seed. The vigor with which such organizations carried on their defense against anti-Semitism, however, evoked the resentment of the American Jewish Committee, which was still bent mainly on proving to Coughlin and Hitler that Jews were not Communists.

Another problem that, in the Thirties, began to concern more and more Jews was the close relation between anti-Semitism and the oppression of the Negro people, both stemming from reactionary circles. It was becoming apparent that racist dogmas of white superiority blended with Hitler's racist "Aryanism." Jews began to be conspicuously active, both as rank-and-filers and as leaders, in supporting the struggle of the Negro masses for total equality and democracy. Thousands of Jews took part in the tremendous movement of white and Negro people that made the Scottsboro Case a national and international issue. In a characteristically hurried frame-up of nine young Negroes on the traditional Southern charge of rape, the Scottsboro, Alabama court sentenced eight of them to the electric chair, sparing the ninth because he was only thirteen.

This outrage might have passed unnoted had not the communist-led International Labor Defense seen the great social issue involved and plunged into the case on April 9, 1931, sparking the great mass movement that signaled a new stage in the struggle for Negro equality. When Joseph R. Brodsky, I.L.D. lawyer, took over the defense of the Scottsboro Boys, he immediately became a target for anti-Semitic attack by Southern white supremacists. In 1934, when the famous criminal lawyer Samuel S. Leibowitz was part of the defense in a re-trial, the prosecution Jew-baited him right in the courtroom. In the second appeal to the United States Supreme Court on February 15-18, 1935, argument by Leibowitz, Walter H. Pollak and Osmond K. Fraenkel helped make constitutional history by winning from the Supreme Court on April 1 a reversal of the conviction on the ground that Negroes had been excluded from the juries that indicted and tried the Scottsboro Boys. Outside the courtrooms, in the long years of activity by petition, resolution and demonstration that saved the lives of the defendants and freed most of them, more and more Jews came into the struggle. Adding substance and depth to such activities was the great work

Franz Boas (1858-1942), anthropologist.

of scholarship performed at this time in the fields of social anthropology and social psychology. Outstanding in the fight to prove the absence of scientific basis for white supremacy was the work of such Jewish scholars as Franz Boaz, Melville J. Herskovits, Otto Klineberg, Ruth Benedict and their many academic disciples. James S. Allen, Philip S. Foner and Herbert Aptheker began to make their significant contributions to the study of the history of the Negro people. Bonds of solidarity between Negro and Jew in the fight against racism were being forged which were to expand tremendously in the Forties and Fifties.

Among the democratic movements of the Thirties, those of the embattled intellectuals and creators of cultural values were of enduring significance. In the colleges the fight against fascism and war attained great heights, influencing millions. Among students, where they were heavily represented, Jews were active at all levels in the communist-led National Student League (born in 1932) and the socialist-led Student League for Industrial Democracy, and then in the American Student Union, the product of the merger of these two in December, 1935. The campus did in fact become, as Roosevelt termed it, a "fortress for democracy." In varying degrees, this student movement extended also into Jewish seminaries, such as the Hebrew Union College, the Yeshiva College, and the Jewish Theological Seminary of America, as well as into the seminaries of other religions. The issue of peace rallied most attention. When the first nationwide anti-war student strike was held on April 12, 1937, there were over 180,000 students in it. Characteristically, Coughlin's *Social Justice* howled that red Jews were running the colleges.

The general cultural and literary renaissance of the Thirties affected the Jews deeply, and they contributed to it with distinction. The concept of the artist as a figure with social responsibility, which was traditional in Jewish life and culture, now came to the fore as the most vital note in American cultural life. At the heart of this upsurge was the concept of proletarian culture, of aesthetic expression wedded to a working class that was conceived as destined to mold the future.

In Jewish life the first expression of proletarian

Zischa Weinper (1892-1957), Yiddish poet.

culture was found among the Yiddish writers. Sharing a common language with the new Yiddish literature of the Soviet Union, which was blooming then, American Yiddish writers were more immediately influenced by it than were American writers as a whole by Soviet literature. (While often healthy, this impact at times turned the Soviet Union into a model to be mechanically imitated.) Centered in the *Freiheit* and its monthly literary journal, *Der Hamer,* this proletarian trend expressed itself in the Union of Proletarian Yiddish Writers of America ("Proletpen"), founded September 13, 1929. Its first "Zamelbuch" appeared in December, 1930 entitled *Union Square.* There was work by already well-known figures like Olgin, Nadir, S. Deiksel and Aaron Kurtz, as well as by relative newcomers like Yossel Cutler, Leib Sobrin, Martin Birnbaum, Moishe Shifris and Sarah Barkan. To show the link to the first generation of proletarian writers, the volume began with a poem by A. Prinz (Ber Green) to Morris Winchevsky on his 75th birthday.

Aaron Kurtz (1891-1964), Yiddish poetry.

As they grew in depth, and therefore in passion and power, these proletarian writers pressed others outside their ranks in the direction of the social theme. In this atmosphere, a Zishe Weinper, with five volumes already behind him, turned from his practice of poetry for poetry's sake, as he tells us in his poetic autobiography (*Pinye,*

1939), to a poetry of social content. Realizing he was

> No longer merely a wanderer,
> No longer alone!

he wrote for the people, who had woven him into their web of solidarity.

At a time when there was so much misery, private woes were recognized as public evils. The crisis had jaggedly thrust into the forefront of artistic consciousness the great common experiences not only of hunger, the fear of it, and its effect on human beings and human relations but also of the new relations and emotions of people working together in a common cause. The idealism, self-sacrifice and modest daily heroism of people struggling against poverty, against war and against social injustice, particularly of the main victims, the Negroes, became new, exciting themes. The Spanish Civil War was a special magnet. Just as it attracted thousands of volunteers, it enlisted the deepest feelings of all the proletarian Yiddish writers—and many others. Aaron Kurtz published an entire volume of Yiddish poems and ballads, *"No Pasaran"* (1938). One of them ended thus:

> Six brothers go off to the war:
> Three Flahertys, three Steins:
> The fate of Biscay and Jarama
> Will be the fate of the Jordan and Thames.

Supplementing the achievements of proletarian Yiddish literature were those of the workers' cho-

The Workmen's Circle Chorus of New York, Lazar Weiner, conductor (front row, left), in 1950.

Jacob Schaefer (1888-1936), composer and choral conductor.

ruses. By 1938, there were Freiheit Gesang Far-einen (Freiheit Choral Societies) in 27 cities around the country and six Freiheit Mandolin Orchestras, all affiliated with the Idisher Musi-kalisher Arbeter Farband (Jewish Workers' Music Alliance). The most impressive was the New York chorus, which started in 1923 with Lazar Weiner as conductor. When in 1929 political conflicts led to his resignation, Weiner took over the choruses of the Central Synagogue in 1930 and the Workmen's Circle in 1931 (and has suc-cessfully conducted both choruses ever since). His place was taken by Jacob Schaefer, who had in Chicago already produced six oratorios and can-tatas, of which the most memorable were *Martirer-Blut* (Martyrs' Blood, 1914, text by A. Liessin), *Di Zwelf* (The Twelve, 1922, text by the Soviet poet, Alexander Blok), and *Di Zvai Brider* (The Two Brothers, 1923, text by Peretz). Before his death in 1936 at 48, Schaefer composed such sig-nificant works as *October* (1930, a tribute to the Russian Revolution with texts assembled by Na-thaniel Buchwald), *Geviter* (Thunderstorm, 1933, with texts by American Yiddish poets assembled by J. Greenspan), *Shturm-Foigl* (Storm-Bird, 1934, with Gorky's text translated into Yiddish by Olgin), *A Bunt Mit a Statchke* (1935, A Con-spiracy and a Strike, a folk-operetta, with texts arranged by Buchwald), and *Biro-Bidjan* (1936, text by the Soviet Yiddish poet, Peretz Markish). In addition, Schaefer wrote more than two score songs to poems by the early American Yiddish proletarian poets, as well as by M. L. Halpern, Mani Leib, Meinke Katz, Menahem Boraisha, I. E. Rontch, I. B. Bailin, and Abraham Victor, and also by Moishe Broderzon of Poland and Itsik Feffer of the Soviet Union. His roots in Hebrew liturgical chant, in the Hassidic tune and the

The Jewish People's Chorus of Chicago, about 1948, Eugene Malek, conductor (second row, center); this was the first Jewish workers' chorus founded, and is oldest affiliate of the Jewish Music Alliance.

Yiddish folk melody gave a distinctive character to his compositions on radical themes.

After Schaefer's death, the New York chorus expanded its scope under Max Helfman's direction (1937 to 1948). Renamed the New York Philharmonic People's Chorus, it performed William Schuman's cantata, *This Is Our Time,* at the Lewisohn Stadium on July 4, 1940, with Alexander Smallens conducting the New York Philharmonic Orchestra. The chorus continues to be the pace-setter for the more than 20 similar groups affiliated with the renamed Jewish Music Alliance. Helfman himself composed several impressive works for the chorus, the last one, in 1948, being *The New Haggadah,* text by Itsik Feffer.

No less significant was the proletarian trend in the Yiddish theater. While the Yiddish Art Theater was having a great box-office success with spectacles like the dramatization of I. J. Singer's novel, *Yoshe Kalb* (1932-1933), and the Second Avenue theatres continued to entertain their audiences with banalities and vulgarities, the new note struck by the Artef was artistically and socially important. It is true that, since 1915, there had been (and it is still in existence) a non-

The Yiddish actor Lazar Fried in the Yiddish Art Theater production of "Yoshe Kalb," 1932-1933.

A scene from the Folks-bihne production of Peretz Hirschbein's "Griene Felder" (Green Fields), staged by Jacob Fishman in 1918.

Third act of the Artef production of Maxim Gorky's "Yegor Bulichev," directed by Benno Schneider, sets by M. Zolotaroff.

The first act of the Artef production of Sholem Aleichem's "200,000," directed by Benno Schneider, sets by M. Zolotaroff.

S. Niger (Samuel Charney, 1884-1955), Yiddish literary critic.

Before the decade ended, there was a cultural event in Jewish life with far-reaching consequences. In September, 1936 the Yiddish Cultural Front of France issued a call to all Jewish communities for a world Yiddish cultural congress to coordinate the work of defending modern Yiddish culture against Hitlerism. This grand plan was only partially realized when the Congress finally convened in Paris, September 17-22, 1937. Unity was unattainable even on such a minimum platform. In the United States, the Workmen's Circle and Yiddish Scientific Institute (Idisher Vissenshaftlicher Institut—YIVO), as well as individuals like Pinski, S. Niger and J. Glatstein, refused to participate with communists. On the other hand, the Yiddish cultural leaders of the Soviet Union failed to send a delegation for reasons that were but little understood at the time (apparently the policies that brought about the cessation of Yiddish cultural life in 1948-1949 began to operate in the mid-1930's.)

professional workers' theater company with an excellent repertory, the Freie Idishe Folks-bihne, affiliated with the Workmen's Circle. The Artef, however, was proletarian not only in its acting personnel and most of its audience, but in its radical view of society. At first it sought for agitational ends to portray on stage topical events such as strikes, evictions, the bonus march and the farm revolt. The Artef's real contribution, however, came with its productions of Sholem Aleichem's 'Ristocrats (1930) and 200,000 (1936) and of Gorky's Yegor Bulichev (1934) and Dostigayev (1935), marked by folk-intimacy, humanism and profundity of characterization. (Outside Yiddish circles the Artef attained renown, largely because of the dramatic style it developed under the direction of Benno Schneider, a pupil of Vachtangov.) Gradually the Artef had expanded its horizon from a proletarian theater to that of a people's theater fusing high art with a social-ethical outlook. Simultaneously, however, the Artef overreached itself by moving to Broadway and striving to become a professional theater—with the result that in 1939 it had to suspend operation.

Kalman Marmor (1876-1956), Yiddish literary historian and biographer.

Nevertheless, there were 104 voting delegates from 22 countries, including Palestine. The delegation of 11 from the United States had been elected by a nationwide conference of over 800 representatives of 452 local Jewish organizations held on August 28-29, and constituted a real coalition. The delegation included communists like Moissaye J. Olgin, editor of the *Morning Freiheit,* and well-known non-communist literary figures like Joseph Opatoshu, H. Leivick, David Ignatov and the poet Z. Weinper.

This Congress witnessed the greatest marshalling of Yiddish forces in defense of Yiddish culture ever held. Yiddish was then the language of almost two-thirds of the world Jewish population of 15,500,000. The Manifesto unanimously adopted was drafted by Olgin, Leivick and Ben-Adir of France. "The very existence of the Jewish people," it declared, "is threatened in several countries. The Yiddish language, Yiddish culture, Yiddish cultural institutions built by the sweat and marrow of the Jewish masses, and Jewish cultural workers are the object of continual persecution in various countries. The enemies

B. Z. Goldberg, Yiddish writer.

know very well that culture is a tested weapon in a people's struggle for its national survival. They therefore have undertaken to undermine, uproot and destroy Yiddish culture. . . ."

A Central Committee of the Alveltlicher Idisher Kultur Farband (World Yiddish Cultural Alliance—YKUF), was elected of 100 members, 18 of them from the United States, among them the writers B. Z. Goldberg, Peretz Hirschbein, Ignatov, Leon Kobrin, Leivick, Kalman Marmor, Olgin, Opatoshu, Lamed Shapiro, Weinper and Haim Zhitlovsky, Frank Kirk the painter and Rubin Saltzman, fraternal organization leader. Leivick, closing the Congress, expressed the fervid hope that individuals and organizations that had boycotted the Congress, and the Soviet Jews as a whole, would work with the YKUF.

In the United States, the YKUF began its work immediately and in November, 1938 started issuing a monthly literary journal of high quality, *Idishe Kultur,* which is still current. Scores of women's reading circles and YKUF branches were built. In 1942, YKUF inaugurated a publishing enterprise that became the largest in the

Nachman Meisel, Yiddish literary historian and critic.

Dr. Moissaye J. Olgin (1878-1939), editor of the "Morgen Freiheit," and Paul Novick, who succeeded Olgin in that position in 1939.

Yiddish field, issuing about 70 volumes by mid-century. Among them were novels by Mendele Mocher Seforim, Sholem Asch, Abraham Bick, and Raboy; poetry by B. Lapin, Malka Lee, L. Miller, Joseph Rolnick, Hannah Safran, Dora Teitelboim and Weinper; plays by Kobrin; essays and other prose works by Reuben Brainin, Nathaniel Buchwald, Marmor, Nachman Meisel, Paul Novick, Olgin, B. Rivkin and Zhitlovsky; and works by such Soviet Yiddish writers as David Bergelson, Itsik Feffer, S. Godiner, David Hofstein, "Der Nister," and M. Wiener.

Spurred on by the founding of the YKUF and rivaling it was the Central Yiddish Cultural Organization (CYCO), established in 1938 with its base among those who had refused to attend the Paris congress. CYCO also launched a publishing department, which issued many volumes, by 1950, of the works of Peretz, Moses Hess, the historian Simon Dubnow, the literary critic S. Niger,

and of Leivick, Opatoshu, Ignatov, Asch, Shneour, Reuben Eisland, Baruch Glasman, Pinski, Dymov, A. Leyeles-Glantz and others. If some of the original spokesmen for the YKUF now appeared in CYCO, that was not because Olgin's and Leivick's wished-for unity had finally been achieved, but because the war in 1939 caused new alignments.

Parallel with proletarian culture in Yiddish was proletarian Jewish culture in English, as one phase of general American proletarian culture. An increasing majority of the Jews were already exclusively or primarily English-speaking. By 1930, two million, less than half of the American Jewish population, told the census-taker that Yiddish had been "the principal language" used at home in their childhood. By 1940, the number of those to whom Yiddish was the "mother tongue" declined to 1,751,000. Likewise the Jewish writer born or educated in the United States

Two popular novelists:
Edna Ferber (above) and Fannie Hurst (right).

almost invariably expressed himself in English. Of course Jewish writers in one way or another

reflected in their work the facts that part of their roots lay in the parental culture and that their

Waldo Frank, writer.

Michael Gold, writer.

Isidor Schneider, writer.

living experience, owing to the restrictions in American life, was largely among Jewish people. In the American proletarian trend Jewish writers were heavily represented. When 70 authors in January, 1935 issued a Call for "a Congress of American revolutionary writers," one-third of the signers were Jewish, with Waldo Frank, Michael Gold and Moissaye J. Olgin among the leaders. When the League of American Writers emerged from this Congress on April 26-28, the majority of the Executive Committee of seventeen was Jewish. This proportion decreased as the movement attracted additional hundreds by broadening its platform from anti-capitalism to anti-fascism but the Jewish element continued to be extensive. In the anthology, *Proletarian Literature in the United States,* published in 1935, fully one-half of the 63 contributors were Jewish, among them Ben Field, Michael Gold, Albert Halper, Joshua Kunitz, Clifford Odets, A. B. Magil, Edwin Rolfe and Isidor Schneider.

Many of the Jewish proletarian writers did not deal directly with the Jewish theme, but some did so, very notably. Michael Gold's *Jews Without Money* (1930), was a bitter, passionate, realistic depiction of Jewish life on the New York lower East Side in the first decade of the twentieth century, when tens of thousands of Jews were "caught like my father in poverty's trap." One conviction emerges: "There can be no freedom in the world while men beg for jobs." The very title of the book was a challenge to the anti-Semitic stereotype that all Jews were rich. By 1935, the work had been translated into sixteen languages, including German, Romanian, Italian, Japanese, Ukrainian, Russian, Tartar, Bulgarian, Swedish and Yiddish. By 1940, seventeen editions had been sold out in the United States and it has continued to be reprinted.

There were a few other noteworthy books. Isidor Schneider's *From the Kingdom of Necessity* (1935), was an apparently autobiographical novel charting the hard life of a sensitive person who gropes for solutions and finds his way to Marxism. Albert Halper, having already produced his memorable novels of group life, *Union Square* (1933), *The Foundry* (1934) and *The Chute* (1937), climaxed his career in 1940 with an unaffected, carefully elaborated and moving novel of a Chicago Jewish family of "little people" as it is sucked into World War I (*Sons of the Fathers*). Even the Jewish Publication Society issued what it advertised as a "proletarian novel,"

Meyer Levin, writer.

Tomorrow's Bread by Beatrice Bisno (1938), a pedestrian account of a Jewish garment union organizer in Chicago and New York from the 1890's to the first World War, apparently based upon the career of her father, Abraham Bisno.

Outside the proletarian trend, there were in the Thirties more than a score of noteworthy novels in which Jewish life was central. Of more than passing interest was Charles Reznikoff's *By the Waters of Manhattan* (1930), Daniel Fuchs' *Summer in Williamsburg* (1934) and Waldo Frank's *Death and Birth of David Markand* (1934). Henry Roth's only novel, *Call It Sleep* (1934), presented in a richly textured, intense and deeply imaginative style the life of a timid Jewish immigrant boy oppressed by the grimy and the sordid in Brooklyn and the East Side. More widely read was Meyer Levin's *The Old Bunch* (1937), in which a group of Chicago Jews are shown in a process of "Americanization" that is really a deculturation, a stripping away of the cultural heritage of their parents in the scramble for economic security. Levin's book was in sharp contrast to Irving Fineman's *Hear, Ye Sons* (1933), which had depicted devotion to

Albert Halper, novelist.

Irving Fineman, writer.

Orthodox Judaism as no barrier to success as a lawyer. Persecutions of Jews by the Nazis began to find their reflection in such books as Robert Nathan's *Road of Ages* (1935), in which satire and fantasy were used to show the Jews, driven out of the Western World, forming a vast caravan to the haven offered to them in the Gobi Desert, or in Irving Fineman's *Dr. Addams* (1939), which unfolded the adjustment to American society of a refugee from Hitlerism. Still another kind of Jewish novel achieved notoriety at this time by concentrating on repulsive types of Jews, thus feeding the false stereotypes of all Jews that the Coughlins were spreading. Examples were Ben Hecht's coarse *A Jew in Love* (1930) and Jerome Weidman's *I Can Get It For You Wholesale* (1937) and *What's In It For Me* (1938). The outcry against the last two was so extensive that the publisher "voluntarily" withdrew the books "with the consent of their author" in 1939. Yet the *genre* continued to appear in Budd Schulberg's *What Makes Sammy Run?* (1941) and in others that crop up periodically as one or another Jewish writer turns in fitful disgust upon one or another negative phase of Jewish life that

Budd Schulberg, writer.

Irving Thalberg (1899-1936), Hollywood film director.

S. N. Behrman, dramatist.

he presents in false perspective and outside its proper relation to negative features in American society as a whole.

On the American theater, Jewish writers had a greater impact than on fiction. By 1943 over 100 Jewish playwrights had had their dramas, comedies and musicals performed on Broadway, and Bruce Mantle listed 62 plays by Jews in his annual collections of the ten best plays of the year. In addition to quantity there was also eminence, which was achieved in the Thirties by Elmer Rice, George S. Kaufman, S. N. Behrman, Clifford Odets and Lillian Hellman. The Jewish theme was rare, however, and even Jewish characters not too common, although they are to be found in plays by such writers as Sidney Howard, Sidney Kingsley, Irwin Shaw and John Wexley. John Howard Lawson in *Success Story* (1932) described the rise and fall of a Russian-Jewish

Sidney Kingsley, dramatist.

Lillian Hellman, dramatist.

business man. *We, the People* by Elmer Rice (1933) dealt with anti-Semitism on a college campus.

Pre-eminent was Clifford Odets, incandescent product of the intensity and the zest of the people's cultural movement of the Thirties. "We are living in a time," he was aware, "when new art works should shoot bullets." New genius was apparent when in 1933 *Waiting for Lefty* thundered onto the boards of out-of-the-way theaters and union halls. It dramatized the frustrations, fears and longings that lead workers to strike, in terms of clear action, deft characterization and the taut but lyrical dialogue that became Odets' hallmark. Two years later the Group Theater, founded by Harold Clurman, performed three plays by Odets. *Awake and Sing!* showed the Bergers of the Bronx in a "struggle for life amidst petty conditions." "Life should have some dignity," said Jacob Berger. "Go out and fight so life shouldn't be printed on dollar bills!" And his grandson Ralph at the end did. *Paradise Lost* brought the Gordons to ruin when

Elmer Rice, dramatist.

Clifford Odets (1906-1963), dramatist.

they lost the little pocket-book factory and their home. Yet, his paradise lost, Gordon realized that "the world is in its morning and no man fights alone." *Til the Day I Die* was a jagged, searing melodrama about the work of the communist underground in Hitler Germany locked in unequal combat with the Gestapo. Odets' plays are a brilliant and sensitive social record of the hopes, anxieties and protests of the time.

A unique achievement of this cultural upsurge of the Thirties was the Federal Theater Project of the Works Progress Administration, which had a Jewish Division, as well as an Italian and a French. Yiddish companies in New York, Boston, Chicago, Los Angeles and other areas performed mainly the "literary" plays by Gordin, Dymov, Pinski, Hirschbein, Sholem Aleichem, Chone Gottesfeld, Sholem Asch, Goldfaden, Kobrin and Peretz. They also staged Friedrich Wolf's anti-Nazi drama, *Profesor Mamlock,* translated from the German, and translations of Odets' *Awake and Sing!* and Sinclair Lewis' anti-fascist novel, *It Can't Happen Here.* An attempt to develop an English-Jewish company, which performed Gordin's *Jewish King Lear* and Hirschbein's

The Idle Inn was interrupted when the entire Federal Theater Project was liquidated under the pressure of reactionaries.

As the decade drew to a close, the reality of war in Europe brought vast changes in its train. New dangers and new issues caused new developments, new alignments, new divisions and new efforts at all-embracing Jewish communal unity.

When Hitler began World War II by invading Poland on September 1, 1939, a new and fateful period opened in world history, especially for the Jewish people. Between the two World Wars the Western democracies had demonstrated perhaps their unwillingness and certainly their inability to protect the Jews from Hitler's proclaimed policy of exterminating them. With fierce anti-Semitic attacks rising not only in Germany but also in Poland, Austria, Hungary and Romania. the United States admitted only 48,683 Jews in the six years from 1933 to 1938. Jewish leadership in the United States, intimidated by the anti-Semitic campaigns of the Coughlins and conscious of the millions made jobless by the economic depression, hesitated to bring real pressure on the government for a liberal or even elementarily humane refugee policy; only Jewish labor groups had the courage to advocate changes in immigration laws. During the same six years, 187,671 Jews had been allowed legally into Palestine by the British Administration, an average of 31,278 per year. But on May 17, 1939 Great Britain issued its White Paper, proclaiming it would permit only 10,000 Jews into Palestine in each of the next five years, plus 25,000 refugees at the discretion of the High Commissioner— and after that immigration would be based on Arab consent. This White Paper came after Hitler's annexation of Austria and the annihilation of the Czechoslovakian state had confronted the Jews of those states with new dangers. American Jews protested loudly. The Jews of Palestine prepared to resist the catastrophic order by accelerating the "illegal" immigration. In 1939 and 1940, Jewish immigration into the United States rose to 80,395, while 20,952 Jews entered Palestine legally and about 15,000 "illegally," despite British deportation of thousands of intercepted "illegals."

From the very beginning of the anti-fascist war, the vast majority of American Jews ranged themselves against the hated Nazi Axis. The Jews vigorously supported the Administration policy of formal neutrality combined with "all aid short of war," and were also energetic in all forms of relief work, from "Bundles for Britain" to aid to Greece.

Only in one section of the Jewish population was there disorientation—the left. When on August 23, 1939 the Soviet Union signed a Non-Aggression Pact with Germany, the Jewish left, like the left as a whole, interpreted the act as properly in the self-interest of the Soviet Union. Western democracies were blamed for rejecting the collective security against Fascist aggression advocated by the Soviet Union, and for preferring the policy, announced at Munich on September 30, 1938, of appeasing Hitler, in effect freeing him to turn to anti-Soviet operations. At the same time, the left here drew profoundly mistaken conclusions from the Non-Aggression Pact. They interpreted the diplomatic neutrality of the Soviet Union as requiring on the part of the American left an ideological neutrality between Nazism and Western democracy, or Western imperialism. This kind of neutrality was wrong, and isolated the left from the American people, who were overwhelmingly anti-Nazi. But the left, in a perhaps characteristically doctrinaire fashion, pushed this error to its extreme. The left began to defend its ideological neutrality in terms that seemed to reveal a neutrality of sentiment, an indifference of feeling, expressed in the idea that they did not care whether the Nazis conquered the British and French or vice versa. Such

Lt. Roland B. Gittelsohn of New York, United States Navy Chaplain at Iwo Jima, was awarded an Oak Leaf Cluster.

a position offended both the democratic sense and the anti-Nazi sensibilities of the American people, and outraged the passionate anti-Nazism of the Jewish masses. Many on the left had grave inner conflicts as they tried to force their strong anti-Nazi ideology and deep anti-Nazi hatred into the rigid confines of an erroneous political line. The circulation of the *Morning Freiheit* dropped by about one-fifth to a figure of 20,160 in 1940. Prominent writers like Moishe Nadir left the *Freiheit*. In the YKUF, Leivick and some others quickly resigned. In the shops, tensions among Jewish workers increased. A significant minority of Jews in the general rather than the Jewish left also turned away from that movement. Coalitions established on the basis of an anti-Nazi program were wrecked. At the height of the furore, Olgin, spokesman of the Jewish left and a rare combination of political leader and man of letters, died of a heart attack on November 22, 1939 in his sixty-second year.

Therefore only a small minority of doctrinaire radicals, pacifists and conservative isolationists opposed the Roosevelt program of aiding the Al-

Services for Jewish marines conducted amid the battle wreckage of Iwo Jima by Lt. Leon W. Rosenberg of New York at an improvised altar.

Tank Corps Lt. Raymond Zussman of Detroit, who won the Congressional Medal of Honor, the highest United States award; killed in action, September 21, 1944.

armed forces, thus supplying us with the most accurate, if still incomplete, picture of such activity that we have in relation to any war effort. Jews were in every branch of the service, and saw action in every theater of war. They were at Pearl Harbor and Guadalcanal, at Bataan and Burma, at Okinawa and Iwo Jima, in North Africa and at Anzio Beach in Italy, at Normandy on D-Day and in Germany.

Of the 14,903,213 Americans in the armed forces from December 7, 1941 to August 31, 1945, almost 600,000 were Jews, or about 12 per cent of the total Jewish population. This ratio —about one per cent higher than that of the entire American population—is probably due to the fact that Jews were deferred from Selective Service at a lower rate, owing to their urban concentration, occupational characteristics and their smaller families (they marry later in life than non-Jews). Jewish casualties numbered 35,157, including 8,006 killed in combat and 18,003 wounded. Exceptional service by 36,352 Jewish men and women won for them 61,448 awards. Two Jews won the nation's highest military

lies, but the radicals abandoned that position when Hitler invaded the Soviet Union on June 22, 1941. Thus when Japan, the eastern end of the Axis, bombed Pearl Harbor on December 7, 1941, there was unprecedented unity of sentiment among the Jewish population. This anti-fascist Jewish unity of feeling went even deeper than the national unity of the American people as a whole, for it grew from the awareness that fascism triumphant meant death to the Jews.

In the armed forces and on the battlefield Jews played an honorable and frequently a distinguished part. Although the national unity woven by the war halted the centralized large-scale anti-Semitic campaigns of the Thirties, there were still malicious rumors that the Jews were not doing their share in the war itself. Therefore the National Jewish Welfare Board organized an elaborate Bureau of War Records to compile and publicize the record of Jews in the

Paratrooper Staff Sergeant Isadore S. Jackman of Baltimore, awarded the Congressional Medal of Honor; killed in action, January 4, 1945

Master Sergeant Meyer Levin of Brooklyn, killed in action, January 7, 1943; among his awards was the Distinguished Flying Cross.

Sgt. Abe M. Kuzminsky of Washington, D. C., awarded the Distinguished Service Cross; killed in action, February 27, 1945.

Paratroop Captain Alexander P. Suer of Philadelphia, died of wounds, February 1, 1945.

Lt. Frances Y. Slanger of Roxbury, Mass., the first American nurse killed by Nazi gunfire, October 21, 1944.

award, the Congressional Medal of Honor; 74 received the Distinguished Service Cross; 37 the Navy Cross and 2,391 the Distinguished Flying Cross. Among thousands of Jewish officers six were Major Generals, 13 Brigadier Generals, one an Admiral, two Rear Admirals and one a Commodore.

Jewish heroes were legion. The names and deeds of a few are illustrative. The first Medal of Honor was awarded to Tank Corps Lieutenant Raymond Zussman of Detroit, who personally killed 17 Nazis and captured 92 of them while leading his tanks in liberating a village in France. The second went to Paratrooper Staff Sergeant Isadore S. Jackman of Baltimore, for what the official citation called "intrepidity" in counterattacking and routing two Nazi tanks in Belgium in 1945, falling fatally wounded as a result. Staff Sergeant Schiller Cohen of New York won the Distinguished Flying Cross and other medals as a tail gunner in the first Flying Fortresses to bomb occupied Europe, Africa and Italy. Hyman Epstein of Omaha and the Medical Corps in New Guinea, having saved three wounded comrades despite active Japanese sniping, was killed after bandaging the third one. Sergeant Abe M. Kuzminsky of Washington, D. C., wounded in Germany by a well-hidden machine gun, deliberately exposed himself so that the renewed enemy fire, although it killed him, would reveal the location to his squad, which promptly eliminated the machine-gun nest; Kuzminsky was given the Distinguished Service Cross. Sergeant Meyer Levin of Brooklyn became the first Jewish war hero when, as bombardier in Captain Colin Kelly's plane, he disabled the Japanese battleship Haruna that first day of the war. First Lieutenant Frances Y. Slanger of Roxbury, Mass. was the first American nurse killed by Nazi gunfire, while on frontline nursing duty in Belgium on October 21, 1944. Alexander P. Suer of Philadelphia, a dentist who enlisted as a private, became a Captain of paratroopers, was wounded several times, lost both legs at the Battle of the Bulge in Belgium and died on the operating table. Technical Sergeant Abraham A. Todres of Brooklyn, bombardier, gunner and paratrooper for four years, sank a

Red-baiting. Yes, and Jew-baiting—you may as well put that right on top; it is here. There are lots of people who don't want to discuss bigotry, but I would rather have it in the open than to have it under cover. (*Applause and cheers*)

It is not surprising that Mr. Hitler has called Mr. Roosevelt a Jew for all these years, that the native American fascists have been screaming about the "Jew Deal," and that the Hearst-McCormick-Patterson Axis rarely misses an opportunity when discussing PAC to drag in the fact that I am a Jew and that I was born in Lithuania. And I don't apologize to anybody for it. (*Applause and cheers*)

There is nothing new about any of this. I think it is just as well that we should learn about what has happened abroad, and you won't learn about it if you hush it up. Anti-Semitism and the Bolshevik bogey have been the basic propaganda lines of German, Italian and Spanish fascism for years. Now, they are the basic propaganda lines of American reaction, whether it comes from Louis Waldman, or the Post or any other of their kind. And I can speak that way because

Sidney Hillman in 1944 rejecting "red-baiting" and "Jew-baiting" as a hindrance to the war effort, in an address at a union convention.

Japanese aircraft carrier at the Battle of Midway and a cruiser at Coral Sea, was shot down four times, wounded several times, was captured by the Germans and escaped, worked with the French underground for a month photographing German positions in preparation for D-Day, was decorated 30 times (Distinguished Flying Cross, Air Medal, Croix de Guerre, etc.), and was honorably discharged in 1945. Perhaps the spirit of these and other heroes was summed up by Technician Fifth Grade Harold Katz of New York,

Anna M. Rosenberg at her desk as New York State Regional Director of the War Manpower Commission.

Henry Morgenthau, Jr., United States Secretary of the Treasury, 1934-1945.

Judge Samuel I. Rosenman of New York, an advisor to President Franklin D. Roosevelt.

a medical corps man killed in action in Germany in 1945 while aiding his wounded comrades. In a letter to be read only if he died (a new form of the traditional Jewish "ethical will"?), he explained to his "Dear Mom" that he had asked for a combat assignment "because if Hitler won, my family . . . would certainly suffer more than the families of other soldiers who died in the fight. I felt that I must risk my life, on that point, so that I could earn the right for my family to live in peace and free from race prejudice."

On the home front, Jews participated with the same special zeal in all phases of the popular war effort: civilian defense, morale-building, the battle for production and the financing of the war through Victory loans. In Washington official positions, outstanding contributions were made by Sidney Hillman as Associate Director of the Office of Production Management in 1941 and as Director of the Labor Division of the War Production Board in 1942, and by Anna M. Rosenberg from 1942 to 1945 as New York Regional Director of the War Manpower Commission (in 1950-1953 she was Assistant Secretary of Defense). Important in Roosevelt's cabinet also was Henry Morgenthau, Jr., Secretary of the Treasury from 1934 to 1945.

The deep anti-fascist sentiments of the Jewish people, however, were not easily, or ever, transformed into effective unity in action in support of the war. There were those who refused to subordinate old differences to the demands of the hour. Some could not restrain their hatred for the Soviet government even when it was fighting Hitler's armies. Thus the educational director of the Workmen's Circle, N. Chanin, declared in January, 1942, in its monthly organ, *Freint,* that "the last shot has not yet been fired; it will be fired, and it will come from free America—and by that shot the Stalin regime itself will be shot to pieces."

Political conflicts prevented unity even on such a fateful issue as the opening of the Second Front in France in 1942, as promised in the agreement signed by Roosevelt and Soviet Foreign Minister V. M. Molotov on June 11, 1942. Hitler had already begun his systematic extermination of Jews in Eastern Europe; by January, 1943, two million Jews had been slaughtered. There were very good military reasons for adhering to the agreement, for a cross-channel invasion would have lifted the pressure on the Russians, against whom the Germans had launched a new offensive on June 28, 1942. Compelling Hitler to fight on two fronts could have shortened the war and thus saved lives. Not only the White House but the highest military authorities were all for it. But Churchill, having other imperial strategic ends in view, was opposed. A mission headed by General George C. Marshall and Admiral Ernest King went to London to persuade him to abide by the agreement and mount an offensive in France by the end of September, 1942. When Churchill finally said no, Commanding General Dwight D. Eisenhower "thought that Wednesday, July 22, 1942 could well go down as the 'blackest day in history,' particularly if Russia is defeated in the big Boche drive now so alarmingly under way." (So it was recorded by Captain Harry C. Butcher, Eisenhower's naval aide, in his diary, published as *My Three Years with Eisenhower.*)

For the war, Churchill's veto was a setback. For the Jews it was a catastrophe. When Churchill also failed to deliver on his promise to open a front in France in 1943, the fate of millions of Jews was sealed, for in that year Hitler carried through most of his extermination program for the Jews. Not until June 6, 1944 was the offen-

sive in France begun. Yet in 1942 and 1943, only a small minority of non-Jews and Jews protested the politically motivated decision to delay the Second Front. The Zionists were indifferent and the social-democratic *Forward* red-baited the cry for a Second Front, writing as if only the Russians, and not the whole world, including the Jews trapped in Hitler's grip, would benefit.

During these grim years there were important communal developments in American Jewish life. In the Zionist movement there were major changes. Because the theater of war was in Europe and the Middle East, and because the United States had the largest and best organized Jewish community in the world and was now the largest power with financial interests in the Middle East, the main center of Zionist political activity swung from London to New York. This was signalized by an Extraordinary Zionist Conference held at the Biltmore Hotel, May 9-11, 1942, at which both Chaim Weizmann of London and David Ben-Gurion of Palestine were present. A change in basic policy was adopted. Hitherto the movement had refrained from defining its ultimate aim, but now the Biltmore Program called for "a Jewish Commonwealth" in Palestine. This goal was soon approved by all Zionist organizations here as well as abroad except the Hashomer Hatzair, which continued to favor a bi-national state of Jews and Arabs in Palestine.

A year later Rabbi Abba Hillel Silver of Cleveland, an outstanding Zionist and a vigorous Republican in Robert A. Taft's Ohio camp, initiated what the veteran Zionist Emanuel Neumann called "a turning point in the evolution of American Zionist policy." Silver rejected the traditional Zionist orientation on British power and reoriented the movement on the now superior power of the United States. And, not sharing the New Deal ties of Stephen S. Wise and other leading Zionists, Silver "dared to challenge," Neumann pointed out, "not only the State Department but the attitude of President Roosevelt himself." To influence Washington, Silver built up the strength of Zionist organizations as agencies for molding public opinion. From 67,000 members in the Z.O.A. at the end of the summer, 1943 the number grew to 120,000 a year later.

A delegation of Orthodox leaders, headed by Rabbis Eliezer Silver and Wolf Gold, met with Vice-President Henry A. Wallace in Washington, D. C., on October 6, 1943 to petition for aid to save the Jews from Nazism.

while Hadassah membership increased from 88,-000 to 111,000. Silver's emphases were significant in the crucial years immediately after the war.

In 1943 there were three other major events, although of varying magnitude: the heroic Uprising in the Warsaw Ghetto, the shameful Anglo-American Refugee Conference in Bermuda, and the promising American Jewish Conference. In the Warsaw ghetto a half million Jews had already been exterminated almost unresistingly by the Nazi terror regime through starvation, disease and the scientific gas-chambers. Among the determined remnant of some 40,000 unity was finally achieved of religious, Zionist, socialist and communist Jews and an armed fighting organization built. On April 19, coincidentally the first day of Passover, the Uprising began. Jews with small arms, gasoline-bottles and a consciously disciplined heroism faced the Wehrmacht with tanks, flame-throwers and planes. But Jews were at last killing Nazis and creating another eternal symbol of Resistance to oppression. Organized resistance lasted until mid-July, but it was not until September 23 that the last group left the rubble of the razed Ghetto, arms in hand, to join the partisans in the woods. Sporadic fighting

amid the ruins broke out as late as December, 1943. As news of the Uprising spread it sparked active resistance in other ghettoes under Nazi occupation and even in Nazi concentration camps. In the Vilna Ghetto, the young worker, partisan and poet, Hirsh Glick, at a May Day celebration in 1943 that glowed with reports of the Warsaw Ghetto battle, wrote "Zog Nisht Kaynmol" ("Never Say"), which has become a people's hymn for the Jewish masses in many lands, and in many translations. In Aaron Kramer's English, the first and last stanzas ring:

Never say that there is only death for you
Though leaden skies may be concealing days
    of blue—
Because the hour that we have hungered for
    is near;
Beneath our tread the earth shall tremble:
    We are here!

This song was written with our blood and
    not with lead;
It's not a song that birds sing overhead.
It was a people, among toppling barricades,
That sang this song of ours with pistols and
    grenades!

Henry Monsky (1890-1947), who initiated the American Jewish Conference.

On the first anniversary of the Uprising, April 19, 1944, commemoration meetings stimulated by the American Jewish Conference were held in various cities in the United States, and annually since then April 19 has been observed widely by Jews as a day of rededication to the resistance to tyranny.

Ironically, the day the Warsaw Ghetto Uprising began also marked the opening in Bermuda of the Anglo-American Refugee Conference, April 19-30, 1943. Twelve days of talk and listening were followed by seven months of secret "consideration" of proposals, all of which resulted literally in not a single measure for the rescue of a single Jew. Secretary of the Treasury Henry Morgenthau, Jr., recorded in his diary that "for nearly eighteen months after the first reports of the Nazi horror plan" the State Department took no action. As for the British Foreign Office, the idea of rescuing Jews was embarrassing because some of the rescued would then want to go to Palestine in violation of the White Paper of 1939. Finally Roosevelt responded to increasing

public pressure and on January 22, 1944 by Executive Order created the War Refugee Board "to rescue the victims of enemy oppression who are in immediate danger of death." This action came too late to be very helpful. The few thousand Jews the Board did save suggest how much more could have been done.

A significant part of the pressure on the Administration came from the American Jewish Conference, which at its first session, August 29-September 2, 1943, had dealt at length with the problem of the "rescue of European Jewry." Although its final efforts to develop a permanent Jewish Assembly were unsuccessful, the American Jewish Conference was the most important communal development of the period. Initiated by a preliminary meeting of leaders of 32 national organizations called together in January, 1943 by Henry Monsky, a Zionist at the head of the B'nai B'rith, the American Jewish Conference at its first session demonstrated that it was the most widely representative body that the American Jewish community had ever convened. The 501 delegates represented about 2,250,000 Jews; 378 of the delegates represented 8,486 organizations in 78 cities and 58 regions and the remaining delegates came from 65 national organizations. However, the Conference excluded delegations from two left-wing organizations, the Jewish People's Committee and the Jewish Section of the International Workers' Order, although the application of the latter was supported by a petition reportedly signed by 75,000 Jews. It was argued that the Jewish Section was inadmissible because it was only a dependent part of a general, non-Jewish, organization. At the Second Session, December 3-5, 1944, the Jewish Section having been transformed into the Jewish People's Fraternal Order, an autonomous part of the I.W.O., it was admitted to the Conference; the J.P.F.O. then had 46,000 members in 200 branches in 36 States. The veteran Zionist Louis Lipsky, one of the main architects of the Conference, formulated a basic principle when he declared that ideological positions and differences were irrelevant and that "no group of Jews, claiming to be Jews and acting as Jews, could be excluded from participation in the Con-

New York City Mayor Fiorello H. La Guardia (1882-1947), received the Russian Jewish cultural delegation at the City Hall in July, 1943—left to right: Professor Solomon Mikhoels (1890-1948), actor and director of the Moscow Yiddish State Theater, La Guardia and Red Army Lieutenant Colonel Itsik Feffer, Yiddish poet (1900-1952). Mikhoels died mysteriously in an auto accident and Feffer was framed-up and executed in the Stalin purges.

ference . . ." Immediately thereafter the social-democratic Jewish Labor Committee, which had strongly urged the ideological test for admission, withdrew from the Conference. At the Third Session, February 17-19, 1946, representatives of 150,000 Jewish trade unionists were admitted as the Trade Union Committee for Jewish Unity (later renamed the American Jewish Labor Council). The rejection of the ideological test was one of the achievements of the Conference.

The original Call to the Conference had placed on the agenda the development of action to further the "rights and status of Jews in the post-war world" and to implement the "rights of the Jewish people with respect to Palestine." The Conference opened on August 29, 1943 under the lengthening shadow of the Jewish catastrophe in Europe. The Conference memorandum, *A Survey of Facts and Opinions on Problems of Post-war Jewry in Europe and Palestine,* informed the delegates that almost 3,500,000 Jews had already been exterminated by massacre, gas-ovens, torture, forced labor, epidemics and starvation. "Of those who escaped, 1,600,000 were evacuated by the Soviet Government from Eastern Poland, White Russia and the Ukraine and later transported to various parts of Asiatic Russia. Another 150,000 reached Palestine, the United

Part of the platform at the meeting at the Polo Grounds, New York, July 8, 1943, to greet the Russian Jewish delegation—left to right: Itsik Feffer, Judge Anna M. Kross, Solomon Mikhoels, Dr. Nahum Goldmann, Zionist leader, Ben Gold, head, the International Fur Workers Union, James N. Rosenberg of the Joint Distribution Committee and Rubin Saltzman of the Jewish People's Fraternal Order.

States and other overseas lands." Recognizing the urgency of rescuing Jews, the Conference gave this matter primacy.

Since Zionist affiliates predominated, the Committee on Palestine, headed by Abba Hillel Silver, easily led the Conference to pass a resolution embodying the Biltmore Program of a Jewish Commonwealth based on the Balfour Declaration. Only four delegates, three of them from the American Jewish Committee, voted against the resolution, while the delegations from the National Council of Jewish Women, the Jewish Labor Committee and Hashomer Haztair abstained, the latter because it favored a bi-national state in Palestine. On October 24, 1943, the American Jewish Committee voted to withdraw from the Conference.

In its short life, the Conference expressed the will of the majority of American Jews, especially on overseas issues, mobilizing opinion and presenting it to international agencies such as the United Nations Organization conference in San Francisco in the Spring of 1945, the United Nations Relief and Rehabilitation Administration and the Anglo-American Committee of Inquiry into Palestine. Two issues grew in importance from the first to the fourth, and last, session: the need to include attention to the "American Scene," and the problem of permanency. The prevailing will for permanency, however, was not realized, largely because of differences on the admissibility of the "American Scene," and the Conference was dissolved on December 31, 1948.

V-E Day, victory in Europe, came on May 6, 1945, with the Germans surrendering unconditionally to the United Nations command. The world danced in triumph and relief. Itsik Feffer, the Soviet Yiddish poet, had been prophetic. In the summer of 1943 he had addressed a throng of 57,000 at the Polo Grounds in New York as a delegate, with the great Yiddish actor and director, Solomon A. Mikhoels, from the Jewish Anti-Fascist Committee in Moscow. Feffer had stirred this and many other audiences in the United States and Canada with his poem, "I am a Jew," ending on the final proud assurance:

> I will dance on Hitler's grave,
> I am a Jew.

And Jews joined the victory-day dancing. But for six million Jews, one-third of their number— the ghastliest price paid by any people in the war —there was only the dance of death. Some Jews, stricken with unrelieved despair, saw only the ghastliness. Much of the Yiddish literature became an unending wail of heartbreak and lamentation. Leivick gave most persistent and lofty utterance to this mood in his post-war volumes, beginning with *In Treblinka Bin Ich Nit Geven* (I Was Not in Treblinka, New York, 1945), dedicated to his sister and two brothers who had perished in Hitlerite massacres in White Russia. He feels guilty for being alive; he should have died with his brethren in the gas-ovens of Treblinka. Every foundation has crumbled to dust. Only sorrow blooms forever on the body of young and old. The Leivick mood of negation came to dominate the Yiddish literary scene— to this day.

There were those, however, who saw the tragedy but looked to the future. These anti-Fascist writers had Hirsh Glick's indomitable optimism. Yuri Suhl among others gave mighty voice to this chord woven of anguish and indestructibility. In "Am Yisroel Hai" (The Jewish People Live) he wrote (in my literal translation):

> Weep your fill, my people, over your pain,
>   over your woe,
> Sit out your six-million-fold mourning-week
> And lift yourself up, and stand on your
>   feet again
> And turn to the great tomorrow, with faith
>   in your eye. . . .

> As a monument for generations erect your
>   sorrow,
> Because on tears we cannot build.
> And build we must now from the start,
> And build we will, for the Jewish people
>   live.

Yuri Suhl, Yiddish poet and English-language novelist.

Material aid to the bloody and emaciated remnants of European Jewry and to the Jews in Palestine became more important than ever in the post-war years. The Jewish middle class, which had shared the war-time prosperity of the American business community, was unprecedentedly responsive. In 1946 a pinnacle was achieved when $103,000,000 were collected by the United Jewish Appeal (the fund-raising apparatus founded in 1939 by the United Palestine Appeal, the Joint Distribution Committee and the United Service for New Americans). The contributors constituted 24.9%, and in the smaller communities as high as 34.6%, of the Jews. Of the total sum, 90.5% was raised by gifts of $100 or more made by 19.8% of the contributors. Only four out of a thousand donors gave $5,000 or more, but these big contributions made up 30.8% of the $103,000,000. Of course these big donors influenced the policy governing the distribution of these vast funds, and some criticism developed when this policy

The "Marine Flasher," the first ship carrying Displaced Persons to arrive in the United States, May 20, 1946.

became tinged with Cold War aims. Expansion in fund-raising continued until the peak was reached in 1948, when $193,612,511 were collected, of which $172,475,458 went for overseas Jewish aid.

Aid was given so freely largely because there was extensive activity and many-sided struggle for a decisive solution of the Palestine question. Jews in the Displaced Persons camps, learning that entry into the United States was virtually barred, turned their eyes to Palestine. But the British White Paper of 1939 blocked the way. Prime Minister Clement Attlee disregarded the proposal sent him by President Truman on August 31, 1945 that Britain allow an additional 100,000 Jews to enter Palestine. In vain did Zionists, desperately or callously, publish the warnings of a British military scientist that, in the face of possible aggression against the Suez Canal from the East, "to discontinue full immigration into Palestine means to deny to the

British Empire the finest recruiting material that could be found in the Middle East." (*Palestine*, Nov.-Dec., 1945, p. 9, American Zionist Emergency Council.) Was there ever so bad an argument used in so good a cause? It was such attitudes on the part of the Zionist leadership that made it possible for the American scene to be what Rufus Learsi, historian of Zionism, has called "enlivened and also bedeviled" by two sensation-stirring organizations which identified their outlook with the terrorist tactics of the "Irgun" in Palestine. After vain clamor to recruit a "Jewish Army" and "to rescue the Jews of Europe," these Irgunists in 1944 established the Hebrew Committee for National Liberation, a group of seven Palestinian and stateless Jews headed by Peter H. Bergson, and its "front" organization, the American League for a Free Palestine, of which the chairman was former Senator Guy M. Gillette and its chief spokesman Ben Hecht. In national advertising campaigns for which most of the striking copy was written by Hecht, and through such devices as Hecht's powerful but confusing pageant, *A Flag Is Born* (1946), these groups seized the imagination of hundreds of thousands of Jews and non-Jews. With the large sums raised, the League claimed to have smuggled several shiploads of "illegal" immigrants into Palestine past the British naval blockade. There were of course many other Palestinian groups and a number of Americans who participated in many ways in the running of these "illegals" into Palestine. Many a ship was intercepted by the British Navy and its frustrated Jews interned on Cyprus. When the luckless 4,500 refugees that overcrowded the *Exodus 1947* were seized by the British, the Cypriote camps were already full. Therefore London decided that the Jews be taken back to the British Zone in occupied Germany, where another camp for Jews was readily established.

After the war, Jewish voices were raised, chiefly on the left in the United States and Palestine, proposing that the Palestine issue be placed before the United Nations. The Zionist leadership, however, was opposed, being still confined to thinking in terms of a "British orientation" or, more recently, a "United States orientation." As late as December, 1946 the World Zionist Congress decided against taking the matter to the U. N.

Meanwhile Britain, playing for time and also hoping to tie the United States into an Anglo-American partnership in the enterprise of holding the lid down in a troublesome area, proposed a joint Anglo-American Committee of Inquiry into Palestine. Another inquiry was futile, Stephen S. Wise and Abba Hillel Silver, co-chairmen of the American Zionist Emergency Council, wired to President Truman on October 30, 1945; they urged instead a "joint pronouncement" of a joint policy to carry out the Balfour Declaration. Nevertheless the joint Committee was appointed, began public hearings on January 4, 1946, and on April 22 reported in favor of Britain's admitting 100,000 Jews to Palestine, of continuing the British Mandate, and of eventually replacing it with a United Nations trusteeship agreement. The United States backed the

Albert Einstein (1879-1955).

proposal for 100,000, the British rejected it, and nothing was accomplished. Anglo-American rivalry for position in the Middle East made agreement impossible. Albert Einstein, testifying before the Committee in Washington, had irritatingly but shrewdly called the turn: "the difficulties in Palestine . . . are artificially created by the English," the hearings are a "smoke-screen," and the problem could best be handled by the United Nations. At least one United States member of the Committee, Bartley Crum, was appalled to discover that both the Foreign Office and the State Department were less concerned with the welfare of the Jews than with using the Palestine issue as a pawn in regional maneuvers against the Soviet Union. In other words, the Cold War was on. This post-war chill, with which the Truman administration replaced the combat warmth of the Rooseveltian Grand Alliance with the Soviet Union, was the disturbing context that beclouded the solution of the Palestine question.

Yet the time for solution was ripe. The arena was chosen by British Foreign Secretary Ernest Bevin, Labor Party leader. He was feeling the hard squeeze exerted against the entire British position in the Middle East as United States oil interests, headed by Aramco (the Arabian-American Oil Company, founded in 1944), actively undermined British domination of Middle East oil resources. He was annoyed by Truman's agitation, during the 1946 election campaign, of the sore issue of the entry of 100,000 Jewish DP's into Palestine. Bevin finally erupted in the House of Commons on February 25, 1947 in an ill-tempered speech blaming Truman and the Jews of New York for the difficulties in Palestine, and announcing that he would take the problem to the United Nations. For the first time the Palestine question was to be before a body in which the anti-imperialist forces, together with the small states, could be decisive in shaping a solution, especially when the United States and Britain were divided. Amid mounting indignation at Bevin's anti-Semitic sneers, all sides began preparations for the Special Session of the United Nations on Palestine, set for April 28, 1947. Before the session opened, however, the Truman Doctrine was proclaimed on March 12, 1947, pronouncing the regimes of Greece and Turkey, widely known for their terrorism, to be outposts of American democracy in a policy of containment of the Soviet Union. And, significantly, some Zionist leaders here and in Palestine, eager for support from the United States, promptly offered the services and lives of the Jews of Palestine in the cause of the Truman Doctrine.

Four factors interlaced to bring about the United Nations resolution of November 29, 1947 and the subsequent birth of Israel as a State on May 14-15, 1948. The determined struggle of the Jewish community of Palestine was fundamental. The position of the Soviet Union and its supporters was decisive. The conflict of interests in the Middle East between Britain and the United States enabled the democratic, anti-imperialist and socialist forces to prevail. American public opinion, mobilized primarily by the Zionist movement with the backing of almost the entire Jewish population, including the non-Zionist American Jewish Committee, Jewish Labor Committee and Left-wing organizations, compelled Truman to resist the State Department

and assure United States' votes for the Resolution.

The policy of the United States was, to say the least, devious. For while there was popular sympathy with Jewish aspirations in Palestine, there was also powerful opposition in high places. Dr. Frank E. Manuel in *The Realities of American-Palestine Relations* described four sources of this opposition: State Department diplomats and Pentagon global strategists, oil magnates, Anglophiles who believed alliance with Britain indispensable, and missionaries who wished to develop Christian influence over "upper Arab classes." The military strategists were interested in the Middle East primarily as a "potential base for future military operations against the Soviet." Together with the oilmen, the strategists did not think that for the sake of the Jews it was "worth endangering the oil and the telecommunications and the airports of Arabia." As for the Middle Eastern specialists in the State Department, like their opposite numbers in the British Foreign Office, they agreed with the strategists and the oil operators, and moreover, as Truman has admitted in his Memoirs, "there were some among them who were also inclined to be anti-Semitic." This combination of oilmen, diplomats, strategists, which operated covertly behind the scenes, was combatted only by overt democratic appeals to public sentiment, mobilized mostly by the Zionist movement.

The report of the United Nations Special Committee on Palestine, completed on August 31, 1947, recommended the establishment of independent, democratic Jewish and Arab States in Palestine, with economic unity between them, and with Jerusalem declared an international city. From September 16, when the U.N. General Assembly reconvened, to November 29, when the partition plan was adopted by a vote of 33 for, 13 opposed, and 11 abstaining (barely the two thirds majority required), the U.N. was rife with intrigue, pressure and counterpressure. Britain and the Arab States were against partition. On October 2, Abba Hillel Silver announced that the Jewish Agency, recognized by the U.N. as spokesman for the Jews of Palestine, favored partition, reluctantly but firmly. On

Rabbi Abba Hillel Silver, chairman of the American Section of the Jewish Agency for Palestine, addressing the United Nations Ad Hoc Committee on the Palestinian Question on October 2, 1947, and declaring that the Jewish Agency is prepared to accept the U.N. Partition Plan.

October 11, the United States declared its support, reluctantly and indecisively. The practice of the U.S. delegation in the U.N. of whipping votes into line was notably absent on this issue, much to the gratification of the opponents of partition. Detailing the maneuvers in and out of the U.N. corridors, Dr. Jorge Garcia-Granados, chief of the Guatemalan delegation and member of the UNSCOP, summed up the matter in *The Birth of Israel* as follows: "Partition was not voted under pressure of the United States. It was voted because of the tireless efforts of those in the United Nations and in the world who believed in its justice and historic necessity."

Exactly one week after it had voted for the resolution of November 29 under pressure of American and international public opinion, the United States indicated that what Dr. Garcia-Granados called "the process of sabotage" was under way, with the British leading and the United States following. On December 6, the United States proclaimed an embargo on shipment of arms to the Jewish community in Palestine—while the British continued to arm the Arab States. The vigilant F.B.I. arrested Americans for attempting to smuggle arms to the Jews of Palestine. Then on March 19, 1948, the United States reversed itself completely and proposed to scrap the decision on Partition for a United Nations Trusteeship for Palestine. By that tme, however, the Jewish community in Palestine was determined to proclaim a Jewish State as soon as the British Mandate ended on May 14, 1948, the date Britain had given the U.N. Dr. Garcia-Granados continued: "A last-minute attempt to prevent the Jewish State from coming into existence was made by a powerful coalition composed of exponents of British and pro-Arab oil interests, including certain officials of the American government. . . . representatives of the United States

State Department exerted the strongest possible pressure on Jewish leaders in an effort to persuade them not to proclaim a state. Veiled threats of possible American disfavor, even of severe economic sanctions, were expressed. Nor was the White House totally unassociated with this effort. . . . at one point Mr. Truman's personal airplane, the Sacred Cow, was offered to members of the Jewish Agency Executive then in the United States to fly them to Jerusalem, if they would agree to take up with their colleagues there the possible postponement of a proclamation of independence."

But on May 14, Palestine time (May 15, United States time), the independent State of Israel was proclaimed. Now Truman, surprising the State Department, effected another reversal by immediately extending *de facto* recognition to Israel, thus acknowledging an accomplished fact when he saw one. The same day Guatemala became the first state to grant full *de jure* recognition to Israel, followed a couple of days later by the Soviet Union, the first big power to do so. Not until January 31, 1949, after Israel had virtually won its war of independence and liberation, did the United States recognize Israel *de jure,* of right and in law.

The policy of the Soviet Union was forthright. In his first-hand account, *State in the Making,* David Horowitz, who took part in many of the difficult negotiations as a Jewish Agency liaison officer with the U.N. Special Committee on Palestine (later he became Director General of the Israel Ministry of Finance), acknowledged the Russians' "obstinate espousal of our cause at every stage and in every sector of the U.N. deliberations." Of Semyon Tsarapkin and his assistant, Professor Boris Stein, "Soviet envoys" to the U.N. at the final Special Session on Palestine, Horowitz recorded that they "showed keen sympathy and understanding of our efforts and interests. . . . The unremitting aid that Tsarapkin and Stein gave our cause, and their sharp, direct logic, played an important part in the long series of gains we made and in the sum total of our triumph." At that Session, also, invaluable aid was rendered by Ksawery Pruszynski of Poland, who as chairman of the subcommittee to formu-

late details of the Partition plan, "conducted the proceedings," Horowitz noted, "with the aim of bringing about the creation of a Jewish state"; Pruszynski had already been in Palestine several times and published a "sympathetic book on Jewish upbuilding there."

It was pressure from the Soviet, Polish and other socialist state delegations that had won for the Jewish Agency the right to have Abba Hillel Silver, David Ben-Gurion and Moshe Shertok (Sharett) present the Jewish case in the General Assembly, that promoted the partition plan recommended by the Special Committee, when no other big power was actively supporting it, and that worked to get the votes to make up the necessary two-thirds majority. A turning point had come when, on May 14, 1947, Andrei Gromyko read his historic speech to the first Special Session on Palestine of the General Assembly. Basing himself neither on the Balfour Declaration nor on Zionist theories, Gromyko pointed to the realities that were undeniable: "the situation of the Jewish population, which is without shelter and without means of livelihood." He stressed that "the experience of the past, particularly during the time of the Second World War, has shown that not one state of Western Europe has been in a position to give proper help to the Jewish people and to defend its interests, or even its existence, against the violence that was directed against it from the Hitlerites and their allies." He concluded that "it would be unjust not to take this into account and to deny the right of the Jewish people to the realization of such an aspiration" for "a state of their own." Gromyko's proposal, in the interests of both Jews and Arabs in Palestine, was for a bi-national "dual, democratic Arab-Jewish state," but if Arab-Jewish tensions were so acute that this was impracticable he declared he would support partition.

The militant hostility of the Arab states to the U.N. decision, the sabotage by Britain and the retreat by the United States made the birth of Israel a particularly bloody one. Hundreds of lives had already been lost in fighting against Arab infiltrators and the Transjordan Arab Legion, trained and led by British officers, when, on May 14, 1948, the British completed their with-

Colonel David Michael Marcus, U.S.A. (1901-1948), recipient of the Distinguished Service Cross in World War II, killed June 11, 1948, while commander on the Jerusalem front in Israel's war against the Arab invaders.

drawal and Israel proclaimed its statehood. The following day, full scale invasion was launched against Israel by Egypt, Syria, Lebanon, Iraq and Saudi Arabia. To beat back the invaders, the Israeli people and soldiers had heroism and dedication in abundance, but in tragic short supply were the heavy arms required by modern warfare. Britain, which had virtually incited the attack, continued to arm the aggressors. The United States persisted in the now obviously unneutral embargo. The Israeli government, with special assistance from Israeli communists, turned to the socialist states, and purchased the planes, artillery and tanks from Czechoslovakia that enabled the Israeli army to win the war. Almost 1,000 Americans, a few of them non-Jews, found their way to Israel and put their World War II military experience to use as volunteers in the Israeli armed forces. About 70 died, the best known being the West Pointer, Colonel David Michael ("Mickey") Marcus, killed on the Jerusalem front.

Faced with aggression against Israel, the United

Nations proved impotent. The unity between the U.S.S.R. and the U.S.A., which had been decisive in passing the partition resolution, was broken. On November 4, 1948, over the objections of the Russian and Ukrainian delegations, the United States and Britain went so far as to threaten Israel with sanctions in the Security Council for clearing the Arab invaders out of the Galilee and the Negev. Dr. Frank Manuel has in fact concluded, after studying the data, that the United States had a grave responsibility for the entire war. The Pentagon strategists' "erroneous estimate of Arab military might and tenacity was in no small measure responsible for the original outbreak of the Palestine war. If the military in the United States had supported partition firmly and consistently, the Arab states would not have ventured to invade Israel . . ." United States policy also contributed to British intransigence. Dr. Manuel declared that "the cold fact is that until the close of 1948, Great Britain was abetted in its dog-in-the-manger policy by officials in the United States military and diplomatic establishment." The force of American public opinion had, for the brief time needed to attain the U.N. decision on Partition, suspended the operation of "cold war" calculations as the dominant factor in United States policy in the Middle East. When the "cold war" reasserted itself, Israel was a victim, as it has continued to be to the date of completion of this book in May, 1958.

The political struggle around the United Nations deliberations, the birth of Israel and the victorious repulse of the Arab aggression had developed among the Jewish population in the United States what Dr. Manuel calls "a formidable unity" on the question of Israel. In September, 1945 an opinion poll by Elmo Roper had revealed that 80% of the Jewish population favored a Jewish state in Palestine, 10% opposed it and 10% were undecided; the unity was even larger in 1950. Except for the dogmatically anti-Zionist American Council for Judaism (which since its founding in 1943 has insisted the Jews were only a religious group and not a people and therefore should have no more interest in the Palestine Jewish community and in Israel than any non-Jewish American), the entire Jewish population subordinated its differences on Zionist theory and program to universal sympathy with, friendship for and aid to Israel. This pro-Israel unity cut across class lines. Class differences, however, have emerged on such questions as the specific policies of Israeli governments, attitudes to various classes and political groupings inside Israel, and methods of best aiding the people and State of Israel. Zionist organizations had a spurt of growth, from 400,000 in 1940 to 1,000,000 in 1948. The new membership was joining, not because of the spread of Zionist principles but out of a desire to help establish a Jewish state as a haven for displaced Jews. Some Zionists disparaged this post-war, post-Hitler American brand of Zionism as "refugeeism"

and not "true" Zionism. Once Israel was a reality, membership declined to 750,000 in 1954. Perhaps Hadassah retained a greater proportion of its new membership than did other Zionist groups by developing American Affairs Committees to meet their members' other Jewish interests as well as their desire to help Israel.

For the Jews overseas, these fateful decades had meant large-scale destruction and the uneven beginnings of reconstruction. The Jews in the United States emerged as the largest Jewish community in the world, the most internationally minded in Jewish affairs, the richest and most generous, and very highly organized. It faced the mid-century with new consciousness of its strength and with expanding awareness of its problems.

CHAPTER 13: Mid-Century Profile

THE MID-CENTURY YEAR, 1950, was a time not only for the decennial census but for informal semi-centennial inventory—and the Jews took full part in this social accounting. Where *was* the Jewish national group in the United States three centuries after its refugee pilgrims had settled in New Amsterdam? How big was the American Jewish community, what was its social composition, and how was it organized? What was its relation to American life, economically, politically, socially, culturally, and as a communal group? What was its own inner Jewish communal life, culture and structure? What was the relation of the American Jewish community to segments of the world Jewish people in other lands? These questions were complex and there were no simple answers.

Sometimes even the bare facts are elusive or uncertain. Handicapped as statistics of Jews are by the absence of official census data about Jews, Jewish sociology was compelled to rely upon the approximations obtainable by careful estimates. On this basis, it has been determined that in 1950 there were about 5,000,000 Jews in a total population of 150,697,000. Three quarters of the Jews lived in 14 of the largest cities in the country, each with a Jewish population of 45,000 or more; seven of the 14 were on the Eastern seaboard. In the order of the size of their Jewish communities, these cities were New York, Los Angeles, Chicago, Philadelphia, Boston, Detroit, Cleveland, Baltimore, Newark, Pittsburgh, San Francisco, St. Louis, Miami and Washington, D.C. The remaining 25 per cent of the Jews are recorded in more than 1,200 other communities throughout the 48 states. The post-war rapid trend toward the suburbs which has swept the American middle classes has also had its strong impact upon the large Jewish middle class. Patterns of life characteristic of suburbia have already begun to reveal specific Jewish aspects, notably an increase in public Jewish identification, which is very often made through the synagogue center (even by non-religious Jews).

In class composition the Jewish population had changed considerably from the turn of the century, when the proletarian wage-workers were the largest single class; at mid-century, the middle class held that position. There was a small plutocracy, including bankers, big manufacturers, big merchants and other magnates. The huge middle class comprised the manufacturers, merchants and retailers, the artists, scientists, professionals and other intellectuals, both self-employed and salaried, the small proprietors, managers and executives, and some 20,000 farming families (mainly in poultry and dairy, but also in grain, cotton, tobacco, vegetable and fruit farming). There was a substantial Jewish wage-working class, chiefly in New York but also in Philadelphia and Chicago, numbering about 300,000 in the traditional Jewish fields—garment and building trades, food industries, shoe and leather crafts—and undoubtedly tens of thousands more scattered in many other crafts, such as automobile, metal and machine work. They were generally skilled workers and unionized. There was a large group of office, clerical and sales employees of all kinds.

The Jewish trade union and labor movement had also undergone tremendous changes. In 1950 there was no longer a single national trade union in which the Jews were a majority of the membership. The former Jewish unions had grown

Jacob S. Potofsky, president, Amalgamated Clothing Workers of America, American Federation of Labor-Congress of Industrial Organizations.

David Dubinsky, president, International Ladies' Garment Workers' Union of America, AFL-CIO.

in size until the Jewish membership was far outnumbered by the newcomers, Italian, Puerto Rican and other non-Jewish workers, although the leadership remained predominantly Jewish. The International Ladies' Garment Workers' Union of 400,000 had only about 30 per cent Jews. Only about 25 per cent of the 375,000 members of the Amalgamated Clothing Workers and of the 100,000 in the International Fur and Leather Workers' Union were Jewish. Of the 45,000 in the United Cloth Hat, Cap and Millinery Workers, about 45 per cent were Jewish. These percentages have continued to decrease as retiring Jewish workers are replaced by young non-Jewish workers. Strictly speaking, there was no longer a Jewish trade union movement in the sense in which it had existed from the 1880's to the 1920's.

Yet the increase in Jewish consciousness stirred by Hitlerism, anti-Semitism in the United States,

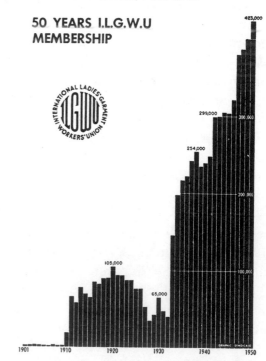

50 YEARS I.L.G.W.U MEMBERSHIP

Official membership chart of the International Ladies' Garment Workers' Union, 1900-1950. Only a minority of the members of this union, however, are now Jewish.

Ralph Helstein, president, United Packinghouse Workers of America, AFL-CIO.

Louis Goldblatt, secretary-treasurer, International Longshoremen and Warehouse Workers' Union, independent.

and the birth of Israel had affected the Jewish trade unionist as well as other Jews. Organized Jewish workers were now active in the general Jewish community. The old trade unionist hostility to Zionism had been replaced by widespread pro-Israel sympathy. All unions with significant Jewish membership, from the fur union on the left of the labor spectrum to the women's garment union on the right, contributed funds to Israeli institutions. In the Jewish community, the influence of the Jewish trade union leaders was exerted largely through the Jewish Labor Committee, with an affiliated Jewish membership of 280,000, and, for a few years from 1946, through its left-wing opposite number, the American Jewish Labor Council.

There was a change also in the temper of the Jewish trade unionists. Once they had made history and smashed the old sweat-shop system by mass, militant, bitter strike struggles. Now the leaders were experts in union-management co-

operation and collective bargaining techniques, but the average wage per hour in the garment industries was among the lowest in the manufacturing trades. The unions now had huge treasuries, and rendered their memberships many welfare services through medical, recreational, educational and pension plans. New members were pleased with these advantages. Old left-wingers who pointed to the failure to maintain wage-scales in the face of climbing prices were ineffective in moving the leadership on such matters. Only in the furriers' union did the old spirit and methods continue at mid-century, despite attacks both by government and the employers. A lockout on April 2, 1948 was answered by the New York Furriers' Joint Council with a general strike of 10,000 mass-picketing furriers who, already averaging $105 for a 35 hour week, won wage-increases, longer paid vacations and other gains (this is a "sick industry" in which there is much unemployment!).

Trade unionists aid Israel: Joseph Breslaw, manager of Local 35, ILGWU, presenting a check to Israel Merom, Histadrut representative, for the Dubinsky Library in Haifa, December, 1950.

In the political outlook of the Jewish trade unionist there was also an evolution. Except in the groups built around the *Morning Freiheit*, the old socialist ideals had become vague and diffuse. The once socialist *Jewish Daily Forward*, as Professor David A. Shannon has pointed out in his history, *The Socialist Party of America*, "had been growing steadily more conservative since the [first] World War." Immediate attention was concentrated on maximum support to New Deal democracy. The tradition of independent political action continued to be more prevalent among Jewish workers than among other American workers, but it was expressing itself in organizations like the American Labor Party and the Liberal Party in New York state. Jewish par-

Hashomer Hatzair Zionist Youth Movement of North America had sent 1,000 young people to Palestine after preliminary training at a Hightstown, N. J. farm. Shown is a scene from the Festival of First Fruits.

ticipation in left-wing activities continued proportionately high.

In the Jewish population as a whole at mid-century, many institutional and cultural changes were noticeable. Conspicuous was the growth in the number of Jews affiliated with religious institutions, part of a general American post-war expansion of religious affiliation. The increase in congregational membership was caused not by a surge of piety—except in minor instances—but by a more acutely felt need for identification with organized Jewish life. From 1945 to 1950, the building of synagogues and temples, especially in suburbia, expanded tremendously, at an estimated cost of $50,000,000 to $60,000,000. About 2,500 Orthodox congregations had a membership of some 200,000 families; 400 Conservative and over 400 Reform congregations had

Congregation B'nai Israel, Millburn, N. J., Percival Goodman, architect, Herbert Feaber, sculptor of "Burning Bush," 1950.

about 150,000 and 100,000 families respectively affiliated. Adding 250,000 otherwise unaffiliated Holy Day seatholders, the number of synagogue-affiliated Jews totaled 1,735,000, or 40 per cent of the Jewish population. The majority of the Jews, particularly in the large cities, however, were still outside the congregations.

Surveys of religious trends were revealing: The fastest growing movement was the Conservative. While attendance at services continued to decline, there was a tendency toward increased ritual ob-

Rabbi Philip S. Bernstein of Rochester, president in 1950 of the Central Conference of American Rabbis (Reform).

Rabbi Max D. Davidson, president in 1950 of the Rabbinical Assembly of America (Conservative).

servance (notably in the Reform movement), especially in rituals practiced at home and during Jewish festivals. The majority of both rabbis and members of Reform congregations were now of East European descent, having displaced the German Jews dominant before the first World War. All three branches, with Reform in the lead, had developed commissions and programs for social action in the cause of social justice. (In June, 1946, the Central Conference of American Rabbis [Reform] and the Rabbinical Assembly of America [Conservative] were among the first organizations in the United States to pass resolutions proposing the outlawing of atomic warfare, and the development of atomic energy for peaceful purposes under public ownership.) The Reconstructionist Movement, to which 5,000 rabbis and Jewish lay leaders adhered (about two-thirds of them Conservative, the remainder Reform), also had a bold program for social change and progress.

The press dealing with Jewish affairs at mid-century consisted of 204 periodicals issued regularly. Of these, 146 were wholly in English, 27 in Yiddish and 11 in Hebrew. The remaining 20

Rabbi Mordecai M. Kaplan, founder of the Reconstructionist Movement.

Some examples of the Jewish press, 1950.

were in two and sometimes in three languages: English and Hebrew, Yiddish and English, German and English, English and Hungarian, English, Hebrew and Yiddish, and so forth. The four daily newspapers were, however, Yiddish, with a total circulation of 199,939, of which the largest was the *Forward,* with 87,596, and the smallest the *Freiheit,* with 14,800. There were 69 weeklies, the most notable being *Congress Weekly,* the Brooklyn *Jewish Examiner,* the Chicago *Sentinel* and the *National Jewish Post.* Of the 59 monthlies, the most prominent were *Yiddishe Kultur* and *Zukunft,* published respectively by the YKUF (Yiddisher Kultur Farband) and the CYCO

(Central Yiddish Culture Organization), *Commentary* (American Jewish Committee), *National Jewish Monthly* (B'nai B'rith), the *Jewish Spectator* (Orthodox), *Jewish Frontier* (Labor Zionist) and *Jewish Life* (left-wing). While most of the weeklies were on a low journalistic level and brashly commercialized, many of them reported news of Jewish life throughout the world more accurately than did most of the Yiddish daily press. The better periodicals also provided an elaborate forum for the discussion of Jewish affairs and the innumerable facets of the Jewish question. As such, the Jewish press was but one part, although a large one, of the foreign language and national group press in the United States at the time. A study in 1948 found 973 publications in 40 foreign languages, the most widely used being Spanish (108 periodicals), Italian (75), German (67), Polish (56), Yiddish (40), Hungarian (30) and French (33). There were also 300 radio programs in 26 foreign languages, with Polish, Spanish, Yiddish and German leading.

Basic to a group's efforts for cultural survival is its educational system. Heightened Jewish consciousness was expressing itself in increased attention to children's education, on which the Jewish community spent more than $25,000,000 in 1950. There were more than 2,700 Jewish school units, with a total registration of over 270,000 pupils. Thus more than 43 per cent of Jewish children of elementary school age that year were attending a Jewish school. The figures also indicate that about 75 per cent of Jewish children "are exposed to some Jewish training" at some time during their elementary school years. For the 130,574 pupils who attended the Sunday schools, their Jewish education was only "rudimentary." However, the 111,238 attending the week-day afternoon schools could have obtained an "extensive" education but for the fact that only three to four per cent of the total number stayed on to be graduated. "Intensive" education was provided for the 21,404 in the Jewish all-day schools (in many of which Yiddish was the language of instruction). These all-day schools were the fastest growing of all Jewish educational institutions, enrolment having leaped from 9,907 in 1945 to 21,404 in 1950, in part because of the post-war influx of East European Hassidic rabbis and their devoted followers. Twenty Jewish teacher training schools tried in vain to keep up with the need for professionally competent personnel in a field not yet ready to meet the salary or status requirements of a profession. In content, the curriculum laid new stress on integrating Jewish religious and cultural values with those of American democratic ideals, on the religio-cultural aspects of Jewish ritual, on aesthetics and on Jewish cultural expression. There were also post-war spurts in two directions: in Jewish high schools, with 5,000 pupils in New

York City alone (constituting 6.5 per cent of the 78,000 Jewish students in the public high schools); and in the study of Hebrew in public high schools, which, begun in New York in 1930, registered 5,200 students in New York, Newark, Boston, Pittsburgh and St. Louis in 1950.

Tenacious, but losing ground steadily, were the Yiddish secular schools of working-class orientation sponsored by the Workmen's Circle, the Jewish National Workers Alliance, the Sholem Aleichem Folks Institute and the Jewish People's Fraternal Order. In 1950, almost one-third of the 20,000 pupils in such schools were in the J.P.F.O. *shules,* with the Workmen's Circle not far behind. In both school systems, since the 1930's the trend had been to a curriculum which combined a more "national" Jewish content with "the spirit of socialism." Noteworthy is the greater earnestness of parents and pupils in these schools: for proportionately twice as many pupils continued to graduation in these Yiddish schools as in the Hebrew schools, and fully half of those graduating went on to the Yiddish secondary schools. Yet the dedication of the grandparents, who generally manage the Yiddish schools, to the perpetuation of Yiddish culture could not check the decline caused by the objective process of linguistic assimilation. The more flexible school administrations began slowly to adapt themselves to the needs of parents who wanted their children to get their secular and progressive Jewish education, if at all, in schools in which the language of instruction was English.

The literary scene at mid-century was diversified. In Yiddish writing, the cleavage between right and left camps sharpened as the Cold War intensified the attack upon the left and upon all dissenters. On all sides there was preoccupation with the Hitlerite catastrophe visited upon East European Jewry, and memorial writings about individuals and entire towns and regions continued to be published. The Warsaw and other Ghetto struggles were an important theme. On the right, the major note in the face of the devastation was one of doom; on the left, there was determination to clear the rubble and begin to rebuild. Menahem Boraisha's distinguished career, in which the two-volume epic poem, *Der*

First National Conference on Jewish Education, December, 1950, in New York, sponsored by the American Association for Jewish Education.

Varieties of Jewish education — right, Mittelshule graduates and faculty, Sholem Aleichem Folk Institute, New York, 1950; below, Temple Israel Religious (Reform) School, New Rochelle, N. Y.

Below, New York Mittelshule, Jewish People's Fraternal Order; bottom, Hanukah Celebration, Workmen's Circle I. L. Peretz School, New York.

Geyer (The Wanderer, 1943) was his highest achievement, was completed by the posthumous publication in 1950 of two long, brooding poems, *Durch Doires* (Through Generations). Posthumous collections of stories appeared by Lamed Shapiro and I. J. Singer. The veteran literary historian, Kalman Marmor, saw his one-volume life and letters of the labor poet, David Edelstadt, issued by YKUF.

At this time, too, new shocks began to jolt the entire Jewish community and especially the American Yiddish reader. The source was the least expected. In the Soviet Union, where the policy of encouraging Yiddish culture had won for that country considerable esteem and innumerable friends, there had been in 1948 and 1949 a sudden, unexplained closing down of all Yiddish theatrical, publishing and press activities outside Birobidjan. The best-known literary figures, many of whose works had been widely read here, disappeared from public life and all communication with them—even private—was broken. There was much wrangling about horrible rumors, genuine concern by the general

Arthur Miller, dramatist.

Jewish public, malevolent denunciations by the right, unpublicized and timid inquiries from the left—and impervious silence by the Soviet Government. By 1950 a cloud of confusion, doubt, fear, bitterness, disbelief, dismay and furtive worry (and some glib dissimulation that even worry was a sign of weakness or error) settled upon the scene. This cloud was not to be dispelled until the blasting revelations of the grim truth of the unjust imprisonment and even in many cases of the execution of these Soviet Yiddish writers began to appear in 1956.

For the English reader, the Jewish theme recurred more and more frequently. Two developments highlighted reader interest in Jews: a bestseller novel, and the popularity of translations of the Yiddish classics. Laura Zametkin Hobson applied her slick-magazine skill in 1947 to *Gentleman's Agreement*, a shiny, tricky novel built on a Sholem Aleichem device (already used by Arthur Miller in *Focus*) of having a non-Jew learn at first hand what it means to be a Jew by being taken for one by anti-Semites. After being serialized in a magazine with 3,000,000

Maurice Samuel, man of letters.

Lion Feuchtwanger (1884-1958), refugee novelist.

Howard Fast, novelist.

Albert Maltz, novelist, dramatist.

Norman Mailer, novelist.

circulation, the book sold 1,250,000 copies, and then reached its largest audience as a Hollywood film. Simultaneously, the way having been prepared by Maurice Samuel's perceptive volumes introducing *The World of Sholem Aleichem* and Peretz as *The Prince of the Ghetto,* a wide audience was being reached by translations of Sholem Aleichem especially, of Peretz and even of the lesser known classic, Mendele Mocher Seforim.

In the mid-century year, the "Jewish" literary event was *The Wall,* an impressive novel of the Warsaw Ghetto under Hitler occupation written by John Hersey, a non-Jew. With astounding verisimilitude of infinite but well-marshalled detail, based on a mountain of documents assembled for him by the American Jewish Committee, Hersey movingly spelled out the suffering, indignity, tragi-comedy, barbarity, treachery, humanity, fortitude, self-sacrifice, heroism and, finally, the triumph of resistance in the Ghetto. If one missed an accurate portrayal of the forces that forged the final unity of the Warsaw Ghetto fighters, one did get the variety of Jewish experience under the spiked heels of the Nazi freebooters and in the shadow of the crematoria. Yet Hollywood, with the Cold War turned on and with Columbia University President Dwight D. Eisenhower exhorting us to "Let bygones be by-

Bruno Walter (1876-1962), orchestral conductor, refugee from Hitlerism.

gones" with reference to the Nazis so that the rearmament of Western Germany could proceed, did not produce *The Wall* but preferred to rehabilitate Rommel as "The Desert Fox."

Fiction by and about Jews in 1950 had its many facets. The unexhausted theme of immigrant life reappeared in *One Foot in America,* the first of a series by Yuri Suhl, who, having published several volumes of Yiddish poetry, now turned to the English-speaking audience with his fiction while continuing to write poetry in Yiddish, a rare example of parallel bi-lingual creativity. With a refreshingly humorous view of his characters and situations, Suhl deftly sketched the "adventures" of an immigrant boy in Brooklyn in the 1920's, amusing his readers without mocking his subjects. The American-born Jewish boy is the focus of *The Sidewalks Are Free* by Sam Ross, which conveys an uncommon awareness of the dignity of labor and the class divisions in the Jewish community. In the tradition of Michael Gold's *Jews Without Money,* this book was a sharp contrast to the recently published novels

Charles Angoff, novelist.

Felix Frankfurter (1882-1965), Associate Justice, U.S. Supreme Court, 1939-1962.

about the Maccabees, *My Glorious Brothers* (promptly awarded a prize by the Jewish Book Council of America and translated into many languages), returned to his excellent and ever more penetrating series of novels about the American Revolution. In *The Proud and the Free,* based on a mutiny of the Pennsylvania Line against overbearing officers, Fast presented Jewish characters as part of the historical picture, as he had done in the entire series from *Conceived in Liberty* on (1939). The works named, while far from exhausting those published in 1950, suggest the variety of subjects and levels of achievement. An even larger number of Jewish writers dealt with the general scene without any Jewish component, or without noting it even when it existed. In every branch of American writing from aesthetics to zoology, Jews participated actively, contributing to American culture without touching the Jewish theme, the basis of American Jewish culture.

While these cultural developments were unfolding, the Jewish population faced many external problems at the mid-century deriving from overt and covert anti-Semitic pressures. "Com-

by Norman Katkov, the effect of whose coarse depiction of Jewish life had been stamped widely as anti-Semitic. The Jewish soldier in World War II, who had appeared marginally in the novels of Norman Mailer and Irwin Shaw, was central in Louis Falstein's *Face of a Hero,* in which the aerial gunner, Ben Isaacs, fights the Nazis with the fused consciousness of a Jew and an anti-fascist. While Isaacs encountered in the army widespread indifference to fascism, no little hostility to Jews and intense contempt for Negroes and Italians, his own grasp of the meaning of fascism was tightened by contact with survivors of the Warsaw Ghetto Uprising in a Displaced Persons' camp. Israel was still too new at mid-century to have stimulated American Jewish fiction, but Murray Gitlin in *The Embarkation* dealt with illegal immigration into Palestine. In historical fiction, Howard Fast, fresh from an excursion that had in 1948 produced his inspiring book

Professor Morris Raphael Cohen (1880-1947), philosopher.

munity relations" work became a major Jewish communal enterprise, and the National Community Relations Advisory Council, set up in 1944, had more than 25 local councils by 1950. The "national unity" developed during World War II had tended to smother the roaring anti-Semitism of the 1930's, but the Cold War fanned the embers. *The American Jewish Year Book* took note of "approximately 50 anti-Semitic groups and 50 periodicals," some of them with circulations of 20,000 and 100,000, operating in 1950. Though they functioned on the margins of public life, their influence was sometimes alarmingly perceived in "respectable circles," as when the *Chicago Daily Tribune* on May 29, 1950 carried a front-page story naming Herbert H. Lehman, Henry Morgenthau, Jr. and Felix Frankfurter as the "secret government of the United States." Occasionally, amid innumerable minor acts of violence, the extremists kindled a blaze of startling proportions. One instance was the well-prepared riots staged at Peekskill, N. Y., on August 27 and September 4, 1949 to prevent an open-air concert by Paul Robeson. Linked menacingly with the blatant anti-Negroism and anti-Communism of the mob that attacked the concerts was the anti-Semitism revealed in stickers, leaflets and outcries. Reporting on its careful investigation of the affair, the American Civil Liberties Union, joined by the American Jewish Congress, the National Association for the Advancement of Colored People, the Council Against Intolerance, the Americans for Democratic Action and the American Veterans' Committee, stated in May, 1950 that "behind the anti-Communist sentiment" of the veterans who organized the attacks "lay prejudice against Negroes and Jews." The increasing connection between anti-Negro and anti-Semitic attitudes, incidentally, was being reflected in joint annual reports, beginning in 1948, by the American Jewish Congress and the N.A.A.C.P., *Civil Rights in the United States, A Balance Sheet of Group Relations*. The report for 1950 "revealed a marked change from the encouraging trend" noted in the first two years.

The occasional dramatic anti-Semitic event that attracted public attention tended only to underline the common experience of the Jewish population with anti-Semitic discrimination in employment, housing selection and social relations, as well as with offensive prejudicial utterance orally or in print. Repeated surveys revealed persistent discrimination against Jews in opportunity and conditions of employment in industrial, clerical, managerial and professional occupations. A 1950 study, by the B'nai B'rith Vocational Service Bureau, of graduates of law, business administration and accounting schools in 1946 and 1947 indicated that Jews had a harder time than non-Jews in finding work, earned about $300 per year less and more often had to find work not related to their training. Insurance and utility companies were found by other surveys to be actively discriminating. Although only a small minority of the Jews directly affected made an issue of this practice, complaints were filed with government agencies administering anti-discrimination laws in Connecticut, Kansas, Massachusetts, Minnesota, New Jersey, Ohio, Oregon, Pennsylvania and Rhode Island. Generally Jews entering the labor market took it for granted that they would be affected by anti-Semitism.

A similar situation existed with regard to housing, particularly in home-owning. Restrictive covenants were not uncommon, and signs either crudely or subtly defining restricted areas were flaunted both in residential and resort areas. The trend to suburbia, encountering the exclusiveness of older residents, sharpened awareness of the problem; sometimes new suburbs were populated, in self-defense, overwhelmingly by Jews.

In social relations, especially those involving the intimacy of the home or the club, Jews became increasingly conscious of the patterns of exclusion. Again this was most marked in suburbia, where social, cultural and to some extent even civic life tends to revolve around church centers. One result was to stimulate increased Jewish organizational and religious affiliation.

The Jewish population was also adversely affected in a particular way by the "Cold War," which generated repressive measures against all critics and dissenters, ranging from communists to the mildest of New York. The Jews in their overwhelming majority had been New Dealers par excellence. Jewish participation in all liberal, progressive and radical movements, whether cultural, social or political, had been conspicuous. Therefore Jews were bound to be among those hardest hit by the blanket attacks of the Cold Warriors on the home front. In 1947, the barometer of intimidation began to fall rapidly. On March 22, 1947, President Harry S. Truman signed his loyalty order affecting millions of federal employees and setting a dread pattern for state and municipal inquisitions. (In 1956, Truman's Secretary of State, Dean Acheson, admitted, in *A Democrat Looks at His Party*: "I was an officer of the Administration and share with it the responsibility for what I am now convinced was a grave mistake and a failure to foresee consequences which were inevitable.") On June 23, 1947 the Taft-Hartley Law was passed, marking the beginning of federal control over the functioning of trade unions; C.I.O. President Philip Murray commented that this was "the first real step toward the development of fascism in the United States." Joseph R. McCarthy in the Senate was concocting his witches' brew of reckless charges of communism, treason and spying. In 1949, he brazenly effected a commutation of the death sentences of the Nazi perpetrators of the Malmedy Massacre of 150 American war prisoners and 100 Belgian civilians at Christmas, 1944. On February 9, 1950 McCarthy falsely charged in Wheeling, W. Va., that the Secretary of State was knowingly employing "205 . . . members of the Communist Party . . . working and shaping policy in the State Department."

Clouds of hysteria masked the sun of the Bill of Rights. Guilt by association became a standard of judgment if not a rule of law as faceless informers filed irresponsible charges. Not conduct but opinion and association became the measure of respectability, employability and even of legality. The air was heavy with suspicion of persons in government employ, federal, state and municipal, of all engaged in education and the mass communication and cultural media, and even of workers in private industry with government contracts. The climate became one of fear. The fear of freedom it was called in 1952 in

a book of that title by Francis Biddle, United States Attorney General from 1941-1945. "Loyalty boards," he explained, developed strange criteria to test what Truman's executive order described as "disloyalty to the Government of the United States" rather than to the United States. Persons were judged not only by what they themselves read, thought or believed but by what their associates, friends or even distant relatives read, thought or believed. The "accused" were asked their views of the capitalist system, of labor activities, of segregation of Negroes, of the internal and foreign policy of Russia. As Chancellor Robert M. Hutchins of the University of Chicago said to a legislative committee in Illinois in 1949, "One who thinks that there are too many slums and too much lynching in America can be called a fellow-traveler, for the Russians say the same."

As the reactionary barrage unfolded, Jews were outstanding among those who bore the brunt of the attack. Thousands of Jews were among the tens of thousands who lost livelihoods, careers, the right to United States residence and even personal liberty as legislative investigating committees, employers, the press, boards of education, immigration authorities and the courts were swept by the hysteria. When Congress on November 24, 1947 cited for contempt ten eminent Hollywood screen-writers—six of them Jewish: Alvah Bessie, Herbert Biberman, Lester Cole, John Howard Lawson, Albert Maltz and Samuel Ornitz—, Rankin of Mississippi made a speech on the floor of the House with clear anti-Semitic innuendoes. Conviction on the same charge had already been secured on June 27, 1947 of eleven members (eight Jewish) of the executive of the Joint Anti-Fascist Refugee Committee, headed by Dr. Edward K. Barsky, for refusing to give names of contributors and of Spanish Republican refugees to the House Committee on Un-American Activities. Of the eleven national leaders of the Communist Party tried under the Smith Act in 1949 on charges of conspiring to teach and advocate violent overthrow of the government, five were Jewish, and the proportion was similar in the subsequent Smith Act trials. All eight teachers with superlative academic records suspended May 3, 1950 by the New York City Superintendent of Schools for refusing to answer questions about political opinion or affiliation were Jews, as were the vast majority of hundreds of teachers forced out of the school system.

The 1950 calendar of intimidation was long and induced among the citizenry what Supreme Court Justice William O. Douglas in 1952 called "the black silence of fear." On September 23, 1950, over Truman's veto, Congress passed the McCarran Internal Security Act, providing for the registration of communist and "communist-front" organizations and their memberships. In November, 1950 the appointment of Anna M. Rosenberg as Assistant Secretary of Defense was met with what the American Jewish Committee described as "the smear of 'Communist' with anti-Semitic overtones." The Senate Armed Services Committee delayed confirmation pending hearings on charges she was a communist concocted by McCarthy, Rep. John E. Rankin, the Mississippi racist, Gerald L. K. Smith, the anti-Semitic agitator, and others. Her vindication on December 19, when the F.B.I. reported the existence of another Anna Rosenberg, did not end

Professor Isidor Isaac Rabi of Columbia University, atomic scientist, Nobel Prize winner, 1944.

the anti-Semitic uses to which the appointment was subjected. Finally came the initiation by the New York State Superintendent of Insurance, on December 18, of the proceeding in the state courts that led to the liquidation of the International Workers' Order and all its affiliates, including the Jewish People's Fraternal Order, which then had a membership of about 53,000.

Generally in Jewish high places, fear was in the saddle and rode hard. The National Jewish Welfare Board advised Jewish centers not to allow "controversial speakers" within their portals. Until the Fort Monmouth case late in 1953 the major Jewish organizations evaded defending and assisting Jews affected by the witchhunts. Yet while the "black silence of fear" was pervasive, there were those who had an even greater fear of silence. Under great difficulties they insisted on being heard against the "cold war" and against McCarthyism. There was never total silence. The whisper and the mutter of opposition was always there, and the unmistakable anti-Semitic tinge to McCarthyism made the hesitant chorus of resistance swell. Major Jewish organizations were among the first to pass resolutions condemning at least the methods of McCarthyism and even questioning his aims, and the Jewish community, right, center and left, was the first national group

Dr. Joshua Bloch (1890-1957), formerly chief, Jewish Division, New York Public Library.

Dr. J. Robert Oppenheimer, atomic scientist.

Dr. Jonas Salk, creator of the Salk vaccine to combat infantile paralysis.

Dr. Selman A. Waksman, discoverer of streptomycin and neomycin, awarded the Nobel Prize in 1952.

in the country to record its opposition to McCarthyism. Expressing the deep liberalism and general desire for progress of the Jewish people, the National Community Relations Advisory Council, consisting of the major, even the most conservative, Jewish organizations, opposed the passing of the McCarran Internal Security Act in 1950. An open McCarthyite like Rabbi Benjamin Schultz was completely isolated both from the rabbinate and from organized Jewish life.

One individual of the highest intellectual eminence and moral influence early took his stand in opposition to the repression of teachers, scholars and scientists. Albert Einstein in 1948 commended a teacher, Samuel Wallach, for denying the constitutional right of a Congressional investigating committee to question him on his political beliefs; and five years later, at the height of the McCarthyite wave, Einstein encouraged other teachers and intellectuals "to refuse to testify" and "be prepared for jail and economic ruin" because "this kind of inquisition violates the spirit of the Constitution."

Turning now to the final feature of this mid-century profile of the American Jewish population, its organization, one finds a specific character, the product of the democratic aspects of American life. The Jewish community is Americanized, but it is distinctive. Jews have neither allowed themselves to be melted down, nor have they been willing to melt away. They are more highly organized than ever before. Anti-Semitic exclusiveness in the United States, the Hitler horror and the birth of Israel have contributed

Edward A. Filene (1860-1937), Boston department store magnate.

Bernard F. Gimbel, New York department store magnate.

to the expansion of Jewish consciousness that is at the base of this move to organization. But a decisive factor is the encouragement to pluralistic group life provided by the traditions and institutions of American democracy, and by those who fought for such an application of democracy to the problems of the immigrant groups in the United States. The Jewish community has become quite American not only in the sense that about 75 per cent of the Jewish population is now native-born, but in a pattern unforeseen by those who promoted the reactionary "melting-pot" theory of forced Americanization. In August, 1918 the Superintendent of Schools of New York City defined Americanization as consisting of two things: "an appreciation of the institutions of this country" and "absolute forgetfulness of all obligations or connections with other countries because of descent or birth." High appreciation and extensive use of American institu-

Joseph B. Strauss (1870-1938), engineer who designed more than 400 bridges in many countries, culminating in the Golden Gate suspension bridge, longest in the world (4,200 foot span).

Ernst Bloch (1880-1959), composer.

tions, especially those with democratic foundations, have certainly been revealed by the Jewish population. But American Jews have, by and large, decisively rejected all attempts to induce in them a kind of ethnic amnesia, "the absolute forgetfulness," of their historic ties with Jews in other countries. As part of the world Jewish people, the American Jews express an organized concern with and interest in the status and life of Jews in other lands. The extent of this inter-

Albert Kahn (1869-1942), industrial architect specializing in automobile plants.

Jascha Heifetz, violinist.

est is suggested in part by the fact that in 1950 the Jewish community raised $21,137,053 for Jewish communal affairs in the United States but $172,475,458 for aid to Jews overseas.

American Jewry underwent many changes but it did not, as some had predicted, warned or hoped, fade away. It was expected that the Jews would show a high rate of acculturation: would acquire rapidly the same culture patterns as other Americans with regard to language, clothes and manners, in economic and political pursuits, and in the artistic, recreational and educational life. Despite anti-Semitic pressures, the vast majority of American Jews have absorbed American culture, especially the democratic and progressive aspects of it. But what was unexpected by theorists who based themselves on European experience was that this high rate of acculturation was accompanied by a low rate of assimilation. In the old European experience, especially in Eastern Europe, a high rate of acculturation had led to a high rate of assimilation, that is, to disaffiliation from the Jewish people, to loss of self-identifica-

נעגרינדעט דעם 16טען סעפטעמבער, 1908

רייטער און רײַנער, יוניאן פרינטערס, 121 נארפאלק סטרים,

A landsmanshaft constitution: Kamenets-Podolier Progressive Ladies Association, founded 1908.

tion as a Jew, to disintegration of the Jewish community. Orthodox Jews in Europe had looked upon Reform Jews as assimilated, as almost lost to the Jewish community. In the United States, however, Reform Jews were building ever larger and more stable organizations and were a constructive part of organized Jewish life. In Europe, Yiddish-speaking Jews had regarded those who abandoned Yiddish for another vernacular as assimilated and virtually on the way out of Jewish life. But English-speaking Jews in the United States were not only creating manifold Jewish cultural works in English but were also increasingly active in Jewish communal life. Intermarriage with non-Jews in Europe was definitely the first step to the abandonment of ties with Jewish life. But in the United States not only was the rate of intermarriage low but about half the intermarriages brought the non-Jewish partner into the Jewish community. Thus acculturation had not produced Jewish amnesia or loss of Jewish consciousness or self-identification.

Because of the pressure of the theory of Anglo-Saxon superiority, acculturation to American life had accelerated certain normal processes of Jewish deculturation, that is, the decline in some important aspects of the immigrant Jews, such as the use of Yiddish and the practice of traditional religious observances and of European Jewish folk-ways and customs. Yet this Jewish deculturation had not resulted in Jewish cultural obliteration, either in religious or secular life. The decline in traditional religious observance has been accompanied by an increase of minimal ritual observance, inadequate as this may seem to traditional Jews. The drastic decline in Yiddish cultural life has been accompanied by an upsurge of English-Jewish culture, pallid as it may seem to those who regard Yiddish as essential in Jewish life. The marks that identify the Jews have changed, but Jewish identification remains. This group identification is today a progressive social phenomenon. It helps assure the perpetuation of cherished cultural values at the heart of which is the tradition and ideal of social justice, which meshes with the general American tradition and ideal of democratic rights and personal liberties.

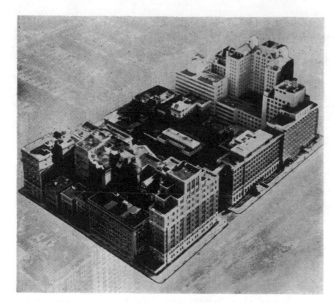

Aerial view of Mount Sinai Hospital, New York.

Significantly, too, Jewish identification is not only private but is primarily public. Jewish identification through Jewish organization is the current important trend. As a result, the majority of the Jewish population is organized, indeed more highly organized than 50 or 30 years ago.

There were 260 national Jewish organizations in the United States in 1950, with innumerable local chapters, branches and lodges, and also many local bodies unaffiliated with central organizations. Of the 260: 54 were religious and educational (chiefly religious); 52 were Zionist or otherwise pro-Israel, while 20 more dealt with overseas aid; 49 were social and mutual benefit groups; 24 were social welfare and philanthropic bodies; 20 were cultural organizations; and 13 were "defense" and political-ideological groups. The biggest increases had taken place in the fields of community relations, central *landsmanshaft* bodies (although the number of individual *landsmanshaften* has fallen greatly), and in social welfare and education. Declining were the number of fraternal orders and fraternities, with labor fraternalism however holding its own (the Workmen's Circle had 70,000, the Jewish People's Fraternal Order 53,000 and the Jewish National Workers' Alliance 30,000 members). Rapid growth was also observable in the number of national youth and women's organizations, with about 20 in each category in 1950. A post-war development had been the burgeoning of local

youth and young adult councils, of which there were 252 in 1950. There were also more than 300 Jewish Centers, with a claimed membership of almost 500,000, serving not only young people, as they had done originally, but also the social and recreational needs of more and more adults.

Besides all these membership organizations, there were 96 professional Jewish social work agencies, 43 of them of the multiple-function type providing services in the fields of child care, family relations, medical care, housing, employment, care of the aged, immigrant aid, and so forth. Post-war expansion had brought the number of Jewish hospitals to 63 in 1950, but half the patients were non-Jewish (in New York, for example, all hospitals receiving public funds are required by law to admit on a non-sectarian basis). Only 12 hospitals had entirely kosher kitchens, 10 served no kosher food at all, and the others provided kosher trays for the small number requesting them. These non-sectarian hospitals were Jewish mainly in the sense that they were supported by Jewish funds and did not discriminate against Jews in employment.

Young Men's Hebrew Association, Lexington Avenue at 92nd Street, New York.

If the Jews had not been melted down or just melted away, it was because they had asserted and won the democratic right to be both Jews and Americans not only as individuals but as a voluntarily organized group with its own culture patterns. When in 1915 Horace M. Kallen had first announced his vital concept of cultural pluralism in his articles in *The Nation,* "Democracy *versus* the Melting-Pot," he had envisioned the possibility of one nation in the U.S.A. with "a cooperation of cultural diversities" or a "commonwealth of national cultures." But he had ended with the question, "Do the dominant classes in America want such a society," or will they turn "the promise of freedom into the fact of tyranny"? The following year, under Kallen's influence, the non-Jewish radical, Randolph S. Bourne, observed in *The Menorah Journal* that for the immigrant it is not "desirable that his cultural soul be washed out of him." Bourne advanced the ideal of "cooperative Americanism . . . a freely mingling society of peoples of very different racial and cultural antecedents, with a common political allegiance and common social ends but with free and distinctive cultural allegiances which may be placed anywhere in the world that they like." He had already elsewhere noted "the failure of the melting-pot" and rejected "any narrow 'Americanism' or forced chauvinism" when he had offered his vision of a "Trans-National America," in which "the most effective integration will be one which coordinates the diverse elements" instead of suppressing or obliterating them. This new radical theory of cultural pluralism challenged both the dominant nativist theory of compulsory assimilation by destroying all immigrant cultures for the greater glory of Anglo-Saxon "Americanism," and also the cosmopolitan socialist theory of eager and rapid voluntary immigrant deculturation for the greater glory of a world culture of the distant future in which all national elements will have been expunged.

The dominant classes' program of cultural leveling, of cultural amnesia, of forced assimilation have not succeeded in the past half century, at least so far as the Jews are concerned. Other national groups of immigrant origin may

The Jewish Theological Seminary of America, Broadway at 122nd Street, New York.

not have maintained their cultural and organizational distinctiveness to the same degree as the Jewish population. But then Hitlerism and Israel have been special influences on all Jews, including those in our own country. In the United States, as part of their democratic struggle, the Jews have developed this highly conscious, highly organized national group. It has its own internal class differences, with the banking, manufacturing, merchandising and real estate plutocracy usually setting the tone and organizational policy, with the middle class weighty because of its sheer bulk, but with the labor forces adding their own interests and emphases. The concern for social justice is still strong in all of Jewish life, especially because of the Jewish labor element's widespread socialist traditions, its deep social idealism, and its universal dedication to New Deal and social welfare programs. One informed observer, Dr. Abraham G. Duker, has however called attention to "the decreasing

Asser Levy School, Public School 19, New York, First Avenue at 12th Street, erected after the American Jewish Tercentenary, 1954.

emphasis on social justice in Jewish religious circles . . . in line with the preferences of the wealthy and middle classes, the growing mainstay of American Jewry, and with the increasingly middle-class character of the rabbinate that serves it." To remedy this situation Dr. Duker proposed increased Jewish education. To this there might be added the desirability of increased activity in all Jewish organized life of the Jewish labor forces and of the professional and other middle class groups that consciously orient to the principles of social justice characteristic of the ideologies of the working class.

Jewish organized life is intensely self-critical and Jeremiahs sprout from all groups, the religious and secular; the Zionist, non-Zionist and anti-Zionist; the Yiddishist, Hebraist and the English-Jewish; the progressives, socialists, democrats, liberals, communists and anti-communists; the bureaucracy and plutocracy and those who seek to democratize Jewish life. Contention is common. Foreboding is especially found among those who mistake the weakening of their own

positions caused by the changes in American Jewish life for a weakening of the American Jewish community as a whole. Yet the forecast seems clear, although not without clouds and even storms. Programmatic and ideological conflicts are not so sharp as they were at the beginning of the century or after the First World War. The issue of Zionism has been side-tracked by a general support for Israel. The religious trends are less antagonistic and embittered, and even the secularists are in their own way observant of many Jewish festivals and are beginning to look with approval upon the liberal social action programs of religious organizations. The issue of language has subsided, more or less resolved by inexorable practice. Political differences were being heightened at the mid-century by the "cold war" and McCarthyism, but the democratic, anti-McCarthyite sentiment of the Jewish people soon reasserted itself in all Jewish circles. The issue of democratic control of organized Jewish life is present but is not being actively pressed. All these issues need to be debated, discussed and partially resolved within the framework of the large areas of agreement that prevail in Jewish life in the face of the widely recognized dangers: the possibility of World War with world-destructive atomic and hydrogen weapons, racism and anti-Semitism at home and abroad, political repression in the form of McCarthyism by that or any other name, the continued threat to the existence of Israel.

In the three centuries of American Jewish experience it has been the struggle for equality and progress, with all the consequent cultural and organizational expressions, that has added the color, depth and forward movement to the content of American Jewish life. This quality has been the basic contribution of the American Jewish national group to the main stream of American democracy. Distinctive national group organization and cultural pluralism have been encouraged by the American democratic tradition because in this way both American democracy and the life of the national groups could best be enriched in this period of our history. An American Jewish community that abandoned its culture and traditions of social justice would have no reason for existence, would serve neither its group nor the general democratic experience. Survival is justified and assured only to the extent that a community continues distinctively to develop its culture and social traditions as it struggles for progress. Increasingly conscious and highly organized, the Jewish population had a justified confidence in its capacity for group survival and in the possibility of such survival in a peaceful world under democratic conditions. It was on this firm ground that the American Jewish community in 1954 faced its Three Hundredth Anniversary and crossed the threshold of its Fourth Century.

CHAPTER 14: Postlude: Past the Mid-Century

Fifteen years past the mid-century, what is the state of the profile we drew in the preceding chapter? What is continued, what is modified, what is new?

In the country as a whole these years have been marked by expanding strife on civil rights and the poverty of the rightless, by a Cold War that did not chill the people's dread of war and the quest for peace through co-existence of nuclear powers, by alarming symptoms of political, social and moral decay, by the attempt to define our national goals in an international arena in which colonialism is being downed by new states emerging from enforced and resentful underdevelopment, by the challenge of new frontiers on the horizons of an undefined "Great Society." All these of course involve and affect the Jewish population too, and Jews and Jewish organizations have been responsive in their diverse ways to all the issues and problems in our land.

Our survey of the Jewish communal structure reveals stability without placidity. A factor for stability is the growth of communal self-criticism to shake complacency. The Jewish vocation of questioning the answers and answering with a question has led to the posing of many questions in many areas of Jewish life. There is evidence of consolidation but no sign of Jewish communal disintegration.

The Jewish population is growing in numbers but declining in relation to the total population, so that 5,600,000 Jews in the United States in 1963 were 2.97 per cent of the total whereas 5,000,000 Jews in 1950 were 3.22 per cent. The Jews are also the most urbanized element in the country: 96.1 per cent live in cities, 87.4 per cent in cities of 250,000 or over, while only .2 per cent live on farms. Jewish residential concentration is also high: 48 per cent live in the Greater New York-Northeastern New Jersey area. The 14 largest cities and metropolitan areas contain 76.6 per cent of the Jewish population: New York City (1,836,000—Greater New York, 2,381,000, or 42.5 per cent of all the Jews in the land), Los Angeles metropolitan (435,000), Philadelphia (330,000), Chicago (285,000), Boston (160,000), Newark (Essex Co.) 100,000, Miami (90,000), Baltimore and Cleveland (85,000 each), Detroit (84,600), Washington, D. C. (80,900), San Francisco (71,-000), St. Louis (57,000) and Pittsburgh (45,000). The cities showing the largest general population growth—Los Angeles, Miami, Washington, D. C., Baltimore and the Newark area—also attracted the largest Jewish population increase.

Jewish immigration from 1950 to 1964 totalled 118,080, averaging only 8,434 per year, or 3.26 per cent of the total immigration. From Israel, it should be noted, there came 36,078 Jewish immigrants, or 30.6 per cent of all Jewish immigration. (From the U. S. A. to Israel from 1948 to 1964 there went only 19,708 Jewish emigrants.) This rate of Jewish immigration may increase under the new immigration reform bill signed by President Lyndon B. Johnson October 3, 1965. Abolishing the racist quota system of the 1920 and 1924 immigration laws, the new law will admit 60,000 more immigrants per year from all countries, but imposes special restrictions on immigration from the Western Hemisphere.

The *relative* decline of the Jewish population may be the result of the low Jewish birth rate. In the 1957 United States religious census it was ascertained that Jewish and Presbyterian women had the lowest fertility rates; "for mothers under

The sanctuary of Temple Emanu-El, Honolulu, Hawaii. Admitted to the Union as the 50th State August 21, 1959, Hawaii in 1963 had about 700 Jews in a population of 69,400.

45, Jewish women are the only ones that have not yet brought into the world enough girls to replace them." Furthermore, the group under 14 is proportionately smaller than in the general population, while the age level at death is higher.

In class composition, the main lineaments are: expansion of the middle class, with strong bases in merchandising, consumer goods manufacturing and the professions, with a shift within the latter to technology and sciences, and some·business administration; significant business positions in new areas like plastics, television, electronics, air-conditioning, frozen foods but continuing insignificance in capital goods industries and virtual exclusion from major executive suites; continuation of a large body (over 300,000) of Jewish workers in industry, especially in New York; and the dwindling of Jewish farm families from 20,000 to 4,000-5,000. It should also be noted that changes in the American economy have outdated the classic concern that the Jewish occupational structure was abnormally weighted in the direction of service rather than production jobs. Since 1953, ours has become the first country in the world in which service jobs outnumber produc-

tion jobs. By 1963, about 55 per cent of American workers were in service jobs and 45 percent in manufacturing. Automation is expected to continue this shift.

In annual income, but not in distribution of wealth, the Jewish population is high: a census sample study in 1957 indicates that 61.8 per cent of Jews had incomes of $5,000 to $15,000 compared to 33.9 per cent for the entire population, or almost as high as that of the Episcopalians. Incidentally, in New York Jewish incomes are generally lower than those elsewhere.

The continuing occupational shift toward the professions is based on the fact that about 75 per cent of Jews of college age are now actually going to college (in 1955 it was 62 per cent), compared to 27 per cent for the general population. In 1963 there were some 275,000 Jewish students attending college, constituting 6.22 per cent of the total college population of 4,420,000. At Harvard, 20.9 per cent of the student body was Jewish; in New York City colleges, 76,000 Jewish students made up only 28 per cent of all Jewish students in colleges. This low proportion is caused by the fact that large numbers of Jewish, like other, students want to get away from home to go to college as a sign of middle class affluence, as a form of rebellion against parental dominance and as a way of escaping the stigma of radicalism that still clings to New York colleges and is considered a handicap to a career.

Among Jewish workers producing goods and services, mostly concentrated in New York, there were two developments that have to be seen against the background fact that New York, which used to be a high-wage area, has slipped into 19th place among United States cities as a low-wage center because of the mass of grossly underpaid Negro and Puerto Rican workers.

One development, a by-product of the civil rights movement, challenged Jewish trade union leadership to integrate the large numbers of Negroes who are already members of Jewish-led unions into the union leadership on all levels and to help upgrade the Negro workers into higher-paid skilled crafts. The serious and widely publicized breach between David Dubinsky and the N.A.A.C.P. was only diplomatically resolved at the May, 1965 union convention when Roy Wilkins, N.A.A.C.P. leader, was a guest speaker. Telling criticism of this Jewish leadership appeared even in *The New Leader* (Daniel Bell, January 21, 1963) and in books like Paul Jacobs' *The The State of the Unions* (1963; the chapter on Dubinsky appeared in *Harper's,* December, 1962). The second, and contrasting, development was the emergence into public prominence of union leaders like Leon Davis of Local 1199 of the Drug and Hospital Workers Union and David Livingston of District 65 of the Retail, Wholesale and Department Store Union, both of whom have provided dynamic, and integrated, leadership to memberships that fully reflect the older white, including Jewish, workers and the growing Negro and Puerto Rican ranks.

The organizational base of the American Jewish population has continued to be extensive and firm. An almost complete listing of *national* Jewish organizations in the latest (1964) *American Jewish Year Book* runs to 207 (community relations, political, cultural, overseas aid, religious, educational, social, mutual benefit, social welfare, Zionist and pro-Israel). The largest memberships are in the Jewish Community Centers, with 714,000 in 1964 in some 350 centers (in 1945 it was 427,000; in 1960, 646,000). The B'nai B'rith has 490,000 members, Hadassah 318,000, the National Council of Jewish Women 125,000, and so on. The overwhelming majority of Jews belong to some Jewish organization, secular or religious, national or local. And the coordinating National Community Relations Advisory Council has expanded to eight national organizations and 76 local Jewish community relations councils (compared with 25 in 1950).

Jewish communal services and philanthropy continue to be major features of Jewish group life. In 1962 and 1963 the annual cost of the main fields of such service was $559,400,000. Fund-raising is therefore a prime preoccupation. During the 1950's, *central* Jewish community campaigns alone raised an annual average of $118,000,000. In 1961, the central welfare fund campaign brought in $125,600,000 and in 1962, $129,600,000. That year, an additional $62,400,-000 was raised independently by 70 national agencies, and another $7,000,000 by local agencies, for a grand recorded total of $199,000,000 (undoubtedly much local Jewish organizational fund-raising is not included in these figures). It is estimated that about 1,000,000 Jews made donations to these campaigns.

Overseas aid to Jews is allotted almost half the total funds raised. In 1961, $94,300,000 went for such purposes, in 1962, $96,600,000—with about 80 per cent going to Israel. Sale of Israel Bonds in the United States from 1951 to 1964 totalled $556,974,000. Including this sum, monies given to Israel from 1948 to 1962 added up to about $1,500,000,000—or an average of $100,000,000 for each of the 15 years. In addition, the Joint Distribution Committee has spent an annual average of $26,607,603 in the 15 years from 1950 to 1964 (the annual average for the five post-war years, 1945-1949 was $53,158,827), of which about one-quarter has gone to Israel and most of the remainder to Europe and Moslem countries. In 1963, the "Joint" served 86,045 Jews in Europe and 83,980 in Moslem lands; in 1964, 89,040 in Europe and 64,165 in Moslem countries (Morocco, Iran, Tunisia, etc.).

At home, Jewish communal service is supplied by an elaborate network of Jewish agencies. The *Yearbook of Jewish Social Service* for 1964 reports 129 family service agencies, 69 child care agencies, 86 homes for the aged, 18 general and special hospitals and 55 clinics. Since 1945, Jewish homes for the aged have about doubled the number of Jews they serve: 73 of them (there were only 55 in 1950) cared for 16,024 persons in 1963. There has also been about an 80 per cent increase since 1945 in the number of patients in Jewish hospitals: 67 of them reported 571,642 patients in 1963. The proportion of Jewish patients continues to decline from the 50 per cent in 1950: in 1963, in the 47 hospitals that report such data, only 31.9 per cent were Jewish patients. This latter fact has led some who believe that Jewish education and culture are very inadequately financed by Jewish communal funds and philanthropy to question the allocation of Jewish funds to Jewish-sponsored hospitals that serve mostly non-Jewish patients. (However, it must not be overlooked that these hospitals serve Jewish patients to a far greater extent than the proportion of Jews in the total population of the country or even in the cities in which the hospitals are located). The facts are that of the total operating income of $279,695,697 reported in 1963 by 60 Jewish hospitals and clinics, $24,581,219 came from Jewish Federation or Welfare Funds (3.8 per cent) and from contributions and membership dues (5 per cent). And the total budget for Jewish education, the critics point out, is only about $60,000,000. Whether the dominant Jewish communal leadership will shift its emphasis, and allocations, from caring for the bodies of Jews to caring for their minds and cultural needs is one of the major issues in the Jewish community.

A significant step in this direction was taken in November, 1959 by the Council of Jewish Federations and Welfare Funds in establishing the National Foundation for Jewish Culture. The basis for the action was a survey report, prepared by a committee of 33 scholars, of the state of Jewish archives, scholarship, research and publications, and of the eight American universities that have Jewish departments and the 13 colleges that offer undergraduate courses in some Jewish studies. With tens of thousands of Jewish graduate students in universities, the report noted that "attracting young men to the scholarly and research fields requires a greatly expanded program of fellowship awards . . . increased employment opportunities, grants-in-aid for travel, for independent research, for extended projects, for increasing publication possibilities . . . so that the potential scholar can be assured that there is not only aid for his initial training but a reasonable prospect for satisfactory placement after graduation and the usual professional opportunities for study, research and creative expression."

Since 1960, the Foundation has awarded 66 fellowships and grants-in-aid, given prizes for 13 masters' theses, encouraged Hadassah, the National Council of Jewish Women and the Workmen's Circle to establish fellowships, aided the endowment of Jewish studies at Syracuse and Roosevelt Universities, given grants to publish research, to reprint a college Yiddish textbook and to issue a student quarterly of the Harvard-Radcliffe Hillel, and stimulated Jewish academicians to found a Conference on Jewish Philosophy. Since from 1951 to 1962 there were 211 doctoral dissertations on Jewish themes in American universities, one can surmise what a stimulus to making Jewish scholarship a profession instead of an avocation a really extensive system of grants could provide. The systematic expansion of a body of professional Jewish scholars, if properly financed by the Jewish community, could do much to shore up the foundations of American Jewish organized life.

On a lesser scale and with even less solid backing, we note the birth, at a conference January 13, 1965 initiated by the American Jewish Congress, of the National Council on Art in Jewish Life, designed to parallel in the graphic arts the functions in their fields of the Jewish Book Council and the Jewish Music Council, both sponsored by the National Jewish Welfare Board. These are all signs of deepening Jewish communal consciousness.

In respect to Jewish religious affiliation, belief and practise, the trend during the past 15 years

Jacob Shatzky (1893-1956), historian, especially of the Jews of Warsaw.

Salo W. Baron, outstanding historian of the Jewish people.

has brought the majority of the Jewish population into congregational folds, but more, apparently, as a comprenhensible American middle class sign of Jewish identity than of Jewish religiosity. The Jewish sociologist C. Bezalel Sherman judges that "The Synagogue has gone even further along the road to secularization than its Christian counterparts." Another scholar, Rabbi Arthur Hertzberg, is worried about the future of Judaism in America. Stressing the importance of "faith, and the personal conduct which flows from it" rather than "institutions and structures," Dr. Hertzberg concludes, "In that deepest dimension [faith] Jewish religion in America is failing amidst its great pragmatic successes."

Notable in current American Judaism, however, is a new surge of social action that reverses "the decreasing emphasis on social justice" seen by Dr. Abraham G. Duker February 7, 1954 (see pages 285-86 above). The stoking of the American social conscience achieved by the United States Supreme Court decision of May 17, 1954, ordering the end of segregation in the schools, sparked an even more active and extensive identification with the civil rights struggle by hundreds of

rabbis and affiliated laymen both in their own communities and in hazardous expeditions to Deep South high-tension areas on the summons of the Rev. Martin Luther King, Jr. Reform and Conservative social action bodies proliferated. Reform opened a Center for Religious Action in Washington, D. C. in December, 1961 as a kind of lobby for civil rights, civil liberties, social welfare and peace programs. Orthodox rabbis also appeared on the social action scene in the past few years. One result has been to enhance the relevance of Judaism in the minds of both congregationally affiliated and secular Jews.

A development of another kind has been the spurt forward of Orthodoxy, especially in its Hassidic expression, based on the post-war immigration of refugees who were devotees of the Hassidic rabbis of Lubavitch, Satmar and Skvir. (American intellectuals, both Jewish and non-Jewish, responded to or paralleled this phenomenon by a literary rather than religious interest in the neo-Hassidism of Martin Buber, 1878-1965, whose *Tales of the Hassidim* in English translation became a vogue and a minor influence.) This strong Orthodox impulse expressed itself primarily in the rapid building of Jewish day schools, about which we shall have more to say later. There was also, however, a bid for the allegiance of Jewish intellectuals with the founding in 1948 of the Association of Orthodox Jewish Scientists, which in 1965 had a quarterly publication, *Intercom,* and some 500 members in nine chapters in eastern and mid-western cities drawn from university faculties, government research and medicine. On the college level, in February, 1960, 80 Orthodox students from 13 eastern campuses founded Yavneh, the National Religious Jewish Students Association, "to provide Jewish education on campus through weekly classes, Gemara *sheurim* [classes] and monthly lectures; to facilitate observance of *mitzvoth* by establishing *minyanim* in dormitories, providing kosher food, solving the problem of exams on the Sabbath; to work in the larger Jewish community, particularly as leaders of youth groups; to unite Jewish students by holding conclaves, weekends, observing Jewish holidays together." By 1965 Yavneh had about 1,200 members on 35 campuses in the east, mid-west and west, a Yavneh House at Princeton with kosher facilities, meeting rooms, library and dormitory space, several periodical publications and a Social Action Committee.

On one important issue, that of separation of church and state, Orthodoxy has split the formerly united Jewish community. Impelled by the desire for financial assistance to their own day school program, the Lubavitcher Hassidim joined forces with the Catholic leadership and in November, 1961 came out in support of Federal aid to religious schools, to be joined later by other Orthodox spokesmen. The bulk of Jewish organized life has held firmly to the basic American democratic principle of separation.

Another aspect of Jewish communal expression, the Jewish press, continues to be extensive, showing decline in some areas and new growth in others. In 1964 there were 171 regularly issued periodicals, 144 in English (including 45 weeklies, 30 monthlies, 31 quarterlies and 13 fortnightlies), 20 in Yiddish (including three dailies) and 7 in Hebrew. Since 1950, the Yiddish dailies have lost half their circulation, dropping from

Examples of Jewish periodicals born, or reorganized, recently.

199,939 for four dailies to 98,344 for three in 1963 (*Forward,* 54,471; *Day-Jewish Journal,* 36,404; *Morning Freiheit,* 7,469). The English weeklies also declined in number from 69 to 45, but the total number of periodicals in English changed only from 146 in 1950 to 144 in 1964. One outstanding quarterly, *The Menorah Journal,* edited since 1915 by the independent and far-ranging Henry Hurwitz (1886-1961), ceased publication with his death. *The Menorah Treasury* appeared in 1964 as a monument to a rare storehouse of almost a half century of Jewish cultural and intellectual life.

The number of "quality" periodicals has been sharply increased since 1950 through monthly magazines like *Israel Horizons* (1952) and *Jewish Currents* (reorganized 1958) and quarterlies like *American Judaism* (reorganized 1951), *Judaism* (1952), *CCAR Journal* (1953), *Or Hamizrahi* (1954), *Midstream* (1955), *Jewish Heritage* (1957), *Zamlungen* (1957) and *Recall* (1959).

New notes of criticism have been sounded of the low standards of too many of the English weeklies and of their lack of independence and, with a few notable exceptions, of controversy. Alarm has also been expressed at the new devel-

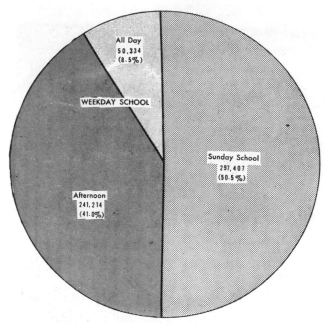

Jewish enrolment of 588,955 pupils, by type of school, in 1963.

opment of newspapers owned by the local Jewish federation and welfare funds in Pittsburgh, Philadelphia, Newark, Omaha, Seattle and St. Louis as liable still further to stifle criticism of the "establishment" and independence.

This Jewish press, it should be indicated, is not a unique phenomenon in American journalism: the American Council for Nationalities Service reported that in 1964 there were 591 periodicals published in the United States in 39 foreign languages (including 59 in German, 45 Polish, 42 Italian, 40 Ukrainian and Spanish, 34 Hungarian and Lithuanian, 30 Czech, 29 Russian and 24 Slovak). Furthermore, in addition to the English-Jewish press, there were 133 periodicals in English for 28 ethnic groups (including 24 periodicals for German-Americans, 13 for Swedish and 12 for Italians). This fact is but another evidence of the persistence of cultural pluralism in our country.

In the basic communal enterprise of Jewish education the growth has been phenomenal. While in 1950 about 2,700 schools with some 270,000 pupils had a budget of over $25,000,000, in 1963 over $60,000,000 was spent on the schooling of more than 590,000 pupils in some 3,700 schools. In the last few years, however, the expansion has slowed down and the figures are now on a plateau. Recent congregational expansion has also affected Jewish education, so that now over 90 per cent of the students are enrolled in congregational schools. In these the Bible "is the heart and core of the curriculum" and "prayers are offered to a greater extent than ever before in the classrooms, at assemblies and at school celebrations," as Dr. Samuel Dinin has noted, although more curricular attention is now being paid to the American Jewish community, American Jewish history and to Israel.

One sign of the maturation of Jewish education is the appearance of searching self-criticism of the quality of this education. Jewish education is "a mile wide and an inch deep" was the startling verdict of the report of a survey commission of the American Association of Jewish Education, published in 1959, drafted by Alexander M. Dushkin and Uriah Z. Engelman. Observing "a rather constant general trend toward more intensive Jewish education for an increasing number of children," the report did not spare criticism of the inadequacy of Jewish school time (90 per cent of the pupils receive instruction only two to six hours a week for three or four years), of the need to break the Bar Mitzva barrier into Jewish high school education, of a teaching staff 60 per cent of which is without "professional pedagogic training" and suffers from "constant and rapid turnover" because of non-professional salary, tenure and retirement provisions, and of the need to develop "in the homes and in the community an atmosphere of respect and desire for Jewish culture and learning."

Other criticism has not been wanting. As early as 1951 Professor Isidor Chein challenged Jewish schools to "take off from the Jewish lives of our youngsters as they live them rather than from our own Jewish lives as we and our ancestors have lived them . . ." With two-thirds of school time spent on Hebrew, Professor Oscar I. Janowsky has pointed out that "When Hebrew is the main subject of the curriculum, a large portion of school time is consumed in learning a limited vocabulary which is quickly forgotten and the effects of Jewish education are thereby minimized." Dr. Zalmen Slesinger as editor of *The Peadagogic Reporter* has directed a continuing stream of criticism at all the weaknesses of Jewish education, stressing the indispensability of making this education *relevant* to the needs of the average child and the Jewish community, so that whatever heritage is transmitted is currently meaningful.

That dissatisfaction with mere quantitative criteria can lead to improvement is suggested by a recent trend to growth in Jewish high school enrolment. Stress on retention as well as recruitment of the pupil has in New York, for example, led to an increase in high school enrolment from 10.9 per cent of the total in 1961-62 to 13.6 per cent in 1964-65, or a leap of 24.7 per cent in four years.

Of course the most conspicuous current trend is the rapid expansion of the Jewish day school, in which the Jewish curriculum is added to the public school curriculum studied from public school texts. From 21,404 day school pupils in 1950, enrolment jumped to 61,000 in 1964, with 303 schools, 93 of them high schools, and an annual budget of about $27,000,000. From 1959 to 1964, 64 new schools were established. Although 42,000 of the total enrolment is in New York City, there are Jewish day schools in 28 states and the District of Columbia. Constituting already over 10 per cent of the entire Jewish school enrolment, the day school is the only one that continues to rise.

It has, incidentally, not escaped public attention that, since a significant percentage of day school pupils do not come from religious homes, part of the turn to these religious day schools, as in the case of Catholic and Protestant parochial schools, is sometimes motivated by parental desire to avoid integration with Negro children. Furthermore, the more democratic sections of the Jewish community recognize the day school movement, like the Christian parochial school drive, as a regressive trend threatening to undermine the public school system, which has been the main force for social integration in our society.

Considering the spurt of Jewish religious schooling, it is remarkable that the secular schools, oriented to the Yiddish language and literature (sometimes in translation), have almost maintained their numerical strength although they are waning relatively. The tenacity of this secular Yiddish movement is suggested by the finding in a 1961 sample survey by the Workmen's Circle Schools that about 70 per cent of their pupils came from parents both of whom were American-born and English-speaking. The largest school network, and most consistent in its mellowed secularism, is an independent, unaffiliated group serviced by the Service Bureau for Jewish Education, which in 1965 had some 4,500 pupils in over 70 schools, including three high schools. Next is the Workmen's Circle with about 65 schools, including seven high schools, and 3,500 students. The Labor Zionist Jewish National Workers Alliance (Farband) schools also have over 3,000 enrolled in 18 five-afternoon-a-week schools, three all-day kindergartens, four high schools and one day school. The Sholem Aleichem Folk Institute has more than held its own since 1950; in 1965 it operated 16 schools with 950 students (including one high school) in the Greater New York area. Apparent in all these school groups, despite their ideological diversity, is a search for the humanist content in Jewish history and culture, religious as well as secular. Although a small minority, they are a distinctive feature in the total picture because of the continuing basic secularization of American Jewish life.

Two more developments in the educational scene are noteworthy. The surge of child education inevitably stimulated the need for parent and general Jewish adult education. Amid profusion and confusion of goals and methods, the spread of adult Jewish education led to the convening February 28, 1965 of a national conference on the subject sponsored by the A. A. J. E. There were 204 delegates from 18 national Jewish organizations discussing this "new frontier" in Jewish education. One result was a National Council on Adult Jewish Education.

Jewish organizationally sponsored summer camps, both resident and day, finally, are being seen more and more as facilities for Jewish education as well as recreation and ritual observance. The numbers reached are high. Under Jewish Community Center auspices alone 275 summer day camps served 70,000 children in

Isaac Bashevis Singer,
Yiddish novelist.

Edward Lewis Wallant (1926-
1962) has left four novels.

Saul Bellow, whose best-selling
"Herzog" won many literary prizes.

1961 and 120 resident country camps had 54,000 campers, and expansion is continuing. In addition there are a growing number of yeshiva-sponsored resident camps, Zionist, secular and other organizationally sponsored camps. A directory of 83 such camps serving the New York area, issued in 1965 by the Association of Jewish Sponsored Camps, indicates the great diversity of sponsorship and also the trend to Jewish educational content in the announced programs.

Turning to the literary scene, we burst into a welter of wide-ranging, voluminous discussion in academic, literary and general intellectual circles of a really new cultural phenomenon: the American Jewish writer is plumb in the mainstream of American fiction, poetry and criticism—successfully, and apparently unhappily, adrift like all his colleagues. Once an outsider, brow pressed against the excluding plate-glass of the literary "establishment," the Jewish writer is now proclaimed as the real insider, although there seems to be a difference of opinion as to whether he has only joined the Establishment or become the Establishment. On all sides we are told with a certain note of restrained jubilance that Jewish writers hold the key Establishment positions on the faculties, in the editorial offices, in the reviews, on lists of esteemed prize-winners and even on vulgar best-seller tabulations.

The editors of *Breakthrough: A Treasury of Contemporary American-Jewish Literature* (1964) declare that "America has at long last caught up with the Jew. His search for identity is its search. Its quest for spiritual meaning is his quest." A Columbia University professor of English literature lectures an audience of Jewish social scientists on the confluence of the widely-touted alienation of the American with the traditional alienation of the Jew. Marie Syrkin, however, steeped in Jewish communal and intellectual life, remarks acutely that these Jewish writers "have added a specific belligerent estrangement from their origin to the general sense of alienation" but asserts that "their general involvement in American life has not been accompanied by a deepening awareness of Jewish identity."

Yet it is a fact—and the Jewish historian Salo W. Baron has called it unique in world Jewish history—that Jewish writers in the 50's and 60's attained general eminence, attention and influence and constitute what is regarded as the literary establishment. Outstanding are such names as Saul Bellow, Irving Howe, Alfred Kazin, Norman Mailer, Bernard Malamud, Philip Roth and the short-lived Edward Lewis Wallant (1926-1962). Outside this trend but still memorable and widely translated is *A Lantern for Jeremy* (1952) by V. J. Jerome (1897-1965), a socially-conscious but elegantly written autobiographical novel of Jewish life in a Polish *shtetl* at the opening of this century.

The seed-bed for this development, it should be noted, lies in the fact that the Hitlerite slaughter of more than two-thirds of the Jews of Europe, the birth and consolidation of the state of Israel, the American experience with pre-war Coughlinite anti-Semitism and with anti-Semitism in our own armed forces during the war—all these had created a receptivity to the Jewish theme in the general American reading public. Post-war Jewish affirmativeness—the reversal of a trend to seek escape from Jewish identity to a much stronger trend to affirm it, no matter how uncertain or confused the content of this affirmation—also contributed to making the Jew in writing and the Jewish writer acceptable.

Herman Wouk's *Marjorie Morningstar* (1954), as best-seller of no literary merit, presented, Professor Syrkin observes, "one of the first Jewish heroines to be accepted widely by the general reading public as a representative American character rather than as a quaint, sinister or romantic alien figure." In paperback, the book sold over 3,000,000 copies as the Hollywood film version was exhibited. In 1958 the Jew as unexpected hero appeared in Leon Uris' *Exodus,* king-size, to lead the best-sellers for a year, then to sell over 5,000,000 in paperback while Hollywood of course multiplied the audience. The same year, Harry Golden's *Only in America,* a best-seller with its soft-focus, nostalgic image of the Jew on New York's East Side a generation ago, brought into public view an amiable and soon ubiquitous raconteur and commentator on American, Southern and Jewish mores who revealed the iron and acid in his character when he dealt trenchantly with the great issue of Negro integration.

Quite another view of the East Side achieved prominence in 1960 when Henry Roth's masterful novel, *Call It Sleep,* all but forgotten since its stillbirth in 1934, was reissued. Winning now instant critical acclaim, it appeared in paperback in 1964 and sold almost 1,000,000 copies in its first year.

In fact the paperback explosion that has revolutionized the book market has included the Jewish book. In 1963 there were 165 paperbacks by Jews on Jewish themes in print, and 20 by non-Jews. The general book-trade became interested in Jewish books. While the Jewish Publication Society grew in membership from 8,400 in 1954 to 12,000 in 1964 (almost reaching the figure of 15,000 it had in 1917, when the Jewish population was only 3,012,000), commercial publishers like Crown, Yoseloff, Citadel, Twayne and Hill and Wang began to issue more Jewish books than did the J. P. S. and many more publishers made sure to include one or two books of Jewish interest on their lists, including of course translations from the Yiddish and the Hebrew. One by-product of this popularization of the Jewish theme was that Arthur Miller, who for 20 years, since *Focus,* had avoided Jewish characters in his plays, introduced them in his *After the Fall* (1963) and made the Jewish element central in his *Incident at Vichy* (1964). Quantitatively, the output of books by Jews on Jewish subjects these 15 years totaled many thousands: in a typical year from May, 1963 to May, 1964 the *Jewish Book Annual 1964-65* listed 290 such books.

Related to this interest in the Jews is the fact that three of the major intellectual controversies of wide public significance dealt with the Jews. In 1961 Professor Raul Hilberg published a monumental tome on *The Destruction of the European Jews,* an exhaustively documented and detailed description and analysis of the Nazi holocaust. But Professor Hilberg also presumed, without thorough study of the available materials and without the scholarly documentation that characterized the main body of his work, to deliver himself, marginally and in passing, of *obiter dicta* about the alleged passivity of the Jews in the face of this destruction and the causes of this "compliance." Although such a work of scholarship had but limited circulation, his marginal comments provoked extensive discussion, rebuttal and refutation in this country (as well as abroad) both in Yiddish and English. While this controversy raged chiefly in the Jewish press, the general press was drawn into a similar and even more extensive and acrimonious debate when Hannah Arendt in 1963 published her *Eichmann in Jerusalem,* first in *The New Yorker* and then as a book. Her popularization of Hilberg's thesis to a large audience, her attack on the Israeli trial of Eichmann, her view of Eichmann not even as human turned monster by Nazism but as simply human, and her imputation of wholesale and decisive collaboration of Jewish leadership with the Nazis in the destruction of the Jews aroused a veritable storm of informed protest and refutation that for months threatened to flood both Jewish and general organs of discussion.

Finally, in 1964, the production of Rolf Hochhuth's *The Deputy* on Broadway caused heated and demonstrative controversy before, during and after the production, which ran for 318 performances. In the published text, on stage and in over 700 articles in periodicals of all kinds, the historic failure of Pope Pius XI publicly to protest the Nazi genocide against the Jews was subjected to intensive examination and debate. And despite the remnants of McCarthyism in American public life, many also got Hochhuth's central message: that Pius had refused to act because in his view the main danger in the war years lay not in Hitlerism but in "Bolshevism."

It is in the context of such a climate of interest in and concern with the Jews that the breakthrough of Jewish writers into the American literary mainstream becomes meaningful and comprehensible. But there is another factor. In the 50's the pressure to conformity was intense. Norman Podhoretz, since 1960 editor of *Commentary* (which in the 50's had in its subtle way been an instrument of this pressure), describes the "revisionist liberalism of the 50's . . . associated with names like Lionel Trilling, Sidney Hook, Daniel Bell and Richard Hofstadter . . . as a species of conformist thinking developed by intellectuals who, motivated in part by a genuine horror of Stalinism and in part by an abject failure of critical nerve, took to celebrating the virtues of American society and the values of the middle-class spirit. I myself have come more and more to see revisionist liberalism as involving an abdication of the intellectual's proper role as a critic of society . . ." In 1958, evaluating a batch of recent novels including some by Bellow and Malamud, Podhoretz perceived that "in losing our taste for ideology we have also lost our capacity for passion." Is it not significant that social passion and social action, then and now, was to be found more often in the rabbinate than in the literati?

The cause of this defection to conformity is tartly defined by Michael Kowal of the Queens College English department in his blunt query in *Judaism* (Fall, 1964) whether this "revisionist liberalism" of the 50's is not "but a euphemism for the central cultural experience associated with this period—McCarthyism? The obscene—and frightening—spectacle of seeing intellectuals degraded and professors dismissed for views held, usually in good faith, 15 years earlier and through imprudence or conviction not renounced when the 'atmosphere' had changed, was a trauma that put this, our generation, off politics for a long time." He adds that his generation has had its social passions quickened, dispelling this trauma, by the civil rights struggle and the terrors of the H-bomb, but such central experiences of our time do not yet seem to have affected the writing —or the conduct—of the literary establishment.

In the realm of Yiddish, two phenomena stand out: the remarkable persistence and resilience of Yiddish writing and publishing, and the new enhanced status of Yiddish language and literature, often in English translation, in academic and literary circles.

Despite the unreplaced drain of heavy casualties among Yiddish writers, the rate of publication is remarkably impressive, with the *Jewish Book Annuals* reporting about 50 or more volumes a year in the last five years, in editions usually of one to three thousand copies. The publishers are either the two main communal enterprises of the Yiddisher Kultur Farband (YKUF) and the Congress of Yiddish Culture (CYCO) or ad hoc committees founded by the author's friends or organizational associates. Bedeviling the situation is the ingrained bitterness between left and right wings, with the dominant right wing generally refusing to acknowledge even the existence of the others, except sometimes for obituary purposes; the only relief is an occasional private gesture of amity.

The bell has tolled in these 15 years for scores of outstanding figures in all camps, including

Abraham Cahan (1860-1951), Abraham Reisen (1872-1953), David Ignatov (1885-1954), Shmuel Niger (1883-1955), Zalmen Libin (1872-1955), Kalman Marmor (1876-1956), Jacob Shatzky (1893-1956), Zisha Weinper (1893-1957), Sholem Asch (1880-1957), N. B. Minkoff (1893-1958), David Pinski (1872-1959), Ossip Dymov (Joseph Perlman, 1878-1959), Moishe Katz (1885-1960), S. Dingol (1887-1961), H. Leivick (1888-1962), Benjamin J. Bialostotzky (1893-1962), Mendl Elkin (1874-1962), Aaron Kurtz (1891-1964), Leibush Lehrer (1887-1964), Haver Paver (Gershon Einbinder, 1901-1965) and A. A. Roback (1890-1965). Even with these and other figures gone, Yiddish writing and culture in our country is still marked by vitality born of tenacity and dedication, and sustained by a physically diminishing but morally unflagging following that is far from exhausted.

Significant, moreover, is the new status that Yiddish is achieving as a language and for its literature. Around the YIVO there have grouped an expanding number of younger academic scholars using Yiddish as a research tool and exploring Jewish subject matter. Courses in the Yiddish language and literature are now being taught in nine colleges and universities. Those having institutes of industrial and labor relations have encouraged the study of Yiddish as an aid in research in American labor and industrial history. The renowned Poetry Center of the 92nd St. Y. M. H. A. in New York now includes readings by Yiddish poets as part of its regular program. Late in 1964, 40 college students who are Yiddish enthusiasts founded a quarterly Yiddish youth journal, *Yugntruf,* a revival of an earlier venture (1941-1949). Early in 1965, the City College in New York announced the formation of an Institute of Yiddish Lexicology to compile a 10 volume dictionary, completing a project begun at the YIVO.

This new public respect for a language not too long ago scorned as a jargon has also helped Yiddish writing to break through into the mainstream in English translation. The pioneer Maurice Samuels was joined in recent years by such popularizers of the value of Yiddish literature as Saul Bellow, Irving Howe, Alfred Kazin and

Isaac Rosenfeld—part of the new literary establishment. Translations of the main works of Sholem Aleichem, Mendele Mocher Sforim and Peretz are available, although the quality and responsibility of the translations vary. Two anthologies brought other Yiddish writers into the American ken: *A Treasury of Yiddish Stories* (1954; paperback, 1958), edited by Irving Howe, a professor of English, and Eliezer Greenberg, a Yiddish poet, and *The New Country* (1961), stories from the Yiddish about life in America, translated and edited by Henry Goodman, a teacher of English. On this crest, a literary cult developed about the Yiddish writer of novels and stories, Isaac Bashevis Singer. Saul Bellow's translation of his little classic, *Gimpel the Fool,* began to make of Singer the darling of the literary magazines. By 1960, when three of his books had appeared in translation, the American Academy of Arts and Letters awarded him a grant, the first ever given an American author not writing in English. In 1955 virtually unknown, Singer by 1965 had seven of his works in paperback, and he had been translated into French, Italian and Swedish. The Yiddish literary world is puzzled by this acclaim, for as David Boroff (1917-1965) indicated in 1962, Singer "is not really in the mainstream of the Jewish tradition. For he deals with the rampageously evil, the cunningly diabolical, the world of terror and nightmare. And this is what has endeared him to the contemporary literary mind so ceaselessly preoccupied with nihilism and disorder." More comprehensible to the Yiddish reader and writer than the zoom to prominence of Isaac Bashevis Singer is the tribute of a year of packed houses won for Sholem Aleichem by Zero Mostel's brilliant Broadway image of Tevye. Between Teyve the *Folksmentsh,* and the bizarre, psychotic and demonic characters of Bashevis Singer, Yiddish culture in English is currently center stage.

Of writing in Hebrew the opposite is true. Although books continue to appear (176 from May, 1962 to May, 1964, of which 142 were religious texts), the Hebrew poet Eisig Silberschlag, surveying the scene, entitled his article, "Development and Decline of Hebrew Letters," and concluded, "The writers who have brought about

Leonard Bernstein, composer and musical director of the New York Philharmonic Orchestra; drawing by René Bouché.

Zero Mostel as Sholem Aleichem's Tevye the Dairyman in "Fiddler on the Roof," Broadway hit, 1964-1965.

this minor renaissance are dead. The few who survive here and in Israel are old and past their prime. And the young are yet to come."

Untouched by the successes of the Jew as literary figure, the noxious stream of anti-Semitism continued to affect American life and to impinge variously on the consciousness of the Jews. In 1958 an A. D. L. survey concluded that "anti-Semitism flows a quiet course, hidden, subtle and pervasive, just as harmful—and even harder to fight" because it was underground. But then, quite above-ground, George Lincoln Rockwell appeared, leading what he called the American Nazi Party with swastikas and jackboots and calling for the gassing of Jews and sending Negroes to Africa. Obviously a lunatic fringe and marginal menace, Rockwell is both a symptom and an omen. For spreading from Cologne in West Germany at Christmas, 1959, a neo-Nazi international loosed a swastika "epidemic" in Western Europe, Latin America —and the United States, where 643 incidents of swastika smearings and acts of violence against Jewish institutions and homes occurred in the first eight weeks of 1960. Two sociologists summed

up their study of this development for the A.D.L. with the warning that "the desecration phenomena indicate that anti-Semitism is a more serious problem in the United States than is generally thought to be the case." The 1964 *American Jewish Year Book* records matter-of-factly that "anti-Semitic propaganda did not diminish" in 1963, that some anti-Semitic periodicals have circulations of 90,000, 30,000 and 27,000, that the forged *Protocols of the Elders of Zion* have been reprinted, that the special Ritual Murder Issue of Goebbels' *Der Stuermer* has been republished here, that the revived Ku Klux Klan is circulating the anti-Semitic materials of other groups, and so on, fringe on fringe on fringe. In that year, too, it was disclosed that at least 15 Nazi war criminals wanted in Europe for their roles in mass murder of Jews had found haven here, but the only demands that these be brought to justice came from the Jewish left and those within hearing of their outcry.

Professor Milton R. Konvitz has also focused attention on another tension-breeding area: conflicts arising from Jews' taking a principled stand for separation of church and state. Following the Supreme Court ruling June 25, 1962 banning organized prayer from the public schools, the Jesuit weekly *America* noticed a spurt of anti-Semitic misinterpretations of the relationship of Jews to this decision. But instead of lashing out at this anti-Semitism, *America* chose, September 1, to issue an editorial warning "To Our Jewish Friends," suggesting that Jews, at the risk of incurring anti-Semitism, consider bargaining away their right to take their stand on American democratic principle as they understood it. Protests from Jews, Protestants and the Catholic *Commonweal* led *America* to retreat with the lament that it had meant no harm . . . Important is Professor Konvitz' call for firmness in Jewish assertion of first-class citizenship rights: "Jews and the Jewish community, in their intergroup relations, will continue to take the calculated risk that what they will claim on the basis of justice and equality may become a power struggle, and that rational argument may degenerate into group antagonism or even bigotry."

Another factor in inter-group, especially Catholic-Jewish, relations is the yellow badge of "Christ-killer" that Catholics for centuries have pinned on the Jews. As recently as the 30's, the American Catholic hierarchy, with minor exceptions, had abetted or tolerated the role of Father Coughlin as the main American propagandist of a savage anti-Semitism. The American Jewish Committee for some years has been directing many efforts towards helping liberal Catholics see the necessity of a formal and binding correction of the record. The readiness of the Church to begin to reconsider its position was perhaps precipitated by the international discussion of *The Deputy* and its spotlighting the sorry record of the Church on the Jews in World War II. Hopes were high that the Vatican Ecumenical Council which opened October 11, 1962 would act on this matter. Under pressure from reactionary bishops and from Arab states that thereby underlined their anti-Semitism, it was not until November 20, 1964 that the Council—voting 1,770 in favor, 185 opposed and seven in favor with reservations—adopted a statement enjoining Catholics: "May they never present the Jewish people as one rejected, cursed or guilty of deicide . . ." American bishops were conspicuous in support of this statement. Yet the pressures against it continue and it is still an open question whether the final session of the Ecumenical Council in September, 1965 will retain it and Pope Paul VI will proclaim it.

Many studies sponsored by the American Jewish Committee have in the past 15 years concentrated attention on the failure of the big corporations—utilities, banks, heavy industry—to admit qualified Jews into the upper echelons of their organization. The "five o'clock shadow" that separates most Jews from non-Jews after working hours as they lead their social lives apart began to increase in significance as it became clear that in big business social exclusion literally bars business integration. The decision-making "executive suite," it seems, has a private door to the social club where decisions are convivially brewed or celebrated. Once the university studies documented the facts, the American Jewish Committee persuaders began to interpret to these exclusive executives how this practise both contradicted democratic theory and might even be bad for business (a Harvard study actually showed that the existing shortage of executives was a result of discrimination against Jews and others in recruiting on college campuses).

The essential and humiliating meaning for Jews of this exclusion from the club and the executive suite is writ large by Professor E. Digby Baltzell in *The Protestant Establishment: Aristocracy and Caste in America* (1964). A Wall Street financier like Bernard Baruch, he stresses, "was never accepted either on The Street or uptown in the society to which his affluence and ability as well as his handsomeness and engaging manner might have led him." His marrying a rich Episcopalian "society" lady opened fewer doors for him than it shut for her and their children. The slights and stings to which the Baruch family was exposed—as well as Henry Ford's *Dearborn Independent's* blatant anti-Semitic attack on him—left their mark on him. Excluded from the Protestant

Bernard M. Baruch (1870-1965).

Establishment's clubs, he shunned public office, made the famous park bench his symbol, and was so lined with bitterness that he once exclaimed, "I could have been President of the United States if I had not been a Jew."

Professor Baltzell is aware of "the psychological damage to the personality of Jews" that flows from such widespread Jewish experience with exclusion or even the report and fear of exclusion. He recognizes that "as a result, there has been a great postwar boom in gilded ghettos, centered around opulent synagogues and country clubs in the upper-middle-class suburbs of all our major cities." Whether the ghetto is gilded, or only silvered or poorly painted, will depend on the class position of the Jews inhabiting it. But Professor Baltzell's analysis is a reminder that ghetto walls are imposed from without and only the interior decoration is applied from within. So long as patterns of exclusion against Jews persist, talk of "self-ghettoization" is delusory and one-sided.

A population so generally aware of anti-Semitic exclusions, no matter how crude or how subtle, has a broad basis for independence of

thought, liberalism, social action and radicalism. Jewish social and political behavior reflects that base as well as the American Jewish traditions of social protest retailed throughout this volume. Yet McCarthyism made its dent and has left its imprint on various parts of Jewish communal life. In general life, President John F. Kennedy recanted symbolically for the nation when on December 2, 1963 he gave to Dr. J. Robert Oppenheimer the Enrico Fermi Award, the highest honor that the Atomic Energy Commission, which had once refused him clearance as a security risk, can bestow. But to this day Jewish communal leadership, perhaps aware that McCarthyite legislation and McCarran acts are still on the books, persists in continuing to exclude progressive and radical Jewish fraternal, cultural and educational institutions from the mainstream of Jewish communality. There has been no public penitence for the crime of silence with which the major Jewish organizations accompanied the McCarthyite act of the dissolution, ordered June 25, 1951 by New York Supreme Court Justice Henry Clay Greenberg (1896-1965), of the International Workers Order and all its affiliates, including the Jewish People's Fraternal Order of 53,000 members (see page 279)—a silence broken only by a memorandum July 25, 1961 circulated to some Jewish organizations jointly by the American Jewish Committee and the A.D. L., and by an article in the Yiddish daily *Tog* August 12, 1952 by B. Z. Goldberg, both of them pointing to the dangerous precedents set by this liquidation of a fraternal order. Many who scorn the antics of a Roy Cohn, once counsel for McCarthy's inquisitorial committee, continue to act on his policies and prejudices. The obsessive "anti-communism" of a David Dubinsky, the Jewish Labor Committee and the *Jewish Daily Forward* feeds this trend both in general American and Jewish life.

Related to McCarthyism is another issue that will not down: whether justice was done in the trial March 6-29, 1951 of Julius and Ethel Rosenberg and Morton Sobell on the charge of conspiracy to commit espionage. The execution of the first two June 19, 1953 and the sentencing of Sobell to a 30 year term were widely questioned both here and abroad. Although Jewish top leadership worked hard to back up the sentences of Judge Irving R. Kaufman and the prosecution by Irving R. Saypol and Roy Cohn, widespread uneasiness in the Jewish community was expressed in the campaign for clemency, supported by personalities like Rabbi Abraham Cronbach (1882-1965) and by such diverse organs as the *Jewish Daily Forward, Morning Freiheit,* the *Jewish Morning Journal, Jewish Life,* the *Brooklyn Jewish Examiner* and the *California Jewish Voice.* A series of books critical of the trial has just been climaxed in mid-1965 by a most challenging volume issued by Doubleday, *Invitation to an Inquest,* by Walter and Miriam Schneir. An official review of the case is in order.

But no matter how many Jewish McCarthyites there may be in Jewish communal life, McCarthyism is alien to the bulk of the Jewish population of all classes. This popular Jewish rejection of reaction was demonstrated again when the danger of the ultra-right loomed and Barry M. Goldwater in 1964 captured the Republican Party nomination for the presidency. Although 27,000,000 voted for Goldwater, he got his lowest support among the Negro voters (only four per cent) and among the Jewish voters (at most 16 per cent), although he obtained 39 per cent of the total vote in the land. Except for the Negroes, no other group or class in the country was as solidly against Goldwaterism as the Jewish population. The minor conservative trend in Jewish political behavior—whether based on class interests, conviction or "Jewish tactical" considerations ("there should be some Jewish reactionaries to show the anti-Semites we're not all reds")—has to be seen in the context of the major fact that, in terms of American political choices, the Jews are among the most steadfastly liberal, with sizable progressive or radical currents. Opposition to communism is of course widespread, but Jews see the "danger on the right" as the main danger and sentiment for peaceful coexistence with socialist-communist states is general. They see the ultra-right danger all the more vividly and concretely in terms of its depiction in the A. D. L. volume by Arnold Forster and Benjamin

Arthur J. Goldberg, chief of the United States delegation to the United Nations, Secretary of Labor, 1961-1962, Associate Justice of the United States Supreme Court, 1962-1965.

R. Epstein, *Danger on the Right.* Their research helped alert the entire country to, among other things, "the sources of finance of the American right wing" among some 70 tax-exempt foundations, 113 business firms and corporations, 25 public utilities and some 250 wealthy individuals. And with the ultra-right reorganizing itself after the defeat of Goldwater, the A. D. L. continues to warn the country as a whole and the Jews of the continuing menace on the right. The N.C.R.A.C. at its annual meeting June 25, 1965 adopted a report calling on its affiliates to "convince the Jewish community and others of the threat posed *directly to Jews* by extremists" like the John Birch Society and other ultra-right groups (italics added).

The sensitive social conscience and the readiness to act upon it has been especially in evidence in the civil rights struggle. From a complicated situation, two related conclusions emerge: that the total record of Jewish participation in the civil rights struggle is the best to be found in the white population, but that it is still

JAMES CHANEY   ANDREW GOODMAN   MICHAEL SCHWERNER

James Chaney of Mississippi, Andrew Goodman and Michael H. Schwerner of New York, murdered in Philadelphia, Miss., June 21, 1964, while they were working for the Mississippi Summer Project. Drawings by Ben Shahn for the Human Relations Council of Greater New Haven.

not good enough in relation to the needs and urgent demands of the Negro people for the actual achievement of equality. Jewish communal leadership is aware both of all that has been done and the much more that needs to be done, and also knows there is a gap between the stated position of leaders and the conduct of members. Sentiment for desegregation is almost universal in the Jewish population. (The Jews in the 13 states of the old Confederacy total only 326,000—less than the Jewish population of Long Island, N. Y.—and make up only six per cent of the United States Jewish population, but even in the South there seems to be more Jewish *sentiment* for desegregation than such a tiny minority dares to reveal or act upon in a hostile climate.)

To turn mass sentiment into mass conduct is the recognized problem of Jewish leadership. This problem was squarely confronted at the annual meeting June 27-30, 1963 of the National Community Relations Advisory Council, which worked out a comprehensive program for action and education for action. Moods in some Jewish circles to hang back from civil rights because of the spread of anti-Semitic attitudes among Negroes are countered by the awareness, as expressed for example in the "Joint Program Plan" adopted at the N. C. R. A. C. annual meeting June 25-27, 1965, that the "struggle for racial equality is inseparable from the pursuit of equal rights for Jews and for all others in our society."

Public discussions between Negroes and Jews have explored such touchy subjects as the pattern often found in Negro ghettos of conflict-breeding economic relations of Negroes who are tenants, employees and customers of Jewish landlords, employers and merchants. These dialogues have clarified the point that anti-Semitism is never justifiable no matter how sociologically understandable and that anti-Semitism is a trap for the Negro people that needs to be combatted not only by Jewish but by Negro leadership.

This Negro leadership has valued highly the extent and quality of Jewish participation in civil rights action both on local levels throughout the North and in such dramatic and demonstrative historic events as took place in Albany, Ga. (1962), the March on Washington (1963), in St. Augustine, Fla. (1964), on the Mississippi Summer Project (1964) and in Selma and Montgomery, Ala. (1965). At the same time, Negro activists have leveled valid criticism that some Jewish groups were not accelerating their own pace of action to keep in step with the heightened pace of the Negro movement. The more advanced sectors of Jewish leadership have warned against the danger that Jews might thus become a brake on the Negro's pace forward. A key area in this danger is the relative confusion in Jewish circles on the complex problem of abolishing racial imbalance in Northern metropolitan school systems. This confusion has even led some Jewish parents to take part in the campaign of movements fighting against school integration in New York. Here, too, N. C. R. A. C. leadership stresses that extensive Jewish parental support for school integration programs depends on "the firmness with which the agencies and responsible leadership hold to their commitments and the effectiveness of the programs of interpretation that are undertaken by the agencies." In fact the best assurance of the continuation of the comparatively high degree of Jewish individual and organizational participation in civil rights action is the continuing, widespread and self-critical public discussion of such problems in the Jewish community.

Recent years have also seen the emergence into the mainstream of public discussion of an approach to the Negroes' situation that was formerly understood only on the left: the demonstration of the inadequacy of the liberal concept of "color-blindness" and the necessity for the concept of a "color-consciousness" that would lead to special efforts to overcome the consequences of a century of post-Emancipation segregation of Negroes. The first government agency on any level to recognize the need for such "color-consciousness" and to repudiate "color-blindness" was the City Commission on Human Rights of New York, headed by the Hon. Stanley H. Lowell (also a vice-president of the American Jewish Congress). The Commission's declaration of October 23, 1963, and Mr. Lowell's defense of that document November 17, 1963 in his address to the Public Employees Lodges of the A. D. L., both reflected and precipitated widespread discussion of the issue raised. Declaring that "society must work affirmatively for integration rather than nega-

tively for desegregation," the Commission proposed special measures and efforts in education, housing and employment "to deal with the historic and existing exclusion pattern of our society." In his address at Howard University, June 5, 1965, President Lyndon B. Johnson underlined the need for such an approach by detailing the oppressive burdens and handicaps that have been imposed on the Negro population.

While paying necessarily special attention to the civil rights struggle as the main domestic issue before the country, the Jewish population was also deeply involved in the prime international issue of preventing nuclear extinction and therefore in all aspects of American foreign policy. Israel's security of course was a special concern. Unremitting Arab intransigence, persistently expressed in such continuing acts as the economic boycott of Israel and the closing of the Suez Canal to Israeli shipping and in flamboyant calls, sometimes even in the United Nations General Assembly, for the elimination of Israel, has united all trends in American Jewish life in the sentiment and resolve that Israel is here to stay. So prevalent is pro-Israel feeling that the very need for a special Zionist movement has been seriously called into question.

Not too well informed about the realities of Israeli life and foreign affairs, American Jewish opinion is far less critical than is Israeli public opinion of many aspects of Israel's internal life and of Israel foreign policy, which since 1951 has been based on a Western orientation in the Cold War. Premier David Ben-Gurion's involvement of Israel with Great Britain and France in a jointly organized attack, beginning October 29, 1956, on the Sinai Peninsula and the Suez Canal, no matter what the claimed justification by Israel, confronted American Jews with a dilemma: Israel's participation could not entirely obsure from most American Jews the fact that the invasion conflicted with their own deep anti-colonial convictions. Jewish and even Zionist leadership was shocked and disoriented by Ben-Gurion's course of action, general Jewish opinion was confused, and there was a sense of relief when the United States government joined with the Soviet government in compelling a withdrawal of all the invading forces, including Israel's. At the same time it should be noted that the sharp anti-Israel edge of the Arab anti-colonialist movement has dulled the perception by most American Jews of what is valid and historically progressive in that movement.

Even more grave was the position into which the Jewish population was maneuvered, despite continual protest by an active minority, with regard to Germany. The State Department having decided, for Cold War purposes, to "let bygones be bygones" and to ignore the Potsdam Agreement calling for the demilitarization, denazification and decartelization of Germany, it devised a way of rehabilitating Germany in Western opinion by involving the Jews, who had suffered most at the hands of the Nazis. This plan gave rise to the reparations agreement worked out between Ben-Gurion and Bonn Chancellor Konrad Adenauer, signed at Luxembourg September 10, 1952 amid mass Jewish uneasiness, tides of moral revulsion and considerable organizational opposition both in Israel and here. One great fear of the opposition was soon realized. The dominant American Jewish leaders speedily put a damper on criticism of West German rearmament, the widespread penetration of West German public life by former Nazis and untried war criminals and the recartelization of the economy under convicted war criminals like Krupp. The vigorously dissenting Jewish minority has all these years been unable to shake off this damper and has been forced to see the bulk of the Jewish population follow the bulk of the American people as a whole in the rebuilding of West Germany into Europe's strongest military and economic power within 20 years after the Allied victory over Hitlerism. Even when there was need for powerful mass protest to press the Bonn government to abolish its Statute of Limitations on war crimes that was to go into effect May 8, 1965, the main Jewish leadership was late and hesitant, and therefore the Jews—and all people —were forced to swallow a mere extension of the Statute to the end of 1969.

More in keeping with the realities of the situation, despite all Cold War and even McCarthyite pressures, was the reaction of the Jewish population on the issue of nuclear warfare. Fear among Jews of the consequences of such conflict was of course not lessened by the fact that, concentrated as they are disproportionately in the major cities of the land, they live in prime target areas of nuclear attack or counterattack. Therefore both affiliated and unaffiliated Jews were an important segment of the active minority that continually pressed our administrations for advances in policy, whether on nuclear disarmament, suspension of nuclear testing, or United States embroilment in Vietnam or the Dominican Republic. On such issues of peace the Central Conference of American Rabbis (Reform) has been repeatedly and cogently outspoken, stimulating similar expressions by other Jewish organizations and leaders.

Too often entangled in the Cold War also was the deepening American Jewish concern with the situation of the Jews in the Soviet Union (see p. 273). Since the 1956 Khrushchev revelations about Stalin's lawless rule, important changes have taken place: the rehabilitation into Soviet society of the dead and living victims, Jews included, of the Stalin terror; the proliferation of Yiddish concerts of music and dramatizations; an amateur but stable Yiddish theater, chorus and dance ensemble in Vilna; the publication of *Sovetish Haimland,* a literary bimonthly (in 1965 a monthly) of high quality and large circulation (25,000—unique in contemporary Yiddish publication); the issuing of six-seven Yiddish books and other evidence of a pragmatic improvement in the Jewish cultural situation—all of which leave it, of course, in far from the flourishing condition in which it was before it was cut down first in 1937 and then in 1948. At the same time, remnants of anti-Semitism continued to appear—in blood libels, in crude atheistic attacks on Judaism that turned into anti-Semitism, in interference with Soviet constitutionally guaranteed rights of believers to the unhampered practice of Judaism. Furthermore, it also became apparent that the practice of forced assimilation—contrary though this is to Soviet theory—had not been abandoned and replaced by a positive socialist program of reconstructing Soviet Jewish cultural institutions in education, theater, press and communal life.

The Cold War atmosphere in which these facts and conclusions emerged bedeviled the entire situation. Cold Warriors, led by the Jewish Labor Committee, engaged enthusiastically in distortion and exaggeration; opponents of the Cold War, although even more concerned with the real issue, tended to defensive apologetics. The Soviet spokesmen, by mechanically denying the very existence of any problem, fed the Cold War extremists. Recognizing the danger of allowing the problem to become a football in the Cold War, more statesmanlike Jewish leaders began to develop a body of authenticated information on the Soviet Jewish situation on which all, including outstanding non-Jewish proponents of peaceful coexistence as well as the Jewish left, could rely. Some of these leaders even realized that the louder voice of the general and Jewish left would perhaps be more persuasive in the far-flung international dialogue with Soviet leadership than the shriller voices of those the Soviet leaders know too well as inveterate Cold Warriors.

The American Jewish Conference on Soviet Jewry, formed in April, 1964 by a score of major Jewish organizations, launched a nationwide campaign in which, unfortunately, the Cold War forces, at first isolated, managed to press to the fore in the year that followed. Ignored too often was the fact that complex political questions like the meaning of forced assimilation could not be resolved by picket lines, demonstrations, resounding orations by Senators with political axes to grind or meetings in Madison Square Garden in which some voices even dared compare, despite the warning of the chairman, the Soviet policy with that of the Nazis—a comparison both utterly false and guaranteed to close Soviet ears to all discussion of the real situation. Two approaches have developed: the clamorous, demonstrative one that inevitably yields to exaggeration and Cold War implications; the principled one that carefully eliminates the Cold War from this area and firmly points to real problems in their real focus and dimensions and discusses how they can be dealt with along lines of socialist theory and practice.

Statesmanlike in his approach is Dr. Nahum Goldmann, president of both the World Jewish Congress and the World Zionist Organization. In an article in the London *Jewish Chronicle* September 4, 1964, widely reprinted in the U. S. A., he warned, "Exaggeration and demagogy, unjust accusations, comparison of the Soviet regime in this regard with the Nazis and similar excesses of propaganda, are not only useless but harmful, both in their possible repercusion on the position of Soviet Jews and in alienating many progressive forces in the world from helping us." He scoffed at the idea that there was an official Soviet policy of anti-Semitism but underscored the view that there was a practise of forced assimilation that contradicted Soviet theory. When Cold Warriors dominated the Madison Square Garden meeting of June 3, 1965, Dr. Goldmann issued another resounding admonition June 10: "Too often the problem is being distorted in its character with the result that accusations are being made against Russia which are not justified and which can only delay the solution of the problem and even harm Soviet Jewry. The problem is not one of persecution in the usual meaning of the word, although there is anti-Semitism in many parts of Russia and the government must be criticized for not acting more vigorously against anti-Semitic incidents. . . . Our only hope is to arouse support through personalities and groups whose opinion is very highly respected by the Soviet government . . ."

While devoting considerable attention to these matters of Jewish relations with non-Jews, with Jews in other lands, and with major contemporary general issues, the American Jewish community has also dealt with some inner communal problems, at least three of which may be noted here. Intermarriage between Jew and non-Jew is a staple issue that periodically rises to the surface for extensive discussion. Communally the problem is approached not primarily from the point of view of the individual rights of the intermarried or even of their personal happiness or welfare but from the point of view of the relation of intermarriage to group survival. American Jews, who generally place the democratic emphasis on the primacy of individual rights as against the requirements of the group (especially "the state"), often reverse themselves in applying their principles to intermarriage and tend to make group rights absolute. But, as was remarked by Rabbi Jacob J. Weinstein, now president of the C. C. A. R., "as long as we choose to enjoy the benefits of a free and democratic society, we must accept the calculated risk of losses to the non-Jewish majority. The only way we can avoid that risk is to move to Israel or island ourselves in one of the Hassidic enclaves in Williamsburg."

Voluminous and alarmed discussion both in rabbinical and secular circles was precipitated by the publication in the 1963 *American Jewish Year Book* of a study of intermarriage in Iowa and in Washington, D. C. by Professor Erich Rosenthal of Queens College. Iowa's experience, with its 8,715 Jews scattered in 12 cities and constituting less than three-tenths of one per cent of the Iowa population, would seem to have little relevance to large Jewish populations concentrated in the 14 largest cities in the countries. And even Washington, D. C., although it is one of these 14, has its sociologically obvious peculiarities as a city with a special character as the seat of government. One of Dr. Rosenthal's findings provoked wide but inconclusive discussion: that Washington men who were foreign born had an intermarriage rate of 1.4 per cent; their sons had an intermarriage rate of 10.2 per cent; the third generation, native born of native parentage, had a rate of 17.9 per cent. All suggested "programs" of dealing with intermarriage remind one of Rabbi Weinstein's observation.

Another continuing and unresolved communal issue has to do with the relation of the American Jewish population to Israel (apart from the practically discredited nonsense about "dual loyalty"). The Zionist view of "the centrality of Israel" has not prevailed in the American Jewish community, which tends to center its life and being in the United States, no matter how much it gives in overseas aid or how committed it is to the survival of Israel. The American-Israel dialogues staged in Israel the past four summers by the American Jewish Congress only underscore the difference between the Israeli and orthodox Zionist approach and that of even such an avowedly pro-Israel group as the Congress. Zionist ambitions about the "Hebraization" of American Jewish life and culture also run up against the questioning of educators who see the centrality of *relevance* in Jewish education.

A mild sensation was created in another area when *Commentary* in April, 1961 printed its symposium on "Jewishness and the Younger Intellectuals," in which a "random group" of 31 (out of 50 queried) professors, novelists, poets, critics, editors, psychiatrists and other professionals under 40 years of age were asked to define their relationship to Jewishness, Jewish culture, the Jewish community and the state of Israel. Since they were selected from the unaffiliated and unorganized sector of the Jewish population, their responses showed considerable distance from the Jewish community. Since the very high percentage of Jews going to college and to graduate schools indicates that the intellectuals are a fast-growing component of the Jewish population, however, the symposium was greeted with more finger-pointing, head-shaking and smug anti-intellectualism than with an awareness of the challenge that the intellectuals were making to Jewish communal life, values and institutions.

Summing up the views of these intellectuals, *Commentary* editor Norman Podhoretz commented that they were "neither vigorously rejecting Jewishness nor enthusiastically rushing toward it. Most of them have something good to say for the Jewish heritage, though very few express any sense of living commitment to it . . . they assume easily, and incorrectly I think, that the American Jewish community is indistinguishable from the middle-class American community in general and bears no sign of the former attributes of the Jewish people." It may be added that these intellectuals, not really knowing the general, non-Jewish, American middle class, exhibit their own parochialism by the gratuitous and false assumption that the Jewish component is the worst possible segment of the middle class. Therefore these distant intellectuals ignore or are ignorant of the still vital intellectual, cultural and progressive traditions to which even the Jewish middle class is still disproportionately responsive.

In closing the first edition of this book, we based our perspective on the continued viability of the theory and practice of "cultural pluralism" in our country (see p. 285). Developments of the past 15 years, and sociological studies of the subject recently published, reenforce this view. Professor Nathan Glazer and Dr. Daniel Patrick Moynihan symbolically entitled their study of "the Negroes, Puerto Ricans, Jews, Italians and Irish of New York City" *Beyond the Melting Pot* (1963). They record "the disinclination of the third and fourth generation of newcomers to blend into a standard uniform national type;" they observe "a distinct identity, albeit a changing one, from one generation to the next;" they conclude that "the ethnic group in American society became not a survival from the age of mass immigration but a new social form" because "ethnic groups . . . are continually recreated by new experiences in America. . . ."

Professor Milton M. Gordon, studying "the role of race, religion and national origins" in *Assimilation in American Life* (1964), found that "the sense of ethnicity has proved to be hardy . . . . the sense of ethnic belonging has survived," although he believes "a more accurate term for the American situation is structural pluralism rather than cultural pluralism, although some of the latter also remains" (he defines structural pluralism as "structural separation on the basis of race and religion").

For these and all the reasons contained in the very texture of these last two chapters, we believe the foundations of American Jewish communal life are still strong and therefore the outlook for the continuity of Jewish group life is good. We agree with Professor Oscar I. Janowsky, who, weighing all the evidence pro and con presented by 19 scholars, concluded the volume he edited, *The American Jew: A Reappraisal,* with the forecast, "American Jewry is not disintegrating. It is in the process of becoming."

EDITOR'S NOTE: *Since Chapter 14 was added for the second edition, it is more convenient to list its references here below; there is no index to this chapter. Abbreviations are listed on page 311.*

P. 288b: Jewish population—*AJYB,* 1964, pp. 6-14; immigration—*AJYB,* 1961, pp. 64-65, 1962, p. 146, 1963, p. 77; *Statistical Abstract,* United Hias Service, October, 1964, p. 6.

P. 289a: Jewish fertility—*AJYB,* 1964, pp. 4-5; C. Bezalel Sherman in *The American Jew, A Reappraisal,* ed. by Oscar I. Janowsky, Philadelphia, 1964, p. 37; class composition—Nathan Reich in Janowsky, pp. 63-64, 74; farm families—*New York Times,* February 6, 1965; service jobs—*New York Times,* June 28, 1965.

P. 289b: income distribution—Reich, work cited, pp. 57, 60; college education—Alfred Jospe, *AJYB,* 1964, pp. 131-34; Robert J. Shosteck, *The Jewish College Student,* Washington, D. C., 1957.

P. 290b: communal services—*AJYB,* 1964; *Yearbook of Jewish Social Service,* 1964; *1964 Annual Report,* JDC.; S. Levy in Janowsky, work cited.

P. 291a: cultural foundation—*National Jewish Cultural Services in America, Appraisals and Recommendations,* 1959, pp. 29-30, *passim;* dissertations—Isacque Graeber in *YIVO Annual of Jewish Social Science,* vol. 13, 1965.

P. 292a: Sherman, work cited, p. 46; Arthur Hertzberg in Janowsky, work cited, p. 103; *AJYB,* 1963, p. 146, 1964, pp. 75ff.

P. 293a: *A Short History of Yavneh,* mimeographed, and *College Years and the Future of American Judaism,* booklet, issued by Yavneh, 1965; federal aid to religious schools, *AJYB,* 1963, p. 147.

P. 293b: press—*AJYB,* pp. 402ff.

P. 294a: criticism of press—David Wolf Silverman in *The Religious Press in America,* New York, 1963, p. 165; Harold Eidlin in *The National Jewish Monthly,* May, 1965; foreign-language press—the American Council for Nationalities Service.

P. 294b: education—budget, Zalmen Slesinger, *The Pedagogic Reporter*, May, 1963, p. 6; curriculum—*AJYB*, 1962, pp. 217-19; survey—Dushkin and Engelman, *Jewish Education in the United States*, New York, 1959, pp. 222, 224, 229, 237, 239; Janowsky, work cited, p. 157, 161; Isidor Chein in *Congress Weekly*, January 15, 1961; Slesinger, *The Pedagogic Reporter*, May, 1961, p. 10; enrolment—*Jewish Education Committee Bulletin*, New York, October, 1964, updated by unpublished data obtained from the Committee·

P. 295a: day schools—*Data Sheet* of Torah Umesorah, New York; *New York Times*, May 16, 1965 for budget.

P. 295b: Service Bureau for Jewish Education, New York, data supplied by I. Goldberg; J. Mlotek in *Kultur un Dertsiung*, Workmen's Circle, New York, May, 1962, pp. 12ff; Farband—data supplied by Leon Rubenstein, director; Sholem Aleichem schools—data supplied by Saul Goodman.

P. 296a: summer camps—*JWB Year Book*, New York, vol. 12, 1961-62, p. 5, vol. 13, 1962-63, p. 11.

P. 296b: Irving Malin and Irwin Stark, *Breakthrough*, New York, 1964, p. 2; Columbia University Professor Steven Marcus, May 18, 1965, at Annual Meeting of the Conference on Jewish Social Studies; Marie Syrkin in Janowsky, work cited, p. 233.

P. 297a: Syrkin, work cited, p. 221; paperback bestseller—*New York Times Book Review*, January 10, 1965; *Paperbound Books of Jewish Interest*, Jewish Book Council, 1963; Jewish Publication Society data—*The JPS Bookmark*, June, 1965, p. 4.

P. 297b: Sampling of criticism of Hilberg—in *Commentary*, November, 1962; in *Dissent*, Spring 1963; in *Jewish Currents*, February, April, May, June, July-August, September, 1962 and April, 1963; K. Shabbetai, *As Sheep to the Slaughter? The Myth of Cowardice*, New York-Tel Aviv, 1963; on Hannah Arendt—sampling the torrent of discussion: *Facts*, A. D. L., July-August, 1963; Schappes, *The Strange World of Hannah Arendt;* in *Commentary*, September, 1963; in *Encounter*, London, January, 1964; *The Times Literary Supplement*, London, April 30, 1964; in *Partisan Review*, Summer, Fall, 1963, Winter, Spring, 1964; Jacob Robinson, *And the Crooked Shall Be Made Straight*, New York, 1965. In the paperback reprint, her corrections and extended Postscript show her essentially unresponsive to the criticism leveled.

P. 298a: On *The Deputy*—Eric Bentley, editor , *The Storm Over The Deputy*, New York, 1964; for its "central message": Grove Press edition, pp. 104, 110, 115-16, 124, 147, 149, 206, and *American Historical Review*, October, 1964, pp. 75-78; Podhoretz quoted from his *Doings and Undoings*, New York, 1964, pp. 7-8, 164.

P. 299b: Yiddish in colleges—Joseph C. Landis in *Judaism*, Fall, 1964, p. 445; grant to Singer—Hasye Cooperman in Janowsky, work cited, pp. 207-08; on quality of translations—Schappes, *Jewish Life*, January, 1954; I. Goldberg, *Yiddishe Kultur*, April and May, 1965; Boroff quoted from *American Judaism*, Spring, 1962; Silberschlag in Janowsky, p. 190.

P. 300a: A. D. L. survey.

P. 300b: Milton Konvitz in Janowsky, work cited, p. 79; Quotation from David Caplovitz and Candace Rogers, *Swastika 1960*, New York, 1961, p. 8; Charles R. Allen, Jr., *Nazi War Criminals in Our Midst*, New York, 1963.

P. 301a: Konvitz, work cited, p. 100.

P. 301b: Harvard study—*New York Times*, May 23, 1965; Baltzell quoted from pp. 33, 316, 323.

P. 303a: Goldwater vote—Harris poll, *New York Post*, January 11, 1964; Facts, A D L, February, 1965.

P. 304a: sentiment for desegregation—Alfred O. Hero, Jr., "Southern Jews, Race Relations and Foreign Policy," *Jewish Social Studies*, October, 1965; Joshua A. Fishman, "Southern City," *Midstream*, Summer, 1961, p. 54.

P. 304b: public discussions—proceedings in *Jewish Currents*, May, 1963 and July-August, 1965; in *Jewish Social Studies*, January, 1965.

P. 305a: N. C. R. A. C. quotation from its Bulletin, *In the Common Cause*, No. 34.

P. 308a: Rabbi Weinstein quotation from *K. A. M. News*, Chicago, May 15, 1964.

P. 309a: Glazer and Moynihan, pp. v, vi, 16, 17.

P. 309b: Gordon quoted from pp. 24-25, 159; Janowsky quoted from p. 399.

Reference Notes and Indexes

Although this is a book for the general reader, I have given essential reference notes for the possible use of the student and scholar. The following abbreviations have been used:

AJA—*American Jewish Archives.*

AJHSP—*American Jewish Historical Society Publications.*

AJYB—*American Jewish Year Book.*

EAH—*Encyclopedia of American History,* ed. by Richard B. Morris, New York, 1953.

JE—*Jewish Encyclopedia.*

JQR—*Jewish Quarterly Review,* Philadelphia.

JSS—*Jewish Social Studies.*

UJE—*Universal Jewish Encyclopedia.*

In the notes, the two columns on the page are designated as *a* and *b*. Thus p. 18a refers to the first column on page 18.

PROLOGUE

Pp. 3a, 4b: Emma Lazarus quotations—Morris U. Schappes, ed., *Emma Lazarus, Selections from Her Poetry and Prose,* New York, rev. ed., 1947, pp. 40, 43.

Pp. 3b, 4a: Columbus quotations— (Samuel Kettell), *Personal Narrative of the First Voyage of Columbus to America,* Boston, 1827, p. 9; Cecil Jane, ed., *The Voyages of Christopher Columbus,* London, 1930, pp. 135-36. In a letter to this author, June 15, 1955, Samuel Eliot Morison acknowledged he had overlooked Columbus' reference to the expulsion of the Jews in his book, *Admiral of the Ocean Sea, A Life of Christopher Columbus,* Boston, 1942, vol. I, p. 193.

Pp. 4-5: Columbus' voyage—Morison, work cited, pp. 92, 136, 147, 187, 190, 192, 193, 194, 263, 338, 364; Cecil Roth, *A History of the Marranos,* Philadelphia, rev. ed., 1947, pp. 271-72; M. Kayserling, *Christopher Columbus and the Participation of the Jews in the Spanish and Portuguese Discoveries,* New York, 1928, needs to be taken with great care.

P. 4b: Charles A. and Mary R. Beard, *The Rise of American Civilization,* New York, 1937, rev. ed., vol. I, p. 8.

P. 4: Columbus a Jew?—this author has found no evidence that he was a Jew, or proof that he was a Marrano.

CHAPTER I

Unless otherwise indicated, sources for this chapter will be found cited in Morris U. Schappes, *A Documentary History of the Jews in the United States, 1654 to 1875,* New York, 1950, rev. ed., 1952, p. 1-13, 565-68 and in Schappes, "Jews in New Amsterdam, 1654: They Fought for Equal Rights," *Jewish Life,* New York, Feb., 1954, pp. 20-25.

P. 9a: Jews in Brazil—Arnold Wiznitzer, "The Number of Jews in Dutch Brazil (1630-1654)," *Jewish Social Studies,* vol. 16, 1954, pp. 111, 113.

P. 9b: *St. Catherine* as the name of the ship, correcting the generally accepted *St. Charles*—Wiznitzer, "The Exodus from Brazil and Arrival in New Amsterdam of the Jewish Pilgrim Fathers, 1654," *American Jewish Historical Society Publications,* vol. 44, 1954, pp. 87, 88.

P. 10: conflict between Stuyvesant and Company—see also interpretation of Harold C. Syrett, "Private Enterprise in New Amsterdam," *The William and Mary Quarterly,* ser. 3, vol. 11, 1954, pp. 546-48; on Jews in Dutch economy, see also Violet Barbour, *Capitalism in Amsterdam in the Seventeenth Century,* Baltimore, 1950, p. 25.

P. 11b: Mose Lumbrozo instead of Ambrosius—Wiznitzer, "The Members of the Brazilian Jewish Community (1648-1653)," *AJHSP,* vol. 42, 1953, p. 394; de Mercado instead of de Mereda—Wiznitzer, p. 394; Sefer Torah returned—I. S. Emmanuel, "New Light on Early American Jewry," *American Jewish Archives,* vol. 7, 1955, pp. 18, 56.

P. 12a: on the oldest tombstone—David de Sola Pool, *Portraits Etched in Stone, Early Jewish Settlers, 1682-1831,* New York, 1952, pp. 9-13, 187-89.

P. 13a: on Jacob Cohen—Berthold Fernow, ed., *The Records of New Amsterdam from 1653 to 1674,* New York, 1897, vol. 2, p. 419; on Rabba Cooty—Fernow, work cited, vol. 6, pp. 151, 259.

P. 13b: on Roger Williams—his book, *The Bloudy Tenent of Persecution,* London, 1644, p. 71, and David C. Adelman, "Roger Williams and the Jews," *Rhode Island Jewish Historical Notes,* vol. 1, 1955, p. 153.

P. 14b: on Jews as strangers—Adelman, "Strangers," work cited, vol. 1, 1954, p. 106; on 1690—Jacob Rader Marcus, *Early American Jewry*, Philadelphia, 1951-1953, vol. 2, pp. 387, 390.

P. 15a: on Rev. Hugh Peters—Winifred King Rugg, *Unafraid*, Boston and New York, 1930, p. 210; I am indebted for this reference to Mr. James J. Green of Brooklyn, New York; on 1662 colony—A. S. W. Rosenbach, "Notes on the First Settlement of Jews in Pennsylvania," *AJHSP*, vol. 5, 1897, p. 195.

P. 15b: on Dr. Lumbrozo—Schappes, *Doc. Hist.*, pp. 13-15, 568; on South Carolina—Charles Reznikoff and Uriah Z. Engelman, *The Jews of Charleston*, Philadelphia, 1950, pp. 5-6; Abram Vossen Goodman, *American Overture*, Philadelphia, 1947, pp. 154-55.

CHAPTER 2

Unless otherwise indicated, sources for this chapter will be found in Schappes, *Doc. Hist.*, pp. 15-44, 568-76.

P. 17b: settling in Georgia—E. Merton Coulter and Albert B. Saye, *A List of the Early American Settlers of Georgia*, Athens, Ga., 1949, pp. x, 1-59; they give the number as 92 instead of 90 because they listed one family twice. See also Jacob R. Marcus, *AJA*, vol. 5, 1953, pp. 128-29.

P. 18a: indentured servants—Edwin Wolf 2nd and Maxwell Whiteman, *The History of the Jews of Philadelphia from Colonial Times to the Age of Jackson*, Philadelphia, 1957, pp. 57, 186; Lazarus Isaac—work cited, pp. 59-60.

P. 18b: Mrs. Hannah Moses—Marcus, *Early American Jewry*, vol. 1, pp. 13-14.

P. 20b: spermaceti industry—Carl Bridenbaugh, *Cities in Revolt, Urban Life in America, 1743-1776*, New York, 1955, pp. 73-74; Marcus, work cited, pp. 131, 134, 136; indigo—Frederick P. Bowes, *The Culture of Early Charleston*, Chapel Hill, N. C., 1952, p. 88.

P. 21a: doctors—Leon Huehner, "Jews in the Legal and Medical Professions in America Prior to 1800," *AJHSP*, vol. 22, pp. 147-65; not voting—Adelman, "Strangers," work cited, p. 104.

P. 21b: anti-Semitism—Bridenbaugh, work cited, pp. 117, 156; Goodman, work cited, pp. 111-14.

P. 22a: Shylock—*The Virginia Gazette*, Williamsburg, Va., September 22, 1752, p. 3, col. 1; Pennsylvania, 1764—Wolf and Whiteman, work cited, p. 45.

P. 23a: Ashkenazim in 1730—D. de Sola Pool, *The Mill Street Synagogue (1730-1817)*, New York, 1930,

p. 49; Rev. John Sharpe, "Proposals for Erecting a School, Library and Chapel at New York, [1713]" *New-York Historical Society Collections*, 1880, p. 343; Wolf and Whiteman, work cited, p. 41.

P. 23b: *hechsher*—Wolf and Whiteman, p. 48; aid to Palestine—Hyman B. Grinstein, *The Rise of The Jewish Community of New York, 1654-1860*, Philadelphia, 1945, p. 440; Wolf and Whiteman, work cited, p. 56; Masons—Samuel Oppenheim, "The Jews and Masonry in the United States Before 1810," *AJHSP*, vol. 19, pp. 2-93; Marcus, work cited, vol. 2, p. 476. By the beginning of the twentieth century, exclusion of Jews from the higher degrees of Masonry forced them to form their own segregated chapters—John Higham, "Social Discrimination Against Jews in America, 1830-1930," *AJHSP*, vol. 47, September, 1957, p. 15.

P. 24a: Union Society—*Minutes of the Union Society . . . from 1750 to 1858*, Savannah, Ga., 1860, pp. 11, 12, 123; Pinto's 1760 prayer—the only known copy is at the Historical Society of Pennsylvania.

P. 24b: Karigal's sermon is at the New York Public Library. Isaac the Scribe—Samuel Oppenheim, "The Chapters of Isaac the Scribe: A Bibliographical Rarity, New York, 1772," *AJHSP*, vol. 22, pp. 29-50; Levy the violinist—Wolf and Whiteman, work cited, p. 33. He has been identified as Nathan Levy (d. 1753, son of Moses Levy of New York), who had settled in Philadelphia in 1737 (AJA press release, *Jewish Criterion*, Pittsburgh, February 21, 1958).

CHAPTER 3

Unless otherwise indicated, sources for this chapter will be found in Schappes, *Doc. Hist.*, pp. 38-40, 45-67, 575-83 and in Schappes, "Jews in the American Revolution," *Jewish Life*, March, 1954, pp. 21-25.

P. 25a: Benjamin Nones—arrived in the colonies in 1772, not as has previously been assumed in 1777, Wolf and Whiteman, work cited, pp. 57, 112.

P. 25b: British mercantalism—Curtis P. Nettels, "British Mercantilism and the Economic Development of the Thirteen Colonies," *The Journal of Economic History*, vol. 12, 1952, p. 114; anti-British coalition—Herbert M. Morais, *The Struggle for American Freedom*, New York, 1944, pp. 158-59, 184ff.

P. 28b: extra-legal organizations—Morais, work cited, pp. 183-84; Salvador in Provincial Congress—Whiteman denies there has been any proof Salvador was elected, *AJA*, vol. 9, April, 1957, p. 59; Governor's description of Parochial Committee—Morais, work cited, p. 181; Marcus, work cited, vol. 2, pp. 346-48.

P. 29a: sending the Declaration of Independence to Amsterdam—Marcus, work cited, pp. 63-64.

P. 29b: Jewish soldier on Sabbath duty—*AJHSP*, vol. 10, p. 163.

P. 31b: number of Loyalists—Merrill Jensen, *The New Nation*, New York, 1950, p. 265; John Adams, *The Works of*, Boston, 1852, vol. 7, pp. 270-271; Richard B. Morris, *Encyclopedia of American History*, New York, 1953, pp. 90, 110.

P. 32b: image of Shylock—James Burgh, *The Art of Speaking*, Newburyport, Mass., 1782, pp. 201-208; Baltimore, 1804, pp. 163-169.

P. 32b: Pennsylvania Constitutional Convention—Wolf and Whiteman, work cited, p. 81; Max J. Kohler, "Phases in the History of Religious Liberty in America with Special Reference to the Jews," *AJHSP*, vol. 11, pp. 68-69.

P. 34a: Haym Salomon—Wolf and Whiteman, work cited, p. 106.

P. 34b: Philadelphia synagogue—Wolf and Whiteman, pp. 115-121.

P. 35b: Christians contribute to synagogue fund —Wolf and Whiteman, p. 143-44; the amounts contributed were listed by Wolf and Whiteman in their original article in *The Jewish Exponent*, November 5, 1954.

CHAPTER 4

Unless otherwise indicated, sources for this chapter will be found in Schappes, *Doc. Hist.*, pp. 68-99; 139-41, 160-63, 168-71, 588-93, 602-07 and in Schappes, "Jews and the Jeffersonians," *Jewish Life*, April, 1954, pp. 21-25.

P. 38a: Jewish population—Reznikoff, work cited, p. 54, 67.

P. 38b: Philadelphia brokers—Wolf and Whiteman, work cited, pp. 184-85; New York Stock Exchange—*One Hundredth Anniversary of the New York Stock Exchange*, New York, 1892.

P. 39a: Bank of New York—Robert A. East, *Business Enterprise in the American Revolutionary Era*, New York, 1938, pp. 327-29; Henry W. Domett, *A History of the Bank of New York, 1784-1884*, New York, 1884, pp. 136-39; Allan Nevins, *History of the Bank of New York and Trust Company, 1784 to 1934*, New York, 1934, p. 4; Bank of the Manhattan Company—*Bank of the Manhattan Company, Chartered in 1799, a Progressive Commercial Bank*, New York, after 1910, pp. 8-10; *An Historical Sketch of the Bank of the Manhattan Company*, New York, after 1920, p. 9; *A Collection of More Than Four Hundred Autographs of Leading Citizens of New York . . . Original Subscribers to the Capital Stock of the Manhattan Company . . . New York, 1919*, p. 13 and numbers 107, 108, 114.

P. 40b: 1788 parade, Philadelphia—Wolf and Whiteman, work cited, p. 150; New York parade—*New York Packet*, August 5, 1788; correspondence with Washington—the complete texts of the entire correspondence are in Schappes, *Doc. Hist.*, Doc. No. 50 and notes thereto.

P. 42a: Constitution and its limitations—Herbert Aptheker, "The Constitution," *Looking Forward*, New York, 1954, pp. 20ff.

P. 42b: *Sefer Haberith*—cited in Jacob S. Raisin, *Centennial Booklet Commemorating the Introduction of Reform Judaism in America at K. K. Beth Elohim of Charleston, So. Ca. Organized 1750*, Charleston, 1925, p. 25, but he gives the wrong place of publication; the copy at the New York Public Library reveals the work appeared in Brünn (Moravia) in 1797 and in Prague in 1799; Nones frees his slave—Wolf and Whiteman, work cited, p. 191; Philadelphia Tammany Society—Wolf and Whiteman, p. 206.

P. 43a: Beth Elohim consecration—Reznikoff, work cited, p. 56.

P. 44a: Jonas Phillips fined—John Samuel, "Some Cases in Pennsylvania Wherein Rights Claimed by Jews Are Affected," *AJHSP*, vol. 5, p. 35; Philadelphia Sunday Law—Wolf and Whiteman, work cited, p. 234.

P. 44b: boxing-match—Wolf and Whiteman, p. 187; Palestinian messenger—Wolf and Whiteman, p. 138; French Jews—Wolf and Whiteman, p. 188; Jewish stereotype in plays—Edward D. Coleman, "Plays of Jewish Interest on the American Stage, 1752-1821," *AJHSP*, vol. 33, pp. 178, 180, 182.

P. 45a: Mrs. [Susanna Haswell] Rowson, *Slaves in Algiers, or, A Struggle for Freedom*, Philadelphia, 1794, pp. i, 11, 13, 15-16, 17, 18, 70-71; R. W. G. Vail, *Susanna Haswell Rowson, The Author of Charlotte Temple*, Worcester, Mass., 1933, pp. 25, 32; *The Cambridge History of American Literature*, New York, 1917, 1944 ed., vol. 1, p. 226; Cumberland's play—the New York edition of 1795 omits the sub-title, "Benevolent Hebrew;" see also Louis I. Newman, *Richard Cumberland, Critic and Friend of the Jews*, New York, 1919.

P. 45b: anti-Semitism in 1790's—Schappes, "Anti-Semitism and Reaction, 1795-1800," *AJHSP*, vol. 38, pp. 115ff.

P. 48a: anti-Semitism against non-Jews—Wolf and Whiteman, work cited, p. 208; Duane and "Jew-Aine"—James Morton Smith, *Freedom's Fetters*, Ithaca, N. Y., 1956, p. 301; Nones' handbill—Wolf and Whiteman, work cited, p. 210; the text is in Schappes, *Doc. Hist.*, Doc. No. 54.

CHAPTER 5

Unless otherwise indicated, sources for this chapter will be found in Schappes, *Doc. Hist.*, pp. 103-80, 593-610 and in Schappes, "The Jews and American Slavery," *Jewish Life*, May, 1954, pp. 15-19.

P. 49b: Reuben Etting's appointment—Dr. Joel Blau informed me on December 22, 1956 that in his forthcoming documentary history of the Jews from 1789 to 1840 he will show that Etting was originally appointed a Federal Marshal in 1791 by George Washington; Jefferson's was thus a reappointment in 1801; appointments of Solomon B. Nones and Benjamin Nones—Wolf and Whiteman, work cited, pp. 291, 216; Solomon Jacobs—Herbert T. Ezekiel and Gaston Lichtenstein, *The History of the Jews of Richmond from 1769 to 1917*, Richmond, 1917, p. 85; Charleston Jewish officials—Reznikoff, work cited, pp. 285-86.

P. 50a: Henry Solomon and Philadelphia health officer—Wolf and Whiteman, work cited, pp. 293, 296, 275; Naphtali Judah—Gustavus Myers, *The History of Tammany Hall*, New York, 1917, p. 51.

P. 52a: Joshua Canter and John Canter—Reznikoff, work cited, pp. 69, 88; George C. Groce and David H. Wallace, *The New-York Historical Society Dictionary of Artists in America, 1564-1860*, New Haven, Conn., 1957, pp. 107-08.

P. 52b: J. N. Cardozo—Joseph Dorfman, *The Economic Mind in American Civilization*, New York, 1949, vol. 3, pp. 79-80; Alexander Brody, "Jacob Newton Cardozo, American Economist," *Historia Judaica*, vol. 15, 1953, p. 166, concluded that "with the disappearance of the issues of which he was exponent, Cardozo was forgotten and the influence of his work proved to be merely ephemeral."

P. 53a: M. M. Noah—as a Jacksonian editor, he nevertheless attacked the Workingmen's Party in 1829, Gustavus Myers, work cited, p. 80; on Noah as playwright, see Lee M. Friedman, *Pilgrims in a New Land*, Philadelphia, 1948, pp. 221-32; about Shylock—Isaac Gomez, Jr., *Selections of a Father for the Use of His Children*, New York, 1820, pp. 326ff; *A Selection from the Miscellaneous Writings of the Late Isaac Harby*, Charleston, 1829, pp. 262-67.

P. 53b: *The Jew of Malta*—*AJHSP*, vol. 33, pp. 196-97.

P. 54b: Abraham A. Massias and Myer Moses—Reznikoff, work cited, p. 104.

P. 55a: Isaac De Young and Philadelphia Jews—Wolf and Whiteman, work cited, pp. 287-89, 292.

P. 55b: at Fort McHenry—Anita L. Lebeson, *Pilgrim People*, New York, 1950, p. 176; Aaron Baroway, "Solomon Etting: 1764-1847," *Maryland Historical Magazine*, vol. 15, 1920, p. 11; Baroway, "The Cohens of Maryland," work cited, vol. 18, 1923, pp. 370-71; Grace Nathan—David de Sola Pool, *Portraits Etched in Stone, Early Jewish Settlers, 1682-1831*, New York, 1952, p. 439.

P. 57b: Philadelphia Benevolent Society—Wolf and Whiteman, work cited, pp. 276-78; New York society—Grinstein, work cited, p. 145; Charleston society—Reznikoff, work cited, pp. 154-55.

P. 59b: Harby quoted—Isaac Harby, *North American Review*, July, 1826, p. 74.

P. 60: I am indebted to Mrs. Louis E. Stern of Westbury, N. Y. for information that clarifies a reference in this letter: the book Rebecca Gratz is discussing is Maria Edgeworth's *Harrington, A Tale*, published in 1817; the name in line six of the manuscript above is Montenero (not Montevaia, as I had read it in my *Doc. Hist.*, p. 138).

P. 62a: Philadelhia Ashkenazim—Wolf and Whiteman, work cited, pp. 225-27.

P. 62a: George Houston as author—the copy in the New York Public Library is marked by I. A. Phillips, 1821 on the title-page; under "By An Israelite" is written, "no Israelite but George Houston." For other literature on early conversion attempts, see A. S. W. Rosenbach, "An American Jewish Bibliography," *AJHSP*, vol. 30 and American Jewish Archives, *Jewish Americana*.

P. 62b: M. M. Noah, *Discourse at the Congregation . . . Shearith Israel*, New York, 1818, pp. 22-23.

P. 63a: on Noah and Charles King—Isaac Goldberg, *Major Noah, American-Jewish Pioneer*, Philadelphia, 1938, pp. 159, 249; "An American Jew's" letter is in the Lyons Scrapbook, No. 1, item 136b, at the American Jewish Historical Society.

P. 63b: Jefferson to Noah—photostat of letter in Lee M. Friedman, *Pioneers and Patriots*, New York, 1943, p. 36; Nathan Nathan's letter—exhibited at the Philadelphia Public Library Tercentenary Exhibition, February 1955, loaned by Dr. S. Weir Newmayer.

CHAPTER 6

Unless otherwise indicated, sources for this chapter will be found in Schappes, *Doc. Hist.*, pp. 181-293, 610-43.

P. 64b: Irish immigration—*EAH*, p. 448; German immigration—Adolf Kober, "Jewish Emigration from Württemberg to the United States of America (1848-1855)," *AJHSP*, 1952, p. 237.

P. 65a: Tyler's message—James D. Richardson, *A Compilation of the Messages and Papers of the Presidents, 1789-1897,* Washington, D. C., 1897, vol. 4, p. 77; transportation—Harold U. Faulkner, *American Economic History,* 5th ed., New York, 1943, p, 282.

P. 65b: East and Central European emigration—Leo Goldhammer, "Jewish Emigration from Austria-Hungary," *YIVO Annual of Social Science,* vol. 9, pp. 359, 361; crossing the Atlantic—Rudolf Glanz, "Source Material on the History of Jewish Immigration to the United States, 1800-1880," *YIVO Annual,* vol. 6, pp. 148, 150; Jacob R. Marcus, *Memoirs of American Jews,* Philadelphia, 1955, vol. 1, pp. 305, 312, 345, vol. 2, p. 155.

P. 66a: "special Jewish pressure"—Glanz, work cited, p. 91; Jewish emigration from Germany—Glanz, "Idn in Amerika far der Massen-Einvanderung," *Gedank un Lebn,* New York, vol. 4, 1946, p. 99; Kober, work cited, pp. 244-45; Russian emigration—S. M. Dubnow, *History of the Jews in Russia and Poland,* Philadelphia, 1916-20, vol. 2, pp. 109, 62-64.

P. 66b: New York Jewish population—Grinstein, work cited, p. 469; in other cities—Bertram W. Korn, *Eventful Years and Experiences,* Cincinnati, 1954, p. 28.

P. 67a: 1850 Census data—Kober, work cited, pp. 230-31; *New-York Daily Tribune,* December 8, 1852, p. 6, col. 3; Jews moving westward—Stuart E. Rosenberg, *The Jewish Community in Rochester, 1843-1925,* New York, 1954, p. 21; Korn, *Eventful Years,* p. 56.

P. 67b: occupations of German Jews—Grinstein, work cited, p. 549; Joshua Trachtenberg, *Consider the Years,* Easton, Pa., 1944, p. 234.

P. 68a: economist on peddlers—Malcolm Keir, *Manufacturing,* New York, 1928, p. 160.

P. 68b: Jewish peddlers—Rudolf Glanz, "Notes on Early Jewish Peddling in America," *JSS,* vol. 7, 1945, p. 120; Fred Mitchell Jones, *Middlemen in the Domestic Trade of the United States, 1800-1860,* Urbana, Ill., 1937, p. 63; Panic of 1837—*EAH,* p. 178; Faulkner, work cited, p. 168; Philip S. Foner, *History of the Labor Movement in the United States,* New York, 1947, vol. 1, pp. 167-68; Jewish benevolence—Marcus, *Memoirs,* vol. 1, p. 368; Isidor Blum, *The Jews of Baltimore,* Baltimore-Washington, 1910, pp. 8-9; Bertram W. Korn, "A Reappraisal of Judah Touro," *Jewish Quarterly Review,* Philadelphia, 1955, p. 576.

P. 69b: mid-west Jewish state—*The Occident,* vol. 1, 1843, pp. 29-31.

P. 70a: New York congregations—Grinstein, work cited, pp. 472-73; Reform congregations—Korn, *Eventful Years,* p. 30; Reznikoff, work cited, p. 200.

P. 70b: Moshe Davis, "Jewish Religious Life and Institutions in America," in *The Jews,* ed. by Louis Finkelstein, Philadelphia, 1949, vol. 1, p. 364; sick-benefit society—Glanz, *YIVO Annual,* vol. 6, p. 141.

P. 71a: True Sisters—Grinstein, work cited, pp. 154, 554; B'nai Israel—same, p. 112; B'nai B'rith—*The Asmonean,* February 7, 14, 21, March 21, July 4, 1851; localism—Korn, *Eventful Years,* p. 30, speaks of a "barely discernible impulse towards national community consciousness"; see also his pp. 35-37.

P. 71b: Damascus case—Schappes, *Doc. Hist.,* contains the only available detailed chronology, with notes and documents: p. 72: for full text of Chasseaud's report, see *Doc. Hist.*

P. 74a: *Israels Herold*—the only known copy, formerly owned by Rabbi Stephen S. Wise, is now in the possession of Mrs. Justine Wise Polier and Mr. Shad Polier.

P. 77a: artists—Irving I. Katz, "Jews in Detroit Prior to and Including 1850," *Bulletin, Detroit Historical Society,* February, 1950; Reznikoff, work cited, p. 88; journalists—Cohn: Isaac Markens, *The Hebrews in America,* New York, 1888, p. 267; Jonas: Bernard Postal and Lionel Koppman, *A Jewish Tourist's Guide to the United States,* Philadelphia, 1954, p. 141; Kursheedt: Korn, *JQR,* 1955, p. 576n; Jonas B. Phillips—*Universal Jewish Encyclopedia,* vol. 8, p. 493; Penina Moise—*Secular and Religious Works of Penina Moise,* with Brief Sketch of Her Life. Compiled and Published by Charleston Section, Council of Jewish Women, Charleston, 1911, pp. 68, 212-13, 177, 1-5.

P. 77b: early Jewish Publication Society—Maurice Jacobs, "Sixty Years of The Jewish Publication Society of America," typescript, 1948; Korn, *Eventful Years,* p. 45; Rosenbach, work cited, Nos. 565, 566, 585, 586, 607, 609, 610, 611, 612, 633, 634, 668.

P. 78b: duel over "Shylock"—Lebeson, work cited, p. 226; *AJA,* vol. 7, 1955, pp. 73-81; anti-Semitism in *Volksfreund*—Glanz, *YIVO Annual,* vol. 6, p. 132; quotations from Leeser, *The Claims of the Jews to an Equality of Rights,* Philadelphia, 1841, pp. 5, 82. By 1840, five of the 26 states in the Union still had constitutional provisions discriminatory against Jews—Connecticut, New Hampshire, New Jersey, North Carolina and Rhode Island (Stanley F. Chyet, "The Political Rights of the Jews in the United States: 1776-1840," *AJA,* April, 1948, p. 67).

P. 79a: peddlers as "Shylocks"—Luke Shortfield (John Beauchamp Jones), *The Western Merchant,* Philadelphia, 1849, p. 184; Rosh Hashana in Baltimore—*The Asmonean,* vol. 2, September 27, 1850, p. 181.

P. 79b: I. M. Wise and Taylor—Marcus, *Memoirs,* vol. 2, pp. 117-18.

CHAPTER 7

Unless otherwise indicated, sources for this chapter will be found in Schappes, *Doc. Hist.*, pp. 37-38, 99-102, 118-21, 134, 293-301, 312-33, 349-508, 573-74, 593, 596-97, 599, 612, 643-44, 648-49, 656, 664-714, and in Schappes, "The Jews and American Slavery," *Jewish Life*, May, 1954, pp. 15-19, and "The Jews and the Civil War," June, 1954, pp. 22-26.

P. 81b: slave population—Faulkner, work cited, p. 327.

P. 82a: cotton—*EAH*, p. 479; industrial production —*EAH*, p. 495; German immigration—Kober, work cited, p. 237; Jews in New York—Grinstein, work cited, p. 469; immigrants in slave states—Maurice R. Davie, *World Immigration*, New York, 1949, p. 232; Faulkner, work cited, p. 325.

P. 82b: Faulkner, work cited, p. 302; "Know-Nothing"—Korn, *Eventful Years*, pp. 59-76; Schappes, *Doc-Hist.*; W. Darrell Overdyke, *The Know-Nothing Party in the South*, Louisiana State University, 1950, pp. 238, 278; Horace Montgomery, *Cracker Parties*, Baton Rouge, La., 1950, p. 153.

P. 83b: Einhorn's *Olath Tamid*—the sixth German edition appeared in New York about 1858; an English translation by Einhorn was published in New York in 1872; Kaufmann Kohler, ed., *David Einhorn Memorial Volume*, New York, 1911, p. 441; *Minhag America*—Isidor Kalisch, *Studies in Ancient and Modern Judaism*, New York, 1928, pp. 10-11; Isaac Mayer Wise, *Reminiscences*, 2d ed., New York, 1945, pp. 343-45.

P. 84a: *Abne Yehoshua*—Joshua Bloch, compiler, *The People and the Book*, New York, 1954, p. 99

P. 84b: Jewish publications—Albert M. Friedenberg, "American Jewish Journalism to the Close of the Civil War," *AJHSP*, vol. 26, pp. 270-73; Wise, work cited, pp. 268-69.

P. 85a: Mortara Case—Schappes, *Doc. Hist.*; Bertram W. Korn, *The American Reaction to The Mortara Case*, 1858-1859, Cincinnati, 1957.

P. 88b: Kate R. Pickard's *The Kidnapped and the Ransomed* was reprinted in New York, 1941.

P. 89a: Frémont's slogan—Allan Nevins, *Frémont, The West's Greatest Adventurer*, New York, 1928, vol. 2, p. 496.

P. 89b: Jews in Republican Party—Schappes, "Jews in Lincoln's Third Party," *Jewish Life*, October, 1948, pp. 13-16; Korn, *Eventful Years*, p. 12.

P. 91a: "The Jew's War Song"—*The Jewish Record*, vol. 1, no. 1, September 12, 1862, p. 4, col. 1.

P. 92a: Congressional Medals—*The Medal of Honor of the United States Army*, Washington, D. C. [1948], p. 468; Lew Wallace, et al., *The Story of American Heroism*, New York, 1896, pp. 385-86;

Simon Wolf, *The American Jew as Patriot, Soldier and Citizen*, Philadelphia, 1895, pp. 204-05; letter by Myer Samuel Levy—from the manuscript in the collection of Maxwell Whiteman, Philadelphia; Wolf, work cited, p. 361.

P. 94b: Col. Adolphus H. Adler—Korn, *Eventful Years*, p. 14.

P. 95a: Chaplaincy issue and Order No. 11—in addition to Schappes, *Doc. Hist.* see the detailed chapters in Korn, *American Jewry and the Civil War*, Philadelphia, 1951, pp. 56-97, 121-55; on weaknesses of Korn's book, see Schappes, *Jewish Life*, October, 1951, pp. 28-29 and Louis Ruchames, "The Abolitionists and the Jews," *AJHSP*, vol. 42, 1952, pp. 131-55.

CHAPTER 8

Unless otherwise indicated, sources for this chapter will be found in Schappes, *Doc. Hist.*, pp. 509-63, 714-36 and in Schappes, "Jews and the American Labor Movement, 1850-1880," *Jewish Life*, July, 1954, pp. 17-20.

P. 100a: Radical Reconstruction program—Herbert Aptheker, *A Documentary History of the Negro People in the United States*, New York, 1951, pp. 565-66. For *The Israelite's* contempt for Thaddeus Stevens, see issue of January 11, 1867, p. 6. The draft of the Reconstruction Act of 1866 discriminated against Jews by requiring a Christian oath from members of state Constitutional Conventions, but on the initiative of the Board of Delegates of American Israelites, the final bill omitted this clause—Max J. Kohler, "The Board of Delegates of American Israelites, 1859-1878," *AJHSP*, vol. 29, 1925, p. 105. In North Carolina, the Reconstruction Constitutional Convention in 1868 finally eliminated from the State Constitution the clause requiring all state officers to take an oath on the New Testament.

P. 100b: Memphis riot—Aptheker, work cited, p. 552; Morris Marks—*The Menorah*, October, 1893, p. 284, June, 1895, pp. 426-27, September, 1897, pp. 169-71; Lewis Abraham, "The Jewish-American as Politician," *The American Jews' Annual, 1888*, p. 107; Charles S. Kuh—Guido Kisch, *In Search of Freedom, A History of American Jews from Czechoslovakia*, London, 1949, pp. 126-27; *The Jewish Messenger*, October 27, 1871, p. 6; *Beaufort Republican*, December 21, 1871.

P. 101a: Isaac W. Hirsch and Edwin W. Moise—Reznikoff, work cited, pp. 161-62; Southern historian—E. Merton Coulter, *The South During Reconstruction, 1865-1877*, Louisiana State University Press, 1947, pp. 202-03; see also review of Coulter, *The Confederate States of America*, 1950, by Herbert Aptheker, *History and Reality*, New York, 1955, pp. 107-08, for quotations of other anti-Semitic comments by Coulter. For contemporary observations on Jews in the South, see *The Nation,* vol. 1, July 20, 1865, pp. 76-77; Frances Butler Leigh, *Ten Years on a Georgia Plantation,* London, 1883, p. 302.

P. 102a: statistics on steel, coal, railroads—*Historical Statistics of the United States, 1789-1945,* Washington, D. C., 1949, pp. 187, 142, 200; *EAH,* p. 496, 430, 432.

P. 102b: railroad subsidies—Richard O. Boyer and Herbert M. Morais, *Labor's Untold Story,* New York, 1955, pp. 22, 34, 38; *EAH,* p. 433; Fred A. Shannon, *The Farmer's Last Frontier,* New York, 1945, pp. 64-66; Harry J. Carman and Harold C. Syrett, *A History of the American People,* New York, 1952, vol. 2, p. 92; statistics on manufacturing, population and immigration—*Hist. Stat.,* pp. 179, 64, 26, 25, 29, 34, 36, 30.

P. 103a: trade union figures—*EAH,* p. 521; Boyer and Morais, work cited, pp. 13, 36, 37; Irish miners (Molly Maguires) and railroad strike—Boyer and Morais, pp. 54-63, 12.

P. 104b: Jewish population figures—*AJHSP,* vol. 29, p. 114; Gustav Gottheil, letter in *New-York Tribune,* January 18, 1877, p. 5; Jacob R. Marcus, article in Irving I. Katz, *The Beth El Story,* Detroit, 1955, p. 158; Morris A. Gutstein, *A Priceless Heritage, The Epic Growth of Nineteenth Century Chicago Jewry,* New York, 1953, p. 269; Board of Delegates and Union of American Hebrew Congregations, *Statistics,* Philadelphia, 1880, pp. 9, 15; Rosenberg, work cited, p. 63; Davis, work cited, vol. 1, p. 381; Isaac Friedlander—Glanz, *YIVO Annual,* vol. 6, p. 151; Stettheimer and Bettman—Markens, work cited, p. 161.

P. 105a: Jewish bankers—*UJE,* vol. 4, p. 301; Anna Rochester, *Rulers of America,* New York, 1936, p. 75; Gustavus Myers, *History of Great American Fortunes,* New York, 1909, 1937 ed., pp. 559-60.

P. 106b: clothing production—Judith Greenfield, "The Role of Jews in the Development of the Clothing Industry in the United States," *YIVO Annual,* vol. 2-3, pp. 182-83, 187-88; *EAH,* p. 496; *Hist. Stat.,* p. 183.

P. 107a: Reform Judaism—Peter Wiernik, *History of the Jews in America,* New York, 1912; Samuel S. Cohon, "Reform Judaism in America," *Judaism,* New York, vol. 3, 1954, pp. 344, 346; Davis, work cited, vol. 1, p. 382.

P. 108a: Jewish hospitals—Davis, work cited, vol. 1, p. 375; Gutstein, work cited, pp. 36, 341; *UJE,* vol. 5, p. 470.

P. 108b: philanthropy—Gutstein, work cited, pp. 31, 36, 344; Gottheil, *New-York Tribune,* January 18, 1877, p. 5.

P. 109a: B'nai B'rith—*New-York Tribune.* January 31, 1879; Free Sons of Israel and Kesher Shel Barzel

—Paul Masserman and Max Baker, *The Jews Come to America,* New York, 1932, p. 213; *The Journal of Commerce,* October 17, 1860, full text, Schappes, *Doc. Hist.;* social clubs—Gutstein, work cited, p. 48; Henry Samuel Morais, *The Jews of Philadelphia,* Philadelphia, 1894, p. 194; Jewish Y's—Benjamin Rabinowitz, "The Young Men's Hebrew Associations (1854-1913)," *AJHSP,* vol. 37, 1947, pp. 223-49.

P. 109b: Jewish periodicals—*Jewish Encyclopedia,* vol. 9, p. 625; Gutstein, work cited, p. 36. *The American Hebrew* in 1957 merged with the *Jewish Examiner* to become the *American Examiner;* German preaching—Katz, work cited, pp. 87, 84.

P. 110b: on Dr. A. Jacobi—Schappes, "Two Humanists: Doctors Jacobi," *Jewish Life,* September, 1952, pp. 22-25.

P. 112a: orthodox congregations—Davis, work cited, vol. 1, p. 380.

P. 112b: *landsmanshaften— Di Idishe Landsmanshaften fun New York,* New York, 1938, p. 70. An earlier example is the Netherland Israelitish Sick Fund Society, founded December 10, 1859 (work cited, p. 113) and Grinstein, work cited, pp. 162, 106, traces such societies back to 1826 to the Hebrew Mutual Benefit Society; Isaac Hart to Leeser—Katz, work cited, pp. 192-93.

P. 113a: Yiddish press—Kalman Marmor, *Der Onhoib fun der Idisher Literatur in America* (1870-1890), New York, 1944, pp. 6-11; Wiernik, work cited, pp. 258-59; *75 Yor Idishe Presse in America, 1870-1945,* New York, 1945, pp. 15-21; Philip Cowen, *Memories of An American Jew,* New York, 1932, p. 31.

P. 114b: Jacob Zebi Sobel—Marmor, work cited, pp. 12-14; in 1872 in Odessa, Sobel had published a poem in Hebrew, *Ahaba Hazionot.*

P. 116b: Seligman Affair—Friedman, *Jewish Pioneers,* pp. 267-78; Hugh Bradley, *Such Was Saratoga,* New York, 1940, pp. 187-88; Elizabeth Drexel Lehr, *"King Lehr" and the Gilded Age,* Philadelphia, 1935, p. 22; Higham, *AJHSP,* vol. 47, pp. 11-12.

P. 117b: anti-Semitism—Nina Morais, "Jewish Ostracism in America, *The North American Review,* September, 1881, pp. 265-75; Schappes, *Emma Lazarus, Selections from Her Prose and Poetry,* New York, 1944, rev. ed., 1947, pp. 68-73; Alice Hyneman Rhine, "Race Prejudice at Summer Resorts," *The Forum,* New York, July, 1887, pp. 523-31.

CHAPTER 9

Unless otherwise indicated, sources for this chapter will be found in Schappes, "Jewish Mass Immigration from Eastern Europe, 1881-1914," *Jewish Life,* November, 1954, pp. 18-22 (reprinted in

"*Jewish Life*" *Anthology, 1946-1956*, New York, 1956, pp. 33-42); "The 1880's—Beginnings of Jewish Trade Unionism," *Jewish Life*, September, 1954, pp. 21-24; "The Nineties—Ups and Downs of Jewish Trade Unionism," *Jewish Life*, October, 1954, pp. 17-20.

P. 118a: Jews in New York—*New York Evening Post*, January 20, 1895, p. 8; Ida M. Van Etten in *The Forum*, April, 1893, p. 173.

P. 121a: statistics on steel, coal, etc.—*Hist. Stat.*, pp. 187, 142, 200, 202, 179, 183.

P. 121b: Cleveland and the iron heel—Boyer and Morais, work cited, p. 65.

P. 124a: anti-alienism, anti-Semitism—John Higham, *Strangers in the Land, Patterns of American Nativism, 1860-1925*, New Brunswick, N. J., 1955, pp. 91, 99-100; Higham, "Anti-Semitism in the Gilded Age: A Reinterpretation," *Miss. Valley Hist. Rev.*, vol. 43, 1957, pp. 568, 572, 574-75, 577; Rudolf Glanz, "The Rothschild Legend in America," *JSS*, vol. 19, 1957, pp. 3-28.

P. 124b: AP dispatch—*The Jewish Voice*, St. Louis, August 14, 1896, p. 4; September 25, 1896, p. 4.

P. 125b: agricultural colonies—Gabriel Davidson, *Our Jewish Farmers*, New York, 1943, pp. 195-96; Zunser's song—Sol Liptzin, *Eliakum Zunser, Poet of His People*, New York, 1950, p. 222.

P. 126a: Baron de Hirsch Fund—Wiernik, work cited, p. 289; agricultural colonies—*New Yorker Volkszeitung*, October 23, 1888, p. 1.

P. 127a: Rabbi Jacob Joseph—Abraham J. Karp, "New York Chooses a Chief Rabbi," *AJHSP*, vol. 44, 1955, pp. 129ff; Orthodox education—Leo L. Honor, "The Impact of the American Environment and American Ideas on Jewish Elementary Education in the United States," *JQR*, vol. 45, 1955, p. 473; Davis, work cited, vol. 1, p. 390, 388, 392; free loan societies —Gutstein, work cited, p. 352; *landsmanshaften*— Landsmanshaften, work cited, p. 28.

P. 128b: Jewish Workingmen's Union—Schappes, ed., "Appeal of Jewish Workingmen's Union, 1885," *Jewish Life*, April, 1952, pp. 12-13.

P. 129a: London influence—Herz Burgin, *Di Geschichte fun der Idisher Arbeiter Bavegung in America, Rusland un England*, New York, 1915, pp. 46, 52, 54.

P. 130b: social justice—Eric F. Goldman, *Rendezvous With Destiny, A History of Modern American Reform*, New York, rev. ed., 1956, pp. 84-85; Leonard J. Mervis, "The Social Justice Movement and the American Reform Rabbi," *AJA*, vol. 7, 1955, p. 198, 221; Bernard Martin, "The Social Philosophy of Emil G. Hirsch," *AJA*, vol. 6, 1954, p. 156.

P. 131a: 1890 strike—Schappes, ed., "Jewish Workers' Victory—1890," *Jewish Life*, April, 1953 pp. 15-16.

P. 131b: DeLeon Jewish—DeLeon reported he was born December 14, 1852 in Curaçao, British West Indies (*Daily People*, March 19, 1906). His parents were Jews, Salomon and Sarah (Jesurun) DeLeon, now buried in the cemetery of the Liberal Congregation of Curaçao (*Dictionary of American Biography*, vol. 5, p. 222; Letter to this writer, August 23, 1957 by Dr. I. S. Emmanuel of Curaçao, author of *Precious Stones of the Jews of Curaçao*). On February 14, 1879, in *The Reformer and Jewish Times*, New York, Daniel DeLeon had a long communication, "Should the Jews Celebrate Christmas?" (reference supplied by Dr. Jacob R. Marcus, AJA). Later DeLeon began to deny his Jewish parentage or to equivocate about it (*DAB*; DeLeon's second wife denied he was Jewish, according to a letter to this writer, July 26, 1957, by Arnold Petersen, national secretary of the Socialist Labor Party; Joseph Schlossberg, a Socialist Labor Party associate of DeLeon's, reported in *Der Tog*, New York, December 29, 1952, that DeLeon told him he was not aware that there were any Jews among his ancestors).

P. 132b: National Council of Jewish Women—Mildred G. Welt, *AJYB*, vol. 46, 1944-45, p. 65; Gutstein, work cited, pp. 308-09; Educational Alliance— S. P. Rudens, *AJYB*, vol. 46, p. 76. The base for the Council was the Jewish middle class: in 1890, a Census survey of 10,000 families showed almost 4,000 had one servant, 2,000 had two and 1,000 had three or more (John S. Billings, *Vital Statistics of Jews in the United States, Census Bulletin, December, 1890*, Washington, D. C.)

P. 133a: Zionist beginnings—Isidore S. Meyer, ed., *Early History of Zionism in America*, New York, 1958, articles by Shlomo Noble, "Pre-Herzlian Zionism in America as Reflected in the Yiddish Press," Anita Libman Lebeson, "Zionism Comes to Chicago," Maxwell Whiteman, "Zionism Comes to Philadelphia," Herbert Parzen, "The Federation of American Zionists (1897-1914)."

P. 133b: 1897 resolution, C.C.A.R.—Namoi Wiener Cohen, "The Reaction of Reform Judaism in America to Political Zionism (1897-1922)," *AJHSP*, vol. 40, 1951, p. 365; 1899 resolution, U.A.H.S.—Max Raisin, *A History of the Jews in Modern Times*, New York, 1937, 5th ed., pp. 331-32; B'nai B'rith positions—*The Menorah*, September, 1897, p. 136.

P. 134a: socialist attitude—*Die Arbeiter Zeitung*, August 1, 1890, translated in *Jewish Life*, April, 1953, p. 16; Spanish-American War—Schappes, "Jewish Labor in the Nineties," *Jewish Life*, June, 1950, pp. 14-16.

P. 134b: Haymarket—Schappes, "Haymarket and the Jews," *Jewish Life*, November, 1956, pp. 25ff;

Ernest Bloomfield Zeisler, *The Haymarket Riot*, Chicago, 1956.

P. 136a: Emma Lazarus—Schappes, *Emma Lazarus, Selections from Her Poetry and Prose*, rev. ed., New York, 1947; Schappes, *The Letters of Emma Lazarus, 1868-1885*, New York, 1949; Eve Merriam, *Emma Lazarus, Woman with a Torch*, New York, 1956.

P. 136b: Morris Rosenfeld—Aaron Kramer, tr., *The Teardrop Millionaire and Other Poems by Morris Rosenfeld*, New York, 1955.

P. 137a: David Edelstadt—Max Rosenfeld translation in *Jewish Life*, November, 1954, p. 12.

P. 137b: Edelstadt's "In Kamf"—*Jewish Life*, July, 1950, p. 13; Bovshover—Marmor, *Der Onhoib . . .*, pp. 94ff; *Jewish Life*, December, 1950, p. 24; Jacob Schaefer, *"Ich Her a Kol," 22 Selected Songs of*, New York, 1952, pp. 95-106.

P. 138a: Winchevsky—Nathaniel Buchwald in *The Cambridge History of American Literature*, New York, 1918, vol. 3, p. 603; *Jewish Life*, March, 1952, p. 18.

P. 138b: Libin, Kobrin—Buchwald, work cited, vol. 3, pp. 604-06; Jacob Mestel, *70 Yor Teater Repertuar*, New York, 1954, p. 18.

P. 140a: Yiddish theater—on Goldfaden: Jacob Mestel, *Unzer Teater*, New York, 1943, see index; on others. Mestel, *70 Yor*, pp. 23, 25 and index; Buchwald, work cited, pp. 607-09.

P. 141b: Cyrus Adler—Abraham A. Neuman, *Cyrus Adler, A Biographical Sketch*, Philadelphia, 1942, pp. 24-25.

P. 142a: Oscar Straus, *Under Four Administrations*, Boston and New York, 1922, p. 46; Samuel Rosenberg—Benjamin Band, *Portland Jewry, Its Growth and Development*, Portland, Me., pp. 17, 8.

P. 142b: Fanny Bloomfield Zeisler—manuscript biography by Sigmund Zeisler (courtesy of Dr. Ernest Bloomfield Zeisler, Chicago); Robinson Locke, *Collection of Dramatic Scrap Books*, New York Public Library; Jewish Publication Society—Joshua Bloch, *Of Making Many Books, An Annotated List of the Books Issued by the Jewish Publication Society of America, 1890-1952*, Philadelphia,, 1953, pp. 37-64.

CHAPTER 10

P. 144b: Russian agriculture—Bernard D. Weinryb, "East European Immigration to the United States," *JQR*, vol. 45, 1955, p. 516.

P. 145a: pogroms—Cyrus Adler, ed., *The Voice of America on Kishineff*, Philadelphia, 1904; Cowen, work cited, pp. 210-26.

P. 145b: Jewish workers protest—*The New York Times*, October 8, 1905, p. 16; *Jewish Daily Forward*, October 1, 8, 1905, p. 1; December march—*The New York Times*, December 5, 1905; p. 6; *Jewish Daily Forward*, November 6, 7, 30, December 5, 1905; *The American Hebrew*, December 8, 1905, pp. 62, 73-74; December 16, 1905, p. 136.

P. 146a: Straus appointed—Oscar Straus, work cited, p. 210; Thomas A. Bailey, *A Diplomatic History of the American People*, New York, 1944, 2d edition, p. 560.

P. 146b: Jewish poverty—Robert Hunter, *Poverty*, New York 1904, p. 279; Pujo report—Henry Steele Commager, *Documents of American History*, New York, 1949, 5th ed., vol. 2, p. 259; Kuhn, Loeb—W. J. Shults and M. R. Caine, *Financial Development of the United States*, New York, 1937, pp. 438, 443, 459, 462; Samuel Armstrong Nelson, "The Jews of Wall Street," *Leslie's Monthly Magazine*, vol. 60, 1905, pp. 148-49.

P. 147a: Wilson quoted—Richard D. Heffner, ed., *A Documentary History of the United States*, New York, 1952, pp. 218-22; Charles A. and Mary R. Beard, *A Basic History of the United States*, New York, 1944, p. 390.

P. 147b: economic conditions, labor problems—*EAH*, pp. 508, 510; Boyer and Morais, work cited, pp. 139-40, 159, 152, 190-91.

P. 148b: attacks on Negroes and N.A.A.C.P.—Aptheker, *Doc. Hist.*, pp. 800-03, 862, 915, 925; Florence Murray, ed., *The Negro Handbook*, New York, 1949, p. 99; Robert L. Jack, *History of the NAACP*, Boston, 1943, pp. 4-5.

P. 149b: Rabbi Jacob Joseph—Karp, *APHSP*, vol. 44, pp. 180-82; *The New York Times*, July 31, 1902, p. 1; Leo Frank Case—Charles and Louise Samuels, *Night Fell on Georgia*, New York, 1956.

P. 150a: Beilis Case—Alexander B. Tager, *The Decay of Czarism, The Beilis Trial*, Philadelphia, 1935, pp. 75, 122, 216.

P. 151a: "Progressive Era"—Boyer and Morais, work cited, p. 180; the Beards, work cited, pp. 383-85; Socialist Party—David A. Shannon, *The Socialist Party of America, A History*, New York, 1955, p. 78; Nathan Fine, *Labor and Farmer Parties in the United States, 1828-1928*, New York, 1928, pp. 214, 220-21, 225.

P. 151b: "muckrakers"—Rudolf Glanz, "Jewish Social Conditions as Seen by the Muckrakers," *YIVO Annual*, vol. 9, 1954, pp. 308ff.

P. 152a: J. H. Hollander and Republicans—Robert H. Bremner, *From the Depths, the Discovery of Poverty in the United States*, New York, 1956, p. 125; I. K. Friedman—Walter B. Rideout, *The Radical Novel in the United States, 1900-1944*, Cambridge, Mass., 1956, pp. 13, 18.

P. 153a: rabbis and social justice—Mervis, work cited, *AJA*, vol. 7, pp. 196, 176-77.

P. 153b: "progressivism"—Goldman, work cited, p. 144; Richard Hofstadter, *The American Political Tradition*, New York, 1955 ed., p. 225; Steffens quoted by Charles A. Madison, *Critics and Crusaders*, New York, 1947, p. 406.

P. 154a: Brandeis—Arthur S. Link, *Woodrow Wilson and the Progressive Era, 1910-1917*, New York, 1954, pp. 20, 22, 24; Laurence H. Fuchs, *The Political Behavior of American Jews*, Glencoe, Ill., p. 58; Louis D. Brandeis, *Other People's Money and How the Bankers Use It*, New York, 1914, p. 4.

Pp. 155-58: Schappes, "The New Century Opens—Jewish Labor Movement Grows," *Jewish Life*, December, 1954, pp. 19-22.

P. 158b: Jewish socialists—Herz Burgin, "Kurze Geschichte fun der Idisher Arbeiter Bavegung in die Fareynikte Shtaten," *Almanach . . . 10 Yoriger Yubilai, International Workers' Order*, New York, 1940, pp. 248-49; Burgin, 1914, work cited, pp. 683-86.

P. 159a: labor Zionism—*AJYB*, 1916-17, pp. 242-43; 1915-16, p. 307.

Pp. 160-65: Schappes, "The Heroic Period of Jewish Labor, 1909-1914," *Jewish Life*, January, 1955, pp. 20-24; Triangle Fire—Max D. Danish and Leon Stein, *ILGWU News-History, 1900-1950*, New York, 1950, Ch. 4, pp. 5-9; Nachman Meisel, "Der Triangl Feier in licht fun der Idisher Literatur," *Idishe Kultur*, September-November, 1948.

P. 165b: Jewish organization—*AJYB*, 1900-01, pp. 505-06, 623-24; 1915-16, pp. 286ff.

P. 166a: New York Kehilla—Norman Bentwich, *For Zion's Sake, a Biography of Judah L. Magnes*, Philadelphia, 1954, pp. 77-82; *AJYB*, 1917-18, pp. 484-86.

P. 166b: Jewish press—*AJYB*, 1900-01, pp. 636-37; 1914-15, p. 328; Mordecai Soltes, *The Yiddish Press, an Americanizing Agency*, New York, 1925, pp. 186-87, 182-83; Jewish education—Leo L. Honor, Jewish Elementary Education in the United States," *AJHSP*, vol. 42, 1952, pp. 26-28.

P. 167a: secular education—I. Goldberg, "Di Orden-Shulen." *IWO Almanach, 1940*, pp. 69-70; H. Lieberman, *Di Idishe Religion un der Nazional-Radikaler Erziung*, New York, 1915, p. 32; C. Bezalel Sherman, "Nationalism, Secularism and Religion in the Jewish Labor Movement," *Judaism*, vol. 3, 1954, pp. 359, 363; J. Kaminsky, *Forty Years Workmen's Circle, a History in Pictures*, New York, 1940, p. 19.

P. 168a: Yiddish theater—Mestel, *70 Yor . . .* , pp. 16-17, 18-22, and passim; Nathan Ausubel, "The Story of Yiddish," *Morgen Freiheit*, September 18, 22, 1947.

P. 168b: Yehoash—Buchwald, *Camb. Hist. Am. Lit.*, vol. 3, p. 603.

P. 169a: The Young—A. A. Roback, *The Story of Yiddish Literature*, New York, 1940, pp. 262-66; Buchwald, work cited, pp. 604-06; Joseph Opatoshu, *YIVO Annual*, vol. 9, pp. 77-80; Moissaye J. Olgin, *Der Hamer*, November, 1930.

P. 170b: Hebrew culture—Jacob Kabakoff, "Hebrew Culture and Creativity in America," *Judaism*, vol. 3, 1954, p. 402-03; Eisig Silberschlag, "Hebrew Literature in America: Record and Interpretation," *JQR*, vol. 45, 1955, pp. 418, 422.

P. 171a: Conservative Judaism—Ben Zion Bokser, "Conservative Judaism," *JQR*, vol. 45, 1955, p. 340; *The United Synagogue of America, Report*, 1913, p. 18.

P. 171b: Who's Who—J. L., "The Distribution of Jewish Talent," *The American Hebrew*, October 13, 1905, p. 546; anti-Semitic restrictions—some colleges began to restrict admission of Jews, and social discrimination led to the birth of Jewish fraternities—Higham, *AJHSP*, vol. 47, pp. 16-17. By 1908, 8.5 per cent of male students in 77 colleges were Jewish.

P. 172a: Epstein quoted—Oliver W. Larkin, *Art and Life in America*, New York, 1949, p. 330; *Epstein, An Autobiography*, London, 1955, p. 8; on Stieglitz and Weber—Larkin, pp. 326-27, 359; on Armory Show—Larkin, pp. 362-64; *Catalogue of International Exhibition of Modern Art*, New York, 1913, passim.

P. 173a: Jews in office—*AJYB*, 1915-16, p. 342; 1900-01, p. 506; Maxwell N. Whiteman, *AJA*, vol. 9, 1957, p. 60; *Who's Who in America*, 1916-17, p. 2214; *AJA*, vol. 9, p. 71.

CHAPTER 11

Unless otherwise indicated, sources for this chapter will be found in Schappes, "World War I and the Jewish Masses (1914-1917)," *Jewish Life*, February, 1955, pp. 16-19, "The Attitude of Jewish Labor to World War I, 1917-1918," *Jewish Life*, March, 1955, pp. 21-24 and "The Jews and the Post-War Reaction After 1918," *Jewish Life*, April, 1955, pp. 23-26.

P. 175b: relief committees—*AJYB*, 1917-18, pp. 200-01.

P. 176a: JDC—*AJYB*, 1919-20, p. 196; ILGWU—*AJYB*, 1918-19, p. 159; furriers—*AJYB*, 1919-20, p. 194.

P. 177b: Wilson and Jews—Fuchs, work cited, p. 57.

P. 178b: peace sentiment—Link, work cited, p. 275, 279; Norris quoted—Ray Ginger, *The Bending Cross, a Biography of Eugene Victor Debs*, New Brunswick, N. J., 1949, p. 340.

P. 179a: Meyer London—Harry Rogoff, *An East Side Epic, The Life and Work of Meyer London,* New York, 1930, pp. 84, 96-97, 128; Julius Kahn—*AJYB,* 1925-26, p. 239.

P. 179b: foreign-born in army—Robert M. Yerkes, ed., *Psychological Examining in the United States Army,* Washington, D. C., 1921, p. 693; Jewish Welfare Board—*AJYB,* 1918-19, p. 92.

P. 180b: Wilson on April 1—Link, work cited, p. 277; the Beards quoted—*The Rise of American Civilization,* vol. 2, p. 643; publications banned—Ginger, work cited, p. 344; IWW—*Bill Haywood's Book,* New York, 1929, pp. 324, 367-68.

P. 183a: socialist vote—"In 15 selected Northeastern cities the Socialists had polled 21.6 per cent of the total municipal vote," Shannon, work cited, p. 105.

P. 184b: pogroms—*AJYB,* 1920-21, pp. 282-83, 136, 134, 266; 1919-20, pp. 190, 192; Philip Friedman, "Political and Social Movements and Organizations," *The Jewish People,* vol. 4, p. 168; Lawton Kessler, *YIVO Annual,* vol. 2-3, p. 223; American Jewish Congress—Bernard G. Richards, *Organizing American Jewry,* New York, 1947, p. 23; Lawton Kessler, Aaron Alperin, Jack J. Diamond, *YIVO Annual,* vol. 2-3, pp. 231-35.

P. 185a: Paris Peace Conference—Dr. Joseph Tenenbaum, in a paper read at the Annual Conference of YIVO, January 20, 1958, saw the historic significance of the Paris Conference in that the Jewish people for the first time appeared in international affairs as a publicly organized force based on the East European Jewish mass movements, that American Jewish representatives virtually took over the leadership of European Jewry and that Jews and other groups won minority rights defined in international law, with Yiddish recognized as a language by an international body.

P. 187b: *Protocols of Zion—AJYB,* 1921-22, pp. 367ff; 1922-23, p. 343.

P. 190b: strike of 1921—*AJYB,* 1922-23, p. 34.

P. 194a: Workmen's Circle conflicts—*Workmen's Circle Convention Bulletin,* No. 6, May 7, 1921 (in Yiddish), p. 2; *W. C. Convention Bulletin,* No. 6, May 10, 1922, p. 17; Maximilian Hurwitz, *The Workmen's Circle,* New York, 1936, p. 61; J. S. Hertz, *50 Yor Arbeter-Ring in Idishn Lebn,* New York, 1950, pp. 208-09, 210-24; Rubin Saltzman, *Zu der Geschichte fun der Fraternaler Bavegung,* New York, 1936, pp. 25-53, 274-81, and "First Struggles for Proletarian Order," *Five Years of International Workers Order, 1930-1935,* New York, 1935, pp. 14-22; *W. C. Convention Bulletin,* No. 7, May 7, 1927, pp. 23-24; Bernard D. Weinryb, "The Adaptation of Jewish Labor Groups to American Life," *JSS,* vol. 8, 1946, p. 233.

P. 194b: Zionist membership—Rufus Learsi, *Fulfillment: The Epic Story of Zionism,* Cleveland and New York, 1951, p. 183; *AJYB,* 1921-22, p. 214; Zionism and Reform—Naomi W. Cohen, *AJHSP,* vol. 40, 1951, pp. 382, 389-90, 394.

P. 195a: American Jewish Committee—*AJYB,* 1918-19, pp. 406-07; Passfield White Paper—Chaim Weizmann, *Trial and Error,* New York, 1940, pp. 331-35.

P. 195b: labor attitude—*AJYB,* 1918-19, pp. 156-57, 310; 1919-20, p. 184; Philip Friedman, work cited, pp. 172-73; Joseph Rappaport, *JSS,* vol. 18, 1956, p. 155; *American Labor Year Book,* 1925, p. 145.

P. 196a: Pittsburgh Program—Jacob De Haas, *Louis D. Brandeis, A Biographical Sketch,* New York, 1929, pp. 96-97; Frank E. Manuel, *The Realities of American-Palestine Relations,* Washington, D. C., 1949, p. 206.

P. 196b: defeat of Brandeis—Manuel, work cited, pp. 262-66; De Haas, work cited, pp. 139-45; Philip Friedman, work cited, p. 171.

P. 197a: *Keren Hayesod*—Learsi, work cited, p. 305.

P. 197b: Florida land boom—Harold U. Faulkner, *American Economic History,* 5th ed., New York, 1943, p. 609; Harry Simonhoff, *Under Strange Skies,* New York, 1953, pp. 278-87.

P. 198b: Jews in colleges and professions—*AJYB,* 1920-21, pp. 383-84, 387-89; Ruth Sapinsky, "The Jewish Girl at College," *The Menorah Journal,* 1916, pp. 294-95; Jacob A. Goldberg, "Jews in the Medical Profession—a National Survey," *JSS,* 1939, p. 329; *AJYB,* 1922-23, pp. 110-11.

P. 199a: Jewish population and organizations—Henry S. Linfield, *The Communal Organization of the Jews in the United States, 1927,* New York, 1930, p. 18, 20-21, 31, 45, 92, 94.

P. 199b: communal organization—Linfield, work cited, pp. 113, 115, 109, 58-59, 65-67.

P. 200b: education—Linfield, pp. 52-53, 57.

P. 201b: philanthropic—Linfield, pp. 102, 99; American Jewish Committee—Linfield, work cited, p. 120.

P. 202a: American Jewish Congress—Linfield, work cited, p. 118; federations—Linfield, work cited, p. 123.

P. 202b: Jewish press—Linfield, work cited, pp. 78, 83, 173-75; *AJYB,* 1928-29, pp. 237-41; Soltes, work cited, p. 185.

P. 203a: Yiddish-speaking—Fuchs, work cited, p. 62; *AJYB,* 1918-19, pp. 32, 42.

P. 204a: Yiddish literature—S. Niger, "New Trends in Post-War Yiddish Literature," *JSS,* 1939, pp. 338-39, 344.

P. 204b: English-Jewish press—Linfield, work cited, pp. 173-75.

P. 206: V. J. Jerome, "Moishe Leib Halpern, Rebel Poet," *Jewish Life*, March, 1955, pp. 15-18; N. B. Minkoff, *UJE*, vol. 7, pp. 129-32; Sol Liptzin, *Jewish Book Annual*, vol. 12, 1954, pp. 12-14.

P. 207a: Asch on Debs—*Zukunft*, July, 1920, pp. 401-02.

P. 208a: Yiddish theaters—Linfield, work cited, p. 131.

P. 208b: Yiddish art theaters—Jacob Mestel, *70 Yor Idisher Teater Repertuar*, New York, 1954, pp. 43-52; Nathaniel Buchwald, *Teater*, New York, 1943, p. 382; David Pinski—B. Rivkin, *Unzere Prozaiker*, New York, 1951, pp. 114-124; Mestel, work cited, p. 58.

P. 211a: proletarian literature—Alexander Pomerantz, *Proletpen*, Kiev, 1935, p. 3; Artef—*10 Yor Artef*, New York, 1937, pp. 12, 14, 19; English-Jewish poetry—Louis Untermeyer, "The Jewish Spirit in Modern American Poetry," *The Menorah Journal*, vol. 7, 1921, pp. 121-29.

P. 214a: Schappes, "Anatomy of 'David Levinsky,'" *Jewish Life*, August, 1954, pp. 22-24.

P. 215a: Joseph Mersand, *Traditions in American Literature*, New York, 1939, pp. 85-86.

P. 215b: Rev. Dr. Felix A. Levy, "Ludwig Lewisohn," *Jewish Book Annual*, vol. 14, 1956-57, pp. 46-56; Stephen Bloore, "The Jew in American Dramatic Literature, 1794-1830," *AJHSP*, vol. 40, 1951, pp. 356-58.

P. 218: Ben B. Seligman, "They Came to Hollywood—How Jews Built the Movie Industry," *Jewish Frontier*, July, 1943, pp. 20-28.

CHAPTER 12

Unless otherwise indicated, references for material on the 1930's will be found in Schappes, "The Thirties—and the Jewish Masses," *Jewish Life*, May, 1955, pp. 17-20.

P. 221b: Bonus March—Jack Douglas, *Veterans on the March*, New York, 1934.

P. 223a: strikes and union membership—*Labor Fact Book III*, New York, 1936, pp. 79-82; *Statistical Abstract of the United States, 1952*, Washington, D. C., p. 195.

P. 223b: white collar unions—Robert R. R. Brooks, *When Labor Organizes*, New Haven, 1937, p. 339; *Labor Fact Book, III*, pp. 115-18.

P. 224a: Lewis statement—Foster Rhea Dulles, work quoted, New York, 1949, p. 317; communists—William Z. Foster, *History of the Communist Party*

of the United States, New York, 1952, pp. 281, 307, 380, 312.

P. 225a: early anti-Nazi books—James Waterman Wise, *Swastika, The Nazi Terror*, New York, April, 1933; Pierre Van Paassen and James Waterman Wise, editors, *Nazism: An Assault on Civilization*, New York, 1934.

P. 225b: Wise quoted—*Challenging Years*, p. 251.

P. 226a: May 10 demonstrations—*The New York Times*, May 11, 1933; *New York Herald Tribune*, May 11, 1933; *Jewish Daily Forward*, May 10, 11, 1933; anti-Nazi boycott—Joseph Tenenbaum, "Anti-Nazi Boycott Movement in the United States," paper read at Annual Meeting, American Jewish Historical Society, February 13, 1955; *Challenging Years*, p. 261; *AJYB*, 1933, p. 54; 1934, p. 131; 1936, p. 191.

P. 226b: *Bremen* incident—*AJYB*, 1936, p.p. 178-79; other incidents—*AJYB*, 1936, pp. 182-85, 187-89; 1937, pp. 211-14.

P. 227a: Jewish Labor Committee—*AJYB*, 1934, p. 142; *Jewish Daily Forward*, February 25, 26, 1934; Melech Epstein, *Jewish Labor in U.S.A., 1914-1952*, New York, 1953, p. 258.

P. 227b: Jewish People's Committee—*Jewish Life*, November, 1938, p. 19; January, 1938, pp. 19-23.

P. 228a: Lincoln Battalion—Edwin Rolfe, *The Lincoln Battalion*, New York, 1939; Alvah Bessie, *Men in Battle*, New York, 1939, 1954; folder, "Death Takes No Holiday in Spain!" by Samuel Levinger Memorial Committee, New York (courtesy Mrs. Elma E. Levinger); Foster Jay Taylor, *The United States in the Spanish Civil War*, New York, 1956; personal interviews with veterans of the Abraham Lincoln Battalion; *Jewish Life*, March, 1938, p. 21.

P. 228b: Palestine immigration—*AJYB*, 1938, p. 573.

P. 231a: anti-Semitic organizations—Donald S. Strong, *Organized Anti-Semitism in America*, Washington, D. C., 1941, pp. 174, 144-45, 146-47; Detroit Board of Health—*AJYB*, 1936, p. 222; 1937, p. 253; "Jew Deal"—*AJYB*, 1935, pp. 153-54; 1937, p. 251; Coughlin—*AJYB*, 1937, p. 254; 1939, pp. 209-10; 1935, p. 156; Strong, work cited, pp. 63, 65; A. B. Magil and Henry Stevens, *The Peril of Fascism*, New York, 1938, pp. 175-96.

P. 232a: Scottsboro case—Haywood Patterson and Earl Conrad, *Scottsboro Boy*, Garden City, N. Y., 1950, pp. 292, 302-06; Allan Chalmers, *They Shall Be Free*, New York, 1951; Quentin Reynolds, *Courtroom: Story of Samuel S. Liebowitz*, New York, 1950, pp. 265, 274-75; *AJYB*, 1933, p. 63; Arthur Garfield Hays, *Trial by Prejudice*, New York, 1933, pp. 90-91, 109, 121-22, 130.

P. 234b: Kurtz's stanza—full text in another English translation in Joseph Leftwich, *The Golden Pea-*

cock, London, 1939, p. 362, and in *Jewish Currents,* New York, February, 1958, p. 15.

P. 235a: Freiheit choruses—I. B. Bailin, *Jacob Schaefer, Zein Lebn un Shafn,* New York, 1938; *IMAF,* New York, April-May, 1934, p. 39; Lazar Weiner—Bailin, work cited, p. 104.

P. 235b: Workmen's Circle chorus—*20 Yeriker Yubilai, Arbeter Ring Chor, 1915-1935,* New York, 1935, pp. 6, 10, 12. In 1922 the Jewish National Workers' Alliance established a chorus conducted by Leo Lowe—*Idish Nazionaler Arbeter Farband, 1910-1946,* New York, 1946, p. 378.

P. 238a: Folks-bihne—*25 Yor Folks-bihne,* New York, 1940, p. 74 and *passim;* Artef—N. Buchwald, *Teater,* New York, 1943, pp. 411-42; *10 Yor Artef,* New York, 1937.

P. 238b: Paris Congress—*Ershter Alveltlicher Idisher Kultur-Kongress,* Stenografisher Baricht, Paris-New York-Warsaw (1938).

P. 240a: CYCO—*AJYB,* 1950, pp. 210, 213; CYCO circular listing publications.

P. 240b: Yiddish language—*16th Census of the United States, 1940, Population, Nativity and Parentage of the White Population, Mother Tongue,* Washington, D. C., 1943, p. 2, Table 1, p. 51, Table 8.

P. 242a: writers' congress—Henry Hart, ed., *American Writers' Congress,* New York, 1935, pp. 11-12, 188; Hart, ed., *The Writer in a Changing World,* New York, 1937, pp. 252, 255; *Proletarian Literature in the United States,* New York, 1935.

P. 244b: American theater—Harold U. Ribalow in *The Jewish People,* vol. 3, pp. 233ff; Ludwig Lewisohn in *Jewish Book Annual,* vol. 9, pp. 6, 8.

P. 246a: WPA Yiddish theater—Mestel, *70 Yor,* p. 61; Hallie Flanagan, *Arena,* New York,, 1940, pp. 68, 124, 127, 224, 228, 277.

P. 246b: Jewish leaders' hesitancy—David Brody, *AJHSP,* vol. 45, p. 239; immigration into Palestine—*The Palestine Year Book,* Washington, D. C., vol. 1, pp. 172-73; Mark Wischnitzer, *To Dwell in Safety,* Philadelphia, 1949, p. 242.

P. 247b: *Freiheit* circulation—printed figures proved unreliable; those used were obtained from past and present managers of the *Freiheit.*

P. 248b: World War II data—I. Kaufman, *American Jews in World War II,* New York, 1947, vol. 1, pp. 27, 174-76.

P. 250a: on Jackman—undated clippings sent by his father, Leo Jackman, Baltimore; on Cohen, Kuzminsky, Levin, Slanger, Todres and Katz—Kaufman, work cited, pp. 69-74, 190-91, 23-25, 147-48, 14-16, 185-87; on Epstein and Suer—I. E. Rontch, "In Dienst fun Folk," *JPFO Almanach,* New York, 1947, pp. 155-56, 157, and Kaufman, work cited, p. 556.

P. 252a: two million Jews—Brody, *AJHSP,* vol. 45, p. 246; Second Front—Butcher, work quoted, New York, 1946, p. 29; Trumbull Higgins, *Winston Churchill and the Second Front,* New York and London, 1957.

P. 252b: Biltmore Program—*AJYB,* 1944, p. 206; full text in American Jewish Conference, *A Survey of Facts and Opinions,* New York, 1943, pp. 140-41; on Abba Hillel Silver—*The American Zionist,* February 5, 1953, pp. 6, 7, 9; Zionist membership—*AJYB,* 1945, p. 171.

P. 253a: Warsaw Ghetto Uprising—the bibliography is tremendous; see Schappes, "Resistance Is the Lesson," *Jewish Life,* April, 1948 and then as a pamphlet; Ber Mark, *Jewish Life,* April, 1956, pp. 16ff; Leo W. Schwartz, ed., *The Root and the Bough,* New York, 1949; Philip Friedman, *Martyrs and Fighters,* New York, 1954.

P. 253b: for Glick's song—Nachman Meisel, *Hirsh Glick un zein Lied, "Zog Nisht Kaynmol,"* New York, 1949, pp. 13-15; full text of Kramer's translation, *"Jewish Life" Anthology,* New York, 1956, p. 134.

P. 254a: commemoration meetings—*Proceedings, American Jewish Conference, Second Session,* p. 56; Bermuda Conference—Wischnitzer, work cited, pp. 246-54.

P. 254b: American Jewish Conference—*Proceedings* of each of the four sessions, Aug. 29-Sept. 2, 1943, Dec. 3-5, 1944, Feb. 17-19, 1946, Nov. 29-Dec. 1, 1947.

P. 255b: Jewish catastrophe—Conference Memorandum quoted, New York, 1943, p. 15.

P. 256a: American Jewish Committee withdraws—*AJYB,* 1945, pp. 170, 583-87.

P. 257a: Suhl's poem—in *A Vort fun Traist, Lieder,* Mexico, 1952, p. 11.

P. 257b: UJA data—*AJYB,* 1948, p. 140.

P. 258b: Bergson's organizations—American League for a Free Palestine, *For Survival and Freedom,* New York, 1946; Rufus Learsi, *Fulfillment,* New York, 1951, p. 350; *AJYB,* 1944, p. 178.

P. 259a: Einstein at hearing—Bartley C. Crum, *Behind the Silken Curtain,* pp. 25-26.

P. 260: on birth of Israel—Manuel, work quoted, Washington, D. C., 1949, pp. 336, 339, 358, 319, 347, 318; A. B. Magil, *Israel in Crisis,* New York, 1950, pp. 23-27; Harry S. Truman, *Years of Trial and Hope,* New York, 1956, p. 164.

P. 261a: Jorge Garcia-Granados, work quoted, New York, 1949, pp. 269, 284-85.

P. 262a: David Horowitz, work quoted, New York, 1953, pp. 271-72, 262.

Times, May 15, 1947; complete text, pamphlet by *Jewish Life.*

P. 263b: Manuel, work cited, pp. 358, 319; Roper poll—*AJYB,* 1946, p. 244.

CHAPTER 13

P. 265a: Jewish population—*AJYB,* 1951, pp. 4, 17-21; 1952, p. 235.

P. 265b: Jewish union movement—*AJYB,* 1952, pp. 59, 62; *New York Times,* May 22, 1950 for Fur union.

P. 267a: union fund contributions—*AJYB,* 1952, p. 64.

P. 267b: fur strike—Philip S. Foner, *The Fur and Leather Workers Union,,* Newark, 1950, pp. 648-50.

P. 268a: *Jewish Daily Forward*—Shannon, work cited, pp. 186, 245.

P. 268b: synagogue building—*AJYB,* 1952, pp. 156-57; religious affiliation—*AJYB,* 1952, pp. 87-88; Conservatism—*AJYB,* 1952, p. 156.

P. 269a: resolutions against atomic warfare—*AJYB,* 1947, p. 144; East European descent—*AJYB,* 1952, p. 155; Jewish press—*AJYB,* 1951, pp. 484-88.

P. 270a: Yiddish dailies—*N. Y. Ayer and Son's Directory,* 1951.

P. 271a: national group press—Yaroslav J. Chyz and Read Lewis, "Agencies Organized by Nationality Groups in the United States," *The Annals of the American Academy of Political and Social Sciences,* March, 1949, pp. 148-58; Jewish education—Israel S. Chipkin, "Jewish Education in the United States at the Mid-Century," in *Jewish Education Register and Directory, 1951,* New York, pp. 20, 11, 30, 39, 50; David Rudavsky, "Trends in Jewish School Organization and Enrollment in New York City, 1917-1950," *YIVO Annual,* X, pp. 10, 59; Uriah Z. Engelman, "Jewish Education," *AJYB,* 1951, pp. 97-98, 109.

P. 271b: Yiddish secular schools—Rudavsky, work cited, p. 65; N. Kamenetsky, *Morning Freiheit,* April 27, 1952; S. Yefroikin, "Yiddish Secular Schools in the United States," in *The Jewish People—Past and Present,* vol. 3, 1948, pp. 145, 150; greater earnestness—Rudavsky, work cited, p. 59.

P. 273a: Soviet Yiddish literature—*Jewish Life,* May, 1956.

P. 273b: *Gentlemen's Agreement*—Harold U. Ribalow in *The Jewish People—Past and Present,* vol. 3, p. 227.

P. 275b: *The Sidewalks Are Free*—review by David Alman, *Jewish Life,* May, 1950; Ludwig Lewisohn, *Jewish Book Annual,* IX, 1950-51, p. 4.

P. 277a: *Chicago Tribune*—*AJYB,* 1951, pp. 63-70.

P. 277b: discrimination in employment—Lois Waldman, "Employment Discrimination Against Jews in the United States—1955," *JSS,* July, 1956, pp. 212-13.

P. 278a: McCarthy and Malmedy—Jack Anderson and Ronald W. May, *McCarthy, the Man, the Senator, the "Ism,"* Boston, 1952, pp. 158-64; Wheeling speech—p. 174; climate of fear—Francis Biddle, *The Fear of Freedom,* Garden City, N. Y., 1952, pp. 186-87, 220-23.

P. 278b: Robert M. Hutchins—David Alison, *Searchlight, An Exposé of New York City Schools,* New York, 1951, p. 241; Hollywood Ten—Gordon Kahn, *Hollywood on Trial,* New York, 1948; New York teachers—Alison, work cited.

P. 279a: William O. Douglas, "The Black Silence of Fear," *The New York Times Magazine,* February 13, 1952; Anna Rosenberg case—*AJYB,* 1952, pp. 135, 555-56; Anderson and May, work cited, pp. 309-13. The Ethel and Julius Rosenberg and Morton Sobell case unfolded later and is thus outside the scope of this Mid-Century Profile.

P. 279b: IWO liquidation—*AJYB,* 1952, p. 554; Fort Monmouth case—*Jewish Life,* December, 1953, p. 4; January, 1954, p. 11; February, 1954, pp. 9-10.

P. 280b: NCRAC opposition—*AJYB,* 1952, p. 555.

P. 281a: Einstein—*Teacher News,* November 6, 1958; May 16, 1953; *Bulletin of Atomic Scientists,* October, 1952; Mrs. Eleanor Roosevelt's TV program, February 12, 1950.

P. 281b: school superintendent—Isaac B. Berkson, *Theories of Americanization,* New York, 1920, p. 59.

P. 283a: funds raised—*AJYB,* 1951, pp. 162-65.

P. 284a: Jewish organizations—*AJYB,* 1951, p. 453-66; Jewish labor fraternalism—*AJYB,* 1952, p. 61; *Jewish Fraternalist,* May, 1947, p. 5; *Der Freint,* June-July-August, 1950, p. 12; youth organizations—*AJYB,* 1952, pp. 198, 201-04.

P. 285a: Randolph S. Bourne, "The Jew and Trans-National America," *The Menorah Journal,* December, 1916, p. 279, 282; Bourne, "Trans-National America," *Atlantic Monthly,* July, 1916, reprinted in Bourne, *The History of a Literary Radical and Other Papers,* New York, 1919 and 1956.

P. 285b: Abraham G. Duker, "Socio-Psychological Trends in the American Jewish Community Since 1900," *YIVO Annual,* IX, p. 177; also Duker, "On Religious Trends in American Jewish Life," *YIVO Annual,* IV, p. 58.

GENERAL INDEX (*A "p" indicates a picture. "Org." and "per." mean "organization" and "periodical."*)